Marketing Strategies, Tactics, and Techniques

Marketing Strategies, Tactics, and Techniques

A Handbook for Practitioners

STUART C. ROGERS

QUORUM BOOKS
Westport, Connecticut • London

Library of Congress Cataloging-in-Publication Data

Rogers, Stuart C. (Stuart Clark)
    Marketing strategies, tactics, and techniques : a handbook for practitioners / Stuart C.
    Rogers.
        p.   cm.
    Includes index.
    ISBN 1–56720–411–2 (alk. paper)
    1. Marketing—Handbooks, manuals, etc.   I. Title.
    HF5415.R567   2001
    658.8—dc21   00–051759

British Library Cataloguing in Publication Data is available.

Library of Congress Catalog Card Number: 00–051759
ISBN: 1–56720–411–2

First published in 2001

Quorum Books, 88 Post Road West, Westport, CT 06881
An imprint of Greenwood Publishing Group, Inc.
www.quorumbooks.com

Printed in the United States of America

The paper used in this book complies with the
Permanent Paper Standard issued by the National
Information Standards Organization (Z39.48–1984).

10 9 8 7 6 5 4 3 2 1

*This book is respectfully dedicated to my colleagues
at the University of Denver's Daniels College of Business,
who welcomed me into a new world.*

Contents

Preface

Businesspeople, professionals, and college students alike are being told that they must develop *marketing strategies* for their ventures to succeed. But, until now, there has not been a single source that lists and defines those concepts simply and succinctly. Here you will find a combined encyclopedia, thesaurus, and how-to manual for strategic marketing planning.

For the more than 1,000 marketing strategies, tactics, and techniques defined, explanations are brief and background basic. The text that supplements the lists of strategies is intended to introduce or explain pertinent topics in a general businesslike manner, with a few observations on practicality and ethics when such are called for.

With no intention to underestimate either the experience or the intelligence of the reader, the fundamentals of marketing are summarized as a foundation for the more sophisticated information which is the heart of this handbook. In addition, marketing trade terms, like "yellow goods," "hypermarche," "stochastic," and "greenwashing," that may not be familiar to some practitioners, are defined.

Because many businesspeople often seem to have trouble with the creative and communications aspects of marketing, those subjects are treated in greater detail than the basic strategies in the first two parts of the handbook. Several appendixes are also included that should be useful to readers who wish to develop formal, written marketing plans, and graduate students who use the case method of study.

As the title suggests, this is meant to serve as an easy-to-use handbook, a memory-jogger for correct terminology to use in strategic planning, an idea-starter, and a source of definitions, as well as a how-to guide on marketing techniques, depending on the reader's need. The descriptors for strategies and/or tactics that are most common are listed first, followed by alternate terms in parentheses; naturally, different industries will favor different terms for the same strategy in some cases.

In addition to definitions by category of marketing strategies and tactics, Parts IV through VII present various marketing techniques that marketing managers might put to good use to further their careers and improve the success of their marketing efforts. It is expected that readers will find this handbook a useful resource that can help them devise strategic solutions to marketing problems and work current strategic marketing terminology and practices into projects involving written marketing and marketing communications plans.

More specifically, the marketing practitioner can perhaps be saved embarrassment when the boss or the board of directors demands an instant answer to a vexing marketing question. A brief look into *Marketing Strategies, Tactics, and Techniques* should provide the perfect immediate response, and deeper study and reflection may reveal ideas that are even more gratifying.

Readers may also wish to use both text and appendices as pilots use checklists before takeoff, to see that they have covered major opportunities in their marketing planning. Or they may use them as handy references when they prepare or review formal, written marketing, advertising, public relations, sales, or other business plans.

Strategies are listed by category in what seem logical orders. A complete, cross-referenced list of them all, in *alphabetical* order, can be found in the index.

Good luck, and good marketing!

Introduction

A LITTLE ETYMOLOGY

Military terminology is remarkably popular in marketing circles. One of the most common examples is the word *campaign* that is used regularly in connection with the communications aspects of marketing programs and which comes from an Old Northern French word meaning "to fight a war."

In much the same vein, the very useful word *strategy* is derived from the ancient Greek for "lead an army," and the word *tactic* is also from ancient Greek for "put in battle formation." The distinction between these two words is clear in their origins: *strategy* refers to the overall conduct of a war, while *tactics* relate to the individual actions in battles that, in aggregate, win or lose wars.

Because the practice of marketing is so highly competitive and even combative, these words are certainly appropriate, and they form an important part of our marketing vocabulary. No doubt other military words—like *mission* and *logistics*, as well as military metaphors like *blitz* (from Nazi Germany's *Blitzkrieg*), *frontal attack, flanking defense,* and so on—will persist. In fact, marketing language may become even more aggressive following publication of books with titles like *Marketing Warfare* and *Guerrilla Marketing—Attack*.

MOSTLY COMMON SENSE

With the help of this handbook, strategic marketing planning can be for you little more than *common sense*. Because strategy in marketing is simply *devising an appropriate overall plan of action* based on several factors, which include the following:

- a definition of your organization
- a description of the product or service you offer
- an indication of your pricing
- who your competition is and what they are doing
- who your various target markets (those you wish to deal with you) and publics (groups you wish to influence) are
- what research you have done and should do
- what motivates your customers or prospects
- your problems and/or opportunities
- your specific objectives and measurable goals
- the name and reputation of your organization, product, or service
- your positioning or brand image
- the message(s) you need to communicate to persuade your target market(s) or public(s)
- the marketing communications techniques you can employ
- the money that must be invested
- the way you will measure your success
- the kinds of people you might employ or retain to help you with your marketing program

A simpler checklist is represented by the *TOAST formula*, which is a handy mnemonic device to recall the most important elements of marketing planning:

- Target market segment
- Objective(s) and goal(s)
- Alternatives to purchase of your product or service, or competition
- Strategy
- Tactics

We'll deal with each of these topics in the pages that follow.

THE FUNCTION OF STRATEGIES

Strategy in marketing planning also means "alternatives." A marketing strategy is simply a statement of what you must *do* out of a myriad of options to accomplish one or more specific objectives, solve problems, or take advantage of opportunities. Looked at a little more carefully, your strategy must involve *who* will be influenced, *what* you want them to do, and finally *how* you are going to get them to do it. This sort of specificity requires, of course, a combination of clear thinking and good judgment based on valid information. The major purpose of this handbook is to suggest what your alternatives in each area of marketing are and to provide accepted terminology so you can call your alternatives by their proper names.

Like military maneuvers, the strategic marketing process is composed of (1) planning, (2) implementation, and (3) control. That should be obvious and basic to good business management.

Although the subject sounds simple so far, you appreciate that in practice the marketing process may be extremely complex. In fact, the assumption that "simple" is the same as "easy" is one of the flaws of many strategic marketing plans. Often a simple strategy statement may seem to solve everything, but in fact too often does *nothing* in and of itself. This is one of the reasons why so many strategic marketing plans get filed and never looked at again—until it's time to write another.

Henry Kissinger is credited with having satirized strategic planning in the federal government when, as U.S. Secretary of State, he suggested that the way to overcome the threat of the Soviet nuclear submarine fleet in the Atlantic was to *boil the ocean.* "That is my strategic plan," he reportedly said, "and now it's up to the rest of you to work out the technical details."

MANY TYPES OF STRATEGIES

Some strategies are planned, but others emerge by a process of organizational evolution and become part of the corporate culture. Sometimes, then, strategic plans are in conflict with strategic reality, and to replace strategies that are seen as "the way we've always operated" can be extremely challenging.

Some strategies are clever and complex, like *forward invention.* Others are extremely simple, like *local distribution.* It seems that most marketing planning and business texts concentrate on the *simple* strategies.

One of the simplest, for example, is *discounting.* You have no doubt observed many times that any slackwit can advise you to cut the price of your product or service—but it takes real marketing know-how to move a product whose price is perceived as high in a competitive marketplace.

Some strategies are commonplace and therefore often taken for granted. For instance, you may recall that an ideal consumer marketing strategy is called the *push-pull* strategy, which means that the marketer will do everything possible to "push" their product into distribution and at the same time everything possible to create consumer demand that will, so to speak, "pull" the product out at the point of purchase.

Although it is far easier to hang labels on strategies *after* plans have been completed than when they are in the making, there are some basically sound ideas you might wish to reflect on as you proceed with your marketing planning.

So what follow, beginning with Chapter 7, are several lists of the most common descriptors of strategies for both consumer and nonconsumer marketing. "Nonconsumer" is a term used to include "organizational," or (more commonly today) "business" marketing, which is composed of professional, commercial, industrial, reseller (or trade), institutional, and governmental targets. Several basic strategies go by different names, and all that are most popular are included. Naturally there is a risk of redundancy, both within categories and from one group of strategies to another, because some strategies cover virtually the same situations and similar objectives in different areas of marketing planning, but they are occasionally included in more than one place for the sake of completeness.

As you review these lists, you should quickly discover those strategies that will be useful in your particular marketing planning. To find strategies by name, check the alphabetical listing in the index at the end of the book.

HOW TO USE THESE LISTS

Successful use of the lists that follow relies on your good judgment enhanced by aided recall. That is, it is far easier to recognize what one needs when one actually *sees* it than to try to bring it to mind without any prompting.

So approach these lists as you would the choice of a treat if you were visiting an ice cream parlor. First decide whether you want a cone, a plate, a soda, or a sundae by looking at chapter headings. Then decide what flavor you want by looking at the appropriate list of selections available. If the perfect choice does not pop right out at you, read the definitions of terms for help.

Remember, you don't have to take plain vanilla every time. There's also fudge swirl, cherry smash, and many more!

Part I

Essentials Before You Strategize

Chapter 1

Marketing Planning versus Business Planning

DISCIPLINE IS VITAL

Strategic marketing planning requires not only creative thinking, but also business discipline. Essential to the development of successful marketing strategies is an understanding of the boundaries of the various functional areas of business, as well as an appreciation of the fundamental components of modern marketing.

As you proceed with strategic planning for a marketing program, you may rely as much on clear thinking, good judgment, and common sense as on case history models of strategies. But, certainly, you must beware of creative ideation without business *discipline*. This is a fault observed among MBA students, as well as among some business leaders.

STAY ON YOUR OWN TURF

For example, in graduate Marketing Strategies courses, an idea commonly advanced by students is to enrich the company by *making a public offering of stock*. What is wrong with this as a *marketing* strategy is that the manner in which a company structures its debt is not a function of marketing, but of finance and top management.

Another idea often presented is to build manufacturing facilities or assembly plants to reduce the length of lines of distribution. But you certainly realize that operations of this nature are the responsibility of manufacturing and top management, not marketing. Marketing might be consulted, but it would be presumptuous for marketing people to make strategic recommendations along this line. Marketing *would*, however, be involved in decisions about locations of warehouses and sales offices, since those are marketing functions involving logistics and personal selling.

How about a strategy that involves launching a profit-sharing program to improve employee morale? A worthy idea, but matters of this type are the province of human resources and top management. While marketing might recommend cash, gift, or award incentive programs for field sales personnel, it would have no business recommending company-wide personnel policies such as profit sharing.

Or it might seem a good idea to acquire another company in a related line of business to increase market share. But this sort of decision normally is made jointly by legal counsel and top management. Again, marketing might be consulted, but the risk of antitrust action by the federal government and the complexities of rights, contracts, and legal obligations are beyond the scope of the corporate marketing function, unless the firm is small and such decisions are made by consensus.

You will find a succinct enumeration of the functional areas of marketing in Appendix 2. How they relate to specific departments and agencies, of course, will vary from one organization to another.

WHAT YOU WILL GAIN HERE

This handbook will enhance your awareness and use of the accepted language of strategic marketing. And your knowledge of proven marketing strategies will certainly *augment* your creative ideation and good judgment, not preempt it.

Additionally, the organization of this handbook will show clearly where business boundaries lie and thereby help avoid fruitless competition with executives in disciplines other than marketing.

A CONSTRUCTION METAPHOR

The sequence of topics in Part I will emphasize the importance of building your house from the foundation up, not from the roof down. This means you must first establish a firm basis for your marketing strategies—the subject of the next five chapters.

Many marketing novices get a product like a new type of prepared soup and want immediately to create a series of television commercials featuring dancing soup cans. Of course, this is great fun and highly creative—but based on nothing more than personal intellectual frivolity. To launch a successful new product or service, one must start at the *beginning* with definitions of target markets, competitive advantages, specific objectives, and measurable goals. That is to say, build from the foundation up, not the roof down. The dancing soup can idea is like the color of the window trim which is among the *last* things to consider in building a house.

So, in addition to recognizing the boundaries of business disciplines, sequence your strategic marketing planning in a *logical* manner. The sequence may not always be the same, but should always be orderly and disciplined, despite the necessity of frequent backtracking, correction of data, and rethinking of strategies and tactics.

To approach strategic marketing planning in a top-of-the-head or off-the-wall fashion is likely to be about as successful as filling out a profit-and-loss statement using a random number table.

Chapter 2

Marketing Research

WHY BOTHER WITH RESEARCH?

It's true that modern marketing is not a science and that considerable art and judgment enter into the planning process. But that does not mean one should trust one's intuition exclusively. Does it really seem logical that your own particular tastes, values, and lifestyle will be the same as those of a market segment composed of people significantly *different* from you in terms of education and attitude toward your business or profession? Research can give you a realistic perspective that "common sense" might ignore.

True enough, you may say, but some things are *obvious*. For example, when Governor George Wallace ran for president of the United States, he did not engage in expensive market research and attitude research like most of the aspirants who have come after him. He said that *everyone knew* what the country wanted and needed. One of his more popular slogans was, "Ask any cabdriver." The fact that he *did not win* suggests that he was not correct in his marketing assumptions.

You will stand a far better chance of developing a winning strategic marketing plan if you take time to research your markets. This does not have to be costly, and it need not take a great amount of your time.

Besides providing guidance such as Governor Wallace might have benefited from, there are five important reasons for conducting marketing research:

1. Marketing research indicates, before you even start planning, what direction you ought to be heading in.

2. Before you spend a lot of money on marketing communications materials (like brochures, displays, and advertising), research can help you predict whether the message you plan to communicate and/or the type of creative and media strategies you devise will have the results you expect.

3. When you are actually running your marketing program, research can indicate whether all is working as planned so that you can change course if necessary.

4. When each marketing effort is completed, research (or evaluation) can show what has actually been accomplished.

5. The data you obtain from research can often provide benchmarks, or points of reference, for designing the next cycle of your marketing activities.

WHY RESEARCH IS OFTEN AVOIDED

For many people the trouble with research is that it doesn't seem much *fun*. To some people, too, research appears only to stand in the way of getting on with their marketing program. But it is an important part of the marketing process, which might be enjoyed more if thought of as a *strategic marketing* function.

Whether you call research methods "strategies," "tactics," or "techniques," they should be considered before you move on to most other marketing considerations because they are necessary for accurately defining target market segments and also in identifying buying motives and buyer behavior.

There are two basic types of research: *primary* and *secondary*. Primary research is the type you conduct yourself and secondary research is the type that has been conducted by someone else—often a syndicated research organization, a trade association, or a government agency. Owing to the vagaries of our language, you should do the secondary research *first*, and the primary *second*—largely because secondary research tends to be less costly and can often provide all the guidance you need in making strategic marketing decisions.

With that in mind, and with no attempt to teach the reader how to conduct marketing research, the following general terminology is included.

SECONDARY RESEARCH

These are the general categories of secondary marketing research:

- *Internal data*—collect and interpret information that already exists within your organization. Be sure to do this *first*.
- *External data*—find information from other sources than your own. These include the following:
- *Industry studies*—other (noncompetitive) companies' primary research. You can sometimes engage in barter for this kind of intelligence.

- *Syndicated data*—such as Nielsen television ratings. By the way, syndicated research firms may also do *customized (primary) research* for fees.
- *On-line databases*—quick and relatively easy, but be sure to check the *reliability* of these types of sources, since there is a great deal of disinformation, misinformation, and outright lies on the Internet.
- *Published tabular data*—such as U.S. government compilations.
- *Directories*—such as Chamber of Commerce and trade association lists.

Consider various formats as well, and do not assume that information you can obtain via the Internet is your *only* source; much exists exclusively in printed form, and much of that is only available for substantial fees. See Appendix 3 for a list of secondary research sources your library and/or Internet connection should provide.

PRIMARY RESEARCH

You do primary research *second* because it is more expensive, more time-consuming, and sometimes more risky in regard to reliability of results.

Primary research is distinguished from secondary research in that you plan, sample, survey, collect, compile, and interpret results directly or with the help of a research firm, rather than get it from published or electronic sources.

Marketing researchers usually divide primary research into two categories: *exploratory* research and *quantitative* research. The academic community refers to the latter as *conclusive* research.

Exploratory research is general in nature, often is the first type of primary research to be conducted, and helps to define more accurately what you are seeking. It tends to be informal in structure, as when you "ask any cabdriver." It comprises:

- *Basic* (or *pure*) *research*—which is conducted for the sake of broadening general knowledge and/or to verify theories.
- *Causal research*—which is conducted to identify cause-and-effect relationships among factors being studied; this is basic to buyer behavior studies.
- *Concept testing*—which is exploratory research to study customers' and prospects' ideas about new, improved, or repositioned products or services.

Once you have defined the research issues more clearly through your exploratory efforts, you can consider conducting *quantitative* research. This involves formal collection of data according to a structured plan and formal analysis of the data to reach a logical conclusion to explain the problem or situation originally defined. Here is basically what you will be seeking:

- *General information*—demographics for consumer marketing (or Standard Industrial Classifications [SICs] and North American Industrial Classifications [NAICs], organization sizes, and function titles for business marketing), psychographics, lifestyles, synchrographics (events in people's lives like graduation, marriage, and retirement that prompt different buying behaviors and permit segmentation), and competitive information.

- *Attitudes*—how your customers or clients feel about your business or organization, your prices or fees, and the goods and/or services they receive from your firm.

- *Awareness*—how much customers, clients, and prospects know about you and your operations, which is particularly important when you want to track the success of public opinion and so-called "educational" efforts you might undertake. The *concept test* refers to evaluation of a new product, service, or idea by exposing a test group to the product or a message about it and soliciting feedback. The *recall test* technique is used to determine the memorability and presumably the success of message delivery; it can be either *aided* or *unaided*.

- *Response*—often analyzed on a test basis to discover how appealing your offer is, which may in turn help in forecasting sales results.

- *Buying* (or *purchase*) *behavior*—how and where the customer currently buys, which is the ultimate information desired by most marketers.

- *Activities, interests, and opinions (AIO)*—factors you can correlate with psychographic profiling for target segment identification.

SAMPLING STRATEGIES

These strategic considerations pertain to the composition of the group of people surveyed in a research study. Identify your target segments, audiences, or publics by geographic factors such as ZIP Codes, demographics, psychographics, synchrographics, usage, and need. For more details on segmentation, see the next chapter and Appendix 5. Usually you can't cover everybody in your research efforts, so consider which of these two techniques would serve your needs best:

- *Probability sample*—where every type of person in a population is represented, this sort of sample is designed to be generalized (or "translated") to a larger population. When you are conducting a *quantitative* study, some type of *probability* sampling should be used.

- *Nonprobability sample*—selected so the likelihood of a particular characteristic being reflected in the sample is minimized or even ignored, this sort of sample is designed so that the results are *qualitative* and therefore they cannot be generalized to a larger population. This type of sampling technique is used with *exploratory* studies.

PROBABILITY SAMPLES

There are several types of *probability* samples, the most common being these:

- *Systematic sample*—the strategy whereby you select every *nth* name from a list or from your files. For example, you have a list of 2,000 business owners available through your Chamber of Commerce, and you can afford a mailed survey of 200 pieces. So you mail to every *tenth* name on the list ($n = 10$).
- *Stratified* (or *optimal allocation*) *sampling*—where you draw the sample to contain a proportion of particular segments to match your customer or client profile, such as 40 percent men ages 18–24 and 60 percent men age 25 and older.
- *Disproportional stratified sampling*—where the sample size for each component is weighted according to analytical considerations.

NONPROBABILITY SAMPLES

Nonprobability samples include these:

- *Random sample*—you select a fraction of a population by "the luck of the draw," as lottery winners are selected.
- *Random digit dialing*—where a sample of a general population is obtained by the use of random numbers to generate telephone numbers to be called and those who answer are interviewed.
- *Convenience sample*—the strategy of choosing to survey anyone who is handy, as with *mall intercept*. This is not likely to provide particularly reliable results but is useful for questions of broad interest, such as whether your signage is visible from the street.
- *Snowball sample*—the first set of respondents may be selected according to probability methods, but *additional* respondents are obtained from the first respondents.
- *Judgment* (or *purposive*) *sample*—where the researcher in selecting the sample decides that certain factors are good parameters for the target population. For example, for mall intercept research, 3 out of 15 local malls might be judged the best in which to conduct surveys.
- *Quota sample*—which includes *representative* (or *statistical*) *sampling*, where people with particular characteristics or interests are included in the sample. For example, at the 3 malls selected out of 15, the researcher might specify that half the people interviewed should be women pushing strollers. This type sample is clearly segmented, but not as carefully structured, generally, as a *stratified sample*.
- *Cluster sample*—entire groups instead of individual elements are randomly selected. An *area cluster sample* means random selection of samples is made from specific geographic areas such as ZIP Codes or census tracts.
- *Specific* (or *census*) *sample*—where more tightly defined targets than general consumer groups are included, such as attorneys or bankers who might refer clients.

You can use the random sampling strategy on such groups, but often they are so limited in size that it is advisable simply to survey the *entire group*. Generally target groups numbering fewer than 1,000 don't need to be sampled but can be efficiently and effectively surveyed in their entirety.

METHODS FOR CONDUCTING MARKETING RESEARCH

Here are the basic research methods you can employ:

- *Self-evaluation research method*—use the product or service yourself to get a first-hand impression of your customers' experiences.

- *Anecdotal research method*—specific incidents are reported, upon which conclusions are based. This is neither scientific nor projectable, but simple and often useful.

- *Observational research method*—people are watched to see what they do in particular circumstances, and their behavior is noted on the assumption it is representative of the behavior of similar people.

- *Mechanical observational research method*—research is conducted by means of electronic or other impersonal means such as meters connected to television sets in viewers' homes.

- *Contrived observational research method*—researchers create an artificial situation in which an hypothesis may be tested.

- *Laboratory research method*—observational research is conducted under carefully controlled conditions.

- *Interview research method*—a single interviewer asks questions of one respondent at a time. *Probing* is a technique to elicit clarifications of responses. *Depth* interviews are usually relatively unstructured and conducted by a qualified psychologist or even psychiatrist (a psychologist with an M.D. degree) to seek hidden factors in the minds of respondents. The latter technique is the basis for what is called *motivational research*, particularly popular in the 1950s and 1960s.

- *A/B research method*—a technique to measure the strength of an appeal or offer, or response to a creative strategy, by running different versions of a marketing communication in two different geographic areas. A popular non-sampling variation of this method that is useful for pretesting advertisements is the *split run test* in periodicals or direct mail when every other name on the distribution list receives the "A" version of an ad and the others receive the "B" version. Response rates, coupon redemptions, or other measures are then compared.

- *In-store research method*—a form of observational research where the environment is an actual store setting, as opposed to a laboratory setting, and particular behaviors are noted.

- *Panel research method*—involves a prerecruited sample of consumers whom researchers measure together. In a *diary panel* (the method of MRI and Simmons) selected consumers record activities and buying behaviors over a period of time. This is called *syndicated research* and is available in both published and tailored forms for significant fees.

- *Scanner-based consumer panel research method*—where participants are provided with *scanners* to record and transmit to the research firm the bar codes (or universal product codes—UPCs) of purchases when they return from shopping. Household information is electronically related to buying behavior to identify trends useful in marketing planning. (See *electronic test market* that follows.)

- *Jury test research method*—pretest technique for evaluating advertisements before they are run in which a panel is asked to evaluate copy and layout in terms of attractiveness, persuasiveness, and other relevant factors.

- *Focus group research method*—particularly useful for discovering fundamental appeals, for developing the basic offer and creative strategy, and even to help find phrases to use in advertising, sales promotion, and publicity copy. Generally 6 to 12 individuals are seated at a conference table, often with one-way mirrors on one wall so the group can be observed without being disturbed as they focus on an issue. Ideally, an experienced moderator encourages discussion and keeps it on track without introducing personal bias. Beware of generalizing focus group results to an entire market segment, however, and don't try to add results together, but treat the results as *informed guidance*. If you need projectable research, you should use other sampling and survey strategies and statistical methods listed in the next section of this chapter.

- *Embedment research method*—where the subjects do not know they are being researched. For example, if you want to test the persuasive power of a television commercial, you could invite a group of people to a purported preview of a pilot for a new television series. As a reward they could pick items from a list of products that includes one or more involved in your test. You collect their checklist choices and show them the pilot, including commercials, one or more of which you are testing. When the screening is over, you apologize for somehow having lost their lists and ask them to fill in new lists. Changes in product choices may be attributed to the effects of the commercial(s) the audience viewed.

- *Test market research method*—select a metropolitan area whose population is representative of the universe you are seeking, launch a marketing program just in that area, and evaluate sales results. Practiced by most consumer packaged-goods marketers in introducing new products, this is a form of statistical sampling combined with observational research that is far less expensive than launching a new product nationwide.

- *Electronic test market research method*—analyze at point of purchase UPC information among a sample of consumers often attracted by a *frequent shopper* or *preferred customer* program. This may be linked with split-cable or other new technological methods for selectively transmitting television commercials to test resultant variations in buying behavior.

- *Cookies research method*—involves files placed by on-line marketers, advertisers, and marketing researchers on the operating systems of consumers' personal computers to track their surfing patterns and gather other private information. A Web page visit can upload one or more *cookies* to Web surfers' computers, and they may remain after surfers have left the Web site. Microsoft is developing software that will let computer users know when this is being done, and the surfer can decide whether to accept or reject the *cookie*. *Third-party persistent cookies* is the term for *cookies* that continue to gather information without the surfer's knowledge.

- *Tracking research method*—where the same sort of information from the same or similar samples is collected at intervals to see how attitudes may be changing or how market shares may be increasing.

TOOLS FOR MARKETING RESEARCH

These are the forms of marketing research or tactics by which you can gather primary research information:

- *Survey research*—questionnaire research to gather information for your marketing plan about customer and/or prospect knowledge, awareness, and attitudes. See Appendix 4 for more on this subject. Several different means to deliver surveys are noted in the following entries.
- *Mall intercept research*—a research tactic where persons are randomly interviewed in shopping malls. There is no opportunity for a clearly defined sample, since anyone who is willing to answer questions is included.
- *Door-to-door research*—allows sample selection by neighborhood, but is limited as to whether an occupant is at home when the interviewer arrives and sometimes biased in that respondents may tell interviewers what they think interviewers want to hear, or what they think will make the interviewer admire them—a problem with mall intercept, too.
- *Telephone research*—offers greater opportunity to select a specific sample of respondents but also can be biased because only particular types of people are likely to cooperate. May cause antagonism in the same way telemarketing sales activities do, especially when a computer voice introduces the survey.
- *Computer-assisted telephone research*—where the interviewer inputs response information directly to a computer.
- *Computer-interactive survey research*—where respondents answer questions displayed on a computer screen. The computer is programmed to present questions in a sequence related to respondents' pervious answers.
- *Internet survey research*—computer-users go to a Web site where they can answer questions displayed.
- *Mail research*—less intrusive than telephone and door-to-door but generally has lower response rates unless a reasonable incentive for cooperation is provided. However, because of relative anonymity, more accurate answers to personal questions such as age and income may be expected.
- *Diary research*—respondents are asked to keep track of opinions, attitudes, interests, and behaviors over specific periods of time.
- *Fax survey research*—questionnaire method using facsimile equipment to transmit and receive.
- *Eye-tracking monitor research*—also called an "eye camera," this device is a mechanical means to record eye movements useful in evaluating responses to print advertising, point-of-purchase materials, and the like.

- *Pupilometer research*—based on a mechanism to measure the diameter of the pupils of subjects' eyes, which may be related to emotional responses to stimuli.
- *Psychogalvanometer research*—the means to measure changes in galvanic skin index or electrical resistance of a subject's skin. Commonly associated with "lie-detectors" but useful for researching unconscious mental processes.
- *Voice-pitch analysis research*—objective measurement of variations of voice pitch that may reveal emotional reactions to stimuli.
- *Projective research*—where respondents are asked what *other* people think, thereby revealing their own often hidden attitudes.
- *Role-playing research*—a common projective technique where respondents act out the way they think others would behave in particular situations or with respect to particular products or services.
- *Thematic apperception test (TAT) research*—respondents explain what is happening in a pictured situation. This may reveal hidden motivations and attitudes toward products. What is called *picture frustration* is a variation of this technique.
- *Word-association research*—a list of words is read one at a time to respondents, who are asked to say the first corresponding word that comes to their mind.
- *Sentence-completion research*—respondents say the first thing they think of to complete a sentence such as "My favorite brand of toothpaste is . . ."
- *Expressive behavior (kinesic communication) research*—in observational research, facial expressions, body language, and tone of voice can not only be subjectively but also mechanically evaluated for clues about subconscious processes.
- *Hidden observation research*—where subjects do not know their behavior is being studied. Useful, for example, in connection with in-store research. This is an effort to minimize the human equivalent of the *Heisenberg uncertainty principle*, which basically holds that the very act of observing and/or measuring any action will to some degree *change* that action.

CAUTIONS

When you conduct primary research of any type, you must keep in mind that your answers will only be *approximate*.

Once you have collected and compiled all your results and begun to interpret what you have accumulated, remember too that research by itself cannot make decisions. It can only *guide* you in making them *yourself*. Poorly prepared and executed, research can lead you far away from the truth. And intelligent interpretation is always called for, no matter how excellently crafted the study.

UNETHICAL RESEARCH STRATEGIES

Pretending to be conducting research when, in fact, the primary objective is something else is by general agreement dishonest and therefore unethical. Common "pseudo-research" practices are these:

- *Lead-generating "survey" research*—popular with some insurance companies which purport, for example, to be conducting national research on attitudes toward healthcare, but in fact are gathering information so that sales representatives can call and pitch their medical insurance policies.

- *Fundraising "survey" research*—practiced for many years by some nonprofit organizations and political candidates who mail questionnaires on timely issues and conclude with a request for a monetary contribution. The information gathered may or may not be compiled and may or may not be used to develop promises made by political candidates.

- *Push-poll activity*—also practiced by some political campaign strategists and not research to discover information at all, but composed of "leading questions" intended to convert respondents to negative opinions about opponents. Also mentioned in Chapter 13, "Competitive Strategies."

- *"Social engineering" activity*—telephoning company employees and, through personal charm and verbal deception, extracting proprietary information. Popularized by computer hackers to gain access to secured databases.

RESEARCHING YOUR COMPETITION

The subject of market intelligence involves serious ethical issues and must be weighed carefully by every conscientious marketing practitioner. But there seems little wrong with keeping your eyes and ears open for indications of how your competitors are spending their marketing dollars, and keeping records of what you discover. Start with the Standard Industrial Classification (SIC) or North American Industrial Classification (NAIC) numbers for your industry and then consider other segmentation variables, according to the guidance in the next chapter.

In addition to the excellent secondary research sources listed in Appendix 3, national marketers can subscribe to *Broadcast Advertisers Reports* (*BAR*) that concern television commercials in 75 markets, *Leading National Advertisers* (*LNA*) that reports on 24,000 brands and their multimedia spending, and *Publishers Information Bureau* (*PIB*) which shows space and costs by brand for indications of approximate historical types of media activities and spending levels of competitors.

Media sales representatives are good sources for competitive information, and this is considered *perfectly ethical* by the marketing merchants, since their mission is to sell their products, services, and media vehicles. In order to initiate and finally close a sale with you, my experience has been that they will generally reveal every piece of information they have at their disposal—even if it has been given to them in confidence. And, in addition, they may even do independent primary research for you at no charge, which of course can involve considerable savings when compared with the costs of conducting your own. But remember in your dealings with them (and with their editorial counterparts—reporters and editors) that today there is *no such thing as "off the record,"* and they may do to you as they do to your competitors.

OTHER INVESTIGATIVE TECHNIQUES

In smaller towns and cities across the United States, overt competitive information gathering for any reason at all is often considered unethical. Although this is not the same as the unethical and increasingly illegal activity of *industrial espionage*, you should nevertheless conform scrupulously to the ethical, legal, and regulatory standards of your community and your industry.

Only if it is acceptable in your area and in your industry or professional community might you try the *mystery shopper* strategy employed by many retailers around the world to check on their own customer services. A variation for the gathering of competitive intelligence is to have someone telephone or visit your direct competitors to see how they handle particular issues and types of prospective customers, and also to inquire about their prices for competitive goods and/or services.

Of course, this must be strictly on the up-and-up, with no attempt at flagrant deception. But to those who say that no matter how it's handled this is wrongful behavior, it might be suggested that there should be nothing unethical in a free-market society with one of your acquaintances asking your competitors about the basics of their business. Persons of honor should have nothing to hide from their customers or clients—*or* their competitors.

However, one should avoid the practice of some marketers who place people in sensitive positions in competitor companies expressly to commit corporate espionage. Nor should one hire away competitors' employees who are willing to share confidential information. This is clearly unethical, immoral, and as unconscionable as "dumpster diving" and wireless telephone surveillance.

Chapter 3

How to Identify and Profile Your Target Markets and Publics for Strategic Marketing Planning

To be successful in your marketing planning and management, before you begin to consider marketing strategies you should evaluate with great care and exactness whom you wish to influence with your marketing program, and base your activities on an affordable mixture of elements that will have the greatest potential effect on *those particular groups*.

This may sound obvious, but it is often overlooked by people eager to forge ahead with their strategic marketing planning.

Target markets—and publics to some degree, too—ideally reflect the following six fundamental qualities:

1. They must share a *common need or desire*.
2. They should constitute a *sufficiently large group* to be worthwhile.
3. They should be *reachable* through modern marketing communications methods.
4. They should be potentially *responsive* to your marketing efforts.
5. They should possess the *means to pay* for what you have to offer, unless your business is not for profit.
6. They should have the *authority* to enter into binding agreements with your organization.

BASIC TYPES OF MARKETS AND PUBLICS

You can easily categorize your potential target markets (those who might or do buy from you) and publics (groups other than customers and prospects whose influence is important to you) according to the general categories that follow. You will not necessarily need to reach all of these segments, but you should consider carefully each group as a possible influence on your marketing program.

- Existing customers or clients.
- Ideal prospects (those you would most like to have as customers or clients, but do not now have).
- Current, potential, and past employees.
- Resellers (dealers [retail] and distributors, brokers, jobbers, etc. [wholesale]) if you do not sell direct.
- Influencers of your customers or clients (such as parents for children's products, and administrative assistants for business accounts).
- The general population in your community.
- Shareholders (if you have been financed by the sale of stock).
- Securities analysts (if you have stock that is publicly traded or need substantial financing).
- Leaders in the financial field (bankers, stockbrokers, and the like).
- Executives (other than yours) in your industry.
- Referral sources (those who may not need your products or services themselves, but who may refer business).
- Managers and executives in businesses other than those in your industry.
- Your suppliers.
- Community leaders and public opinion influencers.
- Representatives of the media.
- Local government officials (municipal, county, parish, and state).
- Federal government officials (elected, appointed, and careerist).
- Perhaps your educational community, including both students and faculty.

MARKET SEGMENTATION

A detailed list of segmentation variables accepted by most marketers and by the mass media is provided in Appendix 5. But to begin your strategic marketing planning, the list that follows here will help you define in general terms who your target markets and publics are so that you can relate them to marketing strategies.

You should continually refine and often redefine your market segments as your marketing program progresses.

CONSUMER MARKETS

With respect to *consumer* markets, the first three items that follow are the most commonly used, but you should consider defining or segmenting your targets with regard to each of the other categories as well. Here is the simplified list:

- geographic factors (most commonly ZIP Code analysis for consumer and many business products; otherwise, census tract, county or parish, state, region, or country)
- demographic characteristics (gender, age, education, income, and the like)
- psychographic or lifestyle considerations (including attitudes, opinions, and interests)
- synchrographic factors (related to major events, occasions, or significant "rites of passage" in people's lives)
- consumer needs
- consumer benefits
- potential response to uniqueness of the product
- potential for satisfaction of consumer wants and needs *other* than the obvious
- potential response to hidden qualities of the product
- possible emotional responses in consumers related to the product or its use
- likely purchase location (store, home, at work, and so on)
- frequency of product purchase and/or use
- usage rate (light, medium, or heavy)
- where product is consumed
- seasonality of product use
- user status (nonuser, ex-user, etc.)
- loyalty status
- consumer readiness stage within the consumer buying cycle
- credit rating

BUSINESS (NONCONSUMER) MARKETS

You should define business, professional, commercial, industrial, reseller (trade), institutional, and governmental markets in terms of the following:

- geographic location
- Standard Industrial Classification (SIC) or North American Industrial Classification (NAIC) which includes the United States of America, Canada, and Mexico
- organizational revenues or company sales volume (annual dollars)
- company production volume (units, tonnage, etc.)
- number of employees
- nature of customer or client requirement (need)
- specific benefit(s) to customer or client

- decision-maker title(s)
- who makes recommendations versus final decisions
- organization's purchasing policies
- uniqueness of the product
- nature of product use
- frequency of product use
- usage rate (light to heavy) or size of orders
- where product is used
- seasonality of product use
- user status (nonuser, ex-user, etc.)
- nature of business relationship and loyalty status
- method of buying-decision-making and/or purchasing (for example, individual decision-making versus buying centers, and centralized versus decentralized purchasing departments)
- buyer readiness stage within the business buying cycle
- reliability and promptness of payment

CONFORMITY TO CATEGORIES IS IMPORTANT

To facilitate tactical implementation of your marketing strategy, be sure that when you refine the profiles of your target markets and publics you use segmentation categories that are compatible with (and preferably identical to) categories used to profile the audiences of the advertising and other marketing communications media you select. For example, Nielsen television research will indicate how many women 18 to 34 years of age you can reach—but you will have no way to calculate your target audience if you specify women 14 to 30 or 25 to 35.

Again, Appendix 5 will guide you in establishing appropriate segmentation categories.

FUNDAMENTAL SEGMENTATION STRATEGIES

- *Mass market*—target everyone.
- *Basic segmentation*—three levels: high tier, middle tier, low tier.
- *Subsegmentation technique*—five levels: high tier, middle tier, low tier, very low tier, ultra-low tier.
- *Matrix* (or *niche*) segmentation—customer or client needs are assumed to be related to the three qualities of price, feature(s), and application(s). These are laid out on a grid or matrix where patterns or "clusters" are plotted, akin to the perceptual mapping discipline but related to acceptance of price, desire for a feature, or need for an application. The densest clusters normally indicate prime target market segments. This is very useful in packaged-goods marketing but rather complex for marketing a professional organization.

KEEP CURRENT

One of the greatest marketing mistakes of all time was Ford's introduction of the Edsel® automobile. Among several major marketing and manufacturing errors that contributed to that costly failure was the company's basing its anticipation of demand for the product on a *ten-year-old* market profile.

The Greek philosopher Heraclitus (ca. 540–480 B.C.) observed, "Nothing endures but change." This and his metaphorical corollary, "You can't step in the same stream twice," should be kept clearly in mind when you identify your target markets. Like Heraclitus' stream, the marketplace and the persons who compose it are constantly changing, and your market intelligence must be kept up-to-date if you are to avoid such disasters as Ford experienced with the Edsel.

YOUR PROSPECT'S SELF-IMAGE

The importance of understanding the *self-image* of prospective customers and positioning products in harmony with diverse self-images has long been appreciated by creative advertising and sales people. However, relating the ways consumers, customers, or prospects view themselves to the *market segmentation variables* noted in this chapter has yet to be mastered. The best we seem to be able to do at present is to try to correlate supposed self-images with current psychographic or lifestyle categories. Discovering the secret of, first, learning what people's self-images actually are (as opposed to what survey respondents might *say* they are) and, second, developing measurable self-image categories which jibe with media research might well be the next great advance for strategic marketing.

Chapter 4

Total Quality Marketing and SWOT Analysis

BACKGROUND

For many years American business and industry ignored the concept of Total Quality Management (TQM) that W. Edwards Deming introduced to Japan. What he did there, though, has been largely credited with the competitive success of Japan over the United States since the end of World War II.

Change for the sake of change is often a mistake, but the nature of TQM is change, and it has certainly been responsible for one of the most amazing shifts in public opinion ever seen: In 1945 "Made in Japan" meant simply *junk* to most Americans. In fewer than 50 years, that perception changed to the absolute opposite, so that "Made in Japan" now means *top quality* to most Americans.

Many highly educated and thoroughly trained professionals, including many marketing practitioners, are so involved in their day-to-day work that they fail to heed Philip Kotler's suggestion that we must *make what we can sell* rather than try to *sell what we can make*. It is a mistake for the marketing professional to believe (as was the case years ago) that most people do not really know what they want and so can be given whatever they probably deserve. Times have changed, and your future success is likely to be in direct proportion to how *customer-oriented* you are with respect to the quality of your goods and services.

Total quality, as the term is used here, is not something noble and remote like liberty and justice for all. It is simply the maximization of productivity, minimization of waste, development of good employee relations, interest in a customer or client orientation, and careful measurement and analysis of results, all rolled into one. It must involve every level and every individual in an organization and must begin with a clear understanding of customer and client needs—which is, of course, the basic marketing concept. In addition, it demands constant attention and improvement.

For total quality *marketing* to work in your organization, you must seek to meet or exceed your customers' needs and expectations with products, services, and customer relations that are clearly superior to your competition. This is no easy task, but is certainly possible.

Quality may cost you a bit in the short term, but it can pay big dividends in the long term—as the Japanese have demonstrated in design and manufacture of electronic and automotive products, and in other industries to which they have devoted their special attention.

WHERE TO BEGIN

You have no doubt already laid the foundation for a total quality marketing program with the implicit understanding of everyone in your organization that you will conform to the written codes of local, state, and national organizations and commonly accepted business standards of *ethical behavior*. Ethics is a complex subject—especially with regard to marketing—and will be treated in more detail in Chapter 40. But you probably have already defined ethical behavior in two parts:

• Consistently doing *the right* things.
• Consistently doing *no wrong* things.

What is the right thing? Generally, that which conforms to commonly accepted business and professional standards as outlined in the American Marketing Association Code of Ethics (Appendix 15), and that which gives you personal and professional pride and satisfaction. And what is the wrong thing? Simply that which violates accepted business and professional standards and/or would make you feel shame if you were to see it reported on the front page of your local newspaper or watch it on the evening news.

PRODUCT DEVELOPMENT

By now you also have a clear idea of which of your products or services, or which of their parts, are most appealing to your customers, prospects, and peers. But you can go a bit further—as have some Japanese who subscribe to the TQM philosophy—and aim to develop one or more products or services that actually *delight* your customers.

This, too, is not a new idea. In fact, it goes by many names in business and industry: *product development, product planning, product modification, brand extension, line extension*—all phrases that mean essentially the same thing: To improve the goods or services offered, so that they will continue to appeal to the target market(s), or begin to appeal to new markets.

The knowledgeable marketer knows that *altering* the product mix (or assortment of goods and services offered) involves substantially less risk than attempting to develop and market an *altogether new* product or service. In hard-goods terms, product development can be divided into these categories:

- *Functional change*—to be useful to more people, to move into a superior position competitively, or simply to appear progressive.
- *Quality change*—with hard goods, this relates to reliability and durability, but service quality is judged by speed, accuracy, efficiency, and courtesy; perceptions may also be related to price.
- *Style change*—subjective determination to gain on competition; but the risk is loss of existing customers.

Some marketers will not want to get involved in these kinds of considerations, but those who do may be surprised at how fruitful a little reflection on the subject may prove. Your immediate aim is probably to persuade customers and prospects to avail themselves of your *current* products or services. But your *long-range* aim should be to create the goods and services they need for the future, and then assure that they are aware of those new goods and services. This approach will make possible a busy, stable, and even growing business.

There are four basic ways to expand what you have to offer:

- Create new products from old products.
- Create altogether new products for the present market.
- Introduce old products to new markets.
- Create new products for new markets (the most risky).

SITUATION ANALYSIS

Basic to strategic marketing planning is completion of a thorough *situation* (or *situational* or *environmental*) *analysis*, wherein several factors are studied:

- *Your industry*—information obtainable from sources noted in Appendix 3 can indicate how large your industry is and how fast it is growing. Also read specialized business publications (trade and professional magazines and newspapers) for your industry which you will find in the three volumes of *Standard Rate & Data Service—Specialized Business Publications* and perhaps academic journals that relate to your industry to determine current industry trends and what *social, technological, economic,* and *regulatory* forces are likely to affect your industry now and in the future. Join business and professional associations that provide industry information to members; attend lectures by leaders in your industry; attend appropriate tradeshows, conventions, and exhibits; and read government publications—particularly for proposed legislation that may affect your industry.

- *Your competitors*—information obtainable from sources noted in Appendix 3 can enlighten you, as can direct observation of your competitors, as suggested in Chapter 13. If your competitors are publicly traded companies you may want to buy their stock so you can receive their annual reports and attend their shareholders meetings. Collect their literature at tradeshows and by responding to their advertising offers of information, read articles in trade magazines about their activities, study their Web sites, and solicit the advice of consultants who are familiar with those companies. In the final analysis you will be trying to determine your *competitive advantage* (which can be defined as attributes such as product quality, brand recognition, value pricing, efficient distribution, memorable advertising, and the like that can cause customers and prospects to perceive your organization's offering as more highly desirable than those of other organizations), how strategically to communicate that competitive advantage, and in what strategic ways you can counter competitive strategies. *Competitive advantage* is also called *differential advantage* or *point-of-difference.*

- *Your customers and prospects (target market[s])*—first, gather information from your own internal records about who your customers are and what their buying patterns may be. Then look to secondary research to determine how large your target markets are, how fast they are growing (if they are), where they are located, and so on. Only after you have completed this sort of research should you engage in primary research, perhaps to determine such things as attitudes, opinions, and interests that you cannot discover elsewhere.

- *Your own company*—conduct internal audits and executive opinion research. To estimate the likelihood of success for your efforts, you will want to evaluate your internal skills, or determine whether you can obtain them, whether you have an intelligent strategic marketing plan (including all the major areas of marketing specified in this handbook), and whether there is full commitment by top management to implement your strategies. Determine the risks of proposed action and try to provide sufficient flexibility in your plan to adjust to unexpected changes. Finally, see that revenue forecasts (the subject of Chapter 36) are reasonable and achievable.

As indicated in Appendix 2, each of these should be described in a separate section of your marketing plan.

Many marketers also favor development of a *SWOT analysis* to emphasize particular areas that represent major problems and opportunities and that should therefore be specifically addressed in the marketing plan.

SWOT ANALYSIS

Today's better marketers rely on three essential questions in the context of improving the products and services they offer:

- What do we *do best*? (Called a "traditional offering.")
- What *might* we do better? (This involves foresight.)
- What *must* we do to succeed? (This, naturally, is related to the need for survival.)

One of the best recent methods to help in this and several other marketing areas is called the SWOT analysis. That easy acronym stands for: Strengths, Weaknesses, Opportunities, and Threats. The first two, of course, apply to *internal* factors, and the last two apply to *external* factors.

Thus, you should consider not only your customers and prospects, but your employees, suppliers, distributors, dealers, and other publics. Look at changes in your business environment that include social, demographic, and cultural; economic; technological and scientific; competitive (both direct and indirect); and legal, governmental, and regulatory (including industry self-regulation).

Identification of critical elements provides a foundation for strategic marketing planning. Let's see how Smythe & Browne, P.C., a hypothetical accounting firm in the Midwest, might measure up on a SWOT analysis grid:

INTERNAL

Favorable Factors	Unfavorable Factors
Strengths	*Weaknesses*
We have provided quality accounting services to our community for 10 years.	We have never made an effort to let people in the area know of us.
We have a good name that is well respected in our community.	We have no "graphic identity" program to enhance our image.
We are making a living.	We should be making a profit.
We have expert personnel who are capable of providing "state-of-the-art" services.	We continue to rely on basic accounting services for most of our volume.

EXTERNAL

Opportunities	*Threats*
New tax laws have made tax preparation so very complicated that only qualified experts can comprehend the rules.	Personal computer programs can do what used to require a qualified accounting professional.
No other accounting firm in our area is doing any media advertising.	There has been considerable media attention lately to financial planning by non-CPA specialists.

Mass marketers consider, in this context, their *product line* or related group of products or services that are sold to the same types of customers, that are used together, and/or that satisfy a particular type of need. When they have more than one product line they often give considerable thought to their *product mix* or the relationships of products or services to one another—particularly as *perceptions* of those relationships may affect consumer awareness and attitudes toward the company and what it has to offer. A *product portfolio* is a company's product mix viewed from a strategic perspective as a set of brands that are at different stages of their product life cycles (PLCs). (The PLC concept is explained in Chapter 8; "Product and Service Strategies.")

FUNDAMENTALS FOR SUCCESS

Here are the fundamentals of total quality marketing:

1. *Quality*—as suggested at the beginning of this chapter, product and/or service quality is considered by many marketing experts today to be the single most important contributor to success.

2. *Timing*—is also crucial to marketing success. This means not only offering what the customer needs, but also providing it when it is needed.

3. *Significantly greater customer benefit*—is also necessary to set your product, service, or business apart from your competition. This is sometimes included in the popular term "competitive advantage." The phrase "comparative advantage," by the way, tends to be used in international marketing in reference to nations rather than companies. The subject of customer benefit is also related to "core competencies" or "distinctive competencies," which are activities that an organization can perform better than other organizations can.

4. *Target markets or publics of sufficient size*—with needs that your product can satisfy certainly are called for. Generally, if you offer something few people need or want, you will soon go broke.

5. *Adequate personnel*—in your firm to do the work required by growing customer demand. This can be especially difficult in fields where workloads vary greatly by time of year, but it must be reckoned with so that customers are not disappointed. Related to this is the need for training, sufficient systems and equipment to maximize productivity, and empowerment of employees to make decisions that satisfy customer needs promptly, aimiably, and reliably.

6. *Availability*—access to customers or clients, or their access to you, is also necessary. If you choose to set up your business strictly to enjoy Wyoming solitude you are probably thinking like a romantic, not like a marketer.

7. *More than customers expected*—the old idea of "a baker's dozen" was giving customers 13 of an item when they asked for 12. By giving a little more, you create a quality image and a perception of value that will not only build customer loyalty, but also generate good word-of-mouth marketing communications.

8. *Careful execution*—of a sound marketing program is required for success. Many products and services that were promising in every other respect have

failed because of faulty planning, ineffective communications, and/or sloppy execution.

IMPLEMENTING A TOTAL QUALITY PROGRAM

Cutting through all the gobbledygook in the business press that deals with TQM, it is apparent that it boils down to *good behavior, good performance*, and providing the customer or client with *good value*.

But total quality for your organization means nothing unless it is implemented, and here are four simple steps to do just that:

- *Commitment*—Begin by encouraging everyone in your organization to strive to equal or exceed your customers' needs and expectations. Many companies today are doing that by the CEO issuing a statement to the effect that everyone is part of the quality improvement effort, that everyone is expected to contribute to the process, and that continuous improvement in products and services is to be the new organizational standard. It should be stressed that the old standard of "close enough" is no longer acceptable; the new standard is excellence in everything the company does. Those employees who don't accept that will certainly be happier working where the standards are not so demanding. And those who accept the charge to produce top quality will quickly realize the sense of pride and accomplishment accompanying their efforts.

- *Evaluation*—Clear identification and description of ideal customers and prospects for your particular operations is the subject of the preceding chapter. Once that is accomplished, all personnel must look constantly for ways to satisfy the needs and expectations of those particular people. After target market(s) identification, suggest that your people ask themselves what bothers or troubles those kinds of people. In other words, *identify a problem*. And keep seeking problems and opportunities at all levels in your firm. Employees should constantly ask themselves questions like these: "Is there something we do that annoys or displeases any of our customers?" "What do we do satisfactorily that we could do even better?" "Is there anything in the company that we can influence that might result in our serving our customers better?" No one should expect to change anything immediately, but reasonable schedules should be expected. In other words, you should not expect early success with respect to quality improvement changes. Good rules from firms that have been successful in TQM are these:

—Keep the changes modest in scope.

—Keep objectives simple.

—Measure your results carefully.

—Don't be too quick to judge success or failure of changes.

—Recognize those who contribute.

—Try to make the program enjoyable as well as productive.

- *Definition*—the problem or opportunity should be clearly defined *in writing*. The means for quality improvement should also be written, along with the anticipated result(s). Then the issue should be thought through with regard to who is affected, both inside and outside the firm, and resources required. Anticipated costs and savings should be calculated, and a cost/value relationship noted. It may be advisable to ask customers early how they feel about the idea and get reactions from them as the idea develops. Remember, it is those people whom you are trying to please in the end, so you need their guidance on a continuing basis. Some people like to create flowcharts to illustrate how quality improvements will work. Although this is clearly important in manufacturing and distribution, it may be less helpful in connection with other operations. Use your own judgment as to whether flowcharting will help. In the end, the written recommendation for each quality improvement should show how much loss or waste is eliminated and how much saving or value is added. The tricky part here, of course, is that what is value to one person may mean nothing to another. Look at the process and ask the following questions:

—Is there a *good reason* for this?

—Has everything that doesn't contribute positively been *eliminated*?

—Will it improve *customer satisfaction*?

—Is the process explained as *simply* as possible so everyone involved can understand it?

—How will we *measure success* on a continuing basis?

• *Execution*—After the quality improvement has been discovered, reflected on, analyzed, evaluated by customers, discussed among employees, written up in proposal form, and approved, it is time to *execute*. Allow time for the idea to work. Ask questions like: "Is this really saving time?" "How much money has this improvement saved this week?" "Are there other improvements or refinements that would help?" "Are our customers happy about this change?" "Are our employees satisfied?" "Have we achieved the goal(s) we set?" "Are our customers *delighted*?" If the idea appears to be a good one based on a reasonable trial period, accept the improvement as *standard operating procedure*. Commend the person(s) responsible and look for new areas in which to improve quality.

CONCLUSION

TQM could represent a separate project equal in scope to the development of a marketing program. But it is included briefly here because it is a timely topic that relates well to strategic marketing planning and that should be considered carefully relative to most written marketing plans.

Chapter 5

How to Set Clear
Marketing Objectives

YOUR ESSENTIAL AIM

In your marketing efforts, you probably want to make the right kinds of people buy your products or avail themselves of your services, and often enough so that your business is at least profitable—and perhaps even *prosperous*.

That certainly is a very reasonable aim. But might you make it somewhat more specific, and thereby more useful in a marketing sense? For example, what *other* possible actions might also be appropriate, how often should they occur, and related to what purchase volume?

The answers might seem easy, but often the *easiest* answers are not the *best* ones.

THE PROCESS

In fact, easy answers are dangerous in marketing because they may lead one to skip the steps of reflection and analysis that are essential to successful strategic planning. And that is why you must look beyond your basic aim to the important discipline of making that aim *specific*. A simple way to systematize your aim is to think of it as requiring these five steps:

1. You must identify from the mass-market universe groups of *suspects* according to your ideal target market definition(s). These are people within your *draw area* (the geographic region from which you attract customers), perhaps segmented not only by ZIP Code or census tract but also according to demographics, psychographics, synchrographics, usage, need, or other segmentation variable.

2. Through a variety of communications techniques, you should elicit attention and interest, measured by any of several forms of research and/or response, which convert the best qualified of the suspects to *prospects*. In business marketing, these are people who contact you for information by writing to you, mailing a business reply card, returning a coupon, calling a toll-free number, or visiting your Web site. They are described by sales people as *inquirers* and their responses as *inquiries*.

3. Additional activity that you direct specifically to these prospects should render a select core of what are called in personal selling *hot prospects*, or individuals with genuine needs, interest in your product, the authority to order, and the financial backing to pay for what they buy. (A neat acronym for this is *MADA*, which stands for the prospective customer needing to have money, authority, desire, and access.) In business marketing they normally identify themselves by requesting that a salesperson call or that a quote be submitted, and are often called *qualified leads* or simply *leads*. In consumer marketing they are people who visit your store, read your direct-response advertisement, or go to your Web site with intent to purchase—in other words, *shoppers*.

4. You can then pursue this manageable number of high-potential people—often through personal contact—and convert them to *customers* or *clients*.

5. By offering fair prices, good value, and conscientious customer service, you can go one step further and stimulate repeat purchase, thereby accumulating a core of *loyal customers* or *regular clients* who will be the foundation of your future business or professional success.

A USEFUL MODEL

It is interesting to see how many of each type of person is required at each successive step in the process suggested here. For example, I have used in business marketing what I call a *"Multiples of Ten"* model that works as follows:

Since an industrial or professional sales rep usually can close only about 1 in 10 personal calls, or convert 1 in 10 qualified leads to a sale, it requires 10 hot prospects (category 3) to acquire *one* first-time customer.

Similarly, only about 1 in 10 inquirers (category 2) actually wants to see a sales rep or obtain a quote, so it takes *100* of them to result in *one* customer. This, by the way, is why it is usually foolish for sales managers and advertising departments to send field sales reps the names and addresses of unqualified inquirers; since only an average of 1 in 100 are likely to be closed, reps quickly learn to consider all names sent to them from headquarters as unprofitable "coupon-clippers."

Going a step further, it is likely that at best only about 1 in 10 moderately qualified people (category 1) will actually ask for more information; so a business marketer must reach *1,000* suspects—or deliver 1,000 effective impressions—to obtain *one* first-time customer.

Since we also have to allow for waste circulation and the necessity of multiple "hits" (calculated as *gross impressions*) in advertising to break through the clutter and obtain a preliminary level of attention and interest, theoretically applying the "Multiples of Ten" model would call for *10,000* gross impressions to obtain 1,000 attentive suspects, 100 inquirers or prospects, 10 hot prospects, and ultimately *one* customer. You might multiply everything by 10 again to estimate the figures required to obtain one *loyal* customer, depending on the attentiveness of your sales personnel and the success of your customer relations efforts.

You can apply any numbers for multiples you think work for your particular industry or product line at each of the five or six levels, and thereby work back arithmetically to the gross impressions your marketing communications plan must achieve to obtain the number of customers you need to succeed.

Then, by factoring in average costs-per-thousand (CPMs) for the particular medium or media mix you choose for your schedule, you can quickly and quite accurately estimate your annual marketing communications or advertising budget. But more about that later in Chapter 37.

A PROFITABLE DISCIPLINE

With the value of executive and managerial time and the cost of overhead rising ever higher, setting clear and specific objectives should be essential to the profitable operation of most businesses and professional practices. To apply this discipline you must ask yourself what you intend your marketing program to *do*. And then, importantly, what the *response* of your ideal customers or clients is to be—or what *specific action* you expect for them to take. That sounds as simple as one-two-three but, like many other aspects of strategic marketing planning, it is by no means *easy* which is probably why the discipline is not more commonly practiced.

SETTING YOUR OBJECTIVES

Objectives are generally considered to be the foundation for strategic marketing planning and should form the basis of almost everything you do with respect to planning, implementation, and control.

The reason is obvious: To determine what should be done and why, to whom it should be done and how, where it should be done and when, to what extent it should be done and for how much, you must have a clear statement of exactly what you *expect* of your marketing program.

Thus, there are three reasons why objectives are important:

• Objectives express for all concerned the agreed-upon expectations of what the marketing program is to accomplish and thereby help to keep the expectations within *reasonable limits*.

- Objectives provide *direction* for all components of the marketing program and help keep all activities in tune with one another.
- Objectives set *standards* by which the success of the various elements of the marketing program can be measured. And by *tracking* your actual accomplishments, daily, weekly, monthly, or quarterly, with regard to your objectives you can adjust or change your strategies if they seem not to be working as you desire.

FUNCTIONAL OBJECTIVES

Although the distinctions will become more important as you proceed with your strategic marketing planning, now is the time to clarify what is meant by different *types* of objectives within a marketing plan. First, look at the scope of your strategic plan, normally a one-year or a five-year plan, and decide whether your objectives are *short-term* (1 to 3 years) or *long-term* (3 to 5, or even as long as 10 years). Then consider the following types of objectives, which relate generally to the departments within an organization that are most likely to do strategic planning:

- *General, corporate, or overall objectives* are those which apply to total operations and are set by top management. An example of this type of objective is "To make a profit this year."
- *Operational objectives* have to do with how a business is run on a daily, weekly, monthly, quarterly, or annual basis. Like general objectives, these are *not* the bases of *marketing* strategies. An example of an operational objective is "To assure that our stores are open 24 hours a day, 365 days a year, including all national and local holidays."
- *Manufacturing objectives* are also outside the responsibility of marketing and relate to matters of production and quality control. An example is "To see that our products meet or exceed the most rigorous standards of U.S. Department of Transportation safety requirements."
- *Marketing objectives* relate to the specifics of marketing planning and are established in the marketing department. This is where strategic marketing planning begins. An example of a marketing objective is "To increase our share of the total breakfast cereal market in the Southwestern Region of the United States."
- *Distribution or logistics objectives* involve how the company wishes to get its product from the point of origin to the end user. For example, "To distribute our potato chips through select food brokers nationwide."
- *Sales objectives* are appropriate for most businesses, although they may not seem altogether appropriate for professionals who are loath to think of themselves as *selling* something. A typical sales objective would read "To sell $1,000,000 worth of our new multi-disk units in Latin America." Sales objectives may be expressed in terms of either sales dollars or units of product, although the former is more common. Professional organizations can express this type of objective in terms of firm revenues, perhaps broken down by type of client or services rendered.

- *Advertising objectives* help to define mass communication choices. An example might be "To make the name of our new brand, Tingle toothpaste, familiar to 40 percent of American heads of household."
- *Sales promotion objectives* relate to offers that prompt prospects to take immediate action. An example might be "To increase repurchase of Goodfellas frozen pizza by distributing in-pack cents-off coupons."
- *Public relations objectives* generally apply to the entire corporate entity, but often involve marketing considerations. They normally involve enhancing perceptions of the company or organization as "a good corporate citizen" concerned with its community, society, and/or the environment. An example is "To demonstrate that our firm is a good neighbor in the community through our continued 50 percent discount to worthy local charities."
- *Publicity objectives* tend to be somewhat less specific than advertising objectives and are often expressed in terms of how much "ink," or media coverage, the company should get. An example related to the PR objective just suggested is "To maintain public awareness that our firm is a good neighbor in the community by attaining no fewer than 40 column inches of editorial coverage of our philanthropic activities in local newspapers."
- *Customer service or client service objectives* relate to making new customers or clients feel welcome and keeping existing patrons convinced that they are important and cared about. One way to express such an objective is "To reinforce in the minds of our company's target market individuals our customer orientation, personal attention, and care."
- *Communications objectives* relate to execution of advertising, sales promotion, public relations, publicity, sales, and customer or client service objectives and might be expressed relative to the foregoing as "By means of daily newspapers and local business magazines to efficiently and effectively reach business executives regularly during the coming year."

As you skim down this list you can see that for the most part each objective evolves from a previous objective and, generally, each becomes more specific in terms of the task(s) to be accomplished.

For example, "To make a profit this year," which is a general or corporate objective, not only may require increased production, but also probably requires a maintenance or increase in share of market, which is a marketing objective. How product reaches the end user is a function of distribution or logistics and significantly affects market share. If market share is measured in terms of company sales as a percent of total industry sales (as it normally is), some sort of sales objective will be necessary to specify the dollars needed to achieve the desired share of market. And in order for people to spend money to provide those dollars, there will have to be an increase, a change, or a maintenance of their awareness, knowledge, opinions or beliefs, curiosity, and/or willingness for trial—all of which are qualities of advertising objectives. Advertising objectives tend to support sales promotion objectives, although sometimes the reverse works better, depending on the market situation and strategy. And advertising may also support public relations activities, and reinforce publicity objectives, especially in organizations practicing integrated marketing communications (IMC). Customer service objectives support all marketing activities from distribution through publicity. And communications objectives are the tactical means that relate to the achievement of sales, advertising, publicity, public relations, sales promotion, and customer or client service objectives.

It is important to understand and apply these distinctions. Too many marketers think they can set, for example, such an *advertising* objective as "Bring in $100,000 in new business." In fact, advertising alone *cannot* "bring in business"—unless the company is a mail order or direct-response marketer—because too many variables uncontrolled by advertising occur between advertising exposure and the final sale.

So think what factors are *directly* involved in each step, and avoid taking shortcuts that can defeat the purpose of strategic marketing planning.

INDIRECT OBJECTIVES

Within the present framework, there are several additional considerations that can influence the specific way you express your objectives, whatever type they might be. Those in the first group relate to what are commonly called *indirect objectives* since they do not involve direct action.

- *Awareness objectives*—are probably the most common in the planning of marketing communications, often expressed as *"create (or increase) awareness."* This generally is useless for strategic planning, though, because "awareness" is so difficult to define, measure, and quantify. Does awareness mean a survey respondent recognizes a brand name, or knows what the branded product does, or specifies the brand when asked to name the top three products in a category, or recalls having seen an advertisement for the product? Although such specificity is seldom seen, "awareness" is commonly noted as the major objective among marketing firms and advertising agencies alike. Because it is expected, you should consider including it in your marketing planning—especially if you can clarify exactly what you wish to achieve.

- *Positioning* (or *brand image*) *objectives*—go beyond simply awareness for a product or service. Chapter 14, "Positioning Strategies," lists several different *types of positioning* that can make this sort of objective specific.

- *Knowledge objectives*—are important whether your business or organization is new or established and you will probably want to set at least one objective that deals with your intentions to *increase knowledge* about your organization and what it stands for, or about features and benefits of your product or service. You might also consider imparting knowledge about where your product can be obtained, how it can be used, how much it costs, if you plan a price increase (which can also serve as a strategy to encourage customers to "buy now"), trade-in or rebate offers, special terms such as financing options, new policies, and guarantees and warranties. An objective related to *increasing knowledge* is stronger than one merely *increasing awareness*, and in general marketing terms will involve steps that include making contact, arousing interest, and creating preference. (For more detail on this, see "The Strategic Steps in Selling" in Chapter 31.)

- *Attitude objectives*—pertain to the need to *change attitude*. This is far from easy to do, but clearly worthwhile, especially if customer or prospect attitudes are negative.

- *Reputation objectives*—are important indirect objectives that relate to the need to *enhance the image* of the organization, its employees, or perhaps even an individual, such as the CEO. You may feel that it would be difficult to do that without a boastful appearance, but this type of objective probably belongs on your list anyway, since if you do not believe in your venture, chances are no one else will either. Consider such factors as your organization's technological leadership, progressiveness, growth potential, good corporate citizenship, fair hiring practices, ethical business dealings, courtesy, and service. You will have already considered the related subject of *product positioning* in terms of product reliability, durability, repairability, style, design, and (of course) quality; but now think, from the customer's point of view, about related *reputation* factors that include ease of ordering, speed and efficiency of delivery, ease of installation, user training, and product maintenance.

- *Confidence objectives*—run along the same line and you might wish to seek to *develop confidence* in your company or brand among any or all of your targets.

- *Goodwill objectives*—are important to public relations activities as well as other types of marketing communications in that they relate to *creating or enhancing goodwill*. As the next chapter will explain, it is particularly important that such an objective as this be further defined with respect to the appropriate target market, checklists for which are included in Chapter 3 and Appendix 5.

- *Competition objectives*—are crucial if your strategic activity is of a competitive nature, the subject of Chapter 13. Commonly marketers specify an objective to *counter competitive claims*.

- *Correction objectives*—are useful if your competition has hurt you, or if you have received bad press. Then an objective could be to *correct false notions* about your company, personnel, product, or service.

- *Recognition objectives*—are popular among consumer packaged-goods marketers in the form of an objective to *build the brand, trade dress, or package recognition*. Most successful brands rely on consumers noticing the brand's distinctive appearance on store shelves.

- *Preference objectives*—are those that intend to lead people to a favorable buying decision. This could be expressed as an indirect objective to *influence preference* and is vital to whether you acquire or lose a prospective customer or client. Therefore, you may wish to set that in some form of an objective so you can consider the many ways to accomplish it.

- *Intention objectives*—should be considered before you move on to action-oriented objectives. Here you express your desire to affect the *intention for action*. Obviously nothing significant will happen until a mental process occurs that culminates in a person deciding to take some sort of action. This can be accomplished by either remote-control or personal communication factors—or more likely by a combination of the two. Intention for action is probably the second most important part of the prospective customer's mental process, outranked in importance only by *direct action*, which is the subject of the next two sections.

DIRECT OBJECTIVES

These are called *direct objectives* because they relate to direct action on the part of the prospect, consumer, customer, or client.

- *Traffic objectives*—are common in consumer marketing and expressed as to *develop or increase traffic* because it is so important to have prospects visit retailers. Unlike those of the retailer, though, the assets of professionals (employees, computers, and so on) are *portable*, which means that the performance of some professional services can be done in many different places. So, although it is important for retailers to have people visit their stores and physically move past their inventories, *traffic* to most business and professional marketers will mean *personal contact* that is made with members of the organization, wherever they may be. So think about both walk-up and drive-up traffic, as well as deploying forces to make direct contact with customers, clients, prospects, and referral sources. "Traffic" in this context, then, is a means to the end of obtaining new business and retaining old business.
- *Coupon objectives*—are perhaps even more common in retailing and relate to sales promotion strategy to increase traffic. Expressed as *coupon redemption*, these can be in the form of straight discounts, limited-time special prices, extra product, and so on—depending on legal and professional restrictions and considerations of personal taste. This item is here because you may want to develop it in the form of a goal, as described in the next chapter. The subject of coupons will be treated in greater detail in Chapter 15, "Offer Strategies," and Chapter 28, "Sales Promotion Strategies."
- *Rebate objectives*—are related to coupon redemption, although involving larger dollar amounts in the form of *rebate return*.
- *Contest objectives*—are also related to sales promotion strategy in the form of *entry in a contest, games, or sweepstakes.*
- *Sampling objectives*—relate to strategies for *trial offers* and *sampling*. The *trial offer* requires a purchase but offers cancellation if the customer is not completely satisfied. *Sampling*, as the term suggests, means a small quantity of a product or service is provided at no charge as a lure.
- *Inquiry objectives*—are particularly important if you are a business marketer to help field sales people obtain new customers. Thus, at least one of your objectives should be to *obtain inquiries* for information, as perhaps when you offer "at no cost or obligation" a folder on several ways to solve a problem through the use of your product(s) or service(s) or information on your Web site. The assumption

here, of course, is that inquirers can be converted somehow to customers or clients. So simply obtaining inquiries should not be an end in itself.

- *Lead objectives*—express your intention to *obtain leads* for follow-up. As noted previously, a *lead* differs from an *inquiry* in that it is a direct request for a personal meeting to discuss possible business, and qualifies a respondent as a *hot prospect* according to "The Process" model described at the beginning of this chapter. Obtaining leads is often their fundamental objective when professional and managerial people agree to speak at social or business meetings on subjects pertaining to their specialties. And it is the reason for including a check-box on ads and reply forms that reads in effect: "Have a representative call me for an appointment to discuss your offer." This often involves *requests for personal demonstrations* and may involve *an incentive for a salesperson's visit*. Sales objectives can be set with regard to *conversions to sales*—that is, what percent of referred leads sales people are able to turn into orders and/or what immediate and long-term dollar value those conversions represent.
- *Volume objectives*—may be expressed in the form of *obtaining larger orders*.
- *Dealer objectives*—relate to intermediaries or resellers and intend to *obtain distributors and dealers* and *get good dealer display space*.
- *Event objectives*—relate to *promoting a buying event*. For ideas on tactics to accomplish this, see Appendix 13, "Special Event List for Retailers and Proven Themes for Sales Managers."
- *Direct order objectives*—these assume that it is possible for the marketer to initiate and close direct sales, or *obtain direct orders*. This is difficult for professional services, but economical and often highly productive for marketers of products. Ethical offers that involve some form of what has traditionally been called "mail order," more recently "direct response" and "direct marketing," and lately "interactive marketing" often include every step in the marketing process. Related objectives of this type can be expressed as *close partially sold prospects*, and *prompt impulse purchases*.

You will find it fairly easy and very productive to express these objectives in *quantitative terms*, according to the suggestions for establishing clear and measurable marketing *"goals"* that appear in the following chapter.

ADDITIONAL ACTION OBJECTIVES

Harder to categorize as "indirect" versus "direct" objectives are the following you might also wish to consider:

- Open new markets (geographic, demographic, psychographic).
- Retain present customers.
- Increase consumer or customer demand.
- Convert users from competitive products or services.
- Encourage specifying your brand name rather than a generic name.

- Cause nonusers to become users.
- Encourage regular purchase.
- Suggest new uses for the product.
- Encourage purchase of larger sizes.
- Encourage greater buying frequency.
- Remind users to buy now.
- Build morale of your sales organization.
- Maintain good working conditions for employees.
- Contribute positively to society in general.

OBJECTIVES FOR EACH ACTIVITY

You should have *at least one* objective for each of the major marketing areas in your plan—specifically pertaining to: your market, product or service, packaging, pricing, distribution or logistics, competition, positioning, marketing communications and media, sales promotion, public relations, publicity, personal selling, customer service, management, and perhaps budgeting.

You should then convert each into at least one *measurable goal*, according to the discipline outlined in the following chapter. After you have completed those steps in the planning process, you can logically, realistically, and imaginatively select appropriate and innovative strategies, tactics, and techniques from the lists that begin with Chapter 7.

Chapter 6

How to Convert Objectives to Measurable Goals

TERMINOLOGY

The words *objective* and *goal* are often used interchangeably in marketing, but that is not satisfactory. Certainly you want people to *buy your product or service*, but exactly who are those people? Exactly what must you do, and exactly what must they do? How many of them do you want to do it, and do it to what extent—taking into account your capacity to deliver your product or service promptly? And how much time will you allow for what you desire to occur?

Many marketers now distinguish a *goal* as a *specific objective*, a refinement of an objective, or a clearly delineated end that is desirable.

This sort of discipline was endorsed as far back as 1960 by the Association of National Advertisers (ANA) and, although it has not been embraced with the enthusiasm it deserves, if you give it a try you should discover how particularly useful in strategic marketing planning this distinction between objectives and goals can be.

The recommended practice requires that once you have your objectives clearly in mind—and preferably written down—you should try to convert them to measurable goals that express four factors:

1. the specific *job to be done*, which is the basic objective, along the lines described in the preceding chapter
2. the specific *target market or public to be affected*
3. the exact *amount of change* to occur
4. the specific *time period* for the activity

These four crucial elements distinguish a *measurable goal* from a more general *objective*. They are easy to remember if you modify the old rhyme about four helpful serving men: Their names are *What* and *Who*; *How Much* and *When*.

AN EXAMPLE OF A CONSUMER GOAL

Here is how your strategic marketing planning can apply and benefit from *goals* instead of merely objectives.

A *general* objective typical of many companies might be:

> To introduce Savor chewing gum nationwide.

An objective that involves a *feature* might read:

> To create awareness that Savor chewing gum is flavorful, but sugar-free.

An objective involving *communication* might read:

> To reach a young consumer audience through a high-frequency television and print advertising campaign for Savor chewing gum.

None of these is *specific* enough, though, to lead logically to development of innovative and practical marketing strategies.

A measurable goal, on the other hand, might read like this:

> To achieve a 3 share of the sugar-free chewing gum market for Savor brand chewing gum among men and women 18 to 34 years of age nationwide within one year of introduction.

This goal statement makes clear that the marketing target is young adults both male and female, within measurable demographic segments (18–34). It clearly states the anticipated share (3), which in turn can be converted to national sales figures, and it specifies that the goal will be achieved within one year—so that the marketing effort does not become open ended.

AN EXAMPLE OF A BUSINESS (NONCONSUMER) GOAL

Here is how a professional organization could set a similar goal, and with even more specificity:

A *general* objective typical of many organizations might be:

> To introduce our firm, Business Accounting Services.

An objective that involves a *feature* might read:

> To announce that Business Accounting Services serves the accounting needs of both large and small businesses.

An objective involving *communication* might read:

> To create awareness of the advantages of dealing with Business Accounting Services.

As in the consumer product example, none of these definitions is *specific* enough to lead to solid marketing strategies for accomplishment. However, a measurable goal could read like this:

> To build our business account roster, we intend to persuade 23 (or roughly 3 percent) of the owners of the 753 privately held business enterprises in the three-county area surrounding our office to request monthly bookkeeping services by Business Accounting Services within calendar year 20XX.

Now *that* is something the firm's marketers can use for intelligent strategic planning.

The goal statement makes clear that the target market is owners of privately held businesses located most conveniently to the firm, and how many of them there are. It specifies the particular job to be done, the service to be offered, and establishes a reasonable number of *suspects* who can be contacted. This goal statement also states the number of *clients* who can reasonably be added so the firm does not risk being overloaded with new business—something that *can* be a problem if marketing communications are not strategically controlled. (The number of *prospects* and *hot prospects* who can be followed up on, by the way, can be calculated using the model indicated in the preceding chapter.) Finally, this statement gives a specific amount of time in which to accomplish the goal—so there is a clear deadline to be observed by all involved.

AN EXAMPLE OF A GOAL FOR OTHER TARGETS

The same type of measurable goal as that in the preceding example can be developed for *other* marketing influencers who, as indicated in the list in Chapter 3, are not actually customers, clients, or prospects.

Take referral sources for a professional practice, for example, where the measurable goal might read like this:

During our first year of operation, among the 214 branch banks in our immediate area, persuade managers and customer service representatives that Business Accounting Services is a fully reliable firm worthy of serving their customers who ask for recommendations for accounting services.

You will perhaps find that it is a little more difficult to define goals for your other publics than for your ideal customers or clients—but it can be well worth the effort.

WHAT YOU WILL ACHIEVE

When you follow this discipline, you will be armed with your own statements of what you intend to accomplish through your marketing program. They will be specific in terms of the job to be done; the individuals you expect to influence; the quantified action they are to take, change that is to occur, or thought or awareness that is to be conveyed; and the exact time period in which the program is to take place.

With those matters clearly established, you can intelligently consider distinct strategies for every aspect of your marketing program.

In the pages that follow, you will find strategies not just related to research and targeting but also chapters on market strategies; product and service strategies; name, brand, and trademark strategies; packaging strategies; pricing strategies; distribution, logistics, and channel strategies; competitive strategies; positioning strategies; offer strategies; marketing communications and media strategies; types of advertisements and creative strategies; rhetorical creative strategies; product or service-related creative strategies; artistic and emotional creative strategies; logical creative strategies; campaign strategies; copywriting techniques; advertising design, art, and typographic strategies and techniques; television commercial production techniques; selling-letter techniques; electronic commerce and Internet tactics; sales promotion strategies; public relations strategies; publicity strategies; personal selling strategies; objection and closing strategies; customer service strategies; presentation and public speaking strategies; revenue forecasting strategies; budgeting strategies; evaluation strategies; marketing management strategies; and information, message, and ethics considerations for strategic marketing; as well as suggestions on how to write a marketing strategy statement; how to evaluate strategic marketing cases; and many related topics in the form of appendices.

The discipline of converting general objectives to measurable goals is the best possible way to proceed in strategic marketing planning because it gives you a solid foundation for rational decision-making—instead of the blind guesses that otherwise are too often required.

STRATEGIES VERSUS TACTICS

The discipline also helps you logically distinguish between strategies and tactics, explained in the Introduction, which is a mental exercise with which many business people have difficulty.

The line of thinking just described leaves little room for confusion because, as a rule, your *strategies* will be what you envision to accomplish your *objectives*, or broader aims. And the *tactics* you employ—the individual executional elements of your plan—will be the means by which you accomplish your *goals*.

It's just that simple: Objectives are achieved through strategies, and goals are achieved through tactics.

Part II

The Nuts and Bolts of
Marketing Planning

Chapter 7

Market Strategies

BASIC TERMINOLOGY

The word "market" originally meant the gathering or place of assembly for people to engage in trade, but it has broadened in modern marketing to mean a variety of things.

Most often "market" means a particular group of people who share a need or potential desire for what you have to offer. That group can be defined by age, as "the teen market," by occupation, as "the blue-collar market," or by income, religion, race, and a variety of other demographic factors covered in Appendix 5. A market can also be a geographic area, as "the New England market," or relate to an industry, as "the electronics market." In general business parlance it can also refer to demand, as "the housing market," or to supply, as "the labor market," or matters of finance and investment, as in "The (Stock) Market."

The term "consumer market" refers to individual buyers who purchase products generally for personal or family use. The old term "industrial market" related to all other buying activity or, more accurately, the "non-consumer market" which is composed of *professional, commercial, industrial, reseller* (or *trade*), *institutional,* and *governmental* markets. Today the term *"business market"* is popular in reference to all types of nonconsumer markets.

Receptivity to new products, services, and ideas varies among different market segments, but consumers as a whole have been categorized from the first through the last to buy a new product or service or accept a new idea as: *innovators* (roughly 2.5 percent of the population), *early adopters* who often are opinion leaders (roughly 13.5 percent), *early majority* (34 percent), *late majority* (also 34 percent), and *laggards* (about 16 percent). This model relates to *diffusion* strategies, noted in subsequent chapters.

Market strategies usually relate to overall business operations, and influence strategies for each of the basic components of a marketing program, including the basic "*4Ps*" that include *product, price, place* (or distribution), and *promotion* (or marketing communications).

NAMES OF STRATEGIES

These are the proper terms for market-related strategies in common use today, which are listed in what to me is a logical sequence:

- *Single-market* (or *target market*, or *market specialization*) *strategy*—discover one specific market segment with a special need that you can satisfy and direct all your energies there. For example, multivitamin pill marketers have targeted seniors with "silver" products purportedly blended especially for the needs of older people. The *single market* strategy is usually defined in terms of *geographic segmentation* and/or *demographic segmentation* strategies.

- *Niche-market strategy*—select one or more target groups that your competitors do not adequately serve, and offer special benefits. A *niche* differs from a *segment* in that it tends to be smaller and often more specialized in some way. The multivitamin pill marketer who might feature the anti-flatulent chemical simethicone as a component of the company's "silver" multivitamin product would be relying on a *niche-market* strategy. Often *niche-market* strategy is defined in terms of *psychographic segmentation, synchrographic segmentation,* or *need segmentation* strategies. Both *single-market* and *niche-market* strategies work well with the product strategy called *differentiation focus strategy* defined in the next chapter.

- *Cascading strategy*—penetrate a small, carefully defined market segment or niche and grow there without attracting the attention of your competition. Not easy to accomplish, since it relies more on the inattention of competitors than on the innovation of the company employing the strategy.

- *Concentrated* (or *concentration*) *marketing* (or *market*) *strategy*—applies to all the foregoing strategies. It means simply that all marketing efforts will be directed to a particular market segment or niche. *Concentrated marketing strategy* is characterized by Procter & Gamble's classic target of "women 18 to 34" which assumed that women buy most consumer packaged goods, form households at 18, and are brand-loyal (hence resistant to brand switching) by age 35. The term "concentrated" is also used to describe an advertising media strategy.

- *Growth-market strategy*—discover one or more fast-growing market segments, and direct your product or service and your communications to them. The personal computer hardware and software industries are still enjoying this strategy. The more general term *growth strategy* is used to encompass strategies treated separately here: *market penetration, market development, product development,* and *diversification.*

- *Market specialization strategy*—clearly define a specific market segment and offer it the widest range of goods or services you can. Outlets such as Office Max® appear to employ this strategy toward consumers, as do companies that concentrate on their *existing base*, or on *prospecting* (for new customers), and *business marketers* who sell "to the trade" and/or to *professional, commercial, industrial, reseller, institutional*, and *governmental* markets.

- *Diffusion strategy*—where you attract the attention to a new product or service of a market segment that *gradually* adopts it. A good strategy for small companies that lack resources to launch aggressively and/or voluminously.

- *Product specialization strategy*—this is the opposite of *market specialization* strategy, where the marketing thrust concentrates on a single product or service, rather than a broad range of products or services. Payless® shoe stores are an example of this. (See definitions for types of *product lines* in the next chapter.)

- *Market aggregation strategy*—somewhat like *product specialization strategy* in that you create a single product supported by a single marketing program, but you try to reach as many prospective customers as you possibly can. This market strategy relates to *penetration pricing* strategy.

- *Market atomization strategy*—just the opposite of the foregoing, in that each prospective customer is treated as a unique market segment.

- *Multi-market* (or *selective specialization*, or *multisegment coverage*) *strategy*— identify several segments likely to need your product or service and try to develop them all simultaneously. For example, a company like Kodak has targeted three types of picture-takers for sales of their photographic film products: amateurs, advanced amateurs, and professionals.

- *Mass-market* (or *undifferentiated*, or *full-market*, or *total-market*, or *shotgun*) *strategy*—go after any and every type of prospect you can identify and offer a variety of products. This has been the traditional strategy of many consumer packaged-goods marketers who, despite success in years past, have recently been resorting to *other* market strategies.

- *Differentiated marketing strategy*—address a relatively large, and perhaps even a variety of market segments, but tailor marketing programs to the particular needs and interests of each segment. For example, Kodak emphasizes the high resolution of its film to all customers, but may feature faithful reproduction of flesh tones to Caucasians interested in photographing family occasions, but high speed for people interested in photographing sporting events.

- *Local-market strategy*—concentrate on the territory that immediately surrounds your place of business.

- *Regional-market strategy*—concentrate on several contiguous states, such as the Southwest.

- *National-market strategy*—try to cover the entire country.

- *International market strategy*—market existing products and services in other countries in the same way they are marketed domestically.

- *Multidomestic* (or *multinational*) *market strategy*—develop different products and different brand names for domestic products that are appropriate for particular countries in which you do business. The phrase "multinational corporation" (or "MNC") became associated with exploitation years ago and has been somewhat out of favor since.

- *Transnational market strategy*—concentrate on similar needs regardless of geographic or ethnic differences.

- *Global market strategy*—involves standardizing marketing practices in light of cultural similarities, and modifying only when there are significant differences. Observed particularly among business marketers. There is greater economy in these latter two approaches as compared to *multidomestic* or *multinational* strategy.

- *Generational market strategy*—design marketing programs for the special values, attitudes, and behaviors of particular age groups (or "generations").

- *Ethnic market strategy*—appeal to clearly defined racial, nationality, religious, or language segments.

- *Expansion* (or *mobile*) *strategy*—grow by encompassing more existing-market type business.

- *Diversification strategy*—grow by offering new products or services to new or existing customers.

- *Pioneer* (or *first-in*) *strategy*—offer a product that no other company does, or offer it before anyone else does. This strategy targets *innovators* and *early adopters*, but frequently results in failure for the pioneering company, even when the industry may prosper.

- *Early-in strategy*—offer what the first-in company offers soon after they introduce their product. This strategy targets *early adopters* and the *early majority*.

- *Late-entry* (or *follower*) *strategy*—wait to see what works and get into the marketplace after the dust has settled. Offerings of this type are called "me-too products." This strategy has been broken down into four subcategories which relate to competitive strategies (the subject of Chapter 13): *counterfeit* which duplicates the leading product in every detail and is sold on the black market; *clone* which imitates the leading product but introduces slight variations in design and packaging; *imitation* which copies several features but has different strategies for pricing, packaging, advertising, and promotion; and *adaptation* which picks up the general idea but improves the product, often moves into different markets, and becomes a future challenger.

- *Survival strategy*—just hold on until your business prospects or the situation in the marketplace improves. This strategy targets the *existing customer or client base*.

- *Share of market* (or *penetration*) *strategy*—aim at maximizing your market share or the number of your customers and also increasing sales of present products to existing markets. (See *penetration pricing* strategy in Chapter 11.)

- *Share of mind strategy*—aim at developing prospect and customer attention, awareness, and knowledge of your organization, product, or service. This is related to communication strategy, specifically with regard to *share of voice strategy*, which refers to the percent a product's advertising budget represents relative to total advertising expenditures for the entire product category or industry. (Also referred to in Chapter 16.)

- *Share of heart strategy*—related to public relations, this is a strategy through which you aim for customer and prospect goodwill. It is largely practiced by monopolies or near-monopolies.

- *Share of customer strategy*—the term for a combination of *share of heart* and *share of mind* strategies.

- *Retention strategy*—concentrate on keeping the customer sold, on the grounds that it is normally more economical to retain a customer than to get a new one. This is related to *relationship marketing* and *relationship selling* strategies which will be covered in Chapter 31.

- *Reverse marketing strategy*—normally initiated by the buyer rather than the seller, this is the effort by organizational buyers to build relationships with their suppliers and to clearly communicate their needs to which suppliers can respond.

- *Line-stretching strategies*—generally refers to product or service strategies including the term "extension." These will be covered in the next chapter. The three that follow, however, relate directly to markets so are included here.

- *Downmarket stretch strategy*—a company with an established product line may produce a new lower-quality brand to appeal to people who want lower-priced goods, without jeopardizing the upscale image of the existing brand.

- *Upmarket stretch strategy*—going the other way, a mid-range product may reach for a more affluent market segment by introducing a prestige brand with improved quality, added features, and/or increased price.

- *Two-way stretch strategy*—a middle-market brand may extend the line both up and down with regard to the socio-economic descriptors of its target market segments.

- *Forced distribution* (or *selected controlled*) *market strategy*—where a market test for a new product is conducted, and retailers are paid to display the new product.

- *Reciprocity*—applied in business marketing where each marketer purchases the other's product or service. Not favored by U.S. government agencies with business oversight responsibility but a fairly common practice.

You will find that distribution, logistics, and channel strategies, treated in Chapter 12, may suggest refinement of your basic *market* strategies.

Chapter 8

Product and Service Strategies

BASIC TERMINOLOGY

Just as market strategies can dominate a marketing plan, product or service strategies can be the foundation. It depends on whether operations are market-driven, as in most consumer packaged-goods marketing, or product-driven, as in the fields of high technology and destination marketing.

Marketing principles can be applied not only to products (like automobiles), but also to services (like banking), personalities (like politicians), locations (like resort hotels), destinations (like cities), behavior patterns (like condom use), and even ideas (like representative government). What is marketed is often referred to simply as "the product."

Products are classified in general as *consumer products* or *business products*. The latter are sometimes called, quite logically, *nonconsumer products* and include products for *professional, commercial, industrial, reseller* (or *trade*), *institutional*, and *governmental* markets, as defined in the preceding chapter.

Products can also be differentiated as *consumables* and *durables* or *hard goods*. They are also rather logically identified by color: *white goods* are common household appliances (such as washers and dryers) and also "linens" (sheets and towels), *red goods* are food products (the color refers here to meat—although "green" goods traditionally have been fruits and vegetables), *orange goods* are consumer goods such as clothing that must be replaced at intervals, *yellow goods* are nonconsumable high-ticket household products (such as designer refrigerators and stoves which come in colors such as Aztec Gold) that are retained for many years and that tend to have high profit margins, and *brown goods* are electronics (such as television sets and stereo equipment) although the term harkens back to mid-twentieth-century product colors and should probably be updated to *black goods*.

A *product line* is a group of products related to one another in terms of being used together, sold to the same market segment, distributed through the same channel, priced similarly, or capable of satisfying the same sort of customer need. The product lines produced by a company collectively are called its *product mix* or *product assortment*.

A product *line* that contains several different products is referred to as "long." A product *mix* of several different product lines is referred to as "wide." A product *line or mix* that has great variety is referred to as "deep." And a product mix in which all products are related in some way is referred to as "consistent."

Consumer goods may be classified as *convenience goods*, which are purchased regularly with little customer involvement, and which include *staple goods* such as a loaf of bread, *impulse goods* such as a candy bar, and *emergency goods* for crisis situations such as an umbrella when rain unexpectedly begins to fall; *shopping goods*, which consumers compare according to preferred features, such as durability and price; *specialty goods*, which require a more conscientious search for information, and which may also involve higher costs and a significant emotional dimension in the purchase decision; and *unsought goods*, which are products generally bought without prior planning such as an oil painting discovered at an art show that the consumer "can't live without." The latter might also be called an *impulse good*, although they tend to be of lower price.

Business goods can be divided into two classes: *production goods*, which are components of a final product the company produces, and *support goods*, such as tools and related services used in manufacturing. A more detailed classification for business products separates: *installations* (facilities and major equipment), *raw materials* (to be made into manufactured products, like tungsten to make lamp filaments), *process materials* (products made from something else and used in another product, like tungsten filaments used in automobile headlights), *component parts* (manufactured products assembled into larger products, like headlights put in automobiles), *accessory equipment* (used in production or for office activities, like copying machines), *MRO supplies* (maintenance, repair, and operating items, like bond paper for office copiers), and *business services* (intangibles like temporary personnel to operate copiers).

As noted in connection with product *reputation* and *positioning* in Chapter 5, your customers are likely to be particularly concerned with product reliability, durability, repairability, style, design, and (of course) quality. You should also think, from the customer's point of view, about ease of ordering, speed and efficiency of delivery, ease of installation, user training, and product maintenance.

You will see occasional reference in this handbook to *product life cycle* (or *PLC*), a concept criticized by some marketers today, but still helpful in many aspects of strategic marketing planning. The PLC has four phases logically termed "introduction," "growth," "maturity," and "decline," which can be laid out on a line graph with the horizontal axis time and the vertical axis sales dollars or number of units sold. Different market, product, pricing, distribution, competitive, positioning, marketing communications, and budgeting strategies should be planned for each stage of the PLC. On introduction a product is said to be "launched"; when it begins to decline it will either be "relaunched," "revitalized," "remarketed," "extinguished," or "discontinued." When a new product is introduced in a series of geographic areas over a period of time it is said to be "rolled out." Many of the strategies listed in this handbook are useful for *launch, relaunch, remarketing,* and *rollout.*

NAMES OF STRATEGIES

With those factors in mind, you can now consider the basic product strategies:

- *Build strategy*—what most marketing managers want: to put all possible efforts and resources behind the product to make it grow and succeed. This is also a corporate strategy.

- *Positioning strategy*—try to set one or more of your products apart from your competition as unique in the minds of your target market individuals. (More on this in Chapter 14.)

- *Repositioning strategy*—develop a new position for your product based on quality, design, price, or some other factor, as reflected in the unsuccessful theme "This is not your father's Oldsmobile."

- *Negative* (or *contrary*) *positioning strategy*—set your product apart from the competition, usually through derogation of a competitor. This is a popular strategy among some consumer products marketers and politicians but is not recommended for professional services.

- *Core product strategy*—concentrate marketing efforts on your single, most important, or best recognized product.

- *Overlap strategy*—introduce a product that competes with one of your existing products. You run the risk of "cannibalization" of your old product when market share is taken from your old product rather than your competition, but this strategy has proved effective in packaged-goods marketing for many years.

- *Flanker brand strategy*—introduce a related product, as Coca-Cola® did with Diet Coke®. Also a branding strategy.

- *Multibrand strategy*—sometimes used as synonymous with *overlap* strategy, but also when products in a particular line are given distinctly different brand names.

- *Scope strategy*—take your pick of offering a *single* product, a *limited variety* of products, or a *system* of products. This strategy is akin to positioning in that you are perceived as offering something special to special customers.

- *Design strategy*—again, choose from three possibilities: a *standard* product to suit a broad market segment, a basic product *modified* to suit special customers, or a fully *customized* product to compete with companies that offer only standard or slightly modified products.

- *Eurostyle strategy*—"plain vanilla," monochromatic, geometric appearance in product design.

- *Eurobrand strategy*—variations of consumer products that may have been discontinued in the United States but for which there is still potential demand in Europe. This also involves logistics and advertising, and the combined efforts are referred to as *pan-European marketing.*

- *Ethnic product strategy*—manufacture products that appeal primarily to people in clearly defined racial, nationality, religious, or language segments.

- *Augmentation strategy*—add features to your product that competitive products don't offer. These add-ons, of course, should satisfy customer and prospect needs or potential desires.

- *Straight extension strategy*—introduce your product without change to a market altogether new to you.

- *Product adaptation strategy*—alter your product to meet conditions or preferences of your existing market(s).

- *Differentiation focus* (or *product differentiation*) *strategy*—use significant points of difference in your product to appeal to one or more special market segments.

- *Just-noticeable-difference (JND) strategy*—a form of *differentiation* wherein you create one aspect of the product that will set it apart from competition in the eyes of your customers.

- *Retro-style strategy*—do not copy old products, but consider older styles, such as the Chrysler Cruiser® automobile body reminiscent of the 1930s.

- *Backward invention strategy*—reintroduce old forms of your product to satisfy new or foreign needs.

- *Forward invention strategy*—create a new product to satisfy new or unmet needs.

- *Backward integration strategy*—a manufacturing strategy related to marketing; expand supply and production capability by purchasing one or more of your suppliers to reduce costs of materials.

- *Horizontal integration strategy*—also manufacturing-related; acquire one or more competitor companies to increase production capacity and enjoy *economies of scale.* The Federal Trade Commission (FTC) watches this sort of thing carefully with respect to antitrust.

- *New-product strategy*—again, there are three choices: *improve or modify* your existing product, *imitate* competition (perhaps by offering features touted by your competitor), or develop a totally *new* product. The word "new" can be used to describe a product only for its first six months of national distribution. After that, it is not uncommon for packaged-goods marketers to add a feature like "bleaching beads" to a laundry detergent and refer to it for another six months as "new and improved." This is also the strategy often used to extend a product life cycle (PLC).

- *New-uses* (or *market modification*) *strategy*—increase consumption by developing new ways to use your product, as Arm & Hammer® has done with their basic box of baking soda.

- *Diversification strategy*—develop new approaches to existing markets, or just get involved in new ventures to spread your risks. There are three substrategies: *concentric diversification*, where the new activity involves product(s) technically similar to the primary product(s), *horizontal diversification*, where the new activity involves product(s) completely unrelated to the company's current product(s) but that appeal to traditional market segment(s), and *conglomerate diversification*, where product(s) are totally unrelated to current offerings and appeal to new segment(s).

- *Relaunch* (or *revitalization* or *vitalization*) *strategy*—when product sales are declining, provide new marketing activity as if you were introducing a new product.

- *Product modification strategy*—alter characteristics such as performance, reliability, or appearance of an existing product to make it more appealing.

- *Line extension strategy*—use your existing known brand name on a new product in the same general product category, often to enter a new market segment. This usually works best if the new product is in the same category as the old one. For example, the Crest® brand name has been extended from toothpaste to toothbrushes.

- *Brand extension strategy*—use an existing brand name to enter a totally new product class. For example, the Harley-Davidson® brand name has been extended from motorcycles to after-shave lotion and cigarettes.

- *Spin-off strategy*—when a product in a line is given its own trademark so it can stand alone; also in the television industry when a popular character in a sitcom is given his or her own series.

- *Dual branding* and *co-branding strategies*—pair two brand names on one product. These are usually of the same company (*dual branding*) but may also be the brands of two different companies (*co-branding*)—for example, Rollerblade® Barbie® dolls.

- *Gap-filler* (or *line-filler*) *strategy*—develop products that fill empty places in your product or service line.

- *Technology driver strategy*—akin to positioning, in that you develop an image for your organization as a new-product innovator.

- *Continuous innovation strategy*—usually reserved for industry leaders, this means that the company concentrates on developing new products and improving services, distribution, and pricing. For example, the double-edged razor blade to replace the original single-edged safety razor blade.

- *Dynamically continuous innovation strategy*—develop products that disrupt the consumer's normal routine, but do not require learning totally new behaviors. For example, the "twin-track" blade design for the safety razor.

- *Discontinuous innovation strategy*—involves the development of new products that require entirely new consumption patterns. For example, the electric shaver to replace blade razors.

- *Planned obsolescence strategy*—when products are produced to last only a limited time or become outdated, thereby encouraging replacement purchase. Obsolescence is broken down as *physical obsolescence* (automobiles), *technological obsolescence* (personal computers), and *style obsolescence* (women's clothing).

- *Postponed obsolescence strategy*—when technological improvements to products could be made, but are not made until the demand for existing products declines.

- *Fad product strategy*—develop products intended to catch the public fancy for only a short time. Some fad products, such as yo-yos and water pistols, come and go at regular intervals; others, like the Pet Rock®, seem to be one-shots.

- *Product-elimination* (or *product pruning*) *strategy*—drop the products that don't produce the best returns.

- *Price-discount strategy*—offer an equivalent product at a lower price. See Chapter 28, "Sales Promotion," for more on this.

- *Cheaper goods strategy*—offer a lower quality product at a significantly lower price. This appeals to those consumers sometimes referred to in the brewery business as "slugs" who will buy almost anything as long as it's cheap.

- *Prestige strategy*—the opposite of *cheaper goods strategy*, in that you offer a significantly better product at a significantly higher price. This is also related to *pricing* strategies.

- *Value strategy*—aim at total customer satisfaction with regard to the perceived value of your products.

- *Service strategy*—link your product with reliable and needed service(s).

- *Total quality management* (or *TQM*, or *quality*) *strategy*—produce a product of the highest quality you reasonably and affordably can. This strategy is dependent on continuous measurement, and is generally not recommended for companies seeking government contracts, where low price normally beats high quality.

- *Capacity utilization strategy*—use previously unused capacity to produce products. This is more a manufacturing than a marketing strategy, but it can affect marketing planning.

- *Product proliferation strategy*—offer a greater variety of products than your competitors. For example, if your major competitor offers 11 flavors of candy, you might wish to market 17.

- *Reengineering strategy*—create teams to develop functions that customers value and break down the organizational barriers between product lines and company departments.

- *Flattening strategy*—reduce the number of levels in the marketing organization to get closer to the customer.

- *Empowering strategy*—give employees authority to develop new product ideas and processes and to take the initiative.
- *Partner-supplier strategy*—instead of relying on many suppliers, develop close relationships with a few reliable ones. This normally relates to obtaining materials for production.
- *Outsourcing strategy*—really a manufacturing strategy, but related to marketing insofar as better products may be produced at lower cost when produced by or obtained from sources outside the company.
- *Benchmarking strategy*—evaluate the best products on the market and copy the most important features. Also referred to in Chapter 13, "Competitive Strategies."
- *Licensing strategy*—allow other companies to manufacture and market products with your established brand name. It is important that you maintain control of product quality to assure continued respect for your brand name.
- *Joint venture strategy*—work with another company with regard to manufacturing and marketing your products.
- *Retailer assortment strategies*—retailers decide whether their choice of merchandise is to be *exclusive* (a single line from a single manufacturer), *deep* (a wide variety of similar products from several manufacturers), *broad* (a range of different products from different manufacturers), or *scrambled* (many unrelated product lines—as in a rural general store).
- *Mass customization* (or *individualization*) *strategy*—basic products are individually produced to the exact specifications of each customer, including size, color, material, and so on. This customer-oriented strategy has been common in business and automobile marketing for many years and is now being practiced widely in other consumer businesses, such as clothing and banking. It can be especially important in electronic commerce operations.
- *Process-focused production strategy*—unique products are manufactured in small batches following different paths through a factory. Literally a manufacturing rather than a marketing strategy but included here because of its strategic relationship to *mass customization.*

Whatever product strategy you select, keep in mind that the product alone cannot achieve sustained success. There must be a real or potential *need* or *want*, the product must be of *good quality* or *value*, it must become *known* to the target market, it must be *relatively easy to obtain*, and it must be offered at the *right time*.

Chapter 9

Name, Brand, and
Trademark Strategies

THE NAME OF YOUR ORGANIZATION OR PRODUCT

Whether you are naming a new organization or product or considering a name change for an existing one, ask yourself the following questions:

1. Does the name you have been using or are considering *belong to another* organization in operational areas into which you might want to move?
2. Does the name have *negative connotations* that you did not realize when you selected it or that have developed as a result of adverse publicity or coincidence beyond your control?
3. Is the name *geographically restrictive*, while you might wish to expand?
4. Is the name restricted to a *single discipline or specialty*, whereas you might want to grow and diversify?
5. Is the name *technologically outdated* or old-fashioned?
6. Is the name *too long* or cumbersome?
7. Is the name *difficult* to spell or pronounce?
8. Is the name associated with *failure*?
9. Is the name *misleading* in any way?
10. Is the name difficult to *remember*?
11. Does the name fail to reflect all your possible *mergers* or *demergers*?
12. In the fast-changing world of American slang, has the name come to have a *double meaning*—particularly a vulgar meaning?
13. If you're planning to market internationally, does the name suggest something negative or vulgar in a foreign language?

Any one of these considerations might be reason to reject an idea or change an existing name. More than one *yes* would strongly suggest such action.

On the other hand, there may be good reasons for keeping the name your organization or product already has. Without rehashing opposites of the preceding list, the most important considerations are these:

1. All the governmental and legal paperwork have been completed and to change the name would be laborious and expensive.

2. Stationery, checks, company forms, promotional literature, and so on have all been printed with the present name, and even more expense would be involved if they had to be discarded and reprinted.

3. If you have been in business for any length of time, you probably have something invested in the customer, prospect, and peer recognition of your current name, even without heavy advertising exposure.

4. Unless you have been involved in a scandal or other negative publicity, you probably have no serious public perception problems which you would like to moderate by changing the name of your organization or product.

5. As far as you know, neither part nor whole nor acronym for the name of your organization or product has a vulgar or socially offensive meaning.

Generally speaking, only if you are setting up a new organization, planning to expand, or having any of the problems suggested here will a new name be in order.

ALTERNATIVE TACTICS

Here are basic tactics for creating a new name:

1. Use the name of one or more of your principals (Ford Motor Company)
2. Apply a geographic descriptor (*New York Times*)
3. Devise a meaningless combination of letters or sounds (Kodak)
4. Discover a foreign word or phrase (Viva Burrito)
5. Develop a word or phrase that describes operations, products, or services (Healthcare for Seniors)
6. Use a word or phrase that suggests a benefit (Jiffy Lube)

Generally speaking, today's best names for both companies and brands are those that make it possible for the public to understand what is being offered.

1. They are meaningful
2. They are descriptive

3. They are inclusive
4. They are memorable
5. They are persuasive

To communicate one or more of these qualities, the better modern brand name usually suggests the following:

- Product attributes
- Customer benefits
- Marketer or manufacturer values
- Customer culture
- Product personality
- Nature of product use

To test for persuasiveness (point 5) you may wish to apply the classic AIDA formula from the direct mail advertising industry. Each letter in that classic operatic acronym represents a step in the process of persuasion:

- A—attract *attention.*
- I—arouse *interest.*
- D—create *desire.*
- A—call for *action.*

BASIC BRANDING STRATEGIES

Most companies' branding strategy aims at establishing a recognized brand name for products and can be classified as one of the following:

- *Individual brand name strategy*—each product in the line has a different and distinctive brand name, like Lever Brothers' Wisk® laundry detergent.
- *Blanket* (or *family*, or *line*, or *multiproduct*) *name* or *branding strategy*—where all products in the product mix share a brand name, like Betty Crocker® products.
- *Separate family name strategy*—like Eastman Kodak Company's Recordak® line of microfilm products.
- *Company name strategy*—such as IBM prefixes on all its products.
- *Dual branding strategy*—where the company pairs two brand names on one product as with SmithKline Beecham's Aquafresh® ALL™ toothpaste.
- *Co-branding strategy*—where brands from different companies appear together on one product. For example, the Citibank American Airlines® AAdvantage® VISA® credit card.

DEFINITIONS OF TERMS

Several terms are used in connection with brands. Among the most common are *logotype* (or *logo*), *symbol, trademark* (or *mark*), and *signature.*

A *logotype* (or *logo*) is distinctive typography used for an organization name or brand. Examples of logos abound on newspaper mastheads (at the top of the front page) and on consumer packaged goods that you see at your supermarket.

Stylized, simple, significant *nonverbal* identification devices are called *symbols* (not logos—a common error). The rabbit-head profile for *Playboy* magazine and the three-pointed star in a circle for Mercedes automobiles are popular examples.

A *trademark* or *mark* may be a little different from a *symbol* in that it can be composed of symbolic letters and/or numbers, like the three A's in the oval for the American Automobile Association and the sans-serif type that distinguishes 3M products. Of course, the word "trademark" also refers to a product *name* or *brand* of goods.

You may find symbols (or sometimes trademarks) and logotypes used *together*, to reinforce one another, as when RCA employs its letters with the spot-eyed dog listening to an old gramophone. Or another element— particularly a *slogan*—can be featured to create a distinguishing expression of organizational identity, as when General Electric uses its full name, its distinctive cursive GE mark, and the slogan "We bring good things to life."

The *signature* is one or more of these elements often accompanied by an address and/or a telephone number and/or a Web site to invite response. The organizational identification device (logo, symbol, or mark) is a vital element of the signature.

RULES FOR USE OF TRADE NAMES

Notice, by the way, that each brand in the preceding section has been distinguished in several ways. The basic rules are these:

1. Never use a brand name as a generic word or a verb, as in "Be sure you always xerox your contracts."
2. Always use your brand name as a modifier of a generic word, as in "Xerox copiers." (It's okay to use such a name to represent the company, though, as in "I work for Xerox.")
3. Distinguish your brand or trademark by use of initial capital letters, solid capital letters, big and little capital letters, underlining, or a distinguishing typeface that is different from the font in the surrounding material.
4. The letters TM, sometimes circled (™), distinguish a word or phrase as a trademark.

5. An R in a circle (®) means the trademark has been formally registered with the U.S. government.

6. The letters SM, in a circle or not (sm) indicate a service mark—often used to identify slogans as well as the name of a service.

7. A C in a circle (©) indicates copyrighted material—intellectual property (a print ad or a brochure for example) that cannot be copied without permission.

SEMANTIC NAMING STRATEGIES

The words and syllables you put together for your organization's name, your brands, and/or trademarks can rely on any of several semantic techniques:

- *Superlative strategy*—employs puffery words like *best, super*, and *miracle* that are somewhat tiresome today.
- *Comparative strategy*—uses words like *better, faster*, and *superior*. Both of these strategies are permissable in the U.S., but illegal in several other countries.
- *Bandwagon strategy*—uses words like *popular, proven*, and *famous*.
- *Quality strategy*—has been popular in commerce and industry for many years and includes words like *real, genuine*, and *strong*, plus the ever-popular *new* and *improved*.
- *Sexual imagery and innuendo strategy*—of course, *not* recommended.
- *Action-word strategy*—accomplishes AIDA better than most of the other strategies with words like *quick, blast*, and *zip*.
- *Reassuring strategy*—uses words like *complete, accurate*, and *approved*.
- *Reliable strategy*—uses words like *first, genuine*, and *lifetime*.
- *Patriotic strategy*—uses words like *American, national*, and *U.S.*
- *Cost-saving strategy*—uses words like *budget, bargain*, and the names for denominations of *small coins*.
- *Prestige strategy*—particularly used for names of organizations with words such as *institute, center*, and even the somewhat pompous *pavilion*.
- *Benefit strategy*—probably the best strategy of all that relies on the advantage(s) to the customer through words like *easy, simple*, or *complete*.
- *Meaningless strategy*—use made-up (today often computer-generated) words like "Kodak" and "Exxon."
- *Numbers and/or letters strategy*—somewhat related to the *secret ingredient* creative strategy; currently Xs and Zs are popular.
- *Foreign strategy*—words or phrases in a language other than English, often used to convey an exotic or sophisticated image.
- *Internet strategy*—companies involved in electronic businesses and the Internet develop names with an "*e*" prefix or a "*.com*" or "*dot com*" suffix.

OTHER BRANDING STRATEGIES

Several additional naming and branding strategies can be considered after the preceding items are decided on. They are the following:

- *National/international brand* (or *manufacturer['s] brand*) *strategy*—establish a recognized brand name for your product(s) nationwide, or perhaps worldwide.
- *Regional brand strategy*—gain product recognition through branding regionally.
- *Local brand strategy*—defines itself; this is the way many big brands began.
- *Euro-branding strategy*—use the same brand name for a product in all countries of the European Community. The word *euro-brand* is not used with an initial capital letter except at the beginning of a sentence.
- *Flanker brand strategy*—introduce a related product, with a different but related brand name, as Coca-Cola® did with Diet Coke®. This has also been noted as a product strategy.
- *Private labeling* (or *house branding*; or *distributor, dealer, retailer, store,* or *private brand*) *strategy*—provide your retail outlets with your product personalized with their own individual organizational or brand name.
- *Mixed branding strategy*—where you market the same product under your own brand name and also under regional, local, and/or private brand names.
- *Generic branding strategy*—market no-name, unbranded, simply packaged products. This is a good product strategy to use in conjunction with a low-price strategy and is often employed for commodity-type products, as well as for many products sold through military stores.

LET CAUTION GUIDE YOU

Once you have a direction and a purpose, it can be creatively satisfying to name your organization or come up with a brand name for a new product.

An important principle to remember is not to get so close to the name, or so delighted with your own wit that what you devise becomes obscure to your prospective customers. And beware of choosing a name based on publicity or advertising concepts you or your advisers might be considering for the future. That is putting the proverbial cart before the horse.

Although you'll want to be sure that no product of the *same type* as yours already uses the brand name you have chosen, you may use a brand name of a *different* product category. For example, there's *Life*® magazine, Life® cereal, and once—rather daringly—one of the major tobacco companies introduced Life® cigarettes.

Reportedly, the major consumer packaged goods companies have reserved most of the active, polite, monosyllabic English words for their particular future products.

USE OF A SLOGAN

A *slogan* is often simply a modifying or amplifying phrase to accompany your organization or brand name, so is similar, strategically, to a name.

Generally speaking, slogans can be good if they are based on a solid positioning strategy (see Chapter 14) such as *Forbes* magazine's classic "The capitalist tool." But they are more often a waste when they rely on ego and puffery, as with "The *real* professionals." Or when they are so general in nature that any organization could use them, as with a grandiose phrase like "Working toward tomorrow."

As a rule, for both names and slogans, *less is more*.

Chapter 10

Packaging Strategies

WHAT PACKAGING DOES

There's an old saying, "You can sell anything if it's packaged right." The success of products such as the famous Pet Rock® years ago seem to prove the truth of that adage, but more often packaging is not so dramatically successful.

Packaging is intended to provide identification, announce contents and recommended use, and satisfy legal requirements. It also protects products, provides convenience in storing and dispensing contents, and often serves a sales promotion function of some sort, such as through the perceived value of the package itself, or by means of discount coupons that may be imprinted, attached, or enclosed.

Packaging may be *primary*, as the combination printed paperboard box and enclosed waterproof bag to hold breakfast cereal, or *secondary*, as the large corrugated cardboard carton that protects a quantity of primary packages shipped to retail outlets.

NAMES OF STRATEGIES

These are the commonly accepted terms used to describe different packaging strategies:

- *Structural packaging strategy*—relates to the means to accomplish a packaging objective, such as a double box to minimize breakage of glass items, or use of aseptic packaging to extend the shelf-life of a perishable product without refrigeration.

- *Bulk packaging strategy*—large-capacity packages intended to induce the perception of economy or value.
- *Trial-size strategy*—small packages to encourage initial purchase.
- *Sample-size strategy*—packages usually smaller than *trial size*, intended to support the sales promotion strategy of *sampling*.
- *Label strategy*—only a label is attached to the product, thereby saving the expense of an enclosing package.
- *Transparent packaging strategy*—displays the actual product. The *blister pack* with a cardboard back and a clear plastic dome to hold the product is a common example; another of the *transparent* type is *shrink-wrap* packaging.
- *Downsizing strategy*—means reducing the contents of a package while maintaining the original package size. This is related to a price increase strategy.
- *Air-packaging strategy*—the equivalent of *downsizing* except that the small volume in the large box is planned from product introduction. This strategy may fool the customer once but is not likely to encourage repurchase.
- *Filler strategy*—intended to convey the impression of greater value through larger quantity of contents, as with laundry detergents, some of which are more than 90 percent inert "filler" material.
- *Concentration strategy*—also used for some laundry detergents to convey the impression they are helping to clean up the environment by "condensing" their product when, in fact, they simply leave out the filler. Similarly, fruit juices from concentrate may contain reduced amounts of water and therefore can be sold at lower prices than "reconstituted" equivalents.
- *Color-and-design strategy*—because people *do* judge a book by its cover, and often a product by its packaging, the product packaging should "grab" the consumer, particularly in the highly competitive environment of today's self-service supermarkets.
- *Family packaging strategy*—related to *color-and-design* but with the additional consideration that all packages for the company's product have a resemblance to one another, or a common graphic element.
- *Creative packaging strategy*—product benefits are communicated to consumers by the package, including on-pack advertising and/or sales promotion.
- *Package band strategy*—the enhancement of a basic package by means of a paper or plastic strip that wraps around the package and carries promotional copy or a sales promotion offer.
- *Bonus pack strategy*—the package contains a greater amount of the product at the original price and the package is flagged with a shellburst or other attention-getting graphic device that says something like "30% more!"
- *Twin-pack* (or *bundle-pack*) *strategy*—two packages fastened together to support the *bundle* sales promotion strategy, such as a bottle of shampoo and a bottle of conditioner sold for less than the sum of their retail prices. When the second product in a *twin-pack* is offered at no extra cost, it is called a *BOGO* for "buy one get one free." When a strong product (the *carrier*) is sold together with a

weaker product to enhance trial or volume of the latter, the strategy is called *piggyback*.

- *Affluent packaging strategy*—assumes consumers will pay more for an elegantly packaged product. Perfumes and cosmetics commonly use this strategy.

- *Innovative packaging*—something special and unusual will attract consumers who are curious about and intrigued by what is new. For example, the famous L'eggs® plastic egg to contain women's stockings.

- *Deposit-bottle strategy*—not as popular as years ago, but required by law in some states.

- *Recyclable* (or *environmental*) *packaging strategy*—appeals to the environmentally conscious.

- *Biodegradable strategy*—an even better appeal to the environmentally conscious.

- *Reusable packaging strategy*—a good sales-promotion-related strategy, whereby the container can be put to another use after the product is consumed.

- *Premium strategy*—such as Jim Beam® liquor bottles in the form of ceramic automobiles and other collectable items.

- *Sales promotion strategies*—use of on-pack or in-pack *free* or *cents-off* coupons (including *cross-couponing* and *cross-ruffs*); *rebate*, *premium*, and *gift* (*in-pack* or *mail-in*) offers; and other sales promotion strategies as part of the product packaging. See Chapter 28 for more on sales promotion.

Chapter 11

Pricing Strategies

Price of product seems to be more important than ever in marketing today, as evidenced by the growth and variety of retail and Internet discount operations.

Basically, you can try low price to maximize volume, high price to recover investment quickly, or "put it where the cattle can get at it" and let the response of the marketplace suggest appropriate cost/value relationships.

Your pricing strategy may or may not be related to your costs, which are affected by your *core competencies* (what you do best), *economies of scale* (related to your production volume), *economies of scope* (savings made possible by sharing knowledge and technology among different areas of your business), and specific marketing factors suggested in this handbook.

BASIC PRICING STRATEGIES

Here are the common strategies for setting reasonable and acceptable prices:

- *Penetration strategy*—set prices as low as possible to get the greatest number of customers you can and to discourage competition.

- *Skimming* (or *milking*) *strategy*—set prices as high as possible to make as much money as you can from the few customers who can afford your product or service. This is used particularly with new-product introductions and fad-type products.

- *Demand-based pricing strategy*—concentrate on the wants and needs of your customers and set prices where they are acceptable to an acceptable number of customers, often accomplished by trial and error.

- *Fair trade pricing strategy*—no longer permitted in the United States in interstate commerce because of the Consumer Goods Pricing Act of 1975. *Fair trade pricing* meant that manufacturers established retail prices and would not allow discounting by retailers. Enforcement was through threat to remove from the manufacturer's "authorized dealer" list any retailer who discounted the *fair trade* price.

- *Manufacturer's suggested retail price (MSRP or SRP) strategy*—here the manufacturer establishes a reasonable (although sometimes on the high side) price for its product but allows retailers to discount that price in any way they wish. It is useful for establishing a point of reference for the consumer when *discounting* strategies are employed. This is sometimes referred to as *list price, base price, sticker price*, or *sucker price*.

- *Unit pricing strategy*—prices are quoted in terms of per gallon, per pound, and the like.

- *Flexible-price policy* (or *variable price* or *negotiated* or *negotiation pricing*) *strategy*—the same product and quantities are offered to different customers at different prices, depending on their negotiating skills and other factors. This is common among peddlers and antique dealers. It can be argued that the only reason sellers choose to negotiate is so they have a chance to charge *more* than a fair price. Shrewd marketers know their costs and their necessary mark-ups and will generally not sell for less than the sums of the two.

- *One-price policy strategy*—the same price is offered to similar customers who buy the same product in the same quantity under the same conditions. Clearly, a strategy of fairness.

- *Cost-focus strategy*—control expenses so that prices can be lowered in a narrow range of market segments.

- *Cost leadership strategy*—also involves controlling expenses to lower prices in a wide (as opposed to narrow) range of market segments.

- *Price stability* (or *parity pricing*) *strategy*—match your competitors' prices (but beware of accusations of *price-fixing*, which is illegal in the United States).

- *Defensive pricing strategy*—bring your prices to a level where your customers feel sufficient value exists to remain your customers. With this strategy you need not meet your competitor's price directly, since you can rely on loyalty and perceived value to provide your advantage.

- *Beating the competition strategy*—set your prices lower than those of your equivalent competitors (but beware of starting a *price war*).

- *High-option pricing strategy*—used when a product line is declining and competition is minimal or when the product line is new and there is little competition. This allows maximization of profits and relates to *skimming* strategy.

- *Low-option pricing strategy*—relates somewhat to *penetration* pricing strategy, may be used to gain market share, and may also be used to develop a market niche at the low end of a product category. *Low-option* differs from *penetration* in that when you employ this strategy you intentionally try to be the lowest priced supplier, so it is useful for your product to be perceived as lower in quality than your competitor(s). This strategy can succeed because there always seems to be room in the marketplace for the marketer with the lowest price.

OTHER PRICING STRATEGIES

Here are several additional strategies used to determine selling price:

- *Market share strategy*—use price to take share points away from your competition (but beware of accusations of *predatory pricing*).

- *Target-return* (or *target-profit* or *target pricing*) *strategy*—evaluate all expenses and establish prices by adding the desired profit margin above expenses. This plus the next four strategies are sometimes collectively called *cost-oriented pricing strategies*.

- *Cost-plus strategy*—similar to *target-return* in that you calculate costs and add a *flat amount* to cover contingencies and profit.

- *Cost plus fixed-fee pricing strategy*—the supplier is reimbursed for all costs, regardless of what they may be, plus a fixed percentage of production or construction costs.

- *Cost plus percentage of cost pricing strategy*—set the price by adding a fixed percentage to the production or construction cost. These last two tend to be terms used in contracting and business marketing contexts.

- *Markup pricing strategy*—a term used to describe what is added to the cost of the product to establish retail price. This includes both *target-return* and *cost-plus* strategies.

- *Going-rate pricing strategy*—based on surveying the marketplace and conforming price to the median or mode price for competitive products. This sometimes takes the form of what is called *follow-the-leader pricing* or *customary pricing strategy*.

- *Six-X pricing strategy*—classic formula for mail order pricing. Basic cost of product is multiplied by six to establish price to consumers. This covers the SADA (sales, advertising, distribution, and marketing administration expense) of direct marketing. Some marketers not in the mail order business use factors of five or less.

- *Full-cost pricing strategy*—total all costs, including staff, property, other overhead, and even debt in addition to manufacturing, distribution, advertising, and sales costs so that prices can be based on the total and allow the company to recover all costs and more quickly realize a profit.

- *Incremental-cost pricing strategy*—only costs directly related to manufacturing and distribution of the product are considered in setting the price.

- *Perceived-value pricing strategy*—uses the buyer's conception of value rather than the seller's cost as the basis for calculating price.

- *Prestige-pricing* (or *psychological* or *premium pricing*) *strategy*—best for large national companies and luxury goods; akin to *skimming*, but for the longer term, where prices are set high for so-called *snob appeal*.

- *Demand-backward strategy*—determine what customers or prospects are willing to pay and work back to determine what you can deliver for that amount.

- *Value-billing strategy*—usually for services, where prices are set according to how valuable they are agreed to be by customers. This is especially good for setting fees for some types of professional services.

- *Percentage of benefit strategy*—similar to *value billing*; through negotiation accept an agreed-upon percentage of the money you can prove you save the customer or client. You will want to get legal advice on the ethical and legal implications of this strategy in your particular profession or line of business and geographic area.

- *Product-form pricing strategy*—adjust your price for the same product based on the form it takes. For example, Eastman Kodak Company charges widely different prices per square inch for its black-and-white AHU film depending on whether it is 16mm for motion pictures, 35mm for snapshots, single-frames for dental x-rays, 105mm microfiche, or 9-inch plates for photogrammetry.

- *Derived demand pricing strategy*—base prices on the fact that production volume and distribution will be dependent on production of another product, such as steering wheels for new automobiles. *Derived demand* will affect other areas of marketing planning as well.

- *Captive-product pricing strategy*—price the basic product low and make up the difference on the related product. A classic example of this strategy is the traditional pricing of safety razors and blades.

- *Two-part pricing strategy*—involves a fixed fee, plus a variable usage fee. Examples are automobile rental plus mileage and cable television usage plus pay-per-view.

- *Stepped pricing* (or *product-line pricing* or *price-lining*) *strategy*—a company manufactures three models of pocket knife, for example, where the A model has a plain pine wood handle, the B model a polished mahogany handle, and the C model a carved bone handle. The prices for the different models, or price points, may not exactly reflect the actual manufacturing costs.

- *Price-point pricing strategy*—retailers, in particular, use this strategy to segment merchandise in terms of perceived quality and value. For example, a department store may carry men's overcoats priced at $200, $300, and $500 dollars apiece. Consumers tend to buy products at their chosen price points, regardless of whether the actual prices are raised or discounted.

- *Decoy-pricing strategy*—a less-than-ethical application of *stepped* or *price-point* pricing where one model of a product may be priced outrageously above the other so that the customer will perceive tremendous value in the lower-priced equivalent. Alternatively, the decoy can be the lower-priced model, and the added features of the higher-priced equivalent could suggest proportionally greater value to the customer. Either way, this seems to be an inherently deceptive strategy.

- *Optional-feature pricing strategy*—long used in the new car sales business and sometimes referred to as *add-on pricing*.

- *Experience-curve pricing strategy*—reduce the price of your product as you become more adept at manufacturing and marketing it and presumably as volume increases.

- *Byproduct pricing strategy*—calculate the market value of byproducts in the manufacturing process into the price of the basic product. For example, companies like Kodak can sell the chemicals that result from their film processing as *process materials* to be used in the manufacture of other companies' products and thereby reduce their film processing prices.

- *Distribution-channel pricing strategy*—vary price according to your technique of distribution. (See Chapter 12 for distribution and logistics strategies.)

- *Location pricing strategy*—base your price on the outlet through which the product is sold, such as candy in supermarkets, versus vending machines, versus movie theater concession stands.

- *Geographic pricing strategy*—calculate price with regard to the geographic area in which it is to be sold or the distance it must travel to reach its market. This sort of pricing is not considered discriminatory by the FTC since different prices are determined in part by costs to get products to customers at different locations. *Freight-absorption pricing* means that the seller pays the cost of shipping. This is a good strategy for picking up key accounts and for penetrating new markets. This may also be called *delivered pricing*. *Freight allowance pricing* is where the selling price includes costs of transportation, and the seller pays the carrier directly or reimburses the buyer. *Uniform delivered pricing* (or *postage-stamp pricing*) involves the same price to all customers regardless of where the product is delivered. *FOB origin pricing* means that customers pay the factory price of products, plus shipping to their particular location. (FOB means "free on board.") *FOB with freight allowed pricing* is a form of *freight absorption pricing* that means the buyer can deduct freight expenses from the list price of the product. *Freight equalization pricing* means the freight discount varies according to the difference between the cost of shipping from the seller's location and the cost of shipping from a competitor located closer to the buyer. *Zone pricing* is a compromise of the previous two, whereby shipping fees are the same within each geographic region, such as New England or the Pacific Coast. *Basing-point pricing* is where you establish a particular geographic location as your "basing point" and charge customers shipping from that spot, regardless of the place from which products are actually shipped. (Multiple basing points may be established.) *Factory pricing* means prices are reduced to adjust for savings realized when the seller completely avoids all transportation costs.

- *Discounting strategy*—cut prices, or give extra value in services or products, to obtain or retain business. Discounts can be in the form of *cash discounts* for immediate or prompt payment, *price-off* (or *off-invoice*, or *off-list*) *discounts* to encourage distributors and dealers to stock up or carry new products, *quantity discounts* for volume purchases (which include *cumulative quantity discounts* applied to total purchases over a period of time and *noncumulative quantity discounts* based on the size of an individual purchase order), *functional discounts* (or *trade discounts*) for buyers who perform particular functions within the scheme of distribution, *allowances* for a variety of functions performed by retailers, *promotional allowances* specifically for cooperation with advertising and displays, *handling allowances* for such operations as redeeming cents-off coupons, *free goods* including additional product and advertising specialties, *BOGOs* ("buy one get one free"), and *type-of-customer* discounts, as for senior citizens, students, or during "ladies nights" at some nightclubs and bars. The final price that results from discounting strategies is called *market price* or *dead-net price*. Note: When you discount your price(s), beware that the lower price does not become the perceived fair or regular price in the minds of your customers. (See Chapter 28, "Sales Promotion Strategies," for more ideas about discounting strategies.)

- *Promotional pricing strategy*—a popular variation on straight discounting strategy, where you offer two-for-one deals, memberships, or other incentives to buy now.

- *Special-event pricing*—including holiday sales, events like store anniversaries, or even what may seem the ridiculous "Door-buster Sale" and "Truckload Sale," the latter presumably to recognize as a special occasion that merchandise has been delivered in quantity in a truck. But, certainly, consumers like to have a *reason* for a reduced price. (Also covered in more detail in Chapter 28.)

- *Seasonal pricing strategy*—sometimes seasons affect the value and hence the price of a product, as rates for television commercial time that are significantly lower during the summer months. Or seasonal discounts may help to move old stock at retail, as when winter jackets go on sale in February.

- *Time pricing strategy*—prices are adjusted according to time of day or day of the week to even out demand. Hotels and airlines refer to *yield pricing* in this context. Retailers refer to *off-peak pricing* which consists of charging lower prices at those times when sales activity is slack.

- *Cash-and-carry pricing strategy*—involves lower prices than might be expected because the buyer pays cash and transports goods from the point of sale. Thus, the seller saves delivery and possible financing costs, which can be passed along in whole or in part to the buyer.

- *Allowances strategy*—another form of discounting for consumers (different than *dealer and distributor allowances*, noted previously) that involves such devices as *trade-ins* of old products for new.

- *Credit terms strategy*—deferred payment or special loan interest rates "sweeten the deal" for the buyer.

- *Loss leader strategy*—offer a dramatically low price for one or more products—even below cost—to increase traffic and to attract new customers. Popular in retailing and not illegal in the United States as long as the retailer's intent is not to drive competitors out of business.

- *Borax strategy*—offer a product that *appears* to be of great value relative to price—but which is *not*—to attract customers. A strategy of questionable ethics.

- *Bait-and-switch strategy*—also a retailing technique, now strictly against the law in the United States. A product is advertised for an attractive price, but the customer is "sold up" to a more expensive (and presumably better) substitute.

- *Every-day-low-price (EDLP) strategy*—a retail strategy that encourages customer perception that prices are routinely set as low as possible to permit no further discounting.

- *Even-price strategy*—even pricing involves a round number, such as $20.00, which has a solid and straightforward feeling to it.

- *Odd-price strategy*—is, as the term suggests, an odd number off the round figure such as $19.99 or $19.95. It seems ridiculous, but not uncommon, when an automobile dealer advertises a price of $49,999.98. But this seems to suggest to many consumers that instead of $50,000, the car costs "$40,000-something."

- *Magic number strategy*—a popular strategy for discount stores that implies the cost to the customer has been cut as close as possible, as with a price of $17.23.

- *Tax-included pricing strategy*—some retailers calculate their prices so that when local sales tax is added, the total comes out to an even amount. This saves time and trouble making change.

- *Survival* (or *break-even pricing*) *strategy*—set your price to cover fixed and variable costs when staying in business is more important than immediate profits. This should be, of course, a *short-term* strategy.

- *Maximum current profit strategy*—set the price to maximize current profit, cash flow, or return on investment. Another short-term strategy, perhaps effective prior to selling a business.

- *Maximum current revenue strategy*—set price to maximize sales revenue, perhaps to impress potential investors.

- *Product-quality leadership pricing strategy*—when your prices are higher than those of your competition, you may give the impression of quality leadership. Somewhat like *prestige pricing* strategy.

- *Sealed-bid* (or *closed-bid*) *pricing strategy*—used by companies that quote confidentially on individual contracts. Popular in government procurement.

- *Open-bid pricing strategy*—all bidders are aware of all other bidders' quotes.

- *Last-look pricing strategy*—in a bidding situation companies either ask or are asked to take a "last look" at the lowest bid submitted and revise their bid to beat it. This seems to be an ethically flawed practice for both buyer and seller when practiced in connection with *sealed bidding*.

- *High-balling pricing strategy*—the seller quotes a very high price to give room to negotiate downward. Employed in real estate sales, and another strategy of questionable ethics.

- *Low-balling pricing strategy*—the seller quotes the lowest price considered reasonable and, when the customer accepts, the seller explains that the price quoted does not include all that the customer wants. An unethical practice commonly employed by automobile salespeople. A strategy of the same name is practiced by some real estate and other high-ticket brokers who recommend a low price for a product to make a quick sale.

- *Trading down strategy*—a marketer known for selling high-priced products offers lower-priced products. Notable when top fashion designers introduce "affordable" lines. Often the marketer will create a new brand name for the lower-priced product to protect the perceived value of the original product.

- *Trading up strategy*—a marketer known for selling low-priced products offers higher-priced products. The old image may make it hard for consumers to accept the change, though. *Trading down* and *trading up*, of course, are directly related, respectively, to *cheaper goods* and *prestige* product strategies.

- *Slotting allowance* (or *slotting fee*) *strategy*—employed by retailers to increase total revenues by charging suppliers for shelf space. Of questionable ethics, this is a practice likely to be addressed in the future by court judgments or restrictive legislation.

- *Dumping strategy*—predatory pricing strategy employed by foreign companies to capture U.S. markets. Products are sold in the United States for less than it cost to manufacture and deliver them. Federal government agencies have tried to control this, but the practice has decimated such traditional American industries as electronics and steel.

- *Arm's-length pricing*—sometimes required by federal government agencies concerned with *dumping*. A form of enforced *parity pricing*.
- *Gray market* (or *parallel importing*) *strategy*—may occur when products are priced significantly differently in different countries. Operators buy products at retail in low-priced countries and export them to high-priced countries where they can underprice local authorized dealers. Although legal in the United States, this practice is illegal in the European Union.
- *Transfer pricing strategy*—charging a high price to a U.S. subsidiary for an imported product so that the selling price provides minimal profit, resulting in lower taxes to be paid to the U.S. government on the same corporate revenue.
- *Deceptive pricing strategy*—the term for a practice related to *discount pricing* which is based on a "regular retail price" that has not actually been charged. Several department stores and jewelry chains have offered such fictional discounts and received severe fines and other penalties—along with bad publicity and correspondingly negative public relations.

Two other terms relate to pricing strategy, although they are not pricing strategies themselves: *barter*, where products are traded rather than sold for money, and *reciprocity* where companies are both buyers and sellers; for example, an auto manufacturer is covered by an insurance company that buys fleets of cars for its sales representatives. The latter was noted as a *market* strategy.

PRICE-INCREASE STRATEGIES

Here are some special strategies that often relate to the need to increase prices. In implementing some of these strategies beware of accusations of *price gouging*.

- *Demand-oriented pricing strategy*—(different than *demand-based* pricing strategy) prices are set based on consumer demand rather than cost. For example, popular music CDs are characteristically priced higher than lower-demand classical CDs by the same recording company—although the opposite should logically be the case, as with a book-publishing company that would price low-volume business books higher than high-volume novels (see *economies of scale*). Although prices may be lowered when demand is low and/or supply is high, more often this strategy is applied to increase prices when supply is low and demand is high—application of the classic economic theory. Abuse of this strategy is regulated by several government agencies in the United States.
- *Replacement cost pricing strategy*—calculate your price on the basis of fixed and variable costs, profit, plus the cost to *replace* product—not to purchase it in the first place. This strategy is used by gasoline retailers to justify consumer price increases in advance of increases in wholesale prices to them.
- *Anticipatory pricing strategy*—in a fast-changing market, set the price where you expect it to be in the future. This is not the same as *replacement cost* pricing.

- *Delayed quotation pricing strategy*—don't set the price until the product is produced or delivered. This is most appropriate when you have relatively long lead-times.

- *Cost-override* (or *escalator clause*) *pricing strategy*—also for long lead-times, this involves basing price on some sort of index that allows increasing the price relative to inflation or additional work required for completion of a contract.

- *Bundle pricing strategy*—akin to discounting, where you package two or more products (like a bottle of shampoo and a bottle of conditioner) or services together and offer the combination at a reduced price. For these types of strategies, be sure that you offer the *same deal* to everyone who wants to take advantage of the offer because favoritism in some areas of pricing can lead to penalties. See *twin-pack* in Chapter 10 for more on this.

- *Bundling pricing strategy*—notice the slight difference from the foregoing term ("bundle" versus "bundling"), *bundling* is where you offer two or more products or additional features at a lower price than if you sold them separately. For example, auto manufacturers routinely price new cars with particular combinations of features lower than the price would be if the customer had the features installed by the dealer.

- *Unbundling pricing strategy*—you price elements of an original combination separately, as a restaurant might do by changing from a *prix fixe* to an *à la carte* menu.

- *Reduction of discounts pricing strategy*—here revenues are increased when sales representatives cease to offer discounting incentives to customers.

- *Downsizing strategy*—mentioned also in connection with packaging strategies, this involves reducing the contents of a package while maintaining the original package size and price. Although of dubious ethics, this has been a popular means among packaged goods manufacturers to surreptitiously increase prices to consumers.

- *Substitution of ingredients pricing strategy*—involves cutting costs by essentially reducing the quality of components. This and the next two relate to *product* strategies.

- *Reduction of product features pricing strategy*—also a cost-cutting strategy that allows a traditional price to be maintained in the face of increased manufacturing costs.

- *Reduction of services pricing strategy*—another cost-cutting strategy that essentially increases price. For example, free delivery might be eliminated.

- *Larger quantity pricing strategy*—here the manufacturer saves on packaging costs by selling the product in larger sizes. (Related to *bulk packaging strategy*.)

- *Reduction of variety pricing strategy*—the number of different sizes and/or models in a product line is reduced to save costs, hence essentially increasing the price to the customer.

- *Price-adjustment strategy*—if you have a mixed product line, you can reduce the price of some items when you increase the price of others, so you seem only to be *adjusting* your prices rather than increasing them. This strategy is fairly common among retailers such as chain stores and can involve *perceived value* and *prestige* pricing strategies.

- *Act-of-faith pricing*—the pricing component of what is called "act-of-faith marketing," whereby marketers charge whatever they wish to because consumers accept on faith that their prices or fees must be fair and proper. Most insurance is sold on this basis, as are many professional services.

Chapter 12

Distribution, Logistics, and Channel Strategies

BASIC TERMINOLOGY

Distribution refers to getting products to customers and consumers. This may be by means of *ships, railroads, motor carriers, airlines, pipelines, courier* and *express companies,* or *postal services. Freight forwarders* consolidate small shipments, and *intermodal* or *containerized shipping* permits use of more than one mode of transportation, as when a container travels by truck to a railroad depot, is hoisted onto a flatcar, and is transported to a seaport where it is transferred to a ship. If the product is *information,* the means of delivery may be physical or electronic.

All these means of delivery are the strategic equivalents of *media* choices in advertising planning and involve objectives related to such factors as cost, customer need, and convenience.

The military term *logistics* is now being used in marketing to include not only physical distribution but also storage, warehousing, and aspects of getting goods to market that do not exclusively include transportation.

Strategies that apply to making products or services available to customers are included in this chapter. Many of those strategies are also useful for product *launch, relaunch* (or *revitalization*), and *rollout,* mentioned in Chapter 8, "Product and Service Strategies."

FUNDAMENTAL DISTRIBUTION STRATEGIES

The fundamental distribution strategies go by the following names:

- *Intensive* (or *extensive* or *open*) *distribution strategy*—try to get goods or services into as many means of distribution as possible.

- *Exclusive distribution strategy*—allow only one retail outlet in any one geographic area to carry a particular item. Normally reserved for *prestige* goods and services. *Exclusive dealing* is the term for a practice, illegal in the United States, where a reseller is required to handle only one manufacturer's products, to the exclusion of competitive products.

- *Exclusive territorial distributorship strategy*—you grant a reseller sole rights to sell a product in a specific geographic area.

- *Selective distribution strategy*—a compromise between *intensive* and *exclusive* distribution, where you permit a limited number of retailers in an area to carry the same product. (As with *exclusive distribution* strategy, be careful not to open yourself up to accusations of discrimination.)

- *Local distribution strategy*—provide your product or service only to your own immediate geographic area. This strategy and the next three should correspond to the selection for a geographic *market* strategy, treated in Chapter 7.

- *Regional distribution strategy*—cover an area that usually includes several contiguous states, such as the Southeastern region.

- *National distribution strategy*—make your product or service available throughout the country.

- *International (transnational, multinational, worldwide, or global) distribution strategy*—distribute your product outside your domestic area, and even around the world. See Chapter 7 for refinements of definitions of these terms. Specific international *distribution* strategies will be treated separately at the end of this chapter.

- *Direct distribution strategy*—product goes from your manufacturing facility to the customer without *intermediaries* (or *middlemen*). This can be handled in business marketing with personal selling by a direct *field sales* organization.

- *Indirect distribution strategy*—items pass through *intermediaries*, which may number as many as half a dozen between source and final buyer. Intermediaries have many different functions and a variety of names including *wholesaler, broker, agent,* and *jobber.* Strategies related to this aspect of distribution are covered in this chapter's section on "Channel Strategies."

- *Dual distribution* (or *multiple-channel,* or *complementary channel*) *strategy*—make your product or service available to buyers at more than one type of outlet. For example, fashion designers may market through large department stores and also through their own private stores bearing the designer's name.

- *Competitive dealer strategy*—distribute similar but differently branded products through different dealer organizations and encourage competition among your different dealers.

- *Forward integration strategy*—where a manufacturer expands into distribution, often by buying a distribution company to expedite and decrease the costs of its distribution.

- *Horizontal integration strategy*—acquisition of a competitor's company or adding outlets to a chain to increase distribution. The FTC watches this sort of thing carefully for antitrust violations.

- *Disintermediation strategy*—when a reseller bypasses another reseller and buys products direct from a supplier higher up the channel of distribution.
- *Multisite strategy*—duplicate what you have to offer at several different locations.
- *Multiservice strategy*—capitalize on your reputation for a good basic service to market additional services.
- *Pyramiding*—a practice illegal in the United States in which the chain of distribution is artificially expanded by an excessive number of resellers that results in an unfairly inflated retail price.
- *Tying agreement*—another practice now banned by U.S. law whereby a marketer could require that in order to buy a desired product customers also had to buy a second or third type of product.

GENERAL LOGISTICS STRATEGIES

Here are the names of general logistics strategies:

- *Channel leadership strategy*—assume a position of leadership, which is easier to accomplish if your organization is the largest in the logistical operation.
- *Takeover strategy*—as part of a distribution system you might wish to obtain the power to exercise centralized control. This is more extreme than *channel leadership*.
- *Alliance with channel leader strategy*—if yours is a smaller firm and you cannot be the top dog, establish good relations with the channel leader to affect policy in your favor.
- *Limited focus strategy*—again, for smaller firms with limited resources that compete with larger firms, this strategy is to concentrate on one or a few key areas such as automation, communication, or reliability. This is related to *positioning*, the subject of Chapter 14.
- *Partnership strategy*—involves stronger bonds than *alliance with leader* strategy.
- *Private fleet strategy*—you own your own means of delivery. This can relate to the broader strategy of *direct distribution*.
- *Quick response strategy*—as noted in connection with customer service in Chapter 33, *quick response*, especially for retailers, is tremendously important. Grocers aim for a strategy called *efficient consumer response* (or *ECR*).
- *First-in-first-out (FIFO) strategy*—assure systematic rotation of stock through this basic inventory control strategy.
- *Just-in-time (JIT) strategy*—save costs of storage with this inventory technique that delivers exactly what is needed exactly when it is needed. JIT requires careful planning, computer algorithms, and fortunate execution to work well, and tends to be easier in Japan, where it originated and where there are no labor unions, than in the United States where such unexpected events as railroad strikes have spoiled carefully laid plans.
- *Modification strategy*—involves a change in the established means of getting goods or services to buyers.

- *Conflict-management strategy*—when there is strife among members of a distribution system, you might make the effort necessary to get things running smoothly again.
- *Postponement strategy*—a method to minimize risk by delaying large-scale manufacturing and distribution until customer demand has been determined. This is not the same as *dry testing* in the mail order business, now illegal in the United States, where offers were made and products only manufactured *after* order quantities were known.
- *Total quality management strategy*—as noted in Chapter 4, *total quality* should be a major strategic consideration in virtually all areas of marketing, including logistics.

CHANNEL STRATEGIES

Channel strategies can be designated by the *means* noted at the beginning of this chapter, and/or by the following:

- *Direct marketing* (or *mail order* or *zero-level channel*) *strategy*—a specific form of direct distribution where no personal-contact sales personnel or other intermediaries are involved. The newest dimension of this strategy is *Internet marketing strategy*, which is treated in Chapter 27.
- *In-home retailing strategy*—includes door-to-door sales, party sales, *home-TV shopping*, noted separately, and *Internet marketing*.
- *Home-TV shopping strategy*—products are demonstrated on television channels established exclusively for shopping, and sales are closed via *inbound telemarketing* (the buyer calls the seller). Billing is by the television organization and often the costs of video production and air time are covered by the seller's commission.
- *Multilevel marketing (MLM) strategy*—a specialized form of *in-home retailing* popularized by Amway and Mary Kay cosmetics where products travel through a folksy pyramid in which everyone gets a cut of the final purchase price.
- *Fulfillment house strategy*—direct marketing operations of storing, packing, addressing, and shipping are handled for the marketer by a specialty organization. Often these also offer direct mail services and are also called *letter shops*.
- *Retail strategy*—choose one or more types of retail outlets through which to distribute. These include *mass merchandisers* (including *discount houses, club stores* or *warehouse stores, catalogue showrooms, off-price retailers, commissaries* or *company stores, factory outlets, hypermarkets*, and *hypermarches*, the latter being combination department store and supermarket), *variety stores, department stores, grocery stores* (including *chain stores, supermarkets*, and *convenience stores*), *combination stores, general stores, general-merchandise retailers, specialty retailers*, and *limited-line retailers*.
- *Cash-and-carry strategy*—mentioned in connection with pricing strategies, this involves the buyer paying cash and transporting goods from the point of sale. This type of operation can also be defined as *limited-service wholesaling*. Usually

the product line is restricted to related products in categories such as electrical components, lumber, and office supplies.

- *Truck wholesaler strategy*—involves use of a type of wholesaler who sells to, delivers, and is paid in a single operation at the customer's location.

- *Drop-shipping strategy*—intermediaries own the merchandise they sell but do not physically take possession or stock it. They take orders and then have the manufacturer or other reseller ship it to the buyer. Wholesalers who use this form of distribution are called "*desk jobbers.*"

- *Freight forwarder strategy*—firms consolidate small shipments into larger loads and hire carriers to transport them, usually being able to pass along lower rates to marketers than would be charged were products shipped in smaller lots.

- *OEM (original equipment manufacture) strategy*—product is installed as original equipment, as with tape and CD players in new cars.

- *Franchising strategy*—a parent company licenses others to market a product or service using its brand or trade name in exclusive geographic areas. The franchisee gets advice, training, and marketing support from, buys products and/or supplies from, and pays fees and/or a percentage of revenues to the franchisor.

- *Piggyback franchising strategy*—where stores operated by one franchisor sell the products or services of another franchised firm, as when a national brand of fast food is sold in the facility of a nationally advertised gasoline. Not quite the same as *co-branding*, mentioned in Chapters 8 and 9.

- *Manufacturer-sponsoring strategy*—can involve *distributors* on an exclusive basis as Coca-Cola has traditionally done with their bottlers, and/or *retailers* as automobile manufacturers have done with their dealers.

- *Miniwarehouse mall strategy*—uses the type of shopping center where a large warehouse offers space to a variety of resellers which may be either retailers or wholesalers.

- *Retailer (or co-op) strategy*—retail outlets band together and use collective buying power to obtain volume discounts and perhaps faster delivery from suppliers.

- *Wholesaler-sponsored voluntary chain strategy*—as the name suggests, independent retailers agree to help a wholesaler compete with large chain organizations to their mutual benefit.

- *Manufacturer's representative (or manufacturer's agent) strategy*—professional sales people not directly employed by the manufacturer solicit orders. They save the manufacturer the costs of recruiting, training, motivating, compensating, and supervising a company sales organization.

- *Selling agent (or commission merchant) strategy*—a function that goes beyond the *manufacturer's rep*, in that the selling agent is responsible for the entire marketing operations of a producer, including product planning, pricing, marketing communications, and subsequent distribution. Used in such industries as textiles, apparel, and home furnishings.

- *Merchant middleman strategy*—relies on resellers who take title to the products they sell to other resellers.

- *Industrial distributor strategy*—usually requires exclusive distribution and, like *manufacturer's reps*, can save your company the cost of a field sales organization.

- *Mill supply house strategy*—uses general merchandise wholesalers that operate in industrial settings.
- *Merchandise mart strategy*—industry-specific locations allow sellers to show their products to buyers who are primarily resellers.
- *Rack-jobber strategy*—distribute your products through order-takers who keep retail racks supplied with products such as candy bars and potato chips.
- *Facilitator strategy*—includes several of the foregoing strategies, in that intermediaries assist in moving, storing, financing, and insuring products as they make their way toward the ultimate point of sale but normally do not take title to products.
- *Vending-machine* (or *automatic merchandising*) *strategy*—a good way to distribute products for fledgling consumer packaged-goods companies that are not well enough established to break into supermarkets.
- *Tradeshow strategy*—primarily for business marketers, this manner of distribution relies on shows, conferences, and conventions which include exhibits and permit direct selling from the floor. See Chapter 35 for more about tradeshows.
- *Consignment strategy*—goods are provided to retailers, payment for which is required only after the goods have been sold to consumers. Attractive to retailers who avoid inventory costs, and good for manufacturers who cannot get distribution through chain stores.

DEMAND-RELATED STRATEGIES

The following are logistics and distribution strategies that relate directly to consumer or business demand:

- *Push strategy*—through special sales efforts and/or incentive programs, force as much of your product into distribution as possible. This strategy is often associated with trade promotion strategies and sometimes used to unload a line that is to be discontinued.
- *Pull strategy*—through consumer advertising and sales promotion, create a demand for your product at the point of final sale.
- *Push-pull strategy*—combine the previous two strategies to move generally massive amounts of merchandise. This is a common strategy among large packaged-goods marketers.
- *Private labeling* (or *house branding*; or *distributor, dealer, retailer, store,* or *private brand*) *strategy*—aim to broaden your consumer base by offering nationally advertised products as well as *off-brand* products to compete with them. The latter usually carry a lower price and attract price-conscious consumers. More choice generally means more customers.
- *Forward-buying strategy*—resellers, particularly supermarkets, buy more product than they intend to sell during a promotion period in response to manufacturers' discounts. They sell remaining product after the promotion period at higher prices or through other outlets.

INTERNATIONAL DISTRIBUTION STRATEGIES

Following are distribution strategies for international operations:

- *Occasional export strategy*—you are not seriously involved with international trade but do a bit of it.
- *Active export strategy*—using export agents or export merchants or co-op organizations, you make the international market a serious part of your marketing planning.
- *Direct exporting strategy*—where foreign trade is a significant part of your business, you may operate through *traveling sales representatives* who are U.S. sales reps you send abroad, and/or *foreign sales offices or subsidiaries* normally managed by U.S. personnel but staffed by foreign nationals, much in the manner the U.S. government handles its foreign embassies. *Licensing* and *joint ventures* (both mentioned in Chapter 8) and *strategic alliances* (mentioned in Chapter 13) are other means to distribute and market internationally.
- *Indirect exporting strategy*—this is when you sell your goods in a foreign country through wholesale intermediaries, such as *foreign distributors* or *foreign agents*.

Chapter 13

Competitive Strategies

Many businesspeople and some academics today believe we are moving beyond the Production Era (roughly 1860 to 1920), the Sales Era (roughly 1920 to 1960), and the Marketing Era (roughly 1960 to the present) into the *Competitive Era* of business, where the major objective will be to outsmart or even destroy the competition. It is to be hoped that those theorists are mistaken, but some industries today suggest that marketing warfare has evolved to embrace either a philosophy of unconditional surrender or mutually assured destruction.

On the other hand, wholesome competition can benefit the *consumer*.

BASIC CONSIDERATIONS

To begin your competitive strategic planning, you should consider your organization's *core competencies* and look at the benefit(s) to customers or your *competitive advantage(s)*. You can then decide whether your competitive strategy in marketing should be either *proactive* or *reactive*—that is, whether you will be initiating competitive activities or only responding to the actions of one or more of your competitors. You should also decide whether your competitive strategy is to be a *nonprice strategy*, where you emphasize factors other than price in your marketing efforts, or a *pricing strategy*, the subject of Chapter 11.

You can think of your firm's competitive style as one of the following:

- *Laid-back*—where you don't react promptly or strongly to competitor's activities. This works best when your customers are loyal and/or when your firm plans to milk a business.

- *Selective*—where you react only to particular types of competitive attack. For example, you would respond to *cents-off coupon* promotions but not to *type-of-customer* discounting strategy.
- *Tiger*—you respond quickly, decisively, and aggressively to any competitive pressure.
- *Stochastic*—from the Greek meaning "skillful in aiming," this is the term for a competitive approach that is not easily anticipated by competitors. Your competitive strategy may take any form you deem appropriate in a particular situation and at a particular time.

Competitive strategies are also characterized according to the commitment of the organizations and individuals executing the strategies:

- *High-commitment strategy*—fight your competition aggressively, with everything you have.
- *Moderate-commitment strategy*—aim to maintain the status quo in your marketplace.
- *Low-commitment strategy*—take the path of least resistance and just try to survive.

Strategies can further be classified (and more vividly named) as either *defensive* or *offensive*, as follows. (All of these considerations also relate to other strategic areas, as you will see in subsequent chapters.)

DEFENSIVE STRATEGIES

Here are the names of current defensive competitive strategies:

- *Fortress* (or *position defense*) *strategy*—the most basic defensive strategy, and appropriate for market leader companies. In the long run probably doomed, this strategy involves concentrating solely on holding the leadership position.
- *Flanking defense strategy*—employed by larger companies to protect their weaker area(s) or to establish a base for possible counterattack of a competitor's *flank attack* strategy.
- *Flanker strategy*—protect against loss of current customers by developing a back-up market segment with special needs you can satisfy best.
- *Preemptive defense strategy*—protect yourself from competitive attack by attacking them *first*. Naturally, this requires good, up-to-the minute competitive market intelligence.
- *Psychological defense strategy*—scare off your competitor from attacking by leaking misleading information that you are going to do something devastating if you are attacked—such as respond with an enormous price cut.
- *Counterattack* (or *counteroffensive*) *defense strategy*—a strong, direct, and aggressive response to a competitor's attack. Timing is a crucial factor here.

- *Mobile defense strategy*—usually employed by a market leader, this strategy involves broadening the defender's market reach or product diversification in order to strengthen its overall defensive position.

- *Demarketing* (or *contraction defense*, or *strategic withdrawal*) *strategy*—reduce or discontinue offering a product, while maintaining the goodwill of present customers. *Selective demarketing* refers to trying to reduce demand in particular geographic or SIC areas where marketing is not sufficiently profitable.

- *Trimming-deadwood* (or *divest*) *strategy*—stay in business by getting rid of the types of customers or types of business that are not agreeable or profitable to you.

- *Key-markets strategy*—concentrate on your most important customers or target market segments.

- *Relationship strategy*—in terms of business friendships, get closer to your customers than your competitors are. More on this appears in Chapter 31, "Personal Selling Strategies."

- *Harvesting strategy*—stop all marketing efforts, serve the customers you have, and maximize profits. This saves money during the decline stage of the *product life cycle.*

- *Abandonment* (or *product deletion*) *strategy*—quit when you see continuing decline in the product life cycle model. The result of this strategy is referred to as *product extinction.*

OFFENSIVE STRATEGIES

Following are the names of current offensive competitive strategies:

- *Frontal attack strategy*—go after your competition's customers directly by offering lower price, better product, or anything that will lure them away. A high-risk strategy, and usually a failure when a small company attacks a large company.

- *Leapfrog strategy*—develop a product or service package so much better or more advanced than your competition that customers flock to you and ignore your competition.

- *Flank attack strategy*—attract customers from one or more major segments whose current needs are not being perfectly satisfied.

- *Encirclement strategy*—attract a substantial number of new customers from a variety of small and specialized segments where needs differ from those of larger segments.

- *Guerrilla attack strategy*—capture a modest amount of business in several market segments to which your competitors are not paying adequate attention. This strategy requires constant surveillance of the marketplace.

- *Bypass attack strategy*—concentrate on easier target market segments to broaden your base. This may involve diversifying into unrelated products, diversifying into new geographic areas, and/or entering new technological areas.

- *Confrontation* (or *head-to-head,* or *nose-to-nose*) *strategy*—protect against loss of current customers by meeting and beating your competition directly.
- *Market expansion strategy*—attract new customers through aggressive marketing efforts.
- *Distribution innovation strategy*—develop a new distribution technique for an industry, such as Avon did many years ago in the cosmetics field. This is related to the logistics strategy in Chapter 12 called *modification.*
- *Service strategy*—link to your product the needed service(s) that competitive products don't offer.
- *Atmospherics strategy*—a retailing strategy which considers such factors as store design, lighting, temperature, "foreground" (entranceway) and "background" (in-store) music, scents, wall coverings, architecture, décor elements, and display fixtures that can be manipulated to have an effect on consumer moods and buying behavior, time spent in the store, and customer loyalty.
- *Strategic alliance strategy*—develop a good relationship with one or more other companies in your industry to collectively exploit market opportunities. Particularly practiced internationally.
- *Benchmarking strategy*—study the best of the products of your competition—through disassembly, chemical analysis, and the like—to identify what makes them superior to yours. Then change the weak features of your products so they equal or exceed those of your competition.

UNETHICAL COMPETITIVE STRATEGIES

There are a few competitive strategies that no ethical marketer—including these involved in politics—should use.

- *Push-poll strategy*—a highly unethical practice popularized by some political candidates. An interviewer (normally by telephone) pretends to be gathering voter opinion or intention data and asks loaded questions to persuade the respondent of a particular political—usually negative—point of view.
- *Reverse-psychology strategy*—also a political ploy, not practiced much in the United States today, where voters are threatened with harm if they do *not* vote for an opposition candidate. Many people's reaction to such extortionate practice is to vote for the opponent, which is exactly what was intended.
- *Product-related competitive strategies*—as noted in Chapter 8, there are four types of product-related follower-type competitors, and the actions of the first and perhaps the second should be considered unethical: the *counterfeiter* who duplicates the leading product in every detail and sells it on the black market; the *cloner* who imitates the leading product but introduces slight variations in design and packaging; the *imitator* who copies several features but maintains different strategies for pricing, packaging, advertising, and promotion; and the *adapter* who picks up the general product idea but improves it, often moves into different markets, and sometimes becomes a future challenger.

Chapter 14

Positioning Strategies

THE POSITIONING CONCEPT

Essentially, positioning is a process by which a marketer discovers in the mind of the consumer, customer, client, or prospect a *unique niche* for a product or service that will be *meaningful* to such a person. A classic example is the Avis slogan "Avis is only Number 2 in rent-a-cars" and its follow-up with an important implied customer benefit: "We try harder."

The concept that David Ogilvy called *brand image*, and that Al Ries and Jack Trout refined into "positioning," is really rather simple, although poorly understood by many marketing practitioners even today, some of whom think the word refers to where a product is placed on retail shelves. Academics got hold of the idea and broke the single *strategy of positioning* into a dozen sub-strategies. Those and several more are identified in the list that follows.

NAMES OF STRATEGIES

Chapter 8, "Product and Service Strategies," made reference to basic *positioning, repositioning*, and *negative* (or *contrary*) *positioning* strategies. The list of current positioning strategies goes well beyond those basics and in some cases may overlap *name* and *brand* strategies.

- *Preemptive positioning strategy*—the quality selected as the basis for positioning may not be exclusive to the company, product, or service, but the marketer is the *first* to claim it.

- *Superlative positioning strategy*—where the marketer claims to be "number one," "the oldest," "the biggest," or "the best." This is called "puffery" in the United States and is permissible, although illegal in several other countries.

- *Exclusive club positioning strategy*—the marketer claims to be one of the firms that is best in its industry or category, such as a "Big Three automaker" or a "Fortune 500 company."

- *Head-to-head positioning strategy*—compete directly with your closest competitors on similar product attributes to the same target market. A very dangerous strategy for a small company against a large competitor.

- *Differentiation positioning strategy*—search out a market segment that is not being attended to by many competitors where you can set yourself apart. This may involve smaller segments.

- *Positioning by competitor strategy*—use your competitor's image as a point of reference. The subjects for comparison can be cost, speed, dependability, and the like. Avis hit on a great *positioning by competitor* strategy with the slogan "We're number two; we try harder."

- *Positioning by feature(s) strategy*—probably the most common positioning strategy. Of course, the feature you emphasize must be something important to the target market. A good example of this strategy is the classic Volkswagen advertising line "Think small."

- *Positioning by benefit* (or *problem*, or *need*) *strategy*—often an even better approach than positioning by feature, positioning by *benefit* emphasizes what your product or service will do for members of your target market, as in the brand name of Easy Off® oven cleaner.

- *Positioning by quality strategy*—not quite the same as positioning by feature, because this refers to "quality" in the sense of *excellence*. This can be a good strategy for you to employ if perceptual mapping indicates your product or service is high on the perceived quality scale.

- *Positioning by use strategy*—relate your positioning to how the product is used. A classic example was the slogan "the toothpaste for people who can't brush after every meal."

- *Positioning by occasion strategy*—consider the time or instance rather than the nature of the use of your product. For example, Anheuser-Busch advertised "This night is made for Michelob®." This strategy can be related to synchrographic segmentation and has valid application to seasonal products, year-end contracting, and the like.

- *Positioning by target* (or *public*, or *user*) *strategy*—relate your product or service to a particular group of people. For example, Robitussin® cough syrup has positioned itself as the choice of "Dr. Mom."

- *Positioning by cost strategy*—use perceptual mapping to indicate if your product or service is considered inexpensive, modestly priced, or of particularly high value. Then the cost factor can be the heart of your positioning strategy.

- *Positioning by type of product strategy*—use the nature of the product itself as the basis for positioning. Sometimes the product name, company name, or positioning slogan reflects the type of product, like "Jell-O®."

- *Product-class dissociation strategy*—position your product in a different class than its competitors. For example, a planetarium could position itself not as an educational institution but as a recreational facility.
- *Fantasy positioning strategy*—link your product to something with psychological appeal to your target market, as has been done for so many years with "I dreamed I was [some interesting type of person] in my Maidenform® bra." Or the classic Marlboro® fantasy of the brand associated with the idealized American cowboy hero.

The process for developing a *positioning statement* for a marketing plan or a *positioning slogan* for marketing communications has been interpreted and refined by many marketing experts since Ries and Trout popularized the concept. Essentially, nearly all emphasize that the correct approach to the challenge of positioning (always easier in retrospect) is not to create something new and different but to rearrange ideas and associations that *already exist* in the minds of your customers and prospects and connect them to your product, service, or organization.

Chapter 15

Offer Strategies

The *offer* is what the prospect, customer, consumer, or client can expect to receive as a result of a marketing exchange. Normally, it is something that promises to satisfy a conscious or potential want or need in target individuals. It is sometimes called simply "the deal."

APPEALS

Many marketers include in the term "offer" what is called the advertising *appeal*. This involves the basic "WIIFT" acronym ("What's in it for them?") that is such an important consideration in all forms of marketing communications including personal selling. Some strategic planners find it helpful to analyze their appeals or offers in terms of *Maslow's hierarchy of needs* model, usually represented as a stepped pyramid with each level described, from the bottom, as *physiological needs* (air, water, food, sex), *safety needs* (shelter, freedom from physical injury, financial security), *social needs* (friendship, belonging, love), *personal needs* (peer approval, status, prestige), and *self-actualization needs* (career success, worthy offspring, publishing a book). The theory is that lower order needs are strongest and that when a lower order need is unsatisfied it tends to preempt concern for higher order needs. For example, if you haven't eaten for three days, you don't care much about whether your neighbors like you. Marketers try to relate their products and services to the level in the hierarchy that is likely to be the strongest in terms of motivation. Sometimes, of course, a product can relate to more than one level; a fancy food product clearly relates to the physiological level but can also relate to social needs, and even enhance status and self-esteem.

ACTION STRATEGIES

There are several ways to think of your offer. After you have decided on your product and/or service strategy, and then your packaging, pricing, distribution, competitive, and positioning strategies, you should be able to identify your strongest appeal(s), and these will all affect your offer strategy. Naturally, your offer should be stronger, more appealing, and more beneficial than that of your competitor. Since offers are vital to the marketing process, they have been implied in several of the preceding sections and will turn up also in later chapters concerning marketing communications.

Consider now how to encourage immediate action:

- *Limited time strategy*—stresses the urgency to *buy now*. When people think they might miss an opportunity to own something special, they are generally more inclined to purchase.
- *Limited quantity strategy*—implies there are not enough units to satisfy anticipated demand. Both *limited time* and *limited quantity* strategies work well with most sales promotion strategies, which also encourage immediate action, and are also related to the *emergency* (or *urgency*) *close* in personal selling. (Chapter 28 deals with sales promotion strategies, Chapter 32 with closing strategies.)
- *One-to-a-customer strategy*—a variation of the *limited quantity* strategy, this suggests personal exclusivity.
- *Limited group strategy*—might seem discriminatory, but offering a product "only to children under seven" or "seniors only" can have great appeal to a clearly defined market segment, and the FTC rarely prosecutes small marketers for this sort of thing.
- *Discriminating customers only strategy*—a variation of the *limited group* strategy with an *appeal to pride* or *snob appeal* twist. "Only those of cultured taste, sophistication, and breeding will appreciate the work of this remarkable young artist."
- *Price increase strategy*—where you announce a future price increase to encourage customers to buy now at the lower price. Sometimes used unethically to move an old product out of the warehouse to make room for an improved product.
- *Buy-back allowance*—special offer made to wholesalers or retailers to repurchase more of a product after the supply purchased under a *deal* is exhausted.

WARRANTY STRATEGIES

Warranties or guarantees are assurances to customers that often make a significant difference in whether the product is purchased and which therefore constitute part of the *offer*. There are five major warranty (or guarantee) strategies:

- *Express warranty strategy*—written statement of liabilities assumed by the manufacturer for any product defects.
- *Limited-coverage warranty strategy*—written statement that expresses the bounds of manufacturer liability.
- *Full warranty strategy*—no limitations.
- *Implied warranty strategy*—nothing in writing, but assumption is made that the customer and the retailer will be covered in the event of product failure.
- *Lifetime warranty strategy*—a fifth type of warranty that is of questionable legal validity. If "lifetime warranty" means "lifetime of the product" it's no warranty at all. If it means "lifetime of the buyer" that would be hard to enforce with companies going out of business, changing their names, and being acquired by other companies. I met a retailer recently who clarified his claim to this offer strategy by telling me, "The product is covered for my lifetime, or as long as I'm interested in it."

INCENTIVES

No matter how strong your offer, it can be enhanced by what are called "incentives." These can take the form of discounts, premiums, gifts, or other items listed in Chapter 28 as sales promotion strategies. A free book with a customer- or client-needs survey, an additional discount for the first 50 people who respond, and a free travel shaver with the purchase of a top-of-the-line everyday model all work well to enhance and *make more appealing* the basic marketing offer.

The response you get to your marketing communications will be directly related to your offer and also influenced by the way you present it. In other words, the objective, the offer, the incentive to respond, and the response itself are all interrelated.

So after you've decided what you want your target audience to do, decide on the offer that will most effectively and cost-efficiently prompt them to do it. After all, if you offer your prospects *nothing*, they will have no rational reason to respond.

These are the basic things you might offer in order to generate response— *before* you try to initiate a sale:

- Your organizational, product, or service brochure
- Other promotional literature
- Educational materials
- Article reprints
- Other types of printed materials (such as posters)
- Discount coupons
- Special offer (without coupons)
- Free discussion of products or services

- Free discussion of prices or fees
- Free analysis of prospect needs
- Other face-to-face contact
- Visit to your exhibit
- Visit to your office or showroom
- Visit to one of your satisfied customers
- Demonstration of your facilities
- Demonstration of your equipment
- Complimentary sample of your product or service
- Discounted sample of your product or service
- Product or service with money-back guarantee
- Product or service with other refund offer (such as a *cause-related marketing* strategy, defined in Chapters 20 and 29)
- Product or service with rebate offer
- Volume discount offer
- Specially priced combination of goods or services
- Trade-up offer to existing customers or clients
- Videotape or audiotape describing your product or service
- Premium item (primarily as an attention-getter)
- Executive gift (stopping short of a bribe)
- Other reward for customer or client loyalty (theater or sports event tickets, for example)
- Contest or game entry (with no strings attached)
- Sweepstakes offer (check local legality)
- Special offers to referral sources

These offers, you no doubt recognize, could also be called "sales promotion techniques," because sales promotion is primarily marketing's means to get people to take a specific, immediate action related to a sale. Chapter 28 is dedicated to sales promotion strategies, but to facilitate strategic planning it seemed that *offer strategies* should appear here separately.

PRESENTING YOUR OFFER

When response is your primary objective, place your offer as *early* in your copy as you reasonably can. You might even have it dominate a magazine ad by featuring it in the *headline*, developing it in the body copy, and mentioning it again in closing and/or in your call to action. If your medium is direct mail, you might mention it on the *covering envelope* and certainly on your reply device. If your medium is your corporate newsletter, you might make it the topic of your *lead article*.

Toll-free (800, 866, 877, and 888) numbers seem to increase response rates to offers, as do business reply cards (brc) and business reply envelopes (bre) in direct mail and periodical advertising with *bound-in* or *blown-in* cards or envelopes. 900 numbers are *not* toll-free but may reflect lesser (or greater) charges to the caller.

POWER WORDS

Words that have proven useful in prompting action, and hence maximizing response, are those you have seen many times in advertising—because they *work*:

- New
- Improved
- Now
- Free
- Easy
- Urgent
- Exclusive
- Limited-time
- No-risk

Some, not so common, which you might also wish to consider are these:

- How to
- Which
- Money
- Amazing
- Wanted
- At last
- This
- Advice
- You

"You" may be the most important word of all, because it tends to be conversational, focuses attention on what's in the offer for the prospect, and hence encourages involvement.

OTHER TECHNIQUES

You want people to respond and therefore you make them a good offer, perhaps with an additional incentive; and you use the strongest words you can find to motivate them and prompt them to action.

In addition, you must make responding *as easy as possible* for them.

That is why the use of telephone numbers—with a *qualified person* standing by to take name, address, phone number, and other information from the caller—can be fruitful. Information provided via the Internet is also relatively easy and convenient, and available to more people every day. Chapter 27 deals specifically with current electronic commerce and Internet strategies.

Chapter 16

Marketing Communications and Media Strategies

MESSAGE DELIVERY

Marketing communications and media both refer to the *means* by which you deliver your marketing message to your target market or other publics. Here they are called your target "audience." Strategies that have to do with the creative aspects of how you present or package your offer will be treated in Parts III and IV. In keeping with the *4Ps* model of marketing components academics refer to this aspect of the marketing mix as "promotion."

Appendix 6 contains a comprehensive list of marketing communications media types, arranged by general category. As a supplement to this, you might consider tactics that involve *size* and *length* of advertisements, such as the now rare 90-second or 120-second television commercial, versus the split-30, versus the 10-second ID spot; or island positions for fractional-space print ads, versus successive right-hand pages, versus pop-up inserts.

Also tactical are media alternatives that include *advertorials*, or ads that look like editorial material in newspapers and magazines, and *infomercials*, which are 15-minute to one-hour commercial programs that appear to be television talk shows or documentaries but are really extended (albeit entertaining) commercials.

NAMES OF STRATEGIES

The broader strategies related to marketing communications and media are the following:

- *Imitative strategy*—where you simply copy your competition.
- *Comparative strategy*—make objective comparison of your marketing communications techniques with your competitor's. Note that this goes beyond comparison of product features, service, and the like. Some marketers stoop to a derogatory or combative stance, which sometimes proves counter-productive.
- *Traditional strategy*—continue to do what you have done in the past.
- *Innovative strategy*—develop a new and different approach to marketing communications, considering both the means of delivery of your message (media) and your creative execution, strategies for which will be covered later. Recent innovations include *holographic images, CD-ROMs* in magazines, and *sound cards.*
- *Mass media strategy*—take the traditional approach where advertising through television, radio, newspapers, magazines, outdoor, and transit predominates and anything else is considered merely support or "collateral."
- *Alternative media strategy*—use more selective media, such as direct mail, tradeshows, advertising specialties, and the Internet in favor of mass media. Usually this is a strategy for clearly defined target market segments.
- *Integrated marketing communications* (or *IMC*) *strategy*—where you develop a balance of mass media and alternative media for all your marketing communications activities. This is difficult to accomplish in organizations still divided into departments that specialize exclusively in advertising, sales promotion, personal selling, and public relations. (A comprehensive list of marketing communications options that can be integrated appears in Appendix 6.)
- *Database marketing strategy*—collect geographic, demographic, psychographic, synchrographic, media exposure, consumption, and purchasing information to develop customer and prospect profiles which can serve as guidance for targeted media efforts.
- *Interactive media strategy*—where you can communicate directly with members of your target audience through such media as direct mail, telephone, fax, and the Internet.
- *Internal marketing strategy*—unlike most of the strategies in this chapter, *internal* directs the advertising message to your own employees. It is often wise to attend to this before your proceed with your *external* marketing communications strategies.
- *Competitive-parity* (or *defensive budgeting*, or *defensive spending*) *strategy*—research your competitors' reach, frequency, gross rating point, or gross impression levels, or estimate their marketing communications budgets and aim to achieve equivalent *share of voice.* Major criticisms of this strategy are that it assumes your competitor's goals are the same as yours, that planning for your competitor's marketing communications is exactly right, and that information is historical, not predictive. (Chapter 37 has more on budgeting.)
- *Objective and task strategy*—employ a budgeting technique whereby you calculate the costs of specific marketing communications activities on the basis of the clearly defined jobs they must do.

- *Blitz strategy*—engage in all-out media activity at maximum spending levels. This strategy is affordable only for relatively short periods of time.
- *Front-load strategy*—scheduling heaviest advertising at the beginning of the ad campaign.
- *Heavy-up strategy*—occasionally increasing advertising weight, as soft-drink marketers do at holiday times.
- *Flighting strategy*—scheduling on-and-off media activity to give high frequency for limited periods of time, followed by a *hiatus* (no activity), followed by another burst of advertising activity.
- *Blinking* (or *blink*) *strategy*—rapid *flighting*, generally one week on and one week off.
- *Pulsing strategy*—varying the intensity of the advertising, never actually taking a hiatus, as in *flighting* or *blinking*, but saving money by reducing frequency periodically.
- *Best food day (BFD) strategy*—a scheduling strategy by which advertising is run on days when a majority of people do their weekly grocery shopping, which is Wednesday in most of the United States but varies from one part of the country to another. These are the days when marketers and manufacturers run most of their retail *coupons* and *free standing inserts* (*FSIs*), also called *free standing stuffers*, and more generically *ride-alongs*.
- *Continuity strategy*—maintain a consistent level of advertising over a long period of time so that name recognition and/or message retention persist.
- *Concentrated strategy*—limit advertising to specific periods. This term is also used to describe a *market* strategy.
- *Concentration strategy*—aim at a single market segment with your advertising. This term is also used for a *packaging* strategy.
- *Across-the-board* (or *strip programming*) *strategy*—in broadcast advertise at the same time or within the same program five days a week. This is a *high-frequency* strategy presumably to obtain greater levels of awareness among a limited audience.
- *Full-run strategy*—in a newspaper campaign, advertise in all editions of scheduled paper(s).
- *High frequency strategy*—maximize the average number of exposures to a relatively small audience. Good for product introductions to achieve awareness quickly.
- *Broad reach strategy*—plan lower frequency, but aim advertising to achieve exposure among as large a portion of the target audience as possible. This relates to a *mass-market* strategy. Because an advertiser cannot have both *high frequency* and *broad reach* except at staggering cost, the strategic choice for long-term scheduling is normally between *reach* or *frequency*.
- *Back-to-back* (or *piggyback commercial*) *strategy*—two commercials for related products, such as toothpaste and mouthwash, are run in one commercial position. This includes the category called earlier the *split-30*.

- *Double-up strategy*—a possibility most often seen in broadcast advertising when at a commercial break two 15-second spots are run—the first at the beginning and the second at the end of the break with other commercials aired between. The strategy is called *bookends* when, for example, the first segment introduces the product in a *slice-of-life* setting and the second segment shows the subsequent beneficial result. This is not the same as a *split-30* where announcements for two different, but similarly targeted products are placed within a single 30-second slot.

- *Fractional strategy*—similar in principle to *double-up*, you schedule smaller time or space units to increase frequency at little or no significant increase in budget. In print media, a full page ad can be divided into two half-pages separated by editorial material (but preferably not other ads) in the same issue, or placed in different issues to increase reach. Both production and media *unit* costs rise slightly with this strategy, but in theory recognition and recall are increased.

- *Repetition strategy*—running the same commercial two or more times in the same program segment. Thought to increase recall, but likely to speed *wearout*, which means the audience becomes bored with or even irritated by the commercial.

- *Upfront strategy*—employed by large national advertisers to obtain what they believe are the best positions in primetime television programs and other network, cable, and syndicated TV offerings. This involves large buys, usually contracted for one year ahead of time.

- *Opportunistic strategy*—a media buying strategy, largely found in network television advertising, that involves holding back advertising dollars until "opportunistic packages" are offered. Opportunistic packages are unpurchased or cancelled collections of *sponsorships* (complete programs), *participations* (in-program positions), or *adjacencies* (immediately before or after a program) that can be bought on short notice at large discounts.

- *Rate-holder strategy*—another media buying strategy whereby frequency discounts are retained by running smaller space or time units. Usually applied in times of media schedule budget reductions to avoid the advertiser being "short-rated."

- *Buyout strategy*—presumably to save time and money, one-time payments are made to talent in broadcast commercials to avoid having to pay *residuals* (or *re-use fees* or *talent charges*) according to the requirements of the American Federation of Television and Radio Artists (AFTRA) and Screen Actors Guild (SAG).

- *Cost-efficiency strategy*—base your media selections on cost-per-thousand (CPM) calculations, and aim at spending the least amount of money per exposure.

- *Cost-effectiveness strategy*—emphasize the quality of the impressions your schedule can make or the value of the prospect to whom your advertising message is delivered, rather than low cost-per-thousand against the total audience. This can be measured even more carefully in terms of what is called *cost-per-inquiry (CPI)* or *cost-per-order (CPO)* in direct response marketing, *cost-per-hit* on a Web site, or *cost-per-lead* for direct sales operations.

- *Cost-of-sale strategy*—relate your advertising expenditures to amounts of lead conversion to sales. Although conversion from an advertising inquiry or lead to a sale using a field sales force involves factors other than advertising, some managers like to calculate by medium their communications costs-per-sales-dollar or (more commonly) the average sales dollars obtained per marketing communication dollar invested.

- *Paid versus nonpaid (or controlled, or qualified) circulation strategy*—selection of periodicals (primarily specialized business) is based not only on total circulation, but also whether readers pay for their subscriptions or receive them on a complimentary basis. Many media buyers feel strongly about which provides the best possible exposure for advertising, but there seems to be no clear consensus.

- *Horizontal versus vertical strategy*—business magazines are defined as *vertical* if they are edited for a particular Standard Industrial Classification (SIC) category, industry, or profession (such as *Chain Store Age*, *Advertising Age*, and *Journal of the American Medical Association*) and *horizontal* if they reach across industries (such as *Business Week* and *Entrepreneur*). One type or the other may be preferable in a media schedule, depending on the marketing and advertising objectives and goals; more often, a mixture is selected. Consumer magazines of the *vertical* type (such as *Guns & Ammo* and *Southwestern Art*) are called *class magazines* because they go to a particular interest classification—not necessarily because their readers are upscale socioeconomically. *Horizontal* consumer magazines include *People* and *TV Guide*.

- *Passalong strategy*—gross impressions are calculated as the sum of audited primary circulations of periodicals, plus the *passalong* or *secondary readers* ("readers per copy" or RPC) estimated by publishers, presumably based on reliable research. Bigger audience figures tend to mean lower costs-per-thousand, which appeal to some clients. Some advertising managers prefer to ignore passalong.

- *Fixed-position strategy*—broadcast spots are bought without possibility of preemption by a higher-paying advertiser, and in print advertising special positions (such as back covers) are secured at extra cost. In print advertising what is called *preferred position* includes also the type of editorial material in which an ad is placed (such as the sports section of a newspaper) or what page it appears on (such as facing the table of contents in a magazine). This may be expensive but locks in a firm schedule. An *island position* in either print or broadcast means that no other advertising appears adjacent to the island ad.

- *Roadblock strategy*—a broadcast media scheduling strategy to maximize reach by buying the same time slots on as many stations or channels as possible, either network or market-by-market.

- *Run-of-press* or *-paper (ROP)*, or *run-of-station [radio]* or *-schedule [television] (ROS) strategy*—a cost-conscious media strategy that allows newspapers and broadcasters to place ads and spots in any position available in exchange for lower rates to the advertiser.

- *Scatter plan strategy*—in broadcast advertising a schedule that runs commercials in a variety of programs, presumably diversifying the audience and increasing reach.

- *Daypart (or exposure-time) strategy*—for broadcast advertising, consider audience composition and attention at various times of day and schedule accordingly.

Radio is divided into *morning drive time* (6:00 to 10:00 A.M.), *daytime* (10:00 A.M. to 3:00 P.M.), *afternoon drive time* (3:00 to 7:00 P.M.), *night time* (7:00 P.M. to midnight), and *all night* (midnight to 6:00 A.M.); *drive times* are considered *primetime* for radio. Television dayparts are *morning* (7:00 to 9:00 A.M. M–F), *daytime* (9:00 to 4:30 P.M. M–F), *early fringe* (4:30 to 7:30 P.M. M–F), *prime access* (7:00 to 7:30 or 7:30 to 8:00 P.M. Sun–Sat), *primetime* (8:00 to 11:00 P.M. M–Sat and 7:00 to 11:00 P.M. Sun), *late news* (11:00 to 11:30 P.M. M–F), *late fringe* (11:30 P.M. to 1:00 A.M.), and *late night* (1:00 to 7:00 A.M. Sun–Sat). These definitions have been established by the Federal Communications Commission (FCC) for the Eastern time zone and may vary slightly elsewhere. Radio *drive time* is when people drive to and from work; *daytime* traditionally reaches more housewives and retirees; *primetime* for television reaches all-family audiences; *early* and *late fringe time* are more economical; and *late night* reaches swing-shift workers and insomniacs.

- *Display strategy*—this term is used in "print" (magazine and newspaper) advertising, particularly newspaper, to describe the use of blocks of ad space within editorial material.

- *Classified strategy*—a relatively low-cost approach to advertising that uses "want ad" listings in newspapers and some magazines.

- *Small-space strategy*—primarily in the newspaper medium, this involves ads that normally measure only one column in width. A good strategy for achieving *high frequency* at relatively modest cost.

- *Omnibus* (or *catalog*) *strategy*—involves full pages on which many products are featured. A media strategy used heavily by discount stores and auto dealers, it is also a popular means for retailers to obtain co-op advertising dollars from manufacturers—which can sometimes total more than the actual cost of the ad space.

- *Place-based media strategy*—place ads in locations likely to achieve exposure to particular target segments, such as on posters or kiosks in airports to reach business travelers and health clubs to reach persons interested in physical fitness.

- *Donut strategy*—in broadcast commercials, you leave the middle blank, or perhaps only with a background music "bed" so that changing information, such as this week's special sale, can be dropped in (often by a live announcer) without having to remake the entire commercial.

- *Dealer tag strategy*—name, address, and telephone number of local retailers are appended locally to nationally broadcast commercials.

- *Cut-in strategy*—primarily for testing purposes, a scheduled network commercial is replaced with a different commercial or one for a different product. Often used in *test market* research.

- *Image liner* (or *pop-in*) *strategy*—use of short, paid, ID-type announcements that simply identify the advertiser and offer brief messages such as "Al's Autos wishes you safe driving this holiday season." Used, too, for announcements of *underwriting* on public broadcasting.

- *Intercept strategy*—based on a consumer-behavior theory to catch the prospect during the information-search part of the decision-making process and place the advertised product in the "evoked set" of products about which a final buying decision will be made. This relies heavily on co-op and point-of-purchase advertising and is reliant on arresting package design and prominent display on store shelves.

- *Disrupt strategy*—a related consumer-behavior idea that holds if your product is not part of the evoked set, you can disrupt the pattern of routine or habitual decision-making by such sales promotion strategies as *sampling, coupons, discounts,* and *rebates.*
- *Acceptance strategy*—intended to attract attention to a product and motivate prospects to learn more about it through such tactics as *cash awards* for test-driving a car.
- *Share of voice strategy*—as noted in Chapter 7, marketers plan to spend a particular percentage of their industry's total advertising expenditures.
- *Share of mind strategy*—maximize attention, awareness, and knowledge of the organization, product, service, or idea. Measured as a percent of various types of awareness.
- *Share of heart strategy*—maximize customer and prospect goodwill. Largely practiced by monopolies or near-monopolies, this strategy and the preceding are sometimes combined and called *share of customer strategy.*
- *Irritation strategy*—for marketers who wish to try it, aim to make the advertising message so intrusive and annoying (often through high volume, high-speed narration, and bad taste) that the prospect cannot help but notice it. Used by some retail car dealers and a few fast-food franchises, this strategy (sad to say) often works better in terms of awareness and action than more low-key and cultivated efforts.
- *Subliminal strategy*—one of the great frauds of the twentieth century. The idea that we are motivated by forces we cannot see or hear is a paranoid delusion, and people who insist subliminal advertising is being performed, I believe, are either fools or fakes. Subliminal advertising doesn't work, isn't done (because, if it were, at least one practitioner would by now have written a book about how to do it), and would be both unethical and illegal even if it *did* work. The term is included here only for the sake of completeness.

FUNDING

Finally, the way advertising is paid for can be thought of as strategic, the most common methods being these:

- *Sponsorship*—where a marketer develops a TV program such as *Hallmark Hall of Fame* for which they pay in full and in which they are the exclusive advertiser.
- *Cosponsorship*—shared sponsorship of a program developed by or for a large company such as Procter & Gamble that has several different products to advertise, or for two or more noncompeting companies.
- *Participation*—where advertisers buy commercial positions or *announcements* (time) in network or locally originated broadcast programs or national *insertions* (space) in print media vehicles.

- *Adjacency*—commercial position immediately before or after a program, at *station breaks* locally or *chain breaks* in network television scheduling.
- *Spot*—where advertisers buy time for broadcast announcements (called "availabilities" or "avails") or packages of positions in specific geographic areas called "markets" on either network affiliate or network "owned and operated" (*O&O*) stations or independent stations. *Spot print* advertising refers to buying particular metro-area newspapers and local and regional editions of periodicals.
- *Co-op*—where manufacturers reimburse retailers for advertising retailers do on behalf of the manufacturers' products. (Different than *co-op* in distribution and *co-op* sales promotions.)
- *PSA* (or *public service announcement*)—advertising space or commercial time donated to nonprofits by the media. No longer are the media required by government regulation to provide PSAs.
- *Word-of-mouth*—often alluded to in marketing plans as a form of advertising media but not a valid strategic alternative because it cannot be controlled the way paid advertising can. Although there is no cost, there is no guarantee of delivery either, and we cannot calculate gross impressions or reach and frequency figures. But we should still strive to accomplish good *word-of-mouth* by means of product quality, fair prices, efficient distribution, creative marketing communications, honest personal selling, and attentive customer service.

Part III

The Aesthetics of Marketing Planning

Chapter 17

Types of Advertisements and
Creative Strategies

Before you consider advertising creative strategies decide on the *type* of advertisement you need, which will be based on your advertising objective(s). By the way, in the advertising business the word "creative" is often used as a *noun* to mean the creative product as in, "Just wait till you see the new *creative* for this brand." It may also be used as shorthand for the Creative Department as in, "*Creative* wants to shoot the commercial in Paris."

Advertisements (whatever the medium) are normally categorized as one of several types:

- *Product ads*—are straightforward as to their subject matter. The "product" could be a manufactured item, a service, a destination (such as a resort hotel), a location (such as a city), a person (such as a political candidate), or an idea (such as quitting smoking), as noted in Chapter 8.
- *Institutional ads*—deal with companies or other organizations and/or the ideas that they represent, as with nonprofit organizations.
- Both of these types of ads may be further categorized as:
  —*Informational* (or *pioneering*)—normally used to introduce new products or services, to introduce existing products to new markets, or to introduce new companies or organizations. The latter type would be called an *informational institutional* ad.

  —*Persuasive* (or *competitive*)—usually containing considerable information and set up to "sell" members of the target audience.

  —*Advocacy*—usually just of the *institutional* variety, intended to present a position on an issue. Often these relate to public relations objectives rather than advertising objectives.

—*Reminder*—these ads, as the term implies, assume the audience is acquainted with the product, service, or organization and its marketing message and just needs a bit of a jog to continue to remember it. For example, Coca-Cola has been doing *reminder product* ads for more than 100 years.

- *Primary demand ads*—when the marketer attempts to create awareness of, knowledge about, and initial acceptance for a product. When placed by associations these may pertain to an entire product category or industry.
- *Secondary demand ads*—based on the assumption that awareness, knowledge, and acceptance of a product exist, these ads aim primarily at encouraging purchase.
- *Selective demand ads*—when the marketer focuses on a specific brand directed to a specific audience.

The challenge of creativity in advertising and other forms of marketing communications basically is to distill the essence of your message (including your *offer*—direct or implied) and blend it into a context that will achieve maximum impact and memorability among your particular target audience(s) through the particular medium (or media) you plan to use. But that's certainly more easily said than done.

It has been recognized by many marketing practitioners that significant numbers of people, particularly in the advertising business, try to be "creative" without discipline. Sometimes good communications emerge without care and self-control, but the chances for marketing success are much greater when a deliberate, disciplined, and intelligent methodology is used.

It could be argued that creative strategies are closer to *tactics*, since they relate to executional elements of strategic marketing planning. But since people in the advertising business generally refer to their techniques as "strategies," that term is used here.

Your goal in this very subjective area of marketing should be to apply advertising and promotion to contribute to the success of your business— not to create enduring works of art, not to shed the light of wisdom on a benighted world, and particularly not exclusively to entertain. The primary purpose of marketing communications normally is to *persuade*, and creativity in your communications is one of the ways to do that.

This subject has been categorized many different ways, and no one system can be guaranteed as best. My own strategic creative approach relies on the following lists that I believe should be used *after* you have developed essential product or service information, determined your positioning and/ or brand image, and decided on the message you wish to communicate.

Many, but by no means all, practitioners believe strongly in the importance of a *creative work plan* to summarize all the items that should be considered for inclusion in an advertisement, and you will find guidance on that subject in Appendix 8.

By selecting one or more of the *creative strategies* in the four chapters that follow, you will instantly establish the core of what is often called your *creative* (or *copy*) *platform*—a task that otherwise might seem simply impossible. The strategies are divided into four types: Rhetorical Creative Strategies, Product- or Service-Related Creative Strategies, Artistic and Emotional Creative Strategies, and Logical Creative Strategies. The creative (or copy) platform in most advertising agencies expands on the creative strategy in that it often includes objectives of the advertisement, basic elements to be included such as slogans and symbols, target audience profile and needs, product or service claims, advertising appeals and the offer, image or positioning, style, and tone—all of which (and more) are treated as separate topics in this handbook and summarized as elements of a *creative work plan.*

Of course, in practice *more than one* strategy is often used in an advertisement, commercial, printed piece, or Internet ad—so feel free to combine two or more as you think about the best way to appeal to and communicate persuasively with the people you wish to influence.

Chapter 18

Rhetorical Creative Strategies

These creative strategies rely on use of spoken and written language, and many date back to ancient times.

- *Identification*—the oldest type of advertising and promotion, characterized first by trade signs and later by posters, broadsides, and newspaper ads that simply identified particular products or services for sale at specific locations. This strategy was important to establishment of national brands toward the end of the nineteenth century. Today it is often seen in the form of small ads for doctors, banks, or public offerings of securities that are commonly called *tombstone ads* in print advertising, and *button ads* on the Internet.
- *Announcement*—an enhancement of *identification*, also old and well established, this strategy is both bold and direct. It makes no effort to build rapport with the audience or to motivate but just proclaims such things as, "We have fresh herring on Hastings Dock today." Quite reasonably, it is still very popular today in forms such as, "The Center for Holistic Medicine announces the opening of its new facilities in downtown Atlanta," and invitations to visit a Web site.
- *Commanding attention*—ads and promotion pieces that rely on this strategy exist primarily to get people to notice them, but *commanding attention* by itself does not accomplish all that successful marketing communications should accomplish. Specifically, the command should be paid off with information important to the target audience.
- *Denial*—an argumentative type of strategy that many consumers find aggravating. A hypothetical example might be, "You thought there was only one way to apply lawn fertilizer . . . well you're *wrong*." Although popular, a more courteous way to introduce new ideas or correct mistaken opinions might be more effective.

- *Surprise*—involves the unexpected juxtaposition of elements. A good example is the classic Volkswagen ad that featured a three-quarter view of the car above the bold word "Lemon."

- *Challenge*—can be a very effective competitive strategy and also useful in efforts to change behavior by direct assault. A hypothetical example would be, "We challenge you to try our comprehensive small-business computer service for one year and *not* save money." The appeal can be to personal pride or even simple faith, or the marketer can actually make a kind of wager with the prospect, as with the addition of a sales promotion offer of a full refund if the customer is not completely satisfied.

- *Exhortation*—a common action-getting strategy, *exhortation* may also be used as the substance of an entire ad. Somewhat like *announcement* and *challenge*, it communicates strong encouragement or even demand for the prospect to *do* something. For example, an ad headline of this type might read, "Don't wait another day to begin your personal anti-aging program." This strategy requires some explanation of why the exhortation is delivered, so it often works best with a *logical approach* called *reason-why*, covered in Chapter 21. In the commercial world the most extreme form of *exhortation* is the popular phrase, "Buy it *now*."

- *Dogmatism*—observed in such advertising insistences as, "The best that money can buy." Generally speaking, though, this strategy is not particularly effective in these days when people do not hesitate to ask themselves, "Says who?"

- *Authoritarianism*—the advertising strategy that over the years has probably featured more purported doctors than any other. Now forbidden by the FTC, this was sometimes called the *white-coat strategy*, and years ago often included the commercial model also sporting an eye reflector; more recently credibility is enhanced by a stethoscope around the neck of the spokesperson or draped casually over one shoulder, although the lab coats are supposedly prohibited. An interesting enhancement is when an *actor* who portrays a doctor on a television series is the authority figure discussing the features and benefits of a healthcare product. A classic Camel cigarette campaign ran for years with variations on the headline, "More doctors smoke Camels than any other cigarette." (There has been some question in recent years of how the survey samples substantiating those claims were drawn.) Fundamentally, this strategy of *authoritarianism* is based on individuals' willingness to replace their own judgment with that of someone they believe must know more about a subject than they do.

- *Two-sided message* (or *two-sided appeal*)—presents positive and negative sides of a selling proposition, usually of a competitive nature, with emphasis on the positive. A *logical* strategy as well as *rhetorical*, this one appeals to intelligent audiences.

- *Parallel construction*—repetition of form or word sequence, as in "I came, I saw, I conquered"—which included *alliteration* and *rhyme* (mentioned later) in Julius Caesar's original Latin "veni, vidi, vici."

- *Hyperbole*—or "hype" as it is commonly called in connection with advertising and promotion—is extravagance and exaggeration in expression. Often it is meant to do no harm, but simply to attract attention and to create interest, as in the soda fountain billed as "Home of the *half-ton* hot-fudge sundae." Rational consumers would not expect to receive 1,000 pounds of ice cream and fudge, any more than they would want to have the promise fulfilled. But *hyperbole* can be dangerous and unethical in advertising and promotion when it *seems* true, or *might be* true, but is not. Although the strategy is not illegal in the United States (as it is in some other countries) where it is sometimes called "puffery," the conscientious marketer must beware lest enthusiasm manifested in *hyperbole* transcend healthy-spirited exaggeration and enter the realm of deliberate deception.

- *Quotation*—can be strong and persuasive. Famous and historical quotes can work well in print ads and direct mail openings. Unattributed quotes, however— unless they are adages—border on the deceptive and should be avoided.

- *Storytelling* (or *narrative*)—the copy is in the form of a purported experience, tale, fable, or parable. Usually the story or narrative is fictitious, unlike the *testimonial*, *celebrity endorsement*, and *case history* strategies defined in Chapter 21.

- *Pun*—particularly popular among advertising copywriters, as the visual cliché is popular among advertising art directors. How many dozen times have you seen advertising for a savings institution that has exclaimed (as if for the first time) "You can *bank* on us!"? This seems to be a weak way to get attention, despite its popularity, because (even if the pun is a good one) its cleverness distracts the audience from the marketing message. The *pun* is another of the entertainment techniques that may win awards for highly creative advertising, but does little to persuade intelligent people to make important decisions.

- *Idiom*—usually takes the form of a cliché when applied to the creative dimension of advertising. For example, a headline might support the illustration of a pile of poker chips with "You can *bet your bottom dollar* Wheeler bicycles are tough." This does not do much to advance the persuasive process or increase the likelihood of a sale—thus the *idiom* is generally weak in the same ways that the *pun* is weak.

- *Irony*—although sometimes applied in questionable taste to counter competition, *irony* can also be employed in a witty, engaging way by genuinely creative adcrafters. Generally speaking, though, most efforts at *irony* suffer when the message is eclipsed by the creator's attempt at entertainment.

- *Analogy*—lacking in real meaning for the most part, *analogy* can engender a sort of pseudo-logic in the minds of susceptible people and can often spark emotional responses. Two common forms are *metaphor* and *simile*. The former says that one thing *is* another, as "Genteel deodorant is *confidence*," while the latter says that one is *like* another, as "Genteel deodorant is like a breath of fresh air." Sports analogies are popular these days. One particularly inept application you see often during football season reads, "*Touchdown!* Run all the way with Shifting Sands Insurance."

- *Slogan*—can be effective if the words chosen are appropriate and meaningful. But such is the exception rather than the rule. Don't rely on a *slogan* strategy unless it is a particularly strong positioning statement that can gain share of mind among your target audience as a result of your being able to afford frequent advertising exposure.

- *Contrast*—can be an effective strategy, in that it can communicate one or more values very quickly. It is most commonly seen in terms of the happy versus the unhappy shopper (the happy shopper, of course, being the one who bought the advertised product). Note that this strategy is not quite the same as either *side-by-side comparison* or *before and after*, both of which are described under *proof* in Chapter 19.

- *Question*—the strength of the *question* strategy lies in the psychological fact that interrogatory phrases are more arresting to most people than declamatory phrases such as *announcement* headlines. Or put another way, most people tend to get more personally involved in a question than in other forms of human communication. The *question* strategy is especially effective when supported by strategies categorized as *logical* in Chapter 21.

- *Faulty grammar*—employed either to attract attention or to reflect *plain folks* or *salt of the earth* strategy, such as the old rhyme "Winston tastes good like [rather than "as"] a cigarette should."

- *Rhyme*—repetition of final sounds at the ends of lines. There are many forms of *rhyme*, the most common in advertising being the "rhyming couplet"—pairs of successive lines that rhyme and that have the same cadence—such as Texaco's classic "You can trust your car/ to the man who wears the star."

- *Rhythm*—words that provide a beat or regular timing to a sequence of syllables, such as the old "Shave and a haircut, two bits."

- *Alliteration*—repetition of a sound, usually the initial consonant of successive words as in "Peter Piper picked a peck of pickled peppers." This is sometimes called "head rhyme."

- *Plosives*—use of the consonant sounds "b," hard "c" and "k," "d," hard "g," and "p." These sounds can provide impact and corresponding excitement.

- *Onomatopoeia*—use of words that suggest the sounds they represent, such as "pop," "bang," "hush," and "crack."

- *Misleading silence*—trade term for a "lie of omission" or what the FTC sometimes calls "incomplete disclosure." An unethical practice, often dealt with harshly by government watchdogs. For more on this topic, see Appendix 9, "A Test for Honest Advertising."

Chapter 19

Product- or Service-Related Creative Strategies

These strategies are useful to almost all marketers but are most commonly seen in connection with consumer advertising:

- *Name* (or *brand*) *recognition*—is generally handled in one of two ways. The first is to feature the product package design or the organizational identity device (logotype, symbol, or trademark) and is often little more than a dominant illustration of the product package and/or a graphic identity treatment. The second way is to feature a distinctive use of the product or service, always with the "trade dress" (corporate color[s] and/or design) predominant. Used primarily for packaged-goods, this strategy creates recognition of the packaging, so people will reach for the product when they see it in a store. Like the *slogan*, this strategy generally requires a *high frequency* media strategy to be successful.

- *Features*—an advertiser can draw attention to *features* of a product or service in terms of four sub-strategies: style, performance, quantification, or extrapolation. *Style* means essentially appearance, as in "European design elegance." *Performance* relates to what it does, as in, "Pulls the heaviest of loads." *Quantification* involves numbers, as in, "679 components and only one moving part." *Extrapolation* is a more intellectual means to express *features* and sometimes flows over into areas defined separately here. An example of *extrapolation of features* is David Ogilvy's classic ad headline that reads, "At 60 miles an hour the loudest noise in this new Rolls-Royce comes from the electric clock." The pure *feature* is that the car is quiet. A *benefit* treatment might have read, "During a long drive, you'll suffer fewer jangled nerves from road and engine noise." But what Ogilvy did (among other splendid things) was to *extrapolate a feature* by relating it to the almost-silent electric clock, and thereby *implied* a benefit while communicating a remarkable product feature. This advertisement is widely accepted among professional marketers as one of the best ever written—and its long-copy text is almost all *features*.

- *Claims*—although a *claim* is essentially a *feature* without substantiation, such as "Absolutely the best-tasting pie you can buy," it is also a *promise*. The unadorned *claim* strategy experiences relatively low believability today.

- *Benefits*—the difference between a *feature* and a *benefit* is that the former is an attribute of the product, while the latter expresses what the product will *do for the customer*. It is an interesting and often rewarding exercise for the marketing communicator to turn features into benefits. Examples pertaining to installation of a new computer in an organization might look like this:

—*Feature*—"Ajax Accounting has a new, high-speed IBM computer system."

—*Claim*—"Now Ajax Accounting can process your records twice as fast at half the cost."

—*Benefit*—"You can start saving time and money today with Ajax Accounting's new, high-speed computerized bookkeeping system."

Generally, the use of a *benefit strategy* in advertising and promotion is effective because it tells customers or prospects *what's in it for them*.

- *Proof*—because *proof* is the strategy that validates the *claim*, and/or the *feature*, and/or the *benefit*, it is sound, logical, and generally ethical. So it is likely to be among the most persuasive of creative strategies, if it is kept interesting and does not bog down in heavy-handed detail, as often happens in highly technical ads. *Proof* is most commonly accomplished through any of four sub-strategies: *demonstration* (where proof is dramatically shown), *before-and-after* (where an ideal latter condition is contrasted with a former), *side-by-side comparison* (perhaps the best form of competitive product advertising), and *absence of product or service* (or *negative appeal*), which illustrates what is lacking or lost without the advertised item.

- *Related factor*—probably *related factor* is not the most ethical of marketing communications strategies, but it can be marginally acceptable. Basically, it introduces a feature that is not inherent in the product or service itself. For example, "Enjoy *ice-cold* Coca-Cola." Or still one more step removed, "Eat Wheaties with lots of *fresh strawberries* and *dairy cream*." It's just a way of making something appealing because of a factor not inherent in the product or service, so you may see how it can be abused.

- *Secret ingredient*—a strategy as old as the oldest medicine show. The oil companies have used it for years—as in ads that promised "TCP® gives you better performance" and "Drive farther, faster with Platformate®." All the major oil companies have at one time or another touted a different *secret ingredient*. Yet a senior oil company executive told me that all those names have referred to just a single compound produced by Ethyl Corporation and used in the same proportion for the same purpose by all of the oil companies. But when the compound was given a unique *secret ingredient* name and advertised heavily, many drivers were persuaded that they noticed a difference in the performance of their automobiles.

- *Price*—the subject of *price* is often shunned in contemporary advertising but can be expressed in three basic ways: *exact price* ("$875.99"), *range of prices* ("between $500 and $1000"), and *divided cost* ("only $73 per month"). Any of these sub-strategies can have excellent appeal today, even if the advertiser doesn't have the lowest price. Be sure, though, that your representation of price is accurate and honest and do not get trapped by the phony (and illegal) strategy of offering an apparent reduction of a price you have never offered.

- *Savings*—ads that feature *savings* are even more popular today than those that feature *price*. The opposite of *divided cost* (already noted) is *multiplied savings*, as in "Now you can save up to $5,000 on your electric bills over the next ten years." As long as the calculations are honest, though, there should be no objection to this as a means to generate interest among customers and prospects.

- *Non-ingredient*—ads claim what the product does *not* contain, such as saturated fat, salt, sugar, preservatives, and so on. This type of strategy appeals strongly to health-conscious consumers, but may be unethical when the copy implies that *competitive* products contain certain ingredients which they *do not* contain. In that case this advertising creative strategy resembles the *sham issue* public relations strategy mentioned in Chapter 29.

Chapter 20

Artistic and Emotional Creative Strategies

This is the area of marketing in which ad agency people often have the most fun—yet, paradoxically, often serve their clients' interests badly. So eager are many advertising and promotion people to win creative awards from their peers that they lose sight of the fact that their primary responsibility should be to advance the interests of the marketer and serve the *real* needs of the consumer.

An effective way to control this problem is for marketing managers to include a clear advertising creative strategy statement in their marketing plans, and insist that their creative sources adhere to it.

- *Drama*—the emphasis endorsed by Leo Burnett many years ago whereby what he called "the inherent drama" of a product or service should serve as the creative strategy for the advertisement. A classic example of this strategy is David Ogilvy's "Man in the Hathaway Shirt" campaign, which featured an elegant and mysterious gentleman with an eye-patch. This strategy can be used with many of the other strategies noted here in Part III.

- *Borrowed interest*—probably the most common creative strategy in all advertising, where the primary purpose is to attract attention and to get the audience involved in the subject of the advertisement. For example, a classic style of ad for business services illustrates a grainy picture of Babe Ruth hitting one of his home runs under a headline that reads, "Babe Ruth held the *home-run* record and the *strike-out* record at the same time." After a review of Ruth's batting average, the copy concludes that those who want to hit the long balls may also be willing to settle for misses—but that Apex Enterprises will minimize the "strike outs" for its clients. The creators of such work merely wrap the marketing message in an *unrelated* topic they believe will interest the audience and then (sometimes through *analogy*, *pun*, or similar rhetorical strategy) try to relate the two—

hence the term *borrowed interest*. Traditionally the most common *borrowed interest* topics are *sex* (covered separately later), *glamour, leisure, indulgence, wealth, history, war, violence, nature, foreign places, cute creatures* (particularly babies, children, and animals—particularly kittens and dogs), *sympathy, future, fantasy,* and *famous persons.*

- *Green marketing*—the topic of *nature* has been afforded special emphasis lately in advertising by marketers treating issues related to our environment. This strategy is related to *borrowed interest* in that many marketers whose products and services have nothing to do with conservation are seeking to establish some sort of relationship to the public interest in "saving our planet." This has been termed "*green marketing*," and the term "*greenwashing*" has entered our business vocabulary to represent the use of environmental claims as a marketing gimmick.

- *Cause-related marketing*—also involves a sympathetic approach that has grown in the last several years into this important strategy where the marketer somehow provides benefits (such as 1 percent of list price) to a worthy cause if prospects buy the marketer's product. You may not think highly of any of these last three strategies, although they do seem to work well for many advertisers.

- *Occasion* (or *peg*)—could be considered *borrowed interest*, but commonly stands by itself in consumer advertising since it relates the product or service emotionally to a particular day or time of year—as in reminders of Christmas cheer, the loyalty that Mother's Day recalls, the family bonds related to Thanksgiving, and so on. The strategy also can be used when markets are segmented synchrographically, such as advertising a high-quality wristwatch in connection with high school and college graduations.

- *Mood*—this type of advertising has been popular since before the turn of the twentieth century for its clearly emotional appeals to adult consumers—frequently women and pipe-smokers. Although once tried by IBM, it is rarely used in business and professional advertising since the frame of mind of a business or professional decision-maker rarely seems to correlate with the *mood* strategy, which is distinguished by illustrative use of sunsets, masses of flowers, and lovely women (or, as in the IBM campaign, robust corporate executives) strolling along lonely windswept beaches. It may be used alone but more often is enhanced by another strategy—perhaps ironically one of the *logical* strategies covered in Chapter 21. The basic topics of *mood* advertising are *romance, nostalgia, luxury, heroism,* and *security.* Generally it's a harmless strategy, but not particularly strong for high-ticket items.

- *Resonance*—a strategy that attempts to remind the audience of prior experiences. An example might be a cosmetics ad that asks, "Remember your very first kiss?" Resonance is sometimes like *mood*, and sometimes like *nostalgia*, but can be different—as with "When was the last time you had a blow-out at 75 MPH?"

- *Relationship*—this strategy might also appear at first to be merely *borrowed interest*, or even *status* or *snob appeal* (to be covered soon). But it can be far more powerful psychologically. There are two general subcategories. The first I call *association*, whereby the product or service is related to something both appropriate and motivating, such as in a controversial Obsession® perfume ad that associated the product with what appeared to be a sex orgy—not in good taste by any means, but apparently highly motivating to the perfume's particular target audience. The second *relationship* strategy I call *affiliation*, whereby the product or service is related to another product or service that is more technologically advanced or otherwise superior to what is being advertised. A classic application of this strategy used for nearly 100 years involves illustrating a new automobile with an *airplane*. The implication, of course, is that the automobile is fast and powerful and able to do wonderful things like the airplane. Because *relationship* strategies can be used unethically to manipulate people's feelings and perceptions, though, caution is recommended.

- *Slogan*—mentioned in Chapter 9, and sometimes the strategic choice for an advertising campaign. Unless the product is well established, though, more than simply the words will be needed.

- *Jingle*—sometimes an effective and "catchy" way to get your audience to remember your message but criticized by such advertising experts as David Ogilvy who reportedly said facetiously, "If you don't have anything to say, *sing* it."

- *Parody*—can be akin to *borrowed interest* but is often used to ridicule competitive advertising, as *irony* is sometimes used to disparage competitive marketing activity. Because of this negative context, in general it is a creative strategy to be avoided.

- *Trade character*—develop a fictional personality—such as the Energizer bunny, Smokey Bear, the Keebler Elves, or the Budweiser frogs—and create vignettes that make points enhanced by the personification of the organization, product, service, or idea. It can be fun and is often effective with respect to both empathy and memorability.

- *Curiosity*—innocent enough, and a good attention-getter. It may be done with an unusual or paradoxical illustration, or with words that form a riddle or otherwise appeal to those with an inquiring nature.

- *Teaser*—is best done in the form of a campaign, or series of ads, that arouses interest by stretching out the message rather than by cleverly concealing it as in the *curiosity* strategy. A classic example was the series of transit ads that changed each week for five weeks before the opening of the movie, *The Birds*. The first of the series read simply "The" with no punctuation. The following week another word was added to the same layout so that it read, "The Birds"—again with no punctuation. The third ad really got the public interested when it stated (apparently ungrammatically) "The Birds is" without punctuation. The fourth ad read "The Birds is coming" with no period. The fifth week provided the explanation or payoff: "The Birds is coming. (A new motion picture by Alfred Hitchcock.)" This kind of advertising requires not only imagination, but also tremendous administrative skill to see that it runs *exactly* as scheduled. For modest efforts, the risks of bad timing usually outweigh the potential benefits of the *teaser* strategy.

- *Quality*—is simply the clear representation of excellence—so it can be viewed as a blend of *features* and *mood* in many applications. I set it apart because it has proved a useful strategy in the advertising of professional practices as well as upscale, high-ticket consumer products—especially when it is blended with one of what I call the *logical* strategies.

- *Status*—this strategy takes the relatively objective emphasis of *quality* a step further in personal terms and relates the product or service to the socioeconomic level of the target audience—or to what consumer behavior experts call its "membership group."

- *Snob appeal*—goes still further by presenting a context of extreme *status* involving exclusivity and/or luxury. More popular before the Crash of 1929 than in recent times, it has nevertheless been resurrected for today's upwardly mobile superachievers, and appeals to an "aspiration group."

- *Salt-of-the-earth*—is the opposite of *snob appeal* in that it portrays or even glamorizes the downscale lifestyle. It has proved especially effective in beer advertising, with some hunting and fishing product advertising, and for consumables targeted to underachievers.

- *Plain folks*—relates to the style of the copy in an advertisement. It presents the writer (who is usually perceived as the advertiser or marketer) as "just one of the group" to which he or she is writing. There can be a lot of appeal and credibility in this strategy, as evidenced by the L. L. Bean mail order catalog copy and the classic series of magazine ads for Jack Daniel's® whiskey. Depending on your product or company image, you might want to give it a try. But be sure you know your audience well so you can believably talk their language.

- *Slice-of-life*—usually this creative strategy takes the form of minidramas showing how products or services solve problems and/or create happiness. The broadcast media (particularly television) permit sound and motion which enhances the effect of this strategy but, even in print, ads can apply it where one or more illustrations represent moments of a "real life" situation that is explained by the body copy. The strategy works nicely with "*cinema vérité*" or *Candid Camera* or *hidden camera* techniques which are those where performers are not necessarily actors (sometimes called "real people"), and/or do not know they are being filmed.

- *Self-test*—can involve an audience in somewhat the same way as the *question* strategy. Many people enjoy evaluating their tastes and interests against the standards of supposed "authorities" and even determining if they "qualify" for some category or other—like "big spender," "great lover," and so on. Ads set up like such tests in general-interest consumer magazines can get good involvement, readership, and response.

- *Disturbing theme*—has proved effective for nearly a century, particularly in making Americans the world's leading consumers of deodorants, mouthwashes, and other personal hygiene products. I divide the *disturbing theme* strategy into its three most common sub-strategies: *fear, shock,* and *shame.* A classic example that combines all three is the 1920s ad for Listerine® mouthwash headlined "Often a bridesmaid, never a bride" with a dominant illustration of a weeping young woman whose halitosis (a term Listerine advertising introduced into the consumer vocabulary) repelled potential suitors. That ad had such force and memorability that although it has not run for some 80 years, it is still widely quoted. In this strategic context, some copywriters explain, "First you make 'em sick, then tell 'em how to get well."

- *Incongruity*—representation of one or more things that clearly don't logically belong with the product, service, or idea. Characterized sometimes by misuse of the product, as when an insured motorist is shown causing a terrible accident.

This strategy seems to defy logic, but some advertising people find such approaches amusing and claim the strategy is a strong attention-getter—and therefore worthwhile—as if attracting attention were all that an advertisement should do.

- *Bizarre* or *grotesque*—a creative approach that goes beyond mere *shock* or *incongruity* and aims to attract attention through the eccentric, sensational, controversial, repugnant, or even horrifying. Much-talked-about examples are the classic Benetton ads whose illustrations clearly intend to appeal to morbid curiosity by such devices as illustrations of a person dying of AIDS, and a guerrilla fighter carrying a human leg bone in his pocket. Not only the taste of the advertiser, but the ethics and potential effectiveness of a campaign can be questioned when the illustration or headline subject has absolutely nothing to do with the product or service advertised.

- *Sex*—although suggested as a subcategory of *borrowed interest* strategy, *sex* is so prevalent in American advertising (and even more common in some other countries) that it should be mentioned as a special strategy in itself. Perhaps it does little harm as an attention-getter when attractive models with sensuous facial expressions are shown holding or using a product, but the approach probably offends significant numbers of prospects when the female model in a clothing ad appears to be a rape victim or when a television commercial suggests a teenaged boy being lured into a homosexual liaison.

- *Bandwagon*—a proven public relations strategy, *bandwagon* is also commonly used in advertising. Essentially, it tells the target individual that everyone else (or almost everyone of intelligence, taste, or sensitivity) is buying something, using something, or doing something, and that therefore the target individual should do the same. Many Americans are remarkably susceptible to this strategy, although it is ethically flawed when it is untrue.

- *Humor*—always popular and always dangerous. One person's humor is often another person's inanity or insult. Unless you are a seasoned communications genius, you may not wish to risk this strategy in the marketing of your goods or services. After all, you're out for business—not for laughs.

- *Stereotype*—once the *stereotype* (often ethnic) was a very popular attention-getting strategy in advertising and useful for making comparative points. Although it is still used in many parts of the world, it is dangerous in the United States, and even outlawed in some states with respect to portrayal of females, racial and religious types, and many nationalities. Stupid fathers, however, seem still to be popular among creators of television commercials. Most marketers will do themselves no favors, though, by running the risk of antagonizing any group of individuals by means of the *stereotype*, regardless of the letter of the law.

- *The customer as a jerk*—to portray *the customer as a jerk* is a popular strategy often considered an application of *humor*. As with the *stereotype*, I believe, it is not only bad taste, but also bad marketing to risk offending *anyone*—particularly members of your target audience.

- *The nonuser as a loser*—usually not as foolish as portraying *the customer as a jerk*, but it can still be potentially offensive or even insulting to many who may see themselves as being ridiculed in ads using this all too common strategy.

- *Inoculation*—a competitive advertising strategy in which the advertiser mirrors or mimics the competitor's claims or creative executions with the intent of making the audience resistant to the competitive message. Relies on *wearout* and sometimes *ridicule* but is risky because if not executed masterfully, the campaign might simply *reinforce* the competitor's message.

- *Patriotism*—increasingly popular in advertising in the United States since 1980, American flags used to be proscribed—not by law as in many other countries, but by industry agreement. The hippie movement of the 1960s changed many citizens' attitudes toward appropriate use of the American flag, and today you see more and more stars and stripes in ads, along with *borrowed interest* depictions of The White House, the U.S. Capitol building, and other government symbols to lend an air of nationalistic pride to the marketing communications effort.

- *Appeal to pride*—this strategy shares elements with *challenge* and *self-interest of the prospect* but can be a distinct and highly motivating strategy. It is regularly used in connection with very expensive and relatively inessential products like diamond tiaras and also works well for some nonprofit advertising.

- *Apology*—almost exclusively seen in corrective advertising required by the FTC to redress wrongs inflicted by a marketer's prior marketing communications. There appear to be few constructive uses for this creative strategy in the marketing efforts of most ethical marketers, unless they have made an honest mistake and wish to express regret.

- *Goodwill*—this strategy leaves the audience with a warm feeling about the advertiser. It can be applied in a variety of ways and should be a natural outgrowth of the genuine concern marketers have for those with whom they wish to do business. A classic strategy is a December advertisement that runs, "All of us at Sooper-Dooper stores wish you the happiest of holiday seasons, and prosperity in the New Year." This *institutional* ad strategy doesn't do much to persuade toward a sale, but it's nice reinforcement of the business name.

- *Thank-you*—expressing thanks in an ad or mailer was originally a simple and direct way to keep the customer sold, but now is also used as a creative strategy to promote *new* business. This can work either as the overall creative theme of advertisements or as a part of a compound approach with other strategies.

Chapter 21

Logical Creative Strategies

For most ethical marketers, *logical* strategies will be the most useful. You can hardly go wrong when you adopt a communications view that your customer is not stupid, but that your customer is a respected friend. Included here is only one ineffective strategy, *interest of the marketer*, solely for the sake of completeness.

- *Promise*—noted by the great eighteenth-century English literary scholar and critic Samuel Johnson as "the soul of an advertisement," *promise* is inherent in most ads but can also serve solely as the creative strategy.
- *Hard sell*—forceful representation of features and benefits and involving a strong personal-selling-type close to prompt immediate action. This is classified as *logical* rather than *emotional*, because it is logical for advertisers to want their ads to accomplish something specific like product sales, and logical for a prospect to become interested in a product about which the advertiser clearly feels strongly.
- *Soft sell*—a gentle approach to telling the product story, which often involves emotional elements, but which does not push the audience as *hard sell* does.
- *Self-interest of the prospect*—can be the most direct of strategies that appeal to avarice. The most notorious examples probably are the ads for various state lotteries that urge people to "Become a millionaire" by gambling. An appeal to the desire for good products and services, though, can be an effective and ethical creative strategy.
- *Interest of a group*—can be a pleasant and direct type of message presentation, common among nonprofit organizations and might well be applied to commercial, industrial, and professional marketing. A familiar example is, "We need $1.5 million this year to save the spotted owl." In most cases, though, such an appeal as this is not nearly as strong as an appeal to the needs and wants of target individuals.

- *Interest of the marketer*—common among auto dealers, this strategy is reflected in lines like, "We want to sell 100 cars by the end of this month!" Despite the supposition that such a fervent desire would result in severe price cutting (if that's logical), one wonders how by itself this strategy can ever be approved by the advertiser—or accepted by the public. Just because something is commonly done does not prove it is the right thing to do.

- *Alleviation of pain or suffering*—is essentially a promise to perform, in response to a fundamental and possibly pressing need. It is commonly used for both health and beauty aid products and also in solicitation of charitable contributions. Handled honestly and in good taste, the application of this strategy can prove useful for other types of marketing efforts as well.

- *Two-sided message*—also called *two-sided appeal*, mentioned in Chapter 18 as a rhetorical strategy, presents positive and negative sides of a selling proposition, usually of a competitive nature, with emphasis on the positive. It appeals logically to intelligent audiences and nonconsumer buyers.

- *Exposition*—is usually found in technical advertising aimed at technical audiences. It is a "no frills" creative strategy that provides facts and figures in a straightforward and sometimes matter-of-fact style.

- *News story*—essentially advertising that looks like publicity or editorial material. It has become so prevalent in recent years that it has almost reached the point of being resented by significant numbers of people. But if you do have a good story to tell, and editors refuse to run it for you as *news*, you might wish to pay for the space to communicate in this form. But don't be surprised to see the word "advertisement" displayed atop your ad, even though you didn't put it there. Today you will find the *news story* strategy used most effectively by large corporations in crisis management situations—as when they have been accused of something terrible, and the media are beating them up about it and will not present the corporation's side of the issue editorially.

- *Reason-why*—has worked well for at least a century. By its very nature it is logical and therefore appeals strongly to the intellect rather than to emotions and impulses. *Reason-why* can be especially effective under headlines like, "Nine reasons why you should consider improving your vocabulary this fast and easy way."

- *How-to*—is a good problem-solving strategy that also appeals to intellect. It can be used to educate the public on uses of new goods and services and new applications of existing products. The words "how to" often appear in the headline.

- *Problem/solution*—usually mixed in consumer advertising with emotional strategies such as *fear* and *shame*. But it can also be handled in a straightforward manner and be as effective as *how-to*, if developed in a helpful way, such as through a series of ads or flyers discussing specific problems that a product or a service can solve.

- *Question and answer* (or *Q&A*)—a strategy that can be very effective for complex product and benefit stories. Research has shown that people tend to get involved and stay with *Q&A* better than with straight expository prose. There's interest and excitement about it—if the questions are of the type the readers, listeners, or viewers themselves would logically ask and if the answers are simple and enlightening. Often laid out in an editorial format, depending on the medium, *Q&A* can also be treated like a mini news conference for either print or broadcast media.

- *Dialogue*—akin to *question and answer*, *dialogue* can be more dramatic and more believable, if somewhat less informational. It lends itself to a blending with *slice-of-life* strategy and would be effectively presented in the form of a conversation between the marketer and a customer (identified or anonymous), who receives direct and helpful information about something important.

- *Testimonial*—is classic, and one of the most persuasive of all strategies—if the spokesperson is appropriate, believable, and likable—and if the topic is of interest to the audience. *Testimonials* work especially well for industrial products and are used extensively for packaged-goods on television in the form of "hidden camera interviews." Also highly favored in the Orient.

- *Celebrity endorsement*—a form of *testimonial* that relies on the fame and popularity of the spokesperson. This strategy can be stupid, of course, when a professional athlete of questionable intellect extols the engineering advances of a high-tech product—but it can be particularly effective when a celebrity with publicly known problems (such as alcoholism) speaks for a charity or a reliable product or service that can solve those particular problems (such as Alcoholics Anonymous).

- *Case history*—also a timeless and potentially persuasive strategy. Because cautious people tend not to want to be first to try something different, this reassures them that others have found satisfaction, happiness, or riches through the advertised product or service. It may be combined with a *testimonial* (direct or implied) by a large or respected organization or even a *celebrity endorsement* for even greater impact in some instances. Care should always be taken, however, that any kind of guarantee of a good result from an ethical product or a professional service similar to that in the case history is not directly offered. The liability risks for some marketers in these days of creative litigation can be enormous, because poor results and unhappy customers are inevitable even in the best of circumstances.

- *USP* (or *unique selling proposition*)—a strategy developed by the great adman, Rosser Reeves, back in the 1950s. The "big idea," as such is often called in the advertising business, was to boil the entire product story down to one simple fact—an irresistible offer—and hammer it home with another strategy Reeves favored which was previously noted as *hard sell*. One of his classics was a series of television commercials for Anacin which beat the consumer over the head, so to speak, with "fast . . . Fast . . . FAST." If you have a single, clearly differentiating quality that can be communicated as simply, succinctly, and powerfully as Reeves was able to do for Anacin, perhaps you can put this powerful creative strategy to good use.

Part IV

The Execution of Marketing Planning

Chapter 22

Campaign Strategies

In marketing, a *campaign* is a concerted, coordinated, and ongoing effort to persuade a target market, audience, or public. This is normally more effective than one-shot communications efforts. Any campaign strategy should incorporate one or more of the following:

- *Strategy of caution*—which means you should check local codes of ethics and your legal counsel as to whether the creative strategy or strategies you choose are acceptable for your business, industry, or profession in your particular marketing area. Regulations and tastes may vary.
- *Theme strategy*—means if you are planning to employ more than just a single piece of communication in your marketing program, you should seriously consider developing a distinctive and meaningful *theme* for your campaign. Even very small marketing communications programs can benefit by this. A theme gives you something memorable on which to build. Thus it should have meaning; be dramatic; appeal to your audience; and be logical, believable, and appropriate. A good theme should provide a springboard to advance the process of communication and persuasion toward obtaining the prospect as a loyal customer or client. Effective theme strategies in commercial marketing communications are closely connected with positioning strategies. The most successful include Kodak's many variations on *memories* in the context of picture-taking, Ford Motor Company's "Quality is job one" slogan, and Marlboro® cigarettes' American West settings and rugged cowboy smokers, which changed that product from an upscale women's brand to the world's largest-selling cigarette. Once you have an appropriate and effective theme of your own, use it in *all your communications* to make it work hard for you.
- *Harmonics strategy*—A consistent *program* is always more effective than a series of independent communications efforts. The benefit lies in what I call *harmonics,*

which differs from *campaigning* and even *theming* in that it unifies your entire program and involves more than one or two media approaches. You multiply the effectiveness of each of your marketing communications elements by strategic repetition of the same basic material—creative strategy, style, illustrative effects, typography, and other graphic elements—in every aspect of your marketing communications activities. The power of harmonics is in its *cumulative effect*, which in turn relies on its *consistency* of message delivery, and in the building of familiarity with your message, style, and theme, rather than in sheer volume or advertising frequency. This is a part of what is now being called "*Integrated Marketing Communications*," or *IMC*, as if it's something altogether new. In fact, many marketers have been doing this for many years but had no popular buzz-phrase to describe the strategy.

• *Satisficing strategy*—a corporate strategy that can affect all areas of marketing, but most significantly, the areas of advertising and sales. Specific, measurable goals are set and, when achieved, activities *stop*. Thus, if your ad campaign reached its gross rating point goal for the current year by the end of November, you would cancel all your remaining December advertising.

Chapter 23

Marketing Communications Copywriting Techniques

NOTHING TO IT

I once worked with a marketing manager who said, not altogether in jest, "There's nothing to writing copy; all the words you need are in the dictionary, so it's just a matter of picking out the right ones and putting them in the right order."

A copywriter friend at one of the world's largest advertising agencies amplified the thought by remarking, "Ads are easy—you just write like you talk—and there's nothing to writing direct mail; most of us wrote a letter home once a week when we were in school or in the service." Indeed, we all have experience with copy—not only writing it, but also because as Americans we have been exposed to so much of it through our entire lives.

Good marketing communications copywriting requires little more than these three things:

• Sound marketing strategies.
• Good judgment.
• At least a seventh-grade grasp of American English composition.

No fooling! Some of the best marketing communications writers have had little formal education in writing. It can actually be an *asset* not to know all the rules of English composition, grammar, and syntax.

Well, if it's all that easy, why is there so much *atrocious* advertising and promotion?

Largely, I believe, because so few copywriters and art directors take the time you are evidently taking by reading this handbook to assure themselves of *exactly what they are trying to do.*

CARDINAL RULES

You'll be far ahead if you keep in mind ten cardinal rules that underlie the great creative concepts like Kodak's "Remember the day in pictures" and Volkswagen's "Think small." I believe they are absolutely essential to successful marketing communications. Here are the things your copy should do:

1. Communicate basic information.
2. Talk to members of a clearly defined audience.
3. Aim at achieving at least one objective or measurable goal.
4. Address the individual reader's, listener's, or viewer's self-interest.
5. Attract attention, arouse interest, provoke desire, and sometimes call for direct action (the old AIDA formula).
6. Create an empathetic or emotional response in the reader, listener, or viewer.
7. Be simple, succinct, single in purpose, and specific.
8. Offer substance versus platitudes and puffery.
9. Be perfectly truthful, and absolutely believable.
10. Clearly identify the sponsoring product, service, or organization.

In addition to these fundamentals, there are several related precepts that will generally assure you of successful results in writing marketing communications copy. Of course, you can't do *all* of them in any one advertisement, commercial, or piece of literature, but you *can* use this guide as a pilot uses a checklist before takeoff.

The techniques are divided into several categories to keep related ideas together and to aid recall.

PSYCHOLOGICAL TECHNIQUES

1. Establish a *personality* and maintain it consistently throughout your copy, and indeed through your entire campaign. This includes style, manner, and use of language.
2. In addition to personality, try to project an *image* for your organization, product, service, or idea. Decide whether you want it to appear established, dependable, successful, or what have you, and then communicate that quality.
3. Emphasize a *benefit.* As noted in the preceding Cardinal Rule #4, as well as under creative approaches in the preceding chapters, people are interested in what appeals to their own self-interest. As previously suggested, ask yourself, "What's in it for *them?*"

4. Determine a *key idea* and consider making it *memorable* by mnemonic devices such as rhymes, alliterative phrases, initial letters, or acronyms.

5. When you refer to people in your copy, make sure they *relate* to the audience. People generally do not identify themselves strongly with age, geographic, social, and economic groups different than their own. Exceptions are sometimes romantic figures, athletes, and appeals to upward mobility.

6. Use the strongest motivation you can discover. Business and professional people have been found to be most highly motivated by *fear*. Fear of making a mistake, looking foolish, being fired, and the like. Curiously, this fact seems to have been little used historically in business advertising, but has recently begun to appear.

7. Avoid the distasteful. For example, pictures of people in pain tend to repel all but the mentally ill.

MANNER AND TONE TECHNIQUES

8. Make your customers or prospects *part* of your copy; make them feel comfortable in its content.

9. Address your chosen audience on a *selective* basis. Don't try to appeal to *all* people. Remember Confucius' ideal: It is best for the *good* people to love you, and *bad* people to hate you.

10. Try to speak person-to-person directly to an *individual*, rather than to a whole group. This is a refinement of the preceding Cardinal Rule #2, and is also emphasized in Appendix 8 which deals with a *creative work plan*.

11. Direct your copy to the *needs* of your potential customer. This sounds obvious, but many marketers and creative people foolishly address *their own* needs and ignore those of their audience.

12. Concentrate on a *single*, clearly defined message.

13. Do not "scream and yell" at your prospect—either in broadcast or print. No one wants to be lectured like a naughty child or browbeaten into doing business with you. This is sometimes a fine line to tread when you've decided on a *hard sell* strategy.

14. Try not to derogate or insult your audience. Even the common creative strategy of *denial* ("You thought there was only one way to fertilize your lawn? . . . Well, you're *wrong*") can immediately antagonize the very people you might most want to attract. So can *the customer as a jerk*, a far too common consumer advertising strategy.

15. Be aware that *good taste* is important, especially if yours is a professional organization.

16. Remember that *neatness and accuracy* count. Sloppy, careless copywriting is likely to suggest sloppy, careless manufacturing and poor customer service.

17. Put your best foot forward and place the best you have to say or to offer at the *beginning* where the greatest number of people have a chance of being exposed to it. Never try to save the best for last.

DETAILS OF CONTENT TECHNIQUES

18. If it can be done gracefully, you will benefit if you mention your best point *more than once*. Do not be afraid of having your copy called "self serving"—that is its *primary purpose*.

19. Promise something of value, directly or indirectly, positively or negatively. That is, the promise can be either in the form of what can be *gained* or in the form of a suggestion of what will be *lost* if the audience does not take the suggested action. (Remember the creative strategy of *absence of product or service*.)

20. Overall, try to make your audience *clearly understand* what you have to offer. Realize that they don't know all that you do about the subject.

21. At the same time, beware of *talking down* to them.

22. In this context, it is well to tell as simply as you can what your product actually *does*, and how it *works*.

23. Include other details of your product, service, organization, or idea. Particularly those likely to be of interest, such as timeliness, perhaps range of costs, and assurances.

24. Set your product or service apart as *different*, *unique*, and *desirable*. Perhaps you've done this adequately with your positioning concept, but use every opportunity to reinforce and expand on the basic idea.

25. Where possible, provide *proof* in the form of evidence that can be objectively sustained. Empty and groundless claims do little good today.

26. Use trademarks and symbols since they save time in reading and thinking. And even many businesspeople are only marginally capable of reading; some have been found to be functionally illiterate. Meaningful symbols help everybody.

27. Clearly identify your organization as the advertiser, even after you have clearly identified the product. This is not vanity but intelligent business practice. Although it's the tenth Cardinal Rule it is included here as reinforcement. Don't forget to clearly state who you are and how you can be contacted.

28. Although it's more of a design than a copywriting consideration, it's good to keep in mind from the beginning that advertiser identification should be at least 10 percent of the ad area and an equivalent amount of broadcast time.

29. Usually, the *earlier* you mention the advertiser, the better. Especially in broadcast, waiting till the very end to "surprise" the audience may leave them wondering who the sponsor was. Many seasoned marketing communicators even advocate putting the sponsor or product name in the headline and again in the first paragraph of the body copy.

VERBAL TECHNIQUES

30. Make your headline *encourage readership* of the text or body copy. To do so, it should not only be *interesting*, but also should logically lead into your text.

31. Get right to your point. Don't "beat around the bush" or equivocate.

32. Related to that, remember the KISS formula: "Keep It Simple, Stupid."

33. Sequence your message in a logical manner. A good guide for how to do this is in Aristotle's classic work, *Rhetoric*. It's worth reading more than once. Occasional review of the principles of classical *logic* can also be helpful in crafting effective copy.

34. Don't be afraid of long copy. If it tells your story, and is likely to be interesting to your audience, it is the right length. After all, your audience contains the only people you should care about affecting. If you can get them interested in your message, they'll read long copy as well as short. So use enough words to cover your material to *their* satisfaction. Succinctly, but thoroughly.

35. Use *narrative* copy as much as possible. It is appealing and interesting and, it *invites readership*. It allows you to present your organization's personality and establish your image. And it permits the friendly, personal tone that helps to turn a prospect into a customer.

36. Use *exactly* the *same words* each and every time you state features and benefits. This enhances recall. Variations on a theme are not as readily remembered.

37. When appropriate, include natural, appropriate, and believable *questions* and *quotes* in your text to add interest.

38. Generally, try to avoid negatives in headlines, as well as a negative tone in the text. Positive statements are both more pleasant and more productive.

39. Break headlines of more than one line into logical and meaningful phrases. This will help your typesetter when you get to preproduction.

40. Use subheads to help make long copy more readable.

41. Plan subheads to tell a story *by themselves*, so you can communicate something even to the person who merely skims your copy.

42. Use boldface and italic type judiciously and sparingly to add meaning, emphasis, and a conversational tone to your printed words.

43. Remember that ad readership studies show that upwards of *twice* as many people read *captions* as read text. Other research has shown that caption information, linked with a picture, is retained better even than a *headline* or a picture alone. So captions for your illustrations should be mini-ads, pertinent and persuasive in and of themselves, complete with product and advertiser identification.

44. Keep in mind that short paragraphs invite readership.

45. Short sentences are easiest and fastest to understand.

46. Use basic, monosyllabic words. Winston Churchill on the value of Anglo-Saxon roots in English wrote: "*Short* words are best, and *old* words when short are best of all." Think of the short, strong words we use every day—like head, hair, eye, ear, hand, foot, hit, joke, fight, stand, sit, and so on. These are all short old (Anglo-Saxon-root) words. They are the easiest for most people in our society to perceive, to understand, and to retain.

47. Use *active* verbs wherever possible. They add excitement, enthusiasm, and create involvement. The idea is to have a clear *subject* that takes some kind of specific *action*.

48. Employ the linguistic style of your audience, except for special effect. That is "talk their talk"—but generally don't try to write in dialect. That can have the reverse of the effect desired by suggesting that you are ridiculing the reader's speech pattern.

49. Use appropriate trade terms for business audiences and sometimes even colloquialisms of the particular trade.

50. Don't use exotic words, except for *very special* effect. If you do use such words, be sure to explain them clearly and completely.

51. Generally speaking, shun vulgarity, especially obscenity—even though it can be a powerful attention-getter.

52. Try to avoid unsubstantiated claims, and superlatives.

53. Avoid advertising clichés, like, "Yes, folks, its *true!*" and "But wait, there's *more!*" These have been so overused as to make the advertiser appear to be a huckster and to create immediate resistance among some audiences.

54. Try to foresee questions your audience might have and *answer* them in your marketing communications copy.

55. It has long been suspected among advertising people that if they could put the customer's or prospect's *name in the headline*, good readership by the person named would be assured. Today that is possible thanks to computerized production of headlines and texts. Perhaps you have received a mail order catalogue with your name on the cover, or opened a copy of *Time* magazine and seen your name in the headline of an ad. This is an interesting copywriting option to consider, although it has not yet been conclusively proven that this tactic is as powerful as once believed. As it is more frequently used, audiences will become accustomed to it, and the initial impact will probably decrease quickly.

56. If your message is complex, make it easier for your reader with *bullets*, such as have been used in this handbook for unnumbered lists, and also asterisks, arrows, dashes, and marginal marks. They all make reading easier, and hence more inviting.

57. If you have a long list, number your items, as has also been done here. But generally do not do so if they are fewer than four. That insults some people. Especially if you write "There are three reasons why you should do this," and then number the items.

58. For overall organization, remember the guidelines of the famous preacher who explained his success in persuading his congregation simply as, "I tell them what I'm *going to tell* them, then I *tell* them, then I tell them what I *told* them."

59. However you choose to organize your communication, be sure to clearly and succinctly sum up your story at the end of your copy.

60. Know when to end, and do so as *soon* as appropriate.

61. *Never* show your marketing communications copy to an *English teacher*. Good marketing and advertising copywriters break nearly all the basic rules to get their messages through. That does not mean incorrect spelling, and deliberately ignorant treatment of grammar, and syntax—but it *does* mean throwing out all those stupid old rules about not beginning a sentence with a conjunction, always having to have a subject and a predicate to make a sentence, never ending a sentence with a preposition, never splitting an infinitive, and so on. Giving an English teacher a chance to "correct" your copy can be even worse than giving it to a *lawyer*. Either one of those two types of learned professionals is likely to turn it into something even *they* would not want to read.

MORE THAN RULES

Of course, you need more than rules to create effective, hard-working, persuasive marketing communications. The process also takes a certain amount of intelligence—which has been referred to in this context as good judgment—and also self-discipline, time, and patience.

COPYRIGHT

The regulations for copyrighting written and recorded materials in the United States were greatly simplified several years ago. The intent seems to have been to make it possible for nearly everyone to protect their intellectual and creative property easily and inexpensively. Without presuming to give you legal advice, I do suggest that you include a little *c* in a circle (©), your organization's name, and the year—or the line "Copyright [name] 20XX"—on *everything* you write or produce for distribution outside your organization.

You can go one step further and contact the Copyright Office in Washington, D.C., for information on formal procedures, or seek advice from your attorney.

You will work hard developing just the right way to express what you have to offer your customers and prospects. So you should try to protect your investment from competitors who might plagiarize your ideas and copy. A simple copyright notice on all your written, graphic, and recorded work is generally agreed in marketing circles to be a good idea.

Chapter 24

Advertising Design, Art, and Typographic Strategies and Techniques

BASIC ARRANGEMENT

When you have a plain page to work with—whether you're trying to develop an advertisement for a magazine or a newspaper, a product folder, a direct mail piece, or an Internet banner—you have several choices of what to put on it:

- A word or words only
- A picture or pictures only
- A combination of word(s) and picture(s)

When you have a word-picture combination you have several basic choices for your design:

- Word(s) at the top (*headline*), picture at bottom
- Picture(s) at top, words at bottom (*footline*)
- Either one on either side
- Words in the middle

You can break up your page into sections:

- Halves
- Quadrants [quarters]
- Thirds
- Sixths

- Eighths
- And so on

You can divide the page up-and-down, side-to-side, or diagonally, or you can divide it into free-form sections. The possibilities are literally infinite.

Finally, you should decide what color treatment your budget will permit. Your ad can be *black-and-white* (*B&W* or *B/W*), *one-color* (*1C*) other than black, *duotone* (black and a second color combined in the illustration), *two colors* (*2C*), *three colors* (*3C*) which is generally not a cost-efficient choice, *four colors* (or *four-color process,* or *full-color,* or *4C*), or *five colors* which is four-color process with an additional metallic or specially blended ink. Sometimes varnish is applied as a fifth color. There's also *spot color* which means an ad is basically black-and-white with an area of one to four additional colors dropped in to attract attention and/or emphasize a design element.

Warm colors like red and orange are said to be "active" or "aggressive." Cool colors like blue and green are said to be "restful" or "recessive." Brown (called "sepiatone" in printing) suggests bygone times. Black in our society connotes gloom and is symbolic of death. There are many theories about the psychological effects that various colors may have on people, many of which conflict with one another. Nevertheless, some designers and art directors take the presumed emotional values of colors into account when they design their ads.

DESIGN STRATEGIES

Here are several terms for strategies of advertising design:

- *All-copy*—no illustration, just type, which may run all the way across the page or be divided vertically into columns, normally either two or three.
- *Typographic* (or *type specimen*)—also without illustration but uses distinctive headline type as an attention-getter.
- *Long copy* (or *copy heavy*)—has lots of words, often broken by small island illustration(s), plus headline, and sometimes subheads to ease readership.
- *Square halftone*—a common design strategy where the illustration is placed against a white or plain background. The illustration need not be literally square to deserve this designation but is usually rectilinear.
- *Picture window*—a large area of dominant illustration, usually at the top of the ad, but sometimes at the bottom. The "Golden Mean" has been noted as a guide whereby two-thirds of the ad is illustration and the remaining third is devoted to headline, body copy, and signature.
- *Rule of thirds*—as with the preceding design strategy this avoids the symmetry of dividing ads into halves. More interesting and pleasing designs are believed to be based on horizontal and sometimes vertical thirds for placement of key elements.

- *Bleed*—where the illustration in a magazine advertisement extends all the way to the edge of the page or, in outdoor, all the way to the edge of the poster. It may bleed one side (top, for example), or two, three, or four sides of the ad. There often is an extra charge by publishers for this effect.
- *Spread*—a two-page ad where the pages are side-by-side, and the ad is normally continuous across the spine, or "gutter," of the periodical. This is also called *double-truck* in newspaper advertising.
- *Color field*—has a large illustration, often bleed, and frequently in the form of a spread or double-truck but, as the term makes clear, always in color.
- *Frame*—where the illustration surrounds or "frames" the headline, copy, and signature.
- *Band* (or *panel*)—several visual elements are lined up in a column (vertically) or in a row (horizontally). This is a good design strategy by which to show a time-lapse sequence in print.
- *Grid*—several illustrations arranged flush with one another in horizontal and vertical alignments.
- *Checkerboard*—a fractional approach, wherein a page is divided into quarters, two quarters are bought at the half-page rate, and the advertising space is arranged so the sections are diagonal to one another, separated by editorial material. This diagonal arrangement is sometimes used with eighth-page units as well.
- *Half-page double spread*—when quarter-page elements are also bought at the half-page rate and run side-by-side on adjacent pages across the gutter.
- *Mondrian*—named for the abstract artist who arranged rectilinear figures of different colors and sizes on his canvases. Lines or "rules" are used to separate elements, and sizes and shapes should be pleasing to the eye and invite eye movement through the components of the ad.
- *Z-formation*—when we look at ads in our culture, our eyes tend to move from upper left to upper right, then diagonally across the ad to lower left, and across the bottom, ending at lower right, where the advertiser identification or "signature" normally appears. This strategy prescribes that elements in an ad be arranged in a Z pattern.
- *Silhouette*—where the illustration is cut out of its background or "silhouetted" and the copy often wraps around its contours. "White (or negative) space" is often dominant to give an airy, open feeling to the ad.
- *Vignette*—a treatment where the illustration irregularly fades off and blends with the unprinted area (white space) of an ad. This word also refers to a small illustration isolated in the body copy of an ad.
- *Mortise*—means an ad illustration that is a picture within a picture.
- *Cartouche*—usually an oval or oblong scrolled border to surround and frame ad copy, intended to look elegant. Sometimes also of smaller size and used to distinguish a trademark or logotype.
- *Axial*—several elements, either blocks of copy or small illustrations, jut out from either side of a central element like leaves from a branch or branches from a tree.

- *Angular*—the illustration and/or copy is slanted off the normal horizontal arrangement.
- *Montage*—multiple illustrations are cropped in a variety of ways and positioned at angles or overlapping one another.
- *Call-out*—often used in technical and industrial ads, the central illustration (normally the product) has lines from different places to blocks of copy that describe features or explain what each part of the product does.
- *Euro-ad*—design specifically targeting the European market that is generic but takes into account cultural differences among EU nations. Copy in different languages is dropped into a consistent layout.
- *Circus* (or *jumble*)—here anything goes, with headline, illustration(s), copy, and signature apparently randomly arranged. This can be great fun for an art director, but the risk is that the viewer's eyes will not be inclined to travel logically through all the elements of the ad, and that it will therefore fail to communicate effectively.
- *Buckeye*—refers to a crude, poorly designed ad lacking in balance and continuity, that often employs excessive graphic elements. Ads of this type are also generally badly written. They are commonly seen in the advertising of automobile dealers and discount furniture stores. Advertising people call cluttered ads whose elements conflict with one another "busy."

FROM IDEA TO FINISHED AD

Development of the graphic aspect of an advertisement begins with what is called a *thumbnail sketch* (or *loose rendering* or *rough layout*) that simply suggests the basic design idea. The next step is to create what is called a *semi-comprehensive layout* (or *semi-comp*) which contains more detail. From that rendering a *comprehensive layout* (or *comp*) is prepared which shows all elements in place, often with text represented by "greeking" composed of meaningless strings of letters to indicate final copy. Headline and body copy type are set and proofread on *galley proofs* or *type proofs*. Next a *mechanical* composed of final type and illustrations in registered positions is pasted up. A *keyline* specifies exact positions of elements in the ad and a *dummy* indicates final positions of elements for a multipage insert or brochure. The mechanical is photographed to create a *film negative*. Or, in the case of four-color work, *separations* into printing colors (black, magenta, yellow, and cyan) are made. The next step is a *pre-press proof* or *silver print*—what used to be called a *blueline* or *van dyke*, depending on the photo process employed—to show what is on the film shot from the mechanical. If all is correct, neat, and clean, a printing plate or plates are then photographically etched from the film and, finally, a *proof* made from the printing plate or plates. *Progressive proofs* (or *color proofs* or *progs*) are inspected in seven steps on four-color jobs. A *press proof* is a "pull" from the beginning of the print run—a very expensive (and sometimes impossible) time to make any changes.

SUBJECTS FOR AD ILLUSTRATIONS

You can rely on a graphic artist or designer to develop layouts for your ad copy, or you can do it yourself if you prefer. Either way, you may wish to use the following checklist for your layouts and designs. There is some duplication with the copywriting checklist in the preceding chapter for the sake of completeness. Production work should be handled by specialists.

1. As you did for your copy, you should establish a *personality* with your design and artwork and maintain that consistently throughout your individual ads and your entire campaign. This includes visual style, typography, and use of light and color.

2. In addition to personality, try to project an *image* for your product or service. Decide whether you want to appear established, dependable, successful, and so on, and aim at communicating that quality visually as well as with your words.

3. When you show people in ad illustrations, make sure they *relate* to the audience. People generally do not identify themselves strongly with age, geographic, social, and economic groups different than their own. Exceptions are sometimes romantic figures, athletes, and appeals to "upward mobility."

4. Use women tastefully in illustrations. Studies show that men, women, and children *all* respond best to attractive women. This is not to say pin-up girls, although they are still attention-getters among some audiences.

5. "Cute" works well with some audiences. Women in general respond particularly well to *babies* and loveable animals like kittens. As more women have entered executive ranks, we now see babies in business advertising.

VISUAL TECHNIQUES

6. Remember that *neatness* counts. Sloppy, careless layouts suggest sloppy, careless manufacturing and customer service.

7. Advertiser identification should be at least 10 percent of the surface of a magazine or newspaper advertisement.

8. Break headlines of more than one line into logical and meaningful phrases. Aim at vertical balance in the typographic treatment.

DESIGN TECHNIQUES

9. Keep in mind that the *design* of an ad in itself is not worth anything. There must be a *reason* for every configuration.

10. Plan your visual and/or headline to attract *attention* and to stand apart from the clutter of competitive advertising and all the other things that compete for your prospect's attention.

11. Use a dominant graphic as a *hook* to grab attention as well as to differentiate your ad from those of your competitors.

12. Keep your design *simple*. The eye should not be distracted by extraneous, intrusive, and/or conflicting elements.

13. Provide a *logical pattern* for the eye to follow. This contributes to what has been called "inviting readership."

14. See that your layout works to move your audience through the *persuasive* process. The successful print ad should never call attention to itself merely as a "beautiful design."

15. Use "white space" to your benefit to give an open appearance, and to set off important elements.

16. While openness is important, don't get carried away and revel in a nearly blank page—as some trendy art directors recommend. You're paying a good price for the ad pages you buy, so don't *waste* space.

17. Remember that illustrations which arouse *curiosity* work well. They incline the audience to wonder what's going on, and to watch the commercial or read the ad copy to find out.

18. Similarly, illustrations that inspire respect and awe can also be beneficial. This is the basis of many *testimonial* ads. But they should be more original than the rash of "We went to the moon" ads of several years ago. Are you as tired as I am of that NASA photo of the earth from space as an advertising attention-getter?

19. Try to make your illustration not only interesting, but also one that creates involvement and enhances understanding by being *relevant* to your message.

20. Along the same line, size (or scale) your dominant illustration in proportion to its importance.

21. Make the illustration simple and immediately recognizable. Masses of people, for example, generally do not pull in the audience. Macro- and microphotographs—except to select scientific audiences—may be pretty but too often are meaningless.

22. Generally speaking, photographs work better than artwork in terms of appeal, believability, and interest.

23. Illustrations of a product actually *in use* are more believable, and therefore more effective, than most other approaches.

24. For technical communication, the best types of illustrations—in order of importance—are (a) photographs, (b) cutaways, (c) graphs and charts, (d) drawings, and (e) cartoons.

25. Small insert or drop-in illustrations can clarify meaning and add interest. But don't overdo this technique, lest your ad resemble a curio cabinet.

26. Plan the *proportions* of your ad—like the length of your commercials—to the exact specifications of the media vehicle you have selected.

27. Consider using color to make ads both more attention-getting and more memorable. Budget is your main consideration. If you can't afford the additional space costs of color, it is better to go with a well-crafted black-and-white ad than with no ad at all.

28. On the other hand, black-and-white, or black-and-white with spot color, in some contexts creates a special effect. This can be particularly attention-getting for a television commercial.

29. Although *bleed* ads may receive good readership scores, they may not justify their extra cost. (As noted previously, "bleed" means the illustration extends to one or more edges of the page.)

30. Putting a border around copy and illustration may hold a reader's eye on the page.

31. Refer to *Standard Rate & Data Service* (available at most local libraries) for information on production. Or obtain specifications directly from the media.

TYPOGRAPHIC TECHNIQUES

32. Unless your illustration is specially shot for it—with even-toned dark or light backgrounds—do not reverse out or overprint your headline. Research shows that a variegated or tonally varying background behind a headline reduces readership and involvement.

33. Generally speaking, readership of an ad is inversely proportional to the number of different typefaces used. The cleanest and best-read ads today generally use a single typeface for headline, caption, and text.

34. Studies show headlines are best read when set in upper and lower case with "normal" capitalization and punctuation. This includes periods at the ends of headlines currently—but the fashion of whether or not to include terminal punctuation seems to run in 15- to 20-year cycles, so we may soon change again.

35. *Serif* type, like that in our reading primers in grade school, is what most American readers find easiest and most inviting. (Some of the most popular typefaces of this sort are Baskerville, Bodoni, Bookman, Garamond, Goudy Oldstyle, Palatino, and Times Roman.) Exotic faces are interesting for short spurts but do not hold readers through long texts the way the classic typefaces do.

36. Type should be large enough to be noticed and to be read easily. Generally, this means text should be no smaller than 10-point. This is particularly important among older audiences.

37. Use ample "leading" (pronounced "ledding") or spacing between lines of type and paragraphs to ease reading, "10 on 12" and "12 on 15," for example, are good proportions of pica type size to leading.

38. Short lines are easiest to read. Break pages vertically into two or three columns, like the columns in newspapers and business magazines. Since newspapers and

magazines are where your print ads will appear, it makes good sense to use the typographic style readers are accustomed to there.

39. Black type on a white or light background offers the best readership. "Reverses" (light or white type against dark backgrounds) are more difficult to read.

40. Although they are very popular with art directors (many of whom seem not to have achieved the skill of reading), screened images behind or over text discourage sustained readership.

41. Different copy and type treatments superimposed on one another may look great to a designer but are often incomprehensible to a prospective reader.

42. Horizontal orientation of type—especially body copy—will get several times the readership of type running at angles or upside down, according to tests among business executives and adult consumer groups.

43. "Windows," caused by short lines at the ends of paragraphs, enhance readership by "opening up" the text to the eye.

44. "Widows," on the other hand—single words on a line by themselves—make the text look irregular. Rewrite your copy or resize your type, if necessary, to avoid them. (Something we have not done here, because this handbook is not to be read in the same way as an advertisement.)

45. Additional rewriting may be called for to get rid of hyphenated words on successive lines. Like the rule about widows, this is an old typesetter's rule, often overlooked today since the development of computerized typesetting.

46. Many readers favor text justified left and right—in a block like newspapers and business magazines set it. Ragged right in ads is currently popular—but is likely to pass, as it has before.

47. Some studies have shown that a large initial letter on the first paragraph of text (called a "drop cap") increases readership. This technique may have been overdone, though, and might therefore have lost its advantage—especially when you want a "news story" look.

48. Related to copywriting, but clearly a design technique, is to use an "*eyebrow*" or small lead-in line of copy above the headline or key word(s). For example, the headline might read "Spring Clearance Sale," and the eyebrow would read "Limited time."

49. Be consistent in all you do. Make all your communications elements reinforce one another and work together to create a whole greater than the sum of its parts.

50. In particular, when you have selected a typeface for your body copy use *the same face* in *all* your marketing communications. Where reasonable, use a single, consistent headline typeface, too.

51. Do not stint on *quality*. Shoot for the very best you can possibly afford. The perceived value of an advertisement, a commercial, a mailing, a piece of literature, or a Web site correlates in the mind of the target audience with the value of the organization, service, or idea presented. To try to save money indiscriminately on production can cost your total marketing program far more than you save.

THREE CLOSING THOUGHTS

52. If possible, emphasize the direct or implied call to action. A special graphic treatment for the call to action—dashes around the coupon, a vibrant color, or even the corny old tried-and-true "shellburst" of jagged lines surrounding your offer—makes it harder for people to miss the point. As noted previously, a clear call to action gives ads a reason for being, and may even be the single most important element in marketing communications such as direct mail.

53. Although most advertising doesn't literally "sell," it is the first step in a process that should result in a sale. Therefore, it is important that you keep firmly in mind that you are not in the business of either entertainment or the fine arts when you create your materials. Logically, you should aim for *persuasion*— not aesthetic fulfillment.

54. As a marketing practitioner you probably have far better judgment about what your target audiences will respond well to than most art directors and designers. So rely on them for *mechanical* help, but don't let them talk you into anything radical or trendy, as they often try to do to win awards for themselves. It's important that you not appear frivolous, foolish, or in any way embarrass yourself or your organization. And *you* are the best judge of what is acceptable and tasteful. Stick to your guns!

FOOTNOTE

You need more than rules like these to create what is called "breakthrough" and enduring marketing communications. But that is not what most advertisers want anyway. They just want to attract good customers and prospects for an acceptable investment.

By following these guidelines, you should make your materials work well for you, and communicate in ways that will significantly contribute to revenues for your organization.

Chapter 25

Television Commercial Production Techniques

There can be good reasons for not only consumer-products companies, but also nonprofits and professional practices to advertise on carefully selected television availabilities—both commercial and cable.

Once you have defined your offer and message, the creative strategies in Chapters 18 through 21 should give you plenty of ideas for execution.

USE ALL DIMENSIONS

Advertising people have been creating television commercials now for nearly 60 years, yet it's amazing how little many of them seem to have learned.

Special effects change with improving technologies, but the planning techniques and creative strategies commonly employed today suggest that many so-called "creatives" still don't understand what makes the television medium great.

Television is most like face-to-face selling, so demonstrations and direct "pitches" are appropriate. You might not want to use a *hard-sell* strategy, but you could consider just *talking* to your prospects on television, in a compressed form, as you would talk to them if they visited your store or office.

Television allows the viewer to *see*, to *hear*, and to *read*—and it is that combination, linked with motion and color, which has provided television's tremendous impact. Therefore, it is astonishing that often creatives provide for only *one* or *two* of these capabilities in their commercials.

For example, a popular creative approach (usually *announcement*) is to have words "creep" down a black screen with no other visual, and no sound. The viewer presumably sits transfixed in the silence and absorbs every word of the deathless prose. Such spots can look great projected on a big screen and even seem dramatic in the dead silence of the ad agency conference room, but miss the mark when viewed in a normal home environment.

Although the people who develop those kinds of spots think they're very clever—even original—and they are often praised and rewarded by their peers for their efforts; such a creative approach seems to make about as much sense as pulling ignition wires out of a car so the engine will fire on only two cylinders.

Television can also use many different special effects: fast and slow motion, time-lapse, fantasy, animation, quick-cuts (such as the visual collage) as well as sound effects, music, narration, and dramatic dialogue.

It's *your* money you're investing in advertising. So invest it wisely and in the most productive way possible.

WAYS TO DELIVER YOUR MESSAGE

There are basically 16 techniques by which your message can presently be delivered on television:

- *Talking head*—the method most ridiculed in the trade. It's when you run a medium close-up, head-and-shoulders shot of your announcer looking into the lens of the camera and reciting your message (often with the product held close to the face). It can work, as it sometimes does, for U.S. presidents when they deliver important announcements to their constituents. But you will probably be better off if you seek alternative ways of presenting your message on television.

- *Live action*—a term usually used to describe *Candid Camera* or *hidden camera* type interviews or testimonials. "Live-live" means a real-time, not prerecorded, announcement—often made before a live studio audience. Wonderful rapport and occasional "bloopers" can make this interesting, amusing, and even exciting. It is not recommended for amateur performers, though—since even the pros have been burned with *live-live*.

- *"Cinema vérité"*—footage that *appears* to be candid. It may be shot without planning or scripting, but more often in television commercials it is performed to have that appearance—sometimes even using a hand-held camera to give a shaky quality to the image.

- *Dramatization*—a familiar form used in *slice-of-life* treatments, *borrowed interest* "recreations," and the like. A disclaimer is often superimposed or "burned" on the image to indicate that the footage is not documentary.

- *Animation*—cartoons drawn or puppets photographed, one frame at a time, to produce the illusion of real-life action on motion picture film. This traditional approach is terrifically expensive, as you would appreciate, because of the time required to prepare each cell or setting, and expose each onto photographic film. Computer imaging is making this technique faster and more affordable, though.

- *Claymation*—popularized by the famous California Raisins in the classic "I Heard It through the Grapevine" commercial, this is probably more than a passing fad. Clay figures are sculpted, photographed one frame at a time on motion picture film, and changed to create animation from one frame to the next, like drawn artwork or animation puppets.
- *Rotoscoping*—a combination of animation and live action. Very expensive.
- *Freeze frame* (or *stop motion*)—when action stops, and the image is held as a still picture by repeating the same frame. *Freeze frame* is the term used in video production, and *stop motion* in motion picture film. This method, like several of the others here, works when the narration is "voice-over" (VO).
- *Time-lapse*—frames exposed at intervals to compress slow action, such as the opening of a flower, to a speeded-up, intriguing, and sometimes surprising effect.
- *Slow-motion*—the opposite of time-lapse, in that film action is slowed down by shooting more frames per second than normal.
- *Fast-motion*—a variation of time-lapse in that normal action is somewhat speeded up by shooting fewer frames per second than normal.
- *Pixilation*—the technique that takes a series of stills from a sequence and holds them one at a time on the screen to give a nervous, jumpy appearance, similar to dancers seen under a stroboscopic light.
- *Montage* (or *collage*)—still pictures run quickly one after another to suggest a sequence of events or passage of time. Perhaps you have seen a "History of the World in Two Minutes." This compresses a lot of visual material.
- *Matting*—where you can show such things as your announcer filmed or video-taped in a studio against a background of a Hawaiian beach. That effect can also be accomplished with *rear-projection screens*, but the higher technology of *matting* permits interaction with other film or video footage as well as the mixing of live-action with animation.
- *Stock footage*—as with stock (still) photographs, this is motion picture or video material generally provided at modest charge or, at worst, less than original footage would cost. If you wanted, for example, a scene of crowds at Times Square on New Year's Eve, you would be wise to order *stock footage*, rather than to send a camera crew to shoot it for you next December 31.
- *Computer imaging*—where a great future awaits us, but even the present state of the art is exciting. You can input still photos or artwork, or even create original images in a computer, and then manipulate them in an infinite number of ways within the computer. The equipment is expensive, and a trained technician is required for satisfactory results, but some of the effects being achieved are simply astounding.

ADDITIONAL TERMINOLOGY

Here are some basic terms and abbreviations you need to know to understand scripts and/or to specify effects and direct camera movement for television commercials:

- *Long shot (LS)*—camera takes in a broad scene.
- *Full shot (FS)*—may be a long shot, but specifically refers to showing an entire person (head to foot) or product (top to bottom, and/or side to side).
- *Wide shot (WS)*—a long shot with a panoramic perspective; accomplished normally by use of a *wide angle lens*.
- *Medium shot (MS)*—camera takes in moderate amount of scene or subject.
- *Close-up (CU)*—camera close to subject.
- *Extreme close-up (ECU)*—the viewer might see only one eye of the subject's face or a tight detail of the product.
- *Zero-degree angle*—the perspective is from the point of view of the customer, as if the camera lens was the viewers' eyes.
- *Low-angle view*—camera position is *below* position of viewers' eyes. Looking *up* at a subject often has the psychological effect of making it seem important.
- *Worm's eye view*—perspective is very low angle, close to the ground or the floor.
- *Bird's eye view*—perspective is from overhead.
- *Zoom in* or *out*—lens of camera is used to pull subject close or to move it away.
- *Dolly in* or *out*—rig on which camera is mounted moves forward and backward, but focal length of the lens stays the same. Different visual effect than the zoom. To *dolly out* is also called to "pull back" and is most commonly used to reveal something new outside the original scene.
- *Truck left* or *right*—camera rig moves to left or right.
- *Pan left* or *right*—camera turns, usually to follow action; rig on which it is mounted stays still.
- *Swish pan*—a very fast pan to blur the image. Sometimes done apparently to 360 degrees as a transition device.
- *Tilt up* or *down*—camera swivels up or down, rig stays in place.
- *Boom shot*—camera is mounted on levered device that allows it to move up, down, and side-to-side for smooth changes in perspective. The camera can even be moved completely (360 degrees) around the subject.
- *Helicopter shot*—aerial photography that may also move around the action or subject.
- *Fade in* or *out*—screen image burns in or out on screen.
- *Go to black*—direction used to indicate picture should fade out until screen is empty and dark.
- *Cross-fade*—also called "lap dissolve." One image fades in while another fades out behind it.
- *Matched dissolve*—where the dissolving images look alike, as when one person's face fades into another's face.
- *Jump cut*—an abrupt change from one scene or camera angle to another. Should not be used often, as it tends to be disruptive and irritating.

- *Split screen*—two images appear on the screen, but separately, one beside or above the other.
- *Wipe*—one image replaces another by pushing the other off the screen. Electronic editing of videotape permits a wide variety of geometric forms and other treatments of wipes, such as the classic "iris out" from silent movie days when a circle comes in from the outside edges of the screen and gets smaller until the original image is gone.
- *Pop-on* and *pop-off* (or *bump in* and *bump out*)—when images or titles suddenly appear and disappear.
- *Superimpose (SUPER)*—two images appear at the same time on the screen, one on top of the other.
- *Focus in* or *out*—begin scene with camera out of focus and the image a blur, then bring into focus; *focus out* is the opposite. Can also be used for transitions, as fades, but provides a dreamy quality to indicate passage of time or change in location.
- *Super* (or *burn*)—image or type superimposed on the screen image or dropped out to white.
- *Scroll* (or *creep*)—type moves up or down the screen. Usually for long copy.
- *Prism shot*—use of a special lens to create multiples of a single image. Other types of lenses can create *star highlights, halos*, and variations in color and focus.
- *Soft focus*—produced with camera slightly out of focus or, more dramatically, to enhance mood with petroleum jelly on the lens.
- *Vignette*—a term also used in print advertising, this means the central image fades out at the edges of the screen. Also means a series of quick related scenes.
- *Special effects (FX)*—visual elements on film or videotape that are not part of live footage, such as flashes of lightning or people turning into animals. Computer imaging has expanded today's possibilities.
- *SFX*—sound effect(s).
- *Voice-over (VO)*—voice of announcer or performer is *off-camera* (another trade term), so the effect is that the speaker is out of the viewer's sight.
- *Lip-sync*—short for "lip synchronization" or the matching of mouth movement on video or film to the voice track.
- *Segue*—change from one sound to another without interruption, sometimes the audio equivalent of a *cross-fade*. (Pronounced "SEG-way.")
- *Sting* (or *stinger*)—distinctive music to heighten attention.
- *Up/Down/Under/Out*—terms refer to volume of audio track(s): *Up* is louder, *down* is softer, *under* is held at a reasonable level behind spoken words, and *out* means "pot down" until sound is off.
- *Up-and-over*—music or sound effects get louder until spoken words are drowned out.
- *Storyboard*—series of illustrations, accompanied by a *script*, that shows visual sequence of a proposed commercial.

- *Animatic*—film or video rendering of the storyboard with sound that can appear on a screen to give an indication in real time of how a commercial is intended to appear.
- *Answer print*—the first edit of a filmed or videotaped commercial, before corrections or synchronization, to obtain agency and client approval.
- *Dub* (or *dupe*)—copy of audiotape or videotape; *dub* can also mean mixing audio or video tracks into one.

Knowing a bit about this subject can save you from exploitation by those unscrupulous advertising agencies and film and video studios that have a tendency to hide significant overcharges in the bills of unsuspecting clients.

Chapter 26

Selling-Letter Strategies and Techniques

The American publisher and philosopher William Feather observed, "Of all techniques devised for the extension of personality, the letter is the oldest and the most effective."

Yet, although letter writing is a common part of marketing management, many professionals find it one of the most difficult skills to master.

A DIFFERENT TYPE OF COMMUNICATION

Broadcast advertising scripts have a special style, print ads tend to conform to a standard format, technical literature requires something else again, and Web pages can involve revolutionary complexity.

But whether you are drafting a staff directive, confirming a sale, responding to a customer complaint, or selling by direct mail or mail order; whether your letter is typed on corporate stationery, dispatched by fax, or disseminated through e-mail, the discipline of writing a strong, persuasive *letter* is different than writing other types of marketing communications. And that is why it gets special attention here.

ATTRIBUTES OF A GOOD SELLING LETTER

Take a few hours sometime to review personal business correspondence and also direct mail advertising you and your associates are exposed to in a few weeks' time. As you read, you will soon begin to categorize. One group—most likely the smallest—will include communications that read so easily and so convincingly that you want to take the action the writer suggests. It is almost certain you will find they share these characteristics:

- *They are attractive*—the margins are not crowded. Most paragraphs are short, often indented and/or double-spaced between. They *invite readership*.

- *They compel attention*—with either a dramatic headline or an opening paragraph they tell why they exist, and/or why you should read them. They offer specific, believable benefits, or pose problems that apply directly to you. In some cases, like old ballads and folksongs, they may begin with an intriguing narrative that leads ingeniously into a sales story.

- *They concentrate on one point at a time*—usually they treat only one major subject. They do not skip around. Their points are presented in a logical sequence.

- *They prove how the product or service fulfills the promise*—they use testimonials or statements of value that are believable and to the point.

- *They ask for action*—in a very straightforward way, and while you are still receptive to the ideas presented. Their appeal is timed to strike you before you begin to think of objections. And they tell you exactly what you are intended to do.

- *They are easy to read*—with short words, short sentences, short paragraphs. The words flow together. They talk your language, using terms pertinent to your specific profession, discipline, or interest.

- *They are enthusiastic, and sincere*—no halfhearted writing here. You feel that the person whose name appears on the letter truly *believes* in every word. This makes it easy for you to believe, too, and an enthusiastic tone further stimulates your enthusiasm.

- *They are friendly*—with a style that makes you *like* the writer from the start. You realize that you prefer to do business with friends than with pompous strangers.

ABOUT LETTER CAMPAIGNS

If you receive a multipart letter campaign, whether by postal service, courier, fax, or e-mail, you may notice that the experienced writer varies the message from letter to letter. This can be an effective tactic as long as strict attention is paid to the fundamental objective.

When a series of letters is used, all major persuasive points should be listed, but only one point fully developed in each. It's hard to know with certainty, in advance, which point will be the most significant to which prospect. But, by treating each point individually, you will not only reinforce your message, but also eventually find the specific appeal that is exactly right for the largest numbers of people in your target audience.

The action inducement or incentive offered may remain the same from letter to letter or may be made increasingly stronger to suggest a sense of urgency.

And, finally, effective letters and campaigns stay in the middle of the road between glamour and technical or business detail. The best direct mail seems to have been written by neither a poet nor a lawyer.

Essentially, your letter is a salesperson. It should be businesslike and informative. So when you plan and prepare it, neither underestimate the intelligence nor overestimate the knowledge of the men and women whom you expect to read it.

FORMULAS FOR WRITING LETTER COPY

There are few areas of marketing for which quite so many rules, check-lists, and formulas have been created as for letters. This may be because direct mail and mail order have traditionally been the easiest of all advertising media to audit and evaluate. But this may lead also to a false sense of security when you think, "If I just follow *this* particular formula, I will succeed."

Still, effective letters *can* be developed by following a few *guidelines*—but there are no *easy answers* by any means. Some of these cover the same ground but in slightly different ways. Here are those I think are the best, from which I hope you can choose one that works for you:

1. AIDA: Attention—Interest—Desire—Action

AIDA is the oldest—and probably the most widely used—of all the letter-writing formulas. It's so good and so popular because *it works*. In order, each letter stands for something you should try to elicit from your reader:

- attract *Attention*
- arouse *Interest*
- create *Desire*
- and call for *Action*.

Some people add *Conviction* between Desire and Action, but for most letter writing that is not necessary.

2. SSSS: Single—Specific—Selective—Succinct

As noted in Chapter 21, the legendary advertising man Rosser Reeves built a career and a place in the Advertising Hall of Fame out of his concept of the *unique selling proposition*, or *USP*. He created communications that featured one factor that set a product apart from all others in the field, and he did not bother with other information—which he reportedly believed just *confused* the consumer and interfered with the process by which people remember brands, products, features, and benefits. A formula to help you remember how to apply the *USP* strategy to letter writing is *SSSS*. The letters stand for the following:

- *Single*—Choose just *one* idea or proposition.
- *Specific*—Concentrate on that one point in a straightforward manner throughout your letter.
- *Selective*—Talk to *one* person in the clearly defined target audience.
- *Succinct*—Keep words, sentences, and paragraphs short and, when you have said what needs to be said, *stop*.

Some great writers of direct mail use *only* this formula to judge their work.

3. III: Impact—Idea—Identity

All effective letters should be *forceful*, just like effective sales presentations and effective management. A helpful formula to aid you in this area is *III*. The letters stand for these words:

- *Impact*—You must develop a concept or portrayal *powerful* enough to stop your prospect—like *Attention* in the AIDA formula.
- *Idea*—You must concentrate on the basic *purpose* of your letter and that part of your message related to why your prospect should consider your product, organization, or idea—like the *USP*.
- *Identity*—You must clearly communicate *who* or what is sending the message— a very important consideration that is often not given sufficient attention.

4. The 4Ps: Picture—Promise—Prove—Push

This is not the *4Ps of marketing*, but the 4Ps of *letter-writing*:

- Start with a word *picture* of the benefits the reader will gain from your product or service.
- *Promise* how your product or service fits the picture.
- *Prove*, convincingly, what the product or service has done for others.
- And close with a *push*, asking for some kind of immediate action—like the last A in AIDA. The inventor of this formula added, "Write your letters *upside down*. Write the push *first*."

5. Egner's Nine Points

Frank Egner was a publisher who believed strongly in formulas. The following list was his own creation—and reportedly his favorite:

- Write a lead (headline or first paragraph) to create desire as well as to get attention.

- Add an inspirational beginning.
- Give a clear definition of the product or service.
- Tell a success story about the use of the product or service.
- Include testimonials and endorsements from satisfied customers or clients.
- List the special features of the product or service.
- Make a statement of the value of the product or service to the prospective buyer.
- Devise an action-closer that will make the reader want to buy immediately.
- End with a P.S. that rephrases the headline. (Incidentally, readership tests have shown that people—particularly those who receive a lot of mail—often read the postscript *first*, and sometimes little else. So if you can do it comfortably, it's a good idea to *restate* your major point or call to action in a P.S.)

6. T&B: Truth and Believability

It almost goes without saying that you should tell the *truth* in all your marketing communications. But, beyond that, you should strive also for *believability*, because being believed is essential to successful letters. Especially if you were to offer enormous cost savings, for example, or the amazing capabilities of a revolutionary new communications system, you would have to be careful to see that a perfectly honest promise would not be perceived as an exaggeration, or even a blatant lie. Once such a negative impression is created, it is very difficult to recreate the feeling of trust which is essential to successful persuasion. The political experts in Washington, D.C., express this fact very simply and well with the phrase: "Perception is the only reality."

7. Common Sense

One of the best overall tests you can use to judge your letter copy is to ask simply: "Does it tell what my prospect needs to know?" Alternatively, look at your draft and ask the question recommended by the famous direct-response genius, John Caples: "Can anyone reasonably ask of my copy '*So what?*' "

What may matter even more than the formula you use is that you approach your writing task in an *organized*, as well as a creatively responsible, way. Rely on Appendix 8, "Items for a Creative Work Plan," to see that you cover all important factors in your letters.

LONG VERSUS SHORT LETTERS

The ideal length of a good selling letter has been argued for many years and has not yet been resolved. Although conciseness in presenting ideas is important, you must take enough time and space to tell your story *com-*

pletely. You should always try to "telegraph" your message, using as few words and sentences as possible while making your meaning clear. But you should never omit good ideas that contribute to the sales argument simply to save space.

Abraham Lincoln is said to have observed that a man's legs should be long enough to reach the ground. In just the same way a letter should be long enough to do what it's intended to do.

HEADLINE VERSUS SALUTATION

In other forms of marketing communications, headlines are used to attract attention and set the stage for the story to follow. But here we are considering letters, which normally open with a traditional salutation such as "Dear Mr. Smith:" in our culture. Computer letters have given us such travesties as "Dear Mr. Howard D. Smith:" Or, even worse—in the case of Gen. Harold Brown, U.S. Army, Retired—"Dear Gen. Retired:"

Variations by some overly zealous sales types run "Good morning, Mr. Smith!" apparently on the assumption that attending to the mail is the executive's first order of daily business, before leaving for 18 holes of golf.

A headline, by contrast, can skip the personal touch of the salutation and get right into the story with the first line reading something like, "Now there's an easy, inexpensive new way for you to save money in your manufacturing operations . . ."

There are no clear answers as to whether it is best to open with a salutation or a headline. Some experts like the personal touch of the salutation, so if you've got a hot "grabber" that could work as a headline, perhaps you'd like to use *both*—if good taste and accepted practice in your industry and that of your addressee permit.

IDEAS FOR HARDWORKING HEADLINES

Tried and true suggestions for letter headlines are these:

- Provide news.
- Tell your major selling point.
- Promise a benefit and prove it.
- Offer something special.
- Suggest the solution to a specific problem.
- Ask a question that can't be answered by "No."
- Offer a guarantee.
- Paint a picture with words.
- Block up an historic and appropriate quote.

- Start an intriguing story.
- Offer vital information.
- Drop a familiar name.
- Use a testimonial.
- Use a case history.
- Refer to the reader's experience.
- Command. (But use this technique with discretion.)
- Use specific, substantive figures.
- Don't ask whether—ask *which*.
- Remember the power words of marketing communications mentioned in Chapter 15:   New . . . Improved . . . Now . . . Free . . . Easy . . . Urgent . . . Exclusive . . . Limited   time . . . No   risk . . . How   to . . . Which . . . Money . . . Amazing . . . Wanted . . . At last . . . This . . . Advice . . . Plus the all important pronoun *YOU*.

TECHNIQUES TO HELP YOUR LETTERS SELL

It makes no difference whether you are paving the way for a personal call, trying to revive a dormant account, answering an inquiry, or soliciting new business: Every time you produce a persuasive letter, you are—or should be—preselling your product, service, organization, and/or yourself.

Here are some suggestions on how to do it, based on experience over many years, for a wide range of products and services:

- *Keep your letter simple.* That does not mean "writing down" to anyone. It *does* mean avoiding high-flown phrases. Use short words everyone understands. Try to stick with *active* verbs and spare the adjectives. Write as if you were speaking aloud. And, unless absolutely necessary for cultural reasons, avoid antique "businessese" clichés such as, "We anticipate with pleasure the favor of a prompt response," and that sort of phony tone.

- *Do not try to be clever or funny.* To attempt humor and fail is worse than not to have written at all. Few people can successfully write humorous letters especially to a person they have never met—and few business offers lend themselves to joke and jollity. Remember that your ultimate goal often is to predispose a prospect to a sale. And selling is serious business.

- *Make your copy specific.* Use names, places, and exact figures. Tell what happens to whom. "Now save $215.00 on annual lawn care" is far stronger than "Save hundreds of dollars in common landscape maintenance expenses over an average twelve-month period."

- *Know what you want and ask for it.* Be explicit in stating exactly what you want. Your readers are no more—nor less—intelligent than you. And they probably have no more time to spare. Do not make them guess at your purpose. If you want them to take action, say so. Then say it *again*.

- *Always put a "hook" in your letters.* Mail order marketers, in particular, always include a hook in their letters—some extra inducement for taking immediate action. Dangle the hook, set it with a firm snap of logic, reel in your line with rational reasons for action, and gently net the big fish with your close. Like good fishermen, professional letter writers say that the hook, line, and net—well deployed—never fail to increase the catch, which is measurable in terms of *qualified responses.*

Chapter 27

Electronic Commerce and Internet Tactics

RAPID CHANGES

Today, the operations of traditional "brick and mortar" businesses are being significantly affected by electronic commerce, and the changes in business marketing appear to be even more dramatic. Things are changing so fast that some traditional textbooks that treat e-commerce today refer readers to their Web sites for current information.

The word "marketspace" has been coined to describe the electronic marketplace that includes bar-code scanning for marketing research and inventory management, credit card charges and debits, commercial online services, and trade via the Internet.

The International Trade Administration has defined electronic commerce as "any activity that uses some form of electronic communication in the inventory, exchange, advertisement, distribution, and payment of goods and services."

To encompass the enormous potential of electronic commerce, the term "direct response marketing" has been expanded so that we now refer to "interactive marketing." The basic Internet marketing strategies are similar to those of telemarketing: either *push* (like *outbound* telemarketing) where the advertiser dispatches uninvited messages to the audience, or *pull* (like *inbound* telemarketing) where the consumer requests information from the advertiser. *E-mail* and *Usenet* tend to use primarily the *push* strategy, whereas the *World Wide Web* is ideal for the *pull* strategy.

BASIC TERMS

To define our terms, of particular importance currently are the following:

- *The Internet*—a worldwide network of computers that provides users of personal computers at home or at work with access to information electronically. It has been estimated, extrapolating growth since its inception in 1996, that 250 million people—nearly 75 million of them in the United States—will be using the Internet by the year 2005.

- *The World Wide Web*—the part of the Internet that allows information to be accessed in the form of Web pages. Hypertext markup language (html) formats documents so they can be retrieved using a browser program such as Microsoft's Internet Explorer and Netscape's Navigator. A Uniform Resource Locator (URL) identifies each Web site (for example, *www.compusa.com*), and formatted information is delivered from Web sites to personal computers by means of a hypertext transfer protocol (http).

- *Commercial online services*—not directly dependent on the Internet, these offer news, entertainment, and information in electronic form, e-mail communication (plagued with *spam* or unwanted promotional messages, soon likely to be regulated), Internet access, marketing services, and online shopping opportunities to subscribers who pay a monthly fee to services that include America Online, Prodigy, and CompuServe.

- *Usenet*—composed of thousands of discussion groups or "chat rooms" on the Internet. Good publicity-type possibilities, and currently especially useful for gathering market research.

- *Listserv groups*—computer users sign up on "electronic mailing lists" according to their particular interest(s). A message sent to a *listserv* e-mail address will automatically be sent to every name on the *listserv* roster, sort of like "electronic word-of-mouth." Marketers are criticized if they use this medium too commercially.

- *Intranet*—private Internet-type operations for businesses and other organizations that may or may not be connected to the Internet. Useful for communication of marketing, sales, product, and other information to employees and other stakeholders.

- *Extranet*—another business form of electronic communication that connects companies and other organizations with their dealers, distributors, suppliers, and services such as advertising and public relations agencies.

- *Electronic data interchange (EDI)*—a combination of proprietary telecommunication and computer information transfer for inventory control, order entry, billing, payment, and so on.

- *Fax-on-demand*—delivery on request of computer-stored information to customers and prospects via facsimile machines. Requests may be via toll-free numbers, e-mail, or Web site visits. This technique is replacing the traditional "bingo card" in periodicals.

WEB STRATEGIES

Strategic considerations in this context currently include these:

- *Corporate Web sites*—or Web pages for organizations and/or brands (called "home pages") that provide information and sometimes opportunities to buy through personal computers. Some of these are elaborate and costly. While popular, their commercial value is yet to be clearly proven.

- *Marketing Web sites*—of two basic types: *promotional*, where the site is essentially an advertisement or commercial, and *transactional*, where the objective is to obtain direct orders and/or gather marketing research information. A *transactional* Web site may cost the marketer 10 times what a *promotional* Web site costs.

- *Web portals*—well-trafficked Web sites, such as search engines, or common starting pages, such as AOL homepage. The marketer can buy space on a service such as Yahoo!® to advertise products or services.

- *Web communities*—special-interest Web sites such as Women's Network that, like Web portals, sell advertising space to marketers whose target market demographics, psychographics, or synchrographics conform to the communities' profiles.

- *Virtual malls*—collections of *corporate Web sites* that sell products related by category, geographics, or some other factor.

- *Search engines*—take the consumer to Web sites according to interest expressed. Of several types: *hierarchical, spider, concept,* and *robot* (or *"bot"*), the latter especially useful for consumers seeking the lowest price for a CD or a car rental.

- *Cookies*—files placed by on-line marketers, advertisers, advertising networks, and marketing researchers on the operating systems of consumers' personal computers when they visit a Web site to track their surfing patterns and gather other private information. Banner ads can be adapted to reflect varied consumer profiles. See Chapter 2, "Market Research" for more information on this.

FORMS OF ELECTRONIC ADVERTISING

Online advertising can take several forms. The most common currently include the following:

- *Banner ads*—static or animated strips that appear on a computer screen adjacent to information sought, that often make some sort of offer, and that require only a mouse-click to carry the viewer into a more complex marketing message. *Enhanced banner ads* are a newer idea and provide more complete information.

- *Button ads*—small rectilinear treatments of organization or brand names that usually appear at the bottom of a Web page.

- *Sponsorships*—advertising that is integrated with a Web community site. For example, a marketer of a woman's product might buy *sponsorship* on Women's Network.

- *Key word ads*—linked to search engines or Web portals such as Yahoo! If, for example, you are an insurance company, you could have your advertisement appear every time a computer user keyed in the word "insurance."

- *Interstitials* (or *intermercials* or *pop-up ads*)—much like television commercials in that they *may* include video and audio dimensions. *Interstitials* pop up automatically on users' computer screens between the time they click on a Web site and the time it appears. As might be expected, this type of advertising seems to be more effective than banners.
- *Coupons*—can be downloaded and printed on home printers for use in local stores.
- *Web casting*—transmission of information, which can include news and entertainment as well as advertising and promotion based on computer users' expressed interest in that type of information. This is reminiscent of the strategy of developing specialized-interest mailing lists, but is more immediate and active.

OTHER OPTIONS

Public relations and publicity activities can also be made more efficient from a cost standpoint and effective from a time standpoint by posting messages to news groups. Many publications now accept electronic press releases and articles on disks.

We can expect to see further innovations in marketing communications as computer, telecommunications, and other electronic technologies progress.

Part V

Persuasion in Marketing Planning

Chapter 28

Sales Promotion Strategies

Sales promotion is essentially a creative form of price discounting. It differs from advertising in that it provides an *incentive* for customers and prospects to take desired action. Sales promotion is employed in consumer marketing, to influence both ultimate customers and resellers, and in business marketing.

WHAT SALES PROMOTION CAN DO

Here are several general objectives that sales promotion strategies might help you achieve:

1. Introduce your existing product or service to new prospects.
2. Introduce your new product or service to existing customers.
3. Attract new customers to your new products or services.
4. Stimulate repeat business.
5. Revitalize a declining product.
6. Encourage customers to use more of your products or services.
7. Build goodwill among both customers and prospects.

There are several proven sales promotion strategies to accomplish objectives of these kinds, although not all are as effective as others in particular applications. Try to keep track of responses so you can test new strategic approaches and improve your success record.

BASIC SALES PROMOTION STRATEGIES

Since sales promotion is that extra offer that tips over the sale, prompts immediate action, and/or makes the prospect want to do business with you rather than one of your competitors, the key to success lies in devising an addition to your basic offer that seems to the prospect to be a better deal than a similar offer *without* the inducement. Here are the basic strategic means to do that:

- *Coupons*—discount (or *cents-off*) coupons in introductory advertisements or in connection with the announcement of a new or existing product or service are popular. *Free* offers also work well in the form of coupons, often to support *sampling*, covered next. In addition to distribution through magazine and newspaper advertising, coupons can be dispensed in cardpacks to occupant addresses; left as doorknob-hangers; sent by direct mail; enclosed with billing statements; handed out at shows, in malls, and other public places; and/or dispensed on-premises or in or on product packaging. *Self-destruct coupons* are two or more printed so they overlap, and clipping one will destroy the value of the other; this technique is used to test the relative appeal of different products and/or promotions. *Instant-redeemable coupons (IRCs)* are peel-off or tear-off coupons placed on products for use with that product at check-out. *Escalating* (or *refund*) *coupons* are a way to reward consumers for increasing purchases; refunds might be $1 for three purchases, $3 for six purchases, and $5 for eight purchases. *Cross-couponing* is where coupons are offered in or on other products' packages (see Chapter 10) or in their promotions. *Electronic coupons* allow retailers to print out coupons at the check-out counter; this process can be linked to the UPC scanner, so that coupon offers are related to consumer purchases, as specified by manufacturers. As noted in Chapter 27, coupons can also be downloaded and printed on home computers. It is estimated that some 300 billion coupons are distributed annually to U.S. consumers, with redemption totaling some $3 billion, so here is a sales promotion strategy that people in the United States are not only familiar with but that many sincerely appreciate.
- *Sampling*—the strategy that allows you to accomplish several possible objectives by offering a sample of your product or service. *Open-house events* are a form of sampling for some businesses, as are *free consultations* for professional services. With a *sampling* strategy you need to keep your specific objective(s) clearly in mind lest you risk "giving away the store," as retailers warn.
- *Cross-promotions*—two noncompetitive manufacturers cooperate by putting offers for or samples of the partner's products in their packages. (See *package-delivered strategy* that follows.)
- *Tie-in promotions*—two or more brands combine forces to produce programs that involve joint coupons, rebates, contests, and the like.
- *Free product*—more than a sample-size and there is no cost to the consumer. There might be no purchase requirement, but more often one or more other products must be purchased; differs from the *bundle* strategy in that products are not packaged or banded together.

- *Bundle strategy*—akin to *straight discounting*, where you package two or more products (like a bottle of shampoo and a bottle of conditioner) or services together and offer the combination at a reduced price. These are referred to in sales promotion as *price-packs*, that can be of two types: *reduced-price-pack* which is a single package containing more than one product sold at a reduced price, and *banded pack* which is two related products such as a shampoo and conditioner banded together. When a strong product is sold together with a weaker product to enhance trial or volume of the latter, the strategy is called *piggyback*. See *twin-pack* in Chapter 10 for more on this.

- *Bundling strategy*—as mentioned in connection with pricing strategies (which relate closely to sales promotion strategies) there is a difference between *bundle* and *bundling* strategies; *bundling* is where you offer two or more products or additional features at a lower price than if you sold them separately, but do not offer them as a *price-pack*. For example, the auto industry commonly offers new cars with particular combinations of features at lower prices than if the customer had the features installed by the dealer.

- *Trial offers*—are somewhat like *couponing* and *sampling*, but are generally used for more expensive goods and services, and normally involve longer-term commitments. Consumer goods marketers have had success with everything from magazine subscriptions to wristwatches by offering a "10-day free trial" and even longer periods of time.

- *Refunds*—are familiar in the form of the classic mail order offer "Your money cheerfully refunded if you are not completely satisfied." Often a time limit like 30 days is included. In many cases this sales promotion strategy *doubles* volume without significantly affecting profit margins. That is, the new and additional business that the refund offer attracts amounts to far more than the cost of the returned merchandise.

- *Rebates*—became popular several years ago when the automobile industry, in a successful effort to prevent government regulation of price increases, made the consumer familiar with the concept. This strategy has proved so successful in attracting new customers and increasing sales that many other marketers have put it to use. Rebates are offered in many forms, including imprints on packages, *tags, neck-hangers* (or *bottle hangers*), and *tear pads* (or *take-ones*) that are pads of sheets imprinted with a sales promotion offer and sometimes a recipe; these are not immediately redeemable like *coupons*, but may generate a check when mailed to the marketer with proof of purchase. It might seem surprising, but many people will more readily pay a higher price if they get a rebate check in the mail than an equivalently lower price without a rebate check. Of course, marketers benefit from failure by consumers to request rebates prior to an expiration date.

- *Bounce-back devices*—any of a variety of direct-response gimmicks included with a product to encourage repeat sales, to add on accessories, or to sell related products or services. Also used in business direct mail to generate qualified leads, as when a "Please have a sales rep call" card is included as part of a literature fulfillment package.

- *Events*—although considered primarily a public relations strategy, sponsorship of or participation in parades, sports competitions, walkathons, bicycle races, and so on can have sales promotion value. *Events* can serve as good occasions for *sampling*. See Appendix 13 for event theme ideas.

- *Contests, sweepstakes,* and *games*—this category includes a variety of competitions, such as "Complete this statement in 25 words or less," that require some skill or talent (which defines a *contest*), and also random-chance competitions (which are called *sweepstakes*). All have enormous appeal to a wide variety of people. Check your legal counsel, local laws, and your own industry codes of ethics for guidance, and watch in particular for the U.S. regulation that participation in a *contest, sweepstakes,* or *game* cannot require the purchase of goods or services. Beware of the term *lottery* which requires payment or purchase and is therefore "immoral" and illegal in the United States except through government agencies. Be sure, too, that you don't offer more than you can afford to pay if there are lots of winners or a single big winner. Where permissible, this strategy seems to work best for businesses and professional organizations as a goodwill generator and is also useful in attracting new customers or clients. Where ethical, some marketers have found a good variation to be a contest in which *every* entrant wins.

- *Premiums*—a strategy used by banks and insurance companies for many years to attract new accounts and make appointments to sell new policies. A *premium* is anything of modest cost (up to $4 to be tax-deductible, according to the U.S. Internal Revenue Service) that you might wish to give free, or anything of equal or greater value that you might wish to offer at a price that is substantially below the perceived value or normal retail price, but at or above the cost to the marketer who is running the sales promotion program; the latter is called a *self-liquidating premium* or *self-liquidating offer (SLO)*. When proof of purchase is required it is also called a *boxtop offer.* Important to the success of premium promotions is that the item offered is somehow *related* to the goods or services being promoted. For example, a medical organization might offer a free blood pressure log book to each new patient who asks about treatment for hypertension. The sponsor name and telephone number imprinted on the premium can serve double-duty— as a goodwill-builder and also as an advertising reminder to return. Premiums at retail can take the form of *in-pack premiums, near-pack offers* that provide a premium free or at a discount with purchase of an adjacent product (such as a free umbrella with the purchase of after-shave lotion), and *in-the-mail premiums* that can be obtained by consumers who return a box-top or UPC code from a purchased package.

- *Gifts*—when a premium gets to be more than a few dollars in value, it is referred to as a *gift*—a sales promotion strategy for rewarding special customers and clients. For example, top business executives are accustomed to receiving modest gifts (up to $25 to be tax-deductible, according to the IRS) in recognition of their patronage. *Dealer* (or *buying*) *loaders* are gifts offered to resellers for stocking products. Many companies specialize in providing premium and gift items, and publish catalogues from which you can select appropriate items. Just beware the perceived value of the gift is not so great that it might be judged to be a bribe. Premiums and gifts fall under the general category of *advertising specialties*.

- *Incentives*—a word sometimes used to characterize premiums and gifts and mentioned in connection with offer strategies in Chapter 15, this strategy also includes techniques for stimulating employees, especially sales personnel. In those cases the incentive is commonly called a *spiff, push money,* or a *push incentive.* There are numerous opportunities for an *incentive* strategy, including *cash bonuses, trips,* and *products* such as clothing, appliances, and automobiles (sometimes called "pots-and-pans promotions") to motivate employees and retail sales people. *Awards* that include recognition certificates, plaques, trophies, and lapel pins can be more economical but no less effective ways to acknowledge desirable performance. Incentive programs take many imaginative forms, but essentially the strategy is based on the idea that a reward system over and above basic salary or wages and benefits will encourage people to work harder and more productively.

- *Package-delivered strategy*—when coupons, premiums, and other promotional offers are printed on or placed inside a product package. That may be either the manufacturer's or another marketer's package; the general term for the former is *cross-couponing,* and the term for the latter *cross-ruffs,* which would include such promotions as a *cents-off coupon* for Mrs. Butterworth's® syrup in a box of Eggo® frozen waffles. If the offer is advertised on the front of the package, it is said to be *flagged.*

- *Point system*—customers earn points each time they buy from you and can redeem points for prizes or free products. This strategy encourages both additional purchases and continued loyalty. The old consumer marketing system of *trading stamps* had this strategy as its foundation.

- *Credit terms*—deferred payment or special loan interest rates offered to customers, dealers, and distributors alike to "sweeten the deal" for the buyer.

- *Guarantees, warranties,* and *service agreements*—especially when offered "free," or at relatively low cost, this strategy reduces anxiety about the reliability of the product and hence encourages purchase and may enhance loyalty. Look back at Chapter 15 for more along these lines.

- *Indebtedness*—involves providing a product or service free to secure a person as a future customer. For example, a retail tire company fixes flat tires at no charge so customers feel obliged to buy their next new tires there.

- *Straight discounting*—is the sales promotion strategy with which most people are probably most familiar. It involves cutting prices or giving extra value in services or products to obtain or retain business. Discounts can be in the form of *cash discounts* for immediate or prompt payment; *price-off* (or *off-invoice,* or *off-list*) *discounts* to encourage distributors and dealers to stock up or carry new products; *quantity discounts* for volume purchases; *functional* (or *trade*) *discounts* for buyers who perform particular tasks within the scheme of distribution; *allowances* for other functions performed by retailers such as advertising and displays; *free goods* including additional product and advertising specialties; and *type-of-customer* discounts, as for senior citizens, students, or during "ladies nights" at some nightclubs and bars. Note: When you discount your price(s), beware that the lower price does not become the perceived fair or regular price in the minds of your customers. See Chapter 11, "Pricing Strategies," for more ideas about reduced prices.

- *Demotion strategy*—sales promotion strategy that relies heavily on discounting (see Chapter 11). *BOGOs* ("buy one get one free") are common, but risk is diminishing product image and perceived value.
- *Deals*—used extensively in retail sales, discounts are given routinely to special groups. Among professional practices, sources of client referrals and special types of clients may be given extra consideration to show appreciation and to build volume. The practice is generally considered ethical, effective, and so common it has become traditional in many fields.
- *Co-op*—promotions in which more than one manufacturer shares the cost of such marketing communications as direct mail and free-standing inserts. (Different than *co-op* in distribution and *co-op advertising*, the latter where a retailer is reimbursed by the manufacturer.)
- *Loss leader*—Suggested as a pricing strategy, *loss leader* can also be considered a sales promotion strategy in that it is a creative form of discounting that offers a dramatically low price for one or more products to increase traffic and to attract new customers.
- *Allowances*—another form of discounting for consumers that involves such devices as *trade-ins* of old products for new.
- *Clubs*—membership with benefits like a newsletter, lapel pin, discounts, and so on can prove good for sustaining repeat purchase and brand loyalty.
- *Continuity programs*—characterized by "frequent flyer" and "frequent buyer" schemes to encourage repeat purchase and customer loyalty. A related term is *patronage awards*.
- *Friend-of-a-friend promotion*—here current customers are encouraged through gifts, bonuses, and/or discounts to refer friends and acquaintances who might be interested in the product or service. Also called (depending on the industry) *member-get-a-member program* and *third-party referral*.
- *Educational marketing*—a recent concept that involves promoting products through the public education system. Targeted coupons, samples, premiums, and other sales promotion items are delivered to students and parents and are tied in with public relations elements including news, education, scholarships, and grants to schools.
- *Finance allowance*—a trade-oriented sales promotion strategy in which retailers are paid for costs associated with consumer sales promotions.
- *Point-of-purchase* (POP) or *point-of-sale* (POS)—can be the best sales promotion strategy of all for many marketers. *Point-of-purchase* (POP) is the term used in commerce and *point of sale* (POS) in business marketing, and there is a difference of opinion as to whether these are sales promotion or advertising. The category includes *flyers* (also spelled *fliers*, or *circulars*), *folders* (or *leaflets*), *brochures*, *booklets*, *posters*, *tags*, *dump-bins*, *end-caps*, *header* (or *riser*) *cards*, *backer cards*, *shelf talkers*, *stack cards*, *banners*, *wobblers*, *flipcharts*, *sales kits* for reps, and other demonstration and display materials.

- *How-to books, bulletins,* and *tip-sheets*—providing information on how your customers can use your products most satisfactorily has long been a fruitful sales promotion activity, although some companies classify these with *instruction* (or *operator*) *manuals* as customer service items. In recent years, with managers encouraged to cut costs wherever possible, production of such items has declined, although they may be deserving of resurrection. Regardless of how you wish to classify printed materials and other graphic information, you can use them to great advantage for prompting purchase, generating inquiries, qualifying leads, and answering questions with or without the expense of personal sales calls. The more your particular product or service is tailored to the special needs of your target market, the better your printed materials will serve your marketing goals.

- *Thank-you*—beyond entertainment, premiums, gifts, trips abroad, and cash bonuses, often a simple *thank-you* (verbally, by business letter, or perhaps on preprinted thank-you cards) goes a long way to promote continued loyalty within the company and among customers as well. These days it seems to be a basic strategy too often overlooked.

ADVANTAGE AND DISADVANTAGE

Sales promotion efforts are different than most other types of marketing communications activities in that they are *short-term* enticements which are perceived by the recipient as having some degree of *value*. They can be offered to retail prospects and customers (called "consumer sales promotions" or "mippies"), your own employees (called "incentives"), or referral sources and business customers and prospects (called "trade sales promotions").

Their primary *advantage* is that they prompt immediate action, whereas without them the target might hesitate or procrastinate.

Their primary *disadvantage* is that their effects are generally temporary. They do not contribute as much to a long-term relationship as many other forms of marketing communications do. And, when the value is presented in the form of refund, rebate, or discount, there is a risk of the reduced price becoming the perceived *value*, and hence the going rate.

Many marketers now budget significantly more for sales promotion activities than they do for advertising, whereas until a relatively few years ago the budget proportions were the other way around—traditionally 60 percent advertising and 40 percent sales promotion. As mentioned, this probably reflects current demands for marketing managers to produce immediate—rather than long-term—results.

Chapter 29

Public Relations Strategies

SOMETHING DIFFERENT

Public relations differs from advertising, sales promotion, and personal selling in that it *is not limited to marketing* and organizationally is often separated from marketing operations under a designation such as "Corporate Communications Department." Among U.S. federal government agencies, where the term "public relations" cannot be used, it is called "Public Information," "Public Liaison," or "Public Affairs." It is the broadest of all the categories presented here and may involve each of the other marketing communications functions even more than they involve one another. Public relations is what organizations or individuals do to be seen as they see themselves or as they wish to be seen by others.

Fortune magazine has made the simple and widely accepted observation, "Good public relations is good performance publicly appreciated because it is adequately communicated."

Public relations should be looked upon by ethical marketers as the *least tangible of communications* for their products, services, or organizations— and that which is intended to influence honestly the attitudes of various target audiences or *"publics"* as they're called in the PR field.

As far as the criticisms of public relations go, PR efforts need be no more inherently deceptive than any other form of human communication. Marketers who will lie to their customers may also attempt deceptive public relations. But the fact that many marketers of professional services as well as consumer goods elect to launch public relations programs does not automatically make them liars.

ACTIVITY-RELATED STRATEGIES

Public relations is important for one very good and old-fashioned reason: *goodwill*. People will more readily deal with a business or professional organization perceived as competent, honest, fair, caring, and public-spirited than with one *not* perceived as having those qualities. Here are strategies that relate to PR activities:

- *Community affairs strategy*—most marketers should place considerable emphasis in public relations planning on what is commonly called "community affairs." This dimension of public relations requires establishing and maintaining cordial relations with citizens, businesspeople, neighbors, and government personnel in your draw area. It involves displaying sensitivity to issues that concern the community, especially with regard to the effect your presence, your business or organization, and your facilities may have on your neighborhood. Your active participation in local events can build genuine bonds by showing your business and professional friendship and involvement in your community. Purchasing equipment and supplies locally can also demonstrate a small businesses' support of the local economy and corresponding concern for the fiscal welfare of the community and its residents and businesses. Your community affairs, like all your other marketing activities, must pertain to the publics you choose to serve in order for those activities to do you any good in a marketing sense. That is to say, if you own a Mexican restaurant in Denver, you probably will not benefit by marching every year in New York City's St. Patrick's Day Parade. Strange as it may seem, some marketers spend substantial sums of money on just such ill-conceived ventures and then complain, "Public relations just doesn't work."

- *Community service strategy*—your community will also respond more favorably to you, and individuals are likely to be more inclined to avail themselves of your goods and services, if you and others in your organization become involved in community service activities. This does not necessarily mean collecting scrap newspaper on weekends, painting the houses of the elderly, or serving Thanksgiving dinners to the poor. Although those kinds of good works can be personally rewarding and can result in a measure of public esteem if properly publicized, you should also seek activities that will benefit you in the *marketing* sense.

- *Publicity strategy*—see the following chapter for details on this strategy of "getting ink" or media exposure that is so important to effective public relations. This strategy relies heavily on *news releases* (what used to be called *press releases* in the days before the broadcast and other electronic media emerged), *fact sheets, backgrounders, bulletins* (or *updates*), and *bios* (or *biogs* or *biographical sketches*) of people to be publicized.

- *Feature article and byliner strategy*—also covered in the next chapter, informative articles that you provide to appropriate periodicals can gain beneficial exposure for your product, organization, or top people.

- *Interview strategy*—arrange for media people to interview your senior personnel who are experts in particular aspects of your industry.

- *Talk show strategy*—arrange for well-trained representatives of your organization to speak on radio or television "magazine" and interview programs. Prepare them with *talking points* to keep them "on message," and rehearse them regularly to see they communicate well.

- *News conference strategy*—only to be used when you have an important announcement, invite media people to get newsworthy material fast and first-hand.

- *Publications strategy*—this can be as extensive as your budget allows. Usually PR departments are responsible for companies' *annual reports*, but they may also produce *brochures, media kits* (what used to be called *press kits* when newspapers and magazines were the only mass media), and other types of printed materials.

- *Newsletter strategy*—a special strategy under *publications* that can range from a single black-and-white sheet to elegant four-color slick magazine-style periodicals. Although there are far too many newsletters published today, owing to "desktop publishing" software, and far too few good ones, you may wish to communicate information and build goodwill with your customers, prospects, and other publics through this medium that you control completely. Some companies consider this an advertising or a customer service activity rather than PR.

- *Advertising strategy*—useful when you can't get sufficient publicity. Create *house ads* for internal publications, *public service announcements (PSAs)* for a variety or media if yours is a *nonprofit* organization, *image ads* to reflect your reputation and prestige, *issue ads* to take a position or express an opinion on a pertinent matter, or *advocacy ads* that go a step further and support *lobbying* efforts.

- *Event strategy*—used as a goodwill-builder, sponsorship and participation in parades, walkathons, bicycle races, and so on can be a very effective PR strategy. Sometimes tie-ins with sales promotion event objectives is possible, but PR events should not appear too commercial.

- *Open-house strategy*—invite selected publics to tour your offices, factories, and other facilities. These occasions can be extravagant, including even sit-down dining and top entertainment. (See Chapter 35 and Appendix 14.)

- *Party strategy*—somewhat like the open-house but need not be held on company premises. Large hotels and elegant restaurants are good locales.

- *Junket strategy*—fly representatives of the media (reporters, editors, and the like) to interesting places and provide well for them so they will be inclined to say nice things about your people, products, and organization.

- *Executive speech strategy*—a dignified way to disseminate your marketing and PR messages, covered in Chapter 34.

- *Stunt strategy*—the strategy associated with what is called *press agentry*, where you arrange for something unusual to take place—like someone walking a tightrope from your new headquarters building to an adjacent rooftop—in order to obtain media attention and publicity.

- *Film and video strategy*—produce informative material for distribution to schools, colleges, and business and professional groups.

- *Internet strategy*—establish a Web site that will communicate your messages to the growing Internet audience. Chapter 27 contains suggestions on this subject.

- *Crisis management strategy*—many PR departments are responsible for devising worst-case scenarios and developing plans for how to handle them. The ways the media can ruin the reputations of companies and executives who are not prepared to defend themselves have led many large companies to spend millions of dollars on this aspect of PR and publicity. See Appendix 12 for suggestions on how to approach *crisis management.*

You should clearly define your particular target audience(s) or public(s) using the categories suggested in Appendix 5. Then establish your objectives and measurable goals, as described in Chapters 5 and 6, and only then select PR strategies that will contribute to your marketing program by influencing your clearly defined public(s) toward your clearly specified goal(s).

ETHICAL PR STRATEGIES

Here are other basic PR strategies with which you should be comfortable:

- *Testimonial strategy*—here you encourage people with excellent reputations to speak or appear on your behalf. High-profile businesspeople and honest politicians (and there really are many of the latter, despite media reports to the contrary), as well as satisfied customers, are the types it can be advantageous to cultivate in connection with implementing this strategy.
- *Celebrity strategy*—although some people consider the use of celebrities ethically flawed, it is a common marketing communications strategy. Many American sports and entertainment figures earn more from commercial endorsements than they do from their regular occupations. It is a foolish person indeed who does not realize that such spokespersons have been paid well for their product endorsements. So, if it doesn't rub you the wrong way, or (most importantly) if it will appeal to your publics, you should be free to use this strategy. And, by the way, this does not always require cash on the barrelhead. On a local level, for example, you could link up with an appealing personality on your local public radio station, offer a modest amount of underwriting to his or her program, and watch the interesting PR opportunities emerge.
- *Bandwagon strategy*—also mentioned under advertising creative strategies, the *bandwagon* strategy tries to persuade the public that "everyone is doing it." This is sometimes frowned upon by ethical marketers because it is so seldom true; our society is just too diverse to have anything appeal to everybody. But for clearly defined target groups it can be a valid strategy when substantiated by research.
- *Plain folks strategy*—another strategy that can be misused. But, properly handled, it could expand your business into new market segments. Depending on the people you wish to serve, you could present a very modest public image that would make ordinary folk feel you were one of them and consequently incline them to deal with you. It works well for L. L. Bean's mail order sales and for Jack Daniel's® whiskey, for example.

- *Snob appeal strategy*—as noted in connection with advertising creative strategies, *snob appeal* is the opposite of *plain folks* or *salt-of-the-earth* (the most down-scale of all). To use this as a PR strategy as a cosmetic surgeon in private practice, for example, you might join the most exclusive country club or yacht club in your area, buy a house in the most expensive section of town you could possibly afford, and become a sponsor of the opera, symphony orchestra, Shakespeare Society, or whatever else appeals to the crème-de-la-crème of your marketing area. Then be sure to attend all the high-society functions to which you can wangle an invitation, and have your picture taken as often as possible at such events. (By the way, I suggest that you try always to stand on your *far right* side of a group being photographed, so you are the *first* to be mentioned in the caption. This also allows you to hide the liquor glass in your left hand behind the person standing beside you.) See that the photographer or his or her assistant gets the correct spelling of your name, the name of your organization, and your product or service to publish on the social pages. Some people actually enjoy living like this, and it can be very good for business, too.

- *Common enemy* (or *dissociation*) *strategy*—a strategy that can be misused, but very effective when honestly applied. The basic idea behind this strategy is that "the enemy of my enemy is my friend." The PR practitioner can build an immediate bond with the target audience by denouncing people or causes the audience dislikes.

- *Relationship strategy*—you may recall that under advertising creative strategies *relationship* was broken down into *association* and *affiliation*. As a PR strategy, it is applied somewhat differently than in advertising—but is no less powerful as an influencer. For PR purposes, you need to do a careful psychographic analysis of your important publics and discover what causes or charities appeal to your target individuals. Then you can relate your business, activities, or product to that cause or charity. This may manifest itself as simply *donating money* to a nonprofit—amid suitable fanfare and publicity, of course. Or it might mean actually doing *volunteer work* for a cause or an organization. Or it might manifest itself in the old gimmick newly dubbed "*cause-related marketing*," where a portion of revenues is contributed to a charity. For example, if your research revealed that a large proportion of your customers had been Girl Scouts in their youth and supported that organization, you might announce that for every $100 in sales, you were going to donate $1 to the Girl Scouts. You might also become a scout leader, a volunteer executive in the national organization, and offer your help with the annual cookie sale. Similarly, as mentioned in Chapter 20, "Artistic and Emotional Strategies" for advertising, treating issues related to our *environment* can also be good PR. As long as you can honestly relate your products, services, and activities to conservation, you may benefit from what has been termed "*green marketing*." True, these activities might have little or nothing to do with your business or profession—but that's often the nature of this sort of attention-getting, goodwill-building PR activity.

UNETHICAL PR STRATEGIES

Since influencing public opinion has been going on for thousands of years, techniques have evolved that are both good and bad, ethical and unethical. Among those with which you may be familiar, but which you will probably want to *avoid* are the following:

- *Name-calling strategy*—which may also include *stereotyping*, mentioned in connection with advertising creative strategies. As the old saying goes, "If you can't say something good about a person, don't say anything." This is even true when you might feel called upon to defend yourself. Chances are you will attain more stature and credibility with a gentle, rational response than with an angry, vicious, or mean-spirited one. For example, President George H. W. Bush probably did himself considerable damage when he was persuaded in his re-election campaign to refer to his opponents as "those bozos."

- *Stacking the deck* (or *card-stacking*) *strategy*—a common strategy where only *one* side of an argument is presented, and then often in a selective fashion. In PR, as well as in advertising, today a balanced perspective tends to be more credible and hence more persuasive.

- *Straw man strategy*—a strategy popular among politicians and special interest spokespersons who seek to persuade unethically. A weak, artificial antagonist is created and then demolished like a straw man burned in ancient times to remove a curse.

- *Sham issue strategy*—public announcement of opposition to an unpopular idea or action, as if one's opponent(s) or competitor(s) *favored* it.

- *Misquoting strategy*—deliberately false attribution is common in both business and politics, but even more common is taking an actual phrase *out of context* that misrepresents a position. Adolf Hitler and Joseph Goebbels were experts at this.

- *Glittering generalities strategy*—which include pie-in-the-sky promises and extravagant statements that are a form of *hyperbole*. This strategy is commonly used for self-aggrandizement but generally results in low credibility today—except, of course, in national politics, where the public continues to be fooled by this strategy.

- *Ridicule strategy*—a far too common strategy that often involves *irony* and overt *sarcasm*. As you have surely observed, it is frequently used by politicians to demean their opponents. It should have no place in ethical free market competition.

- *Stonewalling strategy*—a strategy popularized by the Nixon team during the infamous Watergate scandal, this involves coldly ignoring legitimate inquiry into a newsworthy situation. *Stonewalling* may please your attorney, who might be concerned that statements you make could be used against you in court but (as recent experience has shown) will do little for your public relations, your media relations, or your business and professional image.

- *Whitewashing strategy*—when an individual or organization has something that could hurt them in the PR sense, they cover it up or "whitewash" it by presenting information (either true or untrue) to distract the media and public.

- *False front strategy*—specifically forbidden in the code of ethics of the Public Relations Society of America (PRSA), this strategy involves establishing an organization with a significant-sounding name to work on behalf of a commercial interest. Both business and professional people can easily and inexpensively create nonprofit organizations to serve their special interests. For example, three or four mediocre plastic surgeons might get together and found a nonprofit organization called something like The Reconstructive Surgeon's Board for Ethical Practice (a fictitious name, as far as I know). Then they could all claim in their marketing communications to be "board certified." In addition, they could present one another with awards for their outstanding ethics, and even issue apparently impartial "official" Board for Ethical Practice news releases about how splendidly they were serving their communities. It's almost amusing how many industrial polluters are being recognized for their environmental concerns and generous contributions to humanity by *false front* nonprofits with names like Citizens for a Healthier Environment—also a *fictitious* name, I trust.

"TO THINE OWN SELF BE TRUE"

Whatever you do with any of these strategies, you should try always to be honest and sincere. As in your use of other strategies connected with your marketing program, if you don't agree in your heart with what your prospective customers value, perhaps you should redefine your target market. That way, you can ethically serve causes that you yourself truly believe are worthwhile.

In practical terms, what this means is that you should relate your business to things that, figuratively speaking, will bring a tear to the eye of your public(s), or at least make their hearts beat a little faster. See that your public appearances and prepared statements in the PR context elevate you and your product or service above your competition. And take every opportunity to have yourself identified with concern for your customers or clients, your industry, your profession, your community, your state, your nation, and our fragile world.

A PR message can be a marketing message of sorts, but since the objective of PR is largely to present your business as a "good corporate citizen," and your employees as public spirited professionals, your PR message should involve as many as possible of the following:

- High credibility
- High visibility
- Emotional impact
- Fundamental values
- Straightforward language and imagery
- Motivational appeal
- Safety appeal (per Maslow's hierarchy)
- Love appeal (charity, not sexuality)
- Appeal for esteem
- Consistency of delivery
- Repetition, repetition, repetition

A good set of rules to double-check your PR strategic planning and execution is this:

1. Do no harm.
2. Tell the truth.
3. Do nothing that would embarrass you if reported as news.
4. Prove the truth of your words through your actions.
5. Listen to your customers and prospects.
6. Think ahead and envision the consequences of your actions.
7. Conduct your PR program as if the future of your business depended on it—because it very well might.
8. At all times stay calm, patient, and pleasant-tempered.

No public relations strategy, tactic, or technique—nor any amount of marketing communications expertise—can make you, your organization, your goods, or your services *what they are not*. Thus, the best public relations program begins with a business or professional lifestyle that is the best you can make it.

Chapter 30

Publicity Strategies

Most marketers need publicity to get the name of their product, service, personnel, or organization better known. In the modern marketplace, though, the marketer's needs and the needs of the media that make publicity possible may not coincide. So the smart marketer must deliberately tailor marketing messages to suit the needs of the media and the interests of their audiences.

Today the famous statements of the old Hollywood moguls that "there is no such thing as bad publicity" and "you can say anything you want about me as long as you spell my name right" are no longer valid—if they ever were. In planning publicity, aim for the *positive*, the *pleasing*, and the *productive*. And be sure that what you try to disseminate is always *important*, *interesting*, and *newsworthy*.

MEDIA STRATEGY FOR PUBLICITY

Print media are probably your most promising publicity opportunities, especially if yours is a relatively small organization. Depending on your product or service, consider special sections of major newspapers because of their high readership and strong reader involvement. If you are a local marketer, use local newspapers not only for news items that will place your name before the public, but also for feature and interview article opportunities, personnel and legal announcements and—important but often overlooked—for *op-ed pieces* (essays that appear in the editorial section) and letters to the editor, wherein you can present your unique positions on significant and perhaps controversial issues. This sort of exposure influences public opinion but, sometimes more importantly, can increase name recognition for your product or service, your organization, and perhaps your important personnel.

In addition, there are numerous local, regional, and national consumer magazines that might carry items to benefit you—if you have a news or human interest angle. Specialized business publications abound that might publish articles about aspects of your business, philosophy, or research that would be interesting to their subscribers. There are also specialized publications limited to metropolitan, state, and regional audiences. And there are weekly, monthly, and neighborhood periodicals that will publish nearly anything written cogently and bylined by a person with a title.

You can also investigate the radio and television stations in your marketing area that might pick up those of your newsworthy releases that are primarily consumer oriented and of general interest. Many opportunities currently exist for appearances by experts on radio talk shows and even television interview programs in some areas. *Standard Rate & Data Service* (SRDS)—available in the business sections of most large public libraries—provides excellent listings in volumes for each type of medium. *Bacon's, Gale Directory of Publications,* and *Ulrich's* are also useful sources for planning publicity. (See Appendix 3 for an extensive list of secondary research sources.)

CREDIBILITY VERSUS CONTROL STRATEGY

Although in North America you can save considerable advertising space and time costs and gain an added measure of *credibility* with publicity as a technique of marketing message delivery (unlike many other parts of the world, where the interested marketer *pays* for editorial exposure), you do sacrifice the direct *control* you have with advertising of the timing and the exact words and illustrations that appear.

If your information is so self-serving that news and features editors aren't interested in it, you should not waste time and money on trying to get publicity but instead put it in the form of *advertising*. Although you have to pay for advertising space and time, you run no risk of being misquoted or of having your message twisted into something you did not intend—not uncommon in today's media climate of investigative journalism, negativism, and competitive sensationalism.

If you compare the costs of professional journalistic writing, preparation and production of releases, photo illustrations, and perhaps travel and entertainment expenses connected with publicity placement against the cost of a media contract for advertising, you may find that it is easier, more reliable, and more economical just to run an ad. So it is foolish to refer to publicity as "free advertising," as some business people do, because it is neither advertising nor is it free.

Publicity material includes not only the basic *news release*, but also *ex-*

clusives (stories or articles provided to one media vehicle alone, as opposed to a general release), *byliners* (articles written by you or your associates, or written by a professional writer under your direction and carrying a *byline*, or the name of the purported author), interview articles, and staff-written features on timely topics. By the way, materials of this type can also be prepared and distributed in *audio* form for radio and *video* form for television.

A BASIC PUBLICITY PROGRAM

To get your publicity program off to the right start, prepare several basic information pieces to be sent to editors of periodicals and to news directors of radio and television stations, packaged in a form sometimes called a "media kit."

These are the essential elements that you should include:

- Background on your organization (called a *backgrounder*).
- Overview of your most important current activities.
- *Bios* (or biographical sketches or personality profiles) of senior people in your organization.
- 5-by-7-inch black-and-white headshots of senior people in your organization, with captions attached to indicate names, titles, and specialties.
- Summary of your organization's accomplishments to date.
- Crisp, top-quality, 8-by-10-inch black-and-white glossy photo of something connected with your organization, such as a new product, work with a customer, an interior view of your office or plant, special equipment you may use, or even the exterior of the building in which your organization is headquartered.
- If affordable, color transparencies or a sheet of color illustrations with the offer to send transparencies for publication.
- Covering letter to editors and news directors (by name) detailing enclosures, asking that the packet be kept on file, offering access to you or your spokesperson for more complete information and opinions on industry matters, and promising regular updates.

Your material should be presented in a form that reflects the highest professional, editorial, and production quality standards you can achieve to encourage retention, reference, and active use by editors. In this way editors and news directors will have a chance to learn what your credits are, what your products and services are, and what your organization means to their readers, listeners, or viewers. In the same way they will be encouraged to develop their own stories about you and your plans, to call you for expert opinion quotes on business or professional news items, and to watch for newsworthy releases that you send them from time to time.

Importantly, you should not be open to the accusation of puffery or self-aggrandizement since you will simply be providing factual information *in the public interest.*

THE NEXT STEP

A fundamental key to success in a publicity program is not only to prepare and distribute excellent background material to begin with, but also to provide regular updates to your media contacts that are interesting, timely, and newsworthy.

To this end you must decide whether you and/or your staff can handle the work or if you'll rely on outside planning and writing help. If you choose the latter course, you must devise a technique of communication to assure that pertinent information will be fed immediately to your planners and writers for conversion into *news release, media update, byliner,* or *feature article* form. The system must be reliable so that nothing important either gets lost or becomes stale. And, of course, the procedure must be relatively easy and convenient for you and for the person or persons you charge with the details of responsibility.

In addition to preparing and disseminating interesting, newsworthy stories, you should have a reliable *media relations* program in place with one or more knowledgeable, persuasive individuals charged with *personal contact* (face-to-face, by telephone, fax, or e-mail) with editorial personnel of the media (reporters, editors, news directors, and others who may help publish or broadcast your information) and syndicated columnists if your publicity program is national in scope.

CLASSIC FORMULA

Important to remember in your publicity activities is the old newspaper reporters' rule on what should be included in a news story. An excellent double-check on publicity items you prepare is the classic *5 Ws and an H:*

- *What* happened?
- *Whom* did it happen to?
- *Where* did it happen?
- *When* did it happen?
- *Why* did it happen?
- *How* did it happen?

That aspect of marketing communications called *publicity* can serve you well as a support for not only your special product, service, and organization news, but also for your executive speeches, shows and meetings, and public relations activities. Appendix 10 describes how to write a news release, and Appendix 11 provides a long list of topics or idea-starters for publicity items.

Chapter 31

Personal Selling Strategies

The most dynamic, and the most potentially productive, of all your marketing communications efforts is called in commerce and industry "personal selling" or simply "sales." No other form of communication in American business receives so much attention and investment of personnel time and organization expenditures. Roughly 15 percent of gross revenues is reinvested in sales nationwide, reflecting belief in the old saying, "Nothing happens until somebody *sells* something."

Sales strategies listed here work for company field sales personnel, manufacturers' representatives, multilevel marketers, retailers, or door-to-door sales people.

THE STRATEGIC STEPS IN SELLING

The model described back in Chapter 5 began with identifying from the mass market a group of people called "suspects," continued through identifying "prospects," then "hot prospects," and concluded with converting those people to "customers" and finally "loyal customers" or repeat purchasers.

The fundamental strategy taught in most sales training classes and reflected in most sales and marketing textbooks begins with what is called "*prospecting*." This means the salesperson or the company develops a list of persons believed to be potential customers. *Inquiries* and *leads*, as defined in Chapter 5, are often an important component of this step with the expectation that there will be "conversion" to sales through the steps that follow.

The next step is called the "*preapproach*" where the sales representative evaluates the people on the list and tries to prequalify them to some extent by determining their needs, interests, accessibility, buying authority, and perhaps willingness and financial capability to purchase.

The next step is the "*approach*," where the sales rep makes contact and tries to set up an appointment.

"*Making the presentation*" follows and includes not only "the pitch," but also listening carefully for information that might help identify needs and guide the sales rep to a more tailored presentation.

Most people resist buying to some extent and will respond to a presentation with either real or fictitious objections. The sales rep's job is to "*overcome objections*" in this model.

When objections have been disposed of, the ideal salesperson reiterates the offer and "*closes the sale*," often by simply asking for an order or a signature on a contract, agreement, or engagement letter.

The final step is called "*follow-up*" to see that the customer is satisfied and to correct anything that might have gone wrong. At this point an *acknowledgement* (or "*ack*") in the form of a receipt, card, or letter (depending on the type of sale) should be delivered to the customer to confirm the order, contract, or payment.

A step often overlooked can be called simply "*collect the money*" which anyone who operates a business knows is not always easy, but vitally important to staying afloat.

McGraw-Hill's famous "Six Steps to the Sale" recommends not just follow-up but a tremendously important strategy they have called "*keep the customer sold.*" This is an idea all too often ignored in both business and personal life. It appears later in this chapter as the strategy called "*relationship marketing*," which redefines the traditional selling process a bit, and "*relationship selling*," which redefines the role of the sales representative.

PROSPECTING STRATEGIES

Strategies sales people use to identify prospects are these:

- *Develop a clear descriptive profile of the ideal prospect*—see Chapter 3 and Appendix 5 for variables to consider.
- *Poll company personnel*—particularly management people and contact people, such as service reps, in your own company.
- *Trade organizations*—gain information through personal contact by attending meetings and through membership lists normally available only to members.
- *Convention and conference attendees*—similar information may be restricted to exhibitors or members of sponsoring organizations.
- *List compilers and brokers*—check *Standard Rate & Data Service Direct Mail Lists* volume for names, addresses, and telephone numbers. A vast variety of specialized lists for both business and consumer marketing use is listed. Names can be qualified by *direct mail* and/or *outbound telemarketing*.

- *Networking*—other (noncompetitive) sales reps may be a good source of leads; many organizations (such as Salesmen With A Purpose or SWAP) exist to help in this activity.

- *Public speaking*—depending on what you are selling, public appearances can generate good leads. (See Chapter 34.)

- *Referral sources*—depending on what you are marketing, and particularly for professional practices, this may be your single most productive prospecting tool. Examples are real estate brokers, bankers, lawyers, and accountants.

- *Sales consultants*—hire a specialist to compile a list of prospects for you.

- *Advertise*—run ads in specialized business and consumer media to gather requests for information, demonstrations, and sales presentations.

- *The Internet*—as with traditional media, use the Internet to obtain responses from qualified prospects. (See Chapter 27.)

- *Cold-calling*—often a waste of time, but can be used in high-density areas for relatively low-ticket items. The term is also applied to telemarketing solicitation, where (depending on the offer) a success rate of only one percent or less is expected.

BASIC FUNCTIONAL STRATEGIES

These are the names by which basic personal selling strategies go:

- *Order-getting strategy*—the proactive strategy suggested by the classic model described earlier in this chapter as "The Strategic Steps in Selling."

- *Order-taking strategy*—reactive or passive strategy suggested by a distribution strategy that involves *rack-jobbers* and *vending machine* (or *automatic merchandising*) *operatives* (called "outside order-takers") and retail sales that involve *retail sales clerks* (called "inside order-takers").

- *Missionary sales* (or *detail rep*) *strategy*—where reps do not ask for orders but provide information and introduce new products, as in the case of personnel from pharmaceutical companies who call on physicians.

- *Sales engineering strategy*—deployment of technically oriented reps who often have engineering degrees and who call on corporate engineers, among others.

TYPES OF SALES PRESENTATIONS

Here are the types of sales presentations that should be considered strategically:

- *Canned sales presentation*—a packaged pitch, often in the form of a recorded slide or video presentation where the rep acts only as projectionist.

- *Formula sales presentation*—step-by-step, often memorized presentation, presented live but too often delivered in a manner suggesting a student reciting a poem.

- *Stimulus-response sales presentation*—here the rep tries various proven actions and phrases to discover the prospect's "hot button." In retail this is sometimes referred to as *suggestive selling* and can be as simple as a waiter carrying a bottle of wine and glasses to your table to suggest what might be a pleasant complement to your meal.
- *Adaptive sales presentation*—where the rep responds to feedback from the prospect and adjusts the pitch accordingly. This type of presentation is dependent on the rep asking lots of questions and paying close attention to the answers.
- *Need-satisfaction sales presentation*—also requires reps to ask questions and be attentive not only to spoken answers but also nonverbal signals that may suggest what prospects need or want.
- *Consultative sales presentation*—the approach suggested in the next two sections, which also involves asking questions and listening to answers, but has a slightly different set of objectives.

RELATIONSHIP MARKETING STRATEGY

One of the newer and more popular concepts you may have encountered has been dubbed *relationship marketing*. I think this is an excellent term because it gets right to the heart of what sales management, personal selling, and customer or client service should be: a solid, win-win relationship between customer and marketing representative. Good selling today, related to the market strategy called *retention*, means building customer and client relationships. That can be presented as a four-step process.

- Identifying customer, client, and prospect needs.
- Matching your products or services to those needs.
- Communicating pertinent information so that the customer or prospect is honestly and ethically persuaded to take the course of action recommended.
- Following up to keep the customer satisfied.

RELATIONSHIP SELLING STRATEGY

The key features of relationship *selling* (as distinguished from relationship *marketing*) are these:

- The role of the marketing or sales representative is that of a *consultant* and the strategy is called "*consultative.*"
- The role of the customer or prospect is that of a person to be *served*, not a lead to be *sold*.
- The marketing or sales representative does not use high-pressure tactics or engage in classic hard-sell behavior, but conscientiously seeks to *identify* and tries to *satisfy* the prospective customer's needs.

- The representative's emphasis is on providing *useful information* and negotiating the best solution to the prospect's problems, rather than engaging in psychological manipulation.
- In turn, the customer reciprocates the salesperson's attentiveness by providing information that can be useful to the salesperson in making future proposals and closing future sales. This aspect of the personal selling relationship has been aptly dubbed *partnership selling* or *partnering*.

NOT EASY

None of these aims is easy to achieve. Nor can your sales representatives be expected to adhere to this code of honor and high ethical standards if you put them on tight quotas or entice them with juicy commissions on contracts. They have to be convinced from the start that their long-term interests and the interests of the company are jointly linked to a low-key, courteous, helpful *relationship* strategy.

They must be encouraged to realize that good relationships will mean repeat business, larger volume of business, and referrals of new prospects. They also have to see proof that the company is behind the relationship marketing philosophy in the form of high-quality advertising, direct mail, printed materials, newsletters, and other tangible evidence of support for their efforts.

OTHER STRATEGIES

Here are several other strategies for selling:

- *Direct marketing strategy*—mentioned in connection with distribution, with *direct marketing*, the entire process of persuading a prospect to buy—including the sales presentation and the close—is accomplished at one time. This may be done via the Internet, mail order catalogues, or direct response advertising in a variety of media.
- *Self-service strategy*—popular in chain stores, customers pick products personally, check them out, and pay for them through a clerk or by themselves electronically with the help of bar code scanners.
- *Moderate-service strategy*—customers in stores that use this strategy are not approached by sales personnel but can find clerks to assist if they need help.
- *Full-service strategy*—found in higher level retail establishments where sales representatives greet customers and help them choose merchandise. Particularly important in fashion boutiques and jewelry stores.
- *Systems selling strategy*—is where a line of products is presented as working together, the implication being that those with the same brand name will function more efficiently and/or economically together than a combination of components from different companies. The FTC is leery of this strategy, as it has hinted at

what it has termed "monopolistic practice," even when there are several competitors in the field.

- *Team selling* (or *conference selling*) *strategy*—is sometimes used with systems selling. Here several different specialists from the vendor company make the sales presentation to the buyer. For example, in addition to the lead sales rep (often titled the Sales Manager), distribution, customer service, and technical support personnel would be included. This is good when an industrial "buying center" is responsible for decision-making. When consumer packaged-goods marketers present with this strategy to resellers (distributors and/or dealers), representatives from the vendor company may also include executives with advertising, sales promotion, and even public relations responsibilities to discuss marketing communications support.

- *Seminar selling strategy*—is where the marketer conducts a presentation akin to an educational program for the customer company's technical staff and other buying decision-makers. This strategy is often used in selling to government agencies and is also employed by professional practices, real estate brokers, and the like to consumer audiences.

- *Add-on* (or *tie-in*) *sale strategy*—when the salesperson gets an order, he or she tries to add something to it, such as a camera bag with the purchase of a camera, or a cup of coffee to accompany a slice of apple pie.

- *Upgrade* (or *selling up*) *strategy*—after the close, offer something slightly better for a little more money, such as rosewood dashboard trim in a new car, or a two-year subscription instead of one-year for only 40 percent more. A very important strategy in *fundraising*.

- *Cross-selling strategy*—when an organization has a broad product mix, they can try to sell customers for one type of product on another, unrelated type of product. For example, a company that offers window tinting for offices could try to interest the buyer in the installation of new window shades which are part of their product mix. More common today is the selling of service agreements with initial purchase of products; this is often related to *suggestive selling*, mentioned earlier.

The next chapter deals with strategies for overcoming objections and closing sales.

Chapter 32

Objection and Closing Strategies

Because the purpose of personal selling is to persuade people to make a buying decision, it is only reasonable that important parts of the process should be to *overcome objections* and *ask for the order*. There are several strategic ways to do those things.

OVERCOMING OBJECTIONS

Many people are afraid to make buying decisions, and some will even invent fictitious reasons for refusing to buy or postponing the sale. Here are basic strategies sales reps use:

- *Accept the objection*—when the prospect has a valid objection, sometimes further discussion will prove it to be relatively unimportant or will lead to a solution.
- *Agree and negate* (or *neutralize*)—the rep may say, "You are absolutely right, and several other customers have been concerned about that feature, but they have found the cost savings more than compensated for it."
- *Acknowledge and convert*—often used with price objections, as when the prospect says the product costs too much and the rep replies that, although the price is high, a cheaper equivalent will last only half as long, proving to be more expensive in the long run.
- *Change perspective*—as when a prospect balks at price, the rep might ask, "Which is more important to you, cost or *value*?"
- *Postpone*—the rep says, "I'll get to that in just a minute, if you'll be so kind as to bear with me."
- *Deny*—when the objection is based on misinformation, disinformation, and perhaps competitive lies, it should be addressed strongly and immediately—but, of course, courteously and diplomatically.

- *Ignore*—a strategy not recommended, but used when a rep may feel that the objection is not particularly important.
- *Multiply the savings and divide the costs*—as noted in connection with advertising strategies, *savings* are important to people today—especially when they are *multiplied*, so that a $9,500 monthly saving could be expressed, "Your company can save up to $570,000 over the next five years." And, similarly, when there are objections to costs, *divide* them, so that a $300,000 purchase could be expressed as "your annual investment of only a little over $800 a day."
- *Action close*—do something to force the prospect to agree to the sale, as when the printer's rep says to the ad manger, "Let's go see your production manager and see if he doesn't agree we're the best shop for this job."
- *Let's call right now*—sometimes prospects will put off buying decisions by saying that their boss must make the final decision. This variation of an *action close* is used by some high-pressure types who believe it often pays to say "Let's call him [or her] right now" and even presume to pick up the prospect's telephone and ask for the extension. Pushy but, when you have nothing to lose, perhaps worth a try.

CLOSING STRATEGIES

If you have selected one or more *sales promotion* strategies as motivators for prospects and customers to make buying decisions, consider them first in your close. They are the added inducement that can tip a buying decision in your favor, noted in Chapter 28 as the "mippie."

In addition, here are some proven rhetorical closing techniques. This is by no means an exhaustive list, but includes those that I believe are the most commonly practiced and successful strategies among sales professionals.

- *Trial close*—this can be thought of as a pre-close test, or it might turn into the actual close. A classic example is "I think I can have this order delivered by Wednesday; would that suit you?"
- *Deliberate misunderstanding close*—perhaps a bit devious, as when the rep knows the prospect favors a file cabinet in beige and says "I'm not sure I have this in *brown*." When corrected that she wants beige, he replies that they *do* have just what she wants that could be delivered Wednesday.
- *Direct close* (or *"ask for the order"*)—the most forthright strategy. An example might be, "Well, now you know all about my firm and our services, so if you have no further questions, will you please sign this agreement?" (Note the tactic of avoiding the intimidating word "contract.") A little more subtle in business marketing is simply to ask for a purchase order number.
- *Assumptive close*—a strategy that might seem a bit pushy to some, but one that can work well for all sales people when handled with style. The representative *assumes* that the prospect agrees to the terms that have been discussed and simply

provides a choice incidental to the primary buying decision. An example would be, "Will monthly billing for your lease be most convenient for you?"

- *Either/or close*—a form of the *assumptive close* that puts the decision in the form of a choice, such as, "Ms. Jones, it appears that your budget this year will only allow you to take advantage of my proposed Service A *or* Service B. Which of the two do you need most at present?"

- *Minor question close*—also *assumptive* but related to something of relatively small importance, as in "Don't you think brown leather upholstery would look great in your new Mercedes?"

- *Eliminate the loser close*—a popular technique in retail sales. When the prospect is looking at two portable radios, for example, the salesperson might say, "There is a big difference in performance, as reflected in their prices; this one lists for $129.95, and this one that's not nearly as good costs $89.95. Now, if I said you could have *either one* for only $109.95, which one *wouldn't* you take?" (This also relies on a $20 discount, of course, to sweeten the deal.)

- *Emergency* (or *urgency*) *close*—a strategy you might have encountered at a car dealership or furniture store. For example, let's say you've zeroed in on a particular sofa you like, but just can't quite decide if you want to look somewhere else for alternatives, and the sales representative says, "If you're really interested in that sofa, you probably should make up your mind *right now*; a guy who said he was going to buy it this afternoon just drove into our parking lot—and this is the *last one* we have in stock." An accounting firm might use such a technique in March when a contact person could say, "As you appreciate, we get very busy around this time of year, and we are nearly booked for 1040 work; however, if you'd like to retain us *now*, I know we can fit you in—but I'm really not sure we can oblige next week."

- *Coming event close*—a popular variation on the basic *emergency close* whereby the prospect is told that a particular item will be discontinued next month, or that a price increase has been scheduled for the near future. Again, whatever you are selling, you should be *honest*—but these two strategies let the prospect know that postponing a decision to buy could mean disappointment.

- *Answer-a-question-with-a-question close*—actually, a selling method that can be used through the entire selling process that works like this for a close: The prospect appears nearly sold and asks, "Do you think you could deliver the merchandise by the end of the week?" The rep replies, "If I guarantee delivery by the end of the week will you approve the order today?" Any special offer, such as a discount, credit terms, operator training, and so on can be used as the basis of the rep's question.

- *Secondary question close*—a variation of the *assumptive close*, the radio sales rep concludes her presentation of reach, frequency, gross rating points, and audience composition by saying, "It's clear, isn't it, that with this schedule you'll be reaching exactly the kinds of people you want often enough to pull them in? [without a pause] Are you sure you want to run 30-second spots, or do you think 60s would give us time to be more persuasive?" This example, by the way, also includes an *upgrade* (or *selling up*) strategy.

- *Special offer* (or *gift* or *something-for-nothing*) *close*—a strategy you might think of as selective sales promotion. Commonly a special offer involves additional products or services as part of a package deal or fast delivery if the prospect agrees to sign now. Or it could involve special discounts, credit, or billing concessions. For a professional organization it could also involve such a promise as, "Mr. Brown, if you agree today to become our client, I can assign Dan Steen, our top tax attorney, to your case."

- *Restatement of objective close*—when the rep has questioned well and listened carefully to discover the customer's objective, that can be restated as being achieved by the product or service, and the sale closed.

- *Summary of benefits close*—a strategy that works nicely with what is sometimes called the *series of yeses*, or the *one-more-yes close*, where the salesperson gets the prospect used to saying *yes* to such questions as "It's important that you stay within your budget, isn't it?" and asks for the order with the last question. As the term *summary of benefits* indicates, the rep lists the product benefits in the form of questions and gets the prospect to agree that each is desirable. At the end of the list, the prospect should have nowhere to turn except to become a customer.

- *Ben Franklin close*—attributed to the great man himself, this involves drawing a line down the center of a sheet of paper or a T shape and making a list of *pros* on the left and a corresponding list of *cons* on the right with regard to a purchase. When prospects see that the positive factors outnumber the negative factors, they will presumably be persuaded to buy.

- *"Reductio ad absurdum" close*—as with classical logic, the rep reduces to absurd the possibility of *not* buying the proposed product. Often this involves painting a word picture similar to the *absence of product* advertising strategy. This close can also be used with the objection-countering strategies noted previously in this chapter as *multiply the savings* and *divide the costs*.

- *Case history close*—describe in detail how a sale to a similar customer resulted in desired benefits. Smart marketing companies write up and distribute case histories to their field sales people as well as to trade magazines and for use in advertisements, and the most successful reps develop their own. Often the most persuasive pitch involves showing how the product or service worked for another, similar customer. It's somewhat related to the *bandwagon* strategy for advertising and public relations.

- *Testimonial* (or *endorsement* or *higher authority*) *close*—this involves a satisfied customer who is respected in the industry whom the rep can telephone from the prospect's office and who will discuss the rep's product or service with the prospect. One of the great benefits of *relationship selling* to sales reps is that it gives them this splendid opportunity to have customers close sales for them.

- *Negative close*—based on a reverse appeal to pride. A prospect is considering the purchase of an automobile and appears excited by its style and features. The salesperson says, "I don't know if this car is right for you; it's pretty pricey, and a lot of people can't qualify for the financing. Are you sure you can?" Being careful not to insult the prospect, the salesperson aims here at offering a *challenge* to the prospect to apply for a car loan to buy the model he wants.

- *One good reason close*—learned from a friend who is the epitome of the genteel and dignified salesman. He has made a career of selling corporate aircraft, which cost millions of dollars apiece—and the choices for which are numerous and varied—so the decision to buy is always difficult for prospects to make. When my friend has provided all pertinent information and has summarized benefits, he simply asks, "Well, Mr. Gates, can you give me *one good reason* why you should not give me a check for $750,000 *right now?*" Delivered respectfully, such a question in such a situation has appeal to intelligent buyers. And this man has closed a lot of sales with this simple and succinct strategy.

- *The puppydog close*—a strategy with a particularly appealing name which is derived from the fact that once people take a puppydog home they are unlikely to return it. The prospect for a new car can't quite make up his mind, and the salesman says, "Listen, you don't have to decide right now. It's Friday and we won't miss this car. Just take it home for the weekend, drive it up in the mountains with your wife, and see if it doesn't do just what you want it to do." (Of course, the prospect must be a good risk and not likely to abscond with the car.) A puppydog close for a professional organization might also mesh with a sampling strategy and go like this: "Let me send Mr. Biggs, our computer systems expert, to work with you for the next week at no cost or obligation on your part. At the end of that time, you can see for yourself how our services can smooth out your operations. And, if for any reason you're not completely satisfied, that will be the end of it, and you will not have spent a single penny."

- *Sympathy close*—clearly an act of desperation, as when a rep says, "You've got to give me this order; I'm three months behind on my rent, my kid needs braces, and my wife is terribly ill." Pathetic and even more pitiful when amplified by floods of tears.

- *Negative option close*—developed in the field of mail order and familiar to nearly every consumer today. (Not the same as *negative close* mentioned previously.) Customers place an initial order and, if they do not subsequently refuse, their silence constitutes agreement to purchase future products. This is a common book-club and music-club selling strategy. In business marketing this type of on-going buying arrangement is called "*till-forbid*," or agreement that the seller should keep sending product until told to stop. And in retailing it may be called *automatic reorder*. *Positive option*, of course, means the opposite—that action must be taken by the customer for every order.

- *Do-something close*—also proven in mail order, the prospect is required to perform some action such as punching out a token and slipping it in a slot. Mail order experts claim that response tests show significantly higher returns when this strategy is creatively applied. It can also be adapted to face-to-face selling situations, and is a natural when a *product demonstration* is the key to a sale.

- *Investment of time strategy*—covers both objections and closing, and is based on the assumption that people (especially busy people) hate to waste time. Therefore, some sales trainers urge salespeople to take lots of time in their sales meetings, thereby causing prospects to invest a great deal of their own time in the sales process. In theory, even if doubts persist, the prospect will nevertheless sign rather than endure the frustration of having wasted time. This raises a serious ethical question, and also makes one wonder at the likelihood of repeat sales to customers closed in this manner.

CLOSING AS CLIMAX

Closing is the climax of the person-to-person persuasion process. It can be as thrilling as hooking a big trout, or crossing the finish line first.

Although some of the strategies suggested here might be employed by unscrupulous marketers as psychological sleight of hand, I urge once again honesty, candor, and that win-win philosophy that is now being called *relationship selling*. Linked with skillful application of your other marketing strategies, closing sales will provide the rewards you honestly deserve.

Chapter 33

Customer Service Strategies and Techniques

Customer (or client) service (also called *customer relations* and *customer support*) no longer means merely having a complaint department. I think of this important marketing function strategically as a combination of pricing, distribution, and public relations.

Many were the mass merchandisers years ago who adopted a "to hell with the customer" philosophy—and failed. Today we see popularity of the *retention* market strategy and the *relationship* marketing and selling strategies, which lead to the following customer service strategies in preference to the old "*caveat emptor.*"

BASIC STRATEGIES

These are basic customer service strategies:

- *The customer is always right*—not always the best strategy in view of the incidence today of consumer fraud (that is, fraud committed against companies and retailers by their customers), but it's often a good one to keep in mind as an ideal.
- *No-questions-asked exchange*—probably one of the reasons for the relatively recent success of the big discount stores and the boom in mail order sales. Years ago exchanging faulty merchandise was an enormous hassle and required shrewd negotiating skills and often threats of legal action by the dissatisfied customer. Today many retailers realize that the goodwill that is the foundation of repeat business can be obtained by fair—even generous—exchange policies.
- *Your money cheerfully refunded*—mentioned as *refund* in connection with sales promotion strategies, has made dealing with discounters and other retailers much more pleasant for consumers in recent years and has contributed significantly to

American consumers' eagerness to spend their money both in stores and through direct response (mail order) and thereby build our economy to the envy of the world.

- *Sufficient lead-time strategy*—in the context of "replenishment time" or "order cycle time," good customer service requires products and services to be available to customers when they want them. Such logistics strategies as *just-in-time (JIT)*, however, may jeopardize sufficient lead time through circumstances beyond the marketer's control.
- *Fast response strategy*—just as customers want products and services when they need them, they tend to demand immediate response to requests for information and inquiries that include requests for proposals and/or quotations (RFP/RFQ). Some organizations establish a 24-hour deadline for customer service responses.
- *Accurate response strategy*—some organizations make their lowest ranking personnel responsible for customer response. This is foolish and wasteful of opportunity since an ignorant clerk can quickly destroy potential for big sales, and the boss seldom if ever is even aware of the loss.
- *Courtesy strategy*—like the *thank-you* strategy mentioned elsewhere, a strategy based on *courtesy* to customers can make transactions pleasant for all parties involved, build good will, encourage repeat business, and create long-term customer loyalty. Like *accurate response*, this strategy requires careful screening of prospective employees to see they are psychologically and culturally suited to being courteous, and also training and suitable rewards for good performance to assure that they consistently apply the principles of civil business behavior.

COMMUNICATIONS TECHNIQUES

Here are some ideas you might wish to consider in connection with your strategic planning for customer service:

- Just as you do in all your marketing efforts, have your people try always to look at situations from your customers' and prospects' points of view.
- Welcome people graciously when they visit your premises.
- Train employees to smile.
- Depending on your industry, address customers and prospects by title and surname unless told by them to be less formal.
- Have staff wear nametags, and be properly attired and neatly groomed.
- Have employees refer to one another with respect.
- Respect your customers' confidences.
- Don't discuss politics or religion.
- Depending on your target markets, hire staff who speak more than English to accommodate your customers.
- Provide a suggestion box for customer use.

- Include personalized covering letters or notes on all information sent to customers and prospects.
- See that your personnel identify themselves by name and company affiliation when they telephone, fax, or e-mail customers.
- Think carefully about whether you really want highly automated telephone answering equipment that requires callers to punch many buttons before they can get an answer to a question or speak to a live person.
- Don't leave callers on hold without checking back to apologize for delay.
- Have your executives place their own telephone calls rather than employing the old ego-boosting technique of having a subordinate "Get Mr. Harris on the phone for me," and then requiring Mr. Harris to wait for the caller to get on the line.
- Do not allow employees ever to hang up in anger.
- Train your people to explain briefly the reason for their call when requesting that a customer call back.
- Along the same line, direct that your people specify dates and times they will be available to take returned calls.
- Conduct an audit of your organization from time to time. The "mystery shopper" technique is often an enlightening way to learn how your customers are being treated. Or telephone your office yourself anonymously and see how you are treated.
- If you don't already have one, start a customer relations training program for new employees, and reminder sessions for all.
- Discharge employees who are careless and rude to customers.
- Provide customers with clearly written warrantees or guarantees. (See Chapter 15, "Offer Strategies," for more on this subject.)
- Keep your facilities neat and clean.
- Provide adequate parking for visitors.
- Minimize the amount of paperwork you ask customers to do.
- Consider appropriate music for facilities, elevators, and telephone hold time.
- Be courteous in your billing procedures.
- Encourage your sales managers occasionally to accompany reps on their customer calls.
- Acknowledge mail and electronic communications immediately and then follow up when time permits with detailed information. For example, an immediate e-mail response might read, "We received your e-mail and will have an answer for you in two days. Thank you for thinking of us."
- Do all you can to keep channels of communication open between your personnel and your customers.

Chapter 34

Presentation and Public Speaking Strategies

TYPES OF PRESENTATIONS

Much of the higher-impact marketing communications that you do probably will involve what appears here under the category of presentations and public speaking.

This includes but is not necessarily limited to the following:

- Executive speeches
- Speeches supported by film or video projection (often called "visualized speeches")
- Slide shows with live presenter(s)
- Electronic projection (such as PowerPoint) with live presenter
- Presentations with chalkboard, pad, or whiteboard
- Demonstrations (usually with a product)
- Seminars
- Staff meetings
- Other business meetings
- Slide/tape presentations
- Electronic audiovisual presentations
- Motion picture presentations
- Videotape presentations
- Audiotape presentations
- Person-to-person (sales) presentations

NATURE OF THE SPEECH

The executive speech offers principals in organizations unique opportunities to gain status, achieve credibility, and win recognition for themselves, and for their organization as well.

Whether supported by film or video projection or not, the executive speech is usually presented by a high-level person with the credentials necessary to address the topic. The speaker is assigned a topic or chooses one of interest to a particular audience. The topic may be controversial but is at least provocative and should be one on which a clear and strong position can be taken.

Many executives today hire professional or semi-professional speechwriters or subordinates to do the planning, research, and writing for them. Others feel they can do a far better job for themselves. It's really not difficult to write your own speech when you start with an abbreviated version of the creative work plan that appears in Appendix 8.

Begin, as you should for other types of marketing communications writing, by cultivating a *positive attitude* toward your prospective audience. And then apply the index card approach to organization. As with other types of writing, you may prefer a different technique, but I have found that—especially for speechwriting—putting each of your key ideas on index cards and then arranging them in logical order is the easiest, most convenient, most thorough, and most flexible technique.

ITEMS TO INCLUDE

Here are the basic items you should consider and record:

1. *Name of organization or group to which you'll speak.* It's also a good idea to note and fix firmly in mind the name of the city where you'll be; the name of the hotel, club, or other facility in which your speech will take place; and the names of the event program manager, and other principal participants. Especially if you develop a heavy speaking schedule involving a lot of travel, it's easy to think that you're in Rochester and not Syracuse, or that the association president is Jim Blinder instead of Tim Bender.

2. *Exact definition of your audience.* People who specialize in public speaking agree that the single most important step in speech preparation and delivery is *audience analysis.* This is much like the discipline of *market segmentation* previously addressed. Be sure you have a detailed description of these people, so you can talk in their terms directly to them about what is likely to interest them.

3. *Specific purpose of your speech.* This may be what *you* want them to do or think, or what *your hosts* want the speech to accomplish. The latter should be laid out for you by the person responsible for programming. If they don't tell

you what they want, be sure to *ask*. If they don't know what they want from you (as is sometimes the case), you are free to develop a topic on your own—but clearly based on your understanding of the audience.

4. *Audience needs, wants, and motives.* This is separated from basic audience analysis because it's important that you concentrate on *what's in it for them.* If you were to have an inappropriate topic suggested to you, you would discuss the matter with the event planners and suggest a better one. For example, if you were an accountant addressing a group of AARP (American Association of Retired Persons) members, you probably would not suggest such a topic as "Tax advantages in purchasing your first home." You might, instead, choose a topic like, "Tax aspects of selling your vacation home."

5. *Why they should do what you want them to do.* Generally speaking, you should neither seek nor accept a speaking engagement that does not have the potential to *benefit your organization.* So, in addition to doing what your hosts want, you will have a kind of *hidden agenda* when you address the group. This personal and professional objective may be something quite simple that you want members of your audience to do, such as to write their Congresspersons about proposed legislation, or even to call your office to discuss a purchase. Be sure to include specific names, addresses, and telephone numbers when you have such an action objective. And remember such unspoken objectives are *for your eyes only.*

6. *Your organization's history.* This is not as important in a speech as it is in an organization brochure, a specialized business publication article, or the like. But you should have the basic facts on hand in case the occasion presents itself to mention them. And you should also prepare a succinct, tightly written script on your background and the organization history for the person who introduces you.

7. *Your manner of doing business.* Look for at least *one* opportunity to drop this discreetly into your speech.

8. *How and why you are better than your competitors.* You would *never* use this as a blatant sales pitch in an executive speech, but market-wise executives have known for years that audiences are remarkably receptive to an anecdote or amusing story that illustrates the superiority of the speaker's organization. Subtlety and understatement—perhaps even a touch of humility or self-effacement—should accompany this tactic.

9. *Information.* This will be the bulk of your speech. Gather as much pertinent information as you reasonably can.

10. *Marketing message.* This may be tricky to handle. Perhaps you want to leave it out entirely, lest you appear to be too self-serving. Certainly, if you do include part or all of your marketing message, be sure that it is done ever so subtly.

You do not need to think of the other six topics of the basic work plan sequence that appear in Appendix 8 for an executive speech. Inclusion of those other items would make your appearance seem too commercial.

STRATEGIES TO ORGANIZE A SPEECH

There are five strategies generally considered first for speech organization. Other refinements of strategy will follow. Decide which of these your speech will be:

- *Topical* (or *categorical*)—present your topics in a logical order.
- *Chronological* (or *sequential*)—consider following the time sequence for topics such as events or explaining a manufacturing process step-by-step.
- *Spatial* (or *geographical*)—present information top-to-bottom, as explaining a company reorganization, or explaining a field sales organization by describing regions east-to-west.
- *Causal*—describe a cause and its effect, which can be different than a *chronological* strategy.
- *Problem-solution*—often a very positive strategy which can lead to a strong conclusion and perhaps a call to action.

HOW TO PLAN A SPEECH

Once your topic has been selected and agreed to by your hosts, rely first on your memory as a source of material to use. The best speeches are those that relate closely to the speaker's own experience and beliefs. Go to a quiet spot, relax, depending on the season and your taste, sip a hot or cold drink (an alcoholic beverage helps some people, but may interfere with the thinking of others), and write down or dictate onto tape all the things you think are appropriate to your subject.

Discuss your topic with associates and other experts in your field and record the most interesting and pertinent of their thoughts.

Transfer the best of your preliminary ideas to index cards—one idea or quote per card.

Then use reference sources, such as some of those listed in Appendix 3, and periodicals of your industry to get specific data (including statistics and authoritative quotes) to document what you have collected. When gathering information from the Internet, be sure sources are reliable, since there is a great deal of misinformation and outright lies presented as fact through that medium. Record your sources exactly so you can provide substantiation if you feel it's necessary or if you are questioned by members of your audience.

As you do this academic-type research, you will probably discover *other* good material that you can use as well. Transcribe the best of that information to index cards, too—again, one idea per card.

Then arrange your cards in the most logical order you can devise, but don't belabor the sorting job at this point. Once that first rough sort is finished, put all your cards aside in a safe place for two to six days.

Your subconscious mind will work on that information without your being aware of it. From time to time, though, over the next several days—often when you least expect it—that mysterious mechanism will hit on an idea. It might be a theme line, perhaps a turn of phrase to express a difficult concept, or an analogy or experience that illustrates and illuminates a point. Your subconscious will cry "Eureka" at the best of its work, and will break through to your conscious mind.

Write down those new ideas on index cards as they occur to you.

When your two- to six-day period of "marinating" of material is complete, take out your cards again, add the new ones with their fresh thoughts, rearrange the deck (perhaps on a large floor), pick the cards up in the sequence that pleases you most, number them in pencil so you can retain the order of your ideas, and now you're prepared to *write a speech*.

HOW TO WRITE A SPEECH

With the wealth of material you have accumulated, the next part of the speechwriting job probably will be to figure out *where to start*. This depends on two major factors: your *objective* and your *audience*. Your objective should remain foremost in your mind as you sequence and develop your points or arguments. But your audience and its interests and values will also affect the sequence of points. This process is called "selective exposure" (more about this in Chapter 40) and involves two strategies:

- If your audience is likely to be *with you*—that is, in sympathy with your position—present your strongest argument *first*, and then support it with other points as you build to your conclusion.
- If your audience is likely to be *against you*, try to "seduce" them by starting with ideas with which they agree, bring in your supporting points, and present your strongest point *last*. The psychology at work here is based on the likelihood that if you present a strong contrary point first, the audience will erect mental barriers and not accept anything you say thereafter.
- Never bury your strongest point or argument in the middle of your speech.

Your opening statement may be dictated by your *selective exposure* strategy. But, if not, *quotations* often serve not only as "ice-breakers," but also to set a tone and a creative direction for the speech.

Most American writers' favorite source is *Bartlett's Familiar Quotations*, published by Little, Brown and Company. Use the index to discover quotations that contain key words you might wish to use, both as an opener, and also sprinkled throughout your speech. More of a British slant can be found in the equally excellent *Oxford Dictionary of Quotations*, published by Oxford University Press. For business speeches, *Thoughts on the Business of Life*, by the late Malcolm Forbes, is a tremendous asset in the creative process. Numerous other sources are available, some arranged by topic as well as author.

Alternatively, you could seek material from books specifically edited to help public speakers, as well as collections of anecdotes and (maybe) jokes. Like humor in advertisements, jokes in speeches can fail and embarrass a speaker; so, if you wish to use this popular technique for warming up and softening up an audience, try your material out on a representative sample of the audience first. Few aspects of an executive speech can be more devastating than a deathly silence after a punchline.

The page format you should use for straight speeches presents the text word-for-word, in a point-size large enough for the speaker to read easily. Some executives use solid capital letters, but normal upper and lower case is easier to read. Directions such as "(PAUSE)" or "(WAIT FOR RESPONSE)" will help pace the speech and minimize the chance of a speaker squelching audience response by hurrying to the next topic.

Speeches supported by film or video projection ("visualized speeches") should indicate slide changes or when film or video footage should run (called "cuing") so that the speaker does not have to tell the projectionist "next slide, please"—always a distraction for the audience.

VISUALIZING THE SPEECH

To visualize a speech, you really should try to start thinking graphically from the start. As your ideas develop, record appropriate visual support along with the words to be spoken so that, when you actually write the script, you can include those elements or suggestions for your visualization.

PowerPoint software makes visualizing a speech relatively easy, but the graphics have become visual clichés. In addition, too many speakers just list key words on their visuals—far too many of them as a rule—which insults more than enlightens the audience, and takes attention away from the speaker.

To develop a really creative presentation, you may have on hand slides or film or video footage which can form the foundation for the visual dimension of your presentation. Or you can shoot new material yourself, or hire a photographer or cinematographer to do the necessary work. You could also consider other sources of illustrative and graphic material, including stock houses and libraries.

It's rather a big job to put together an original, quality audiovisual show, whatever the format, so you might want to seek the help of a professional AV or video producer. The better ones will be listed in your Yellow Pages and also found in creative service directories at your public library.

GOOD STRATEGIC PRACTICES

Here are some basics for public appearance:

- *Put your best foot forward*—consistently groom and dress yourself and your representatives appropriately and appealingly. Don't allow yourself to be photographed or even seen in an unflattering situation. Franklin D. Roosevelt, one of the world's all-time great PR practitioners, was paralyzed from the chest down by polio and moved in a wheelchair, or for very short distances on crutches after he had been locked upright by braces. He had a blanket order that he was *never* to be photographed with either of those symbols of his handicap visible. PR experts agree that few Americans even knew that Roosevelt was handicapped during his presidency and that if the public had known, he would not have been able to win election.

- *Take the floor commandingly*—a strategy essential to your personal and professional public relations. If you are not comfortable with public speaking, join Toastmasters, take a public speaking course, or hire a private coach. Study how to respond to media interview questions. Consider taking a course that involves your performances being videotaped and critiqued by media relations specialists. Even the best of speakers can improve their style and delivery with the right training and conscientious practice.

- *Tell them what they want to hear*—we have all seen clearly in recent years that this is what gets people elected to Congress and to the presidency of the United States. As long as it is not used in a deliberately deceptive fashion, telling your target market what they want to hear can work for you, too. Discover what your market(s) and other public(s) think is important and what their position on the subject is, and concentrate in your public appearances and in your written communications on feeding that material back to them. If what you have to say is contrary to what you honestly *believe*, though, you should consider redefining your publics to include those who agree with you. That way, you can be both effective and honest.

- *Deliver a strong conclusion*—perhaps with a call to action. And, as with other forms of marketing communications, when you have said what needs to be said, *stop*.

UNETHICAL PUBLIC SPEAKING STRATEGIES

Most often used by politicians and leaders of special-interest groups, here are presentation and public speaking strategies to *avoid*. Some of these have been mentioned in Chapter 29, "Public Relations," because PR and speechmaking are so closely related.

- *Faulty causal reasoning*—as the term implies, this is a relationship without logic. For example an anti-gun advocate might state that a majority of suicides involve handguns and conclude that by outlawing handguns we could eliminate suicide as a cause of death.

- *Red herring strategy*—the speaker uses a factor unrelated to the argument to distract the audience.
- *Name-calling strategy*—which may also include *stereotyping*, also mentioned in connection with advertising creative strategies.
- *Stacking the deck* (or *card-stacking*) *strategy*—where only *one* side of an argument is presented, and then often in a selective fashion. Today a balanced perspective tends to be more credible and hence more persuasive.
- *Straw man strategy*—where a weak, artificial antagonist is created, and then demolished like a straw man burned in ancient times to remove a curse.
- *Misquoting strategy*—deliberately false attribution is common in both business and politics, but even more common is taking an actual phrase *out of context* that misrepresents a position.
- *Glittering generalities strategy*—this is the "pie in the sky" rhetoric for which devious politicians are famous and which includes grandiose promises and extravagant statements that are a form of *hyperbole*.
- *Ridicule strategy*—which often involves *irony* and overt *sarcasm*. Frequently used by politicians to demean their opponents. This strategy has no place in ethical free market competition.

TIPS FOR A SUCCESSFUL PRESENTATION

When it comes time for you to deliver your speech or your presentation, here are several suggestions to help make things run smoothly:

1. Chances are that you know far more about your topic than anyone in your audience, so approach your presentation with complete confidence and the self-assurance of the expert that you are.

2. Except for formal policy statements, and to emphasize that you are quoting a source, do not read a script verbatim. Instead, put key words, phrases, and quotes on sequentially numbered index cards, and use them as reminders if you don't work from a word-for-word script. Memorized speeches tend to have a "canned" quality that bores most audiences, and completely impromptu speeches risk skipping important points and well-chosen phrases.

3. Rehearse your presentation before the delivery date. At least two complete run-throughs are essential. More practice will probably make you even better. And rehearse *aloud*, in a tone of voice like that which you plan to use on the show date. This will improve your performance, minimize the glitches that will surely occur if you are not well rehearsed, and also allow you to check the exact running time so you can add or delete material if you're not hitting your time allocation. If you can, have someone listen to your delivery and comment on whether your pace is satisfactory, whether you are projecting your voice well, and whether your posture, eye contact, and general presence convey confidence.

4. Best of all, videotape your speech and critique yourself.

5. If possible, visit the site of the presentation, and even rehearse in the presentation room if you can. Check to see whether you need a public address system,

whether a lectern is provided if you need one, and whether it has a functioning reading light so you can see your script or notes in the dark.

6. Make sure that what you put on your visual aids can be seen at the back of the room and by everyone in the audience—even to the far right and left.

7. At the time of the presentation, dress as becomes your status. It is better to be dressed *more stylishly* than the audience than to be underdressed. Remember, you have to win their confidence and respect *immediately* for your speech to be well received. In addition, grooming and attire are important cues to your audience as to how seriously *you* are taking your subject—and hence how seriously they are to take what you have to say. People who specialize in public speaking generally agree that *navy blue* is the suit, jacket, or dress color that best communicates both authority and sincerity for both men and women.

8. Approach the platform or the front of the room positively and energetically. Some motivational speakers actually *sprint* to the platform when they are introduced. This conveys enthusiasm and excitement, and inclines the audience to be eager to hear what is said.

9. Acknowledge the person who introduced you, and then take a moment to establish eye contact with members of the audience. Greet them without looking at your script or notes, and establish by your bearing that *you* are now in charge of the proceedings. Some very successful speakers give the audience a big smile in those first crucial moments to make friends as quickly as possible.

10. If you are a truly excellent raconteur, you might try to loosen up the audience with a bit of humor. More often than not, though, stale jokes and "a funny thing happened to me on my way here" embarrass audience and speaker alike. Well done, though, a good story or tasteful and *pertinent* gag often proves a good ice-breaker.

11. Use of a lectern gives you a bit of cover, something to hang onto, and a place to rest your index cards out of sight of the audience—so use one if it helps you. On the other hand, a lectern creates a *barrier* between you and your audience, so move away from it as often as possible.

12. If you plan to use a public address system, check it *before* the audience arrives. Do not wait until your introduction is complete and then tap the microphone and deliver that popular and idiotic line, "Testing, 1, 2, 3." If you do not use a mike, adjust your voice to the size of the room and the number of people there.

13. Get right to your task of communicating with every member of your audience. Do not spend a lot of time on introduction and background of your subject. Make sure your audience understands your purpose and what you are going to tell them from the very beginning. It will greatly enhance their attention, comprehension, and recall of your remarks.

14. Adjust your tone and manner to the mood of the occasion. For example, an announcement to your assembled employees that you are cutting staff by 30 percent requires a different tone than an announcement of a handsome year-end bonus.

15. Speak from your diaphragm, through your mouth rather than your nose, and feel your voice reaching out to the far wall of the room. If you are projecting well, you should be able to detect a slight echo of your voice which indicates that you can be heard by all assembled.

16. Overall, your delivery should not call attention to itself. You want people to remember and perhaps even act upon your message, not to exclaim afterward on what a beautiful voice you have.

17. Move as you speak. Approaching the audience indicates interest and concern. Moving away gives them time to reflect on what you have said. Retreats are therefore good times for a brief silence to allow a point to register.

18. Use your body as well as your hands and arms, eyes, and head to emphasize points and to indicate transitions. Make all of your gestures firm and emphatic. Decisiveness of movement conveys confidence and enhances your personal credibility.

19. The larger the room and the more numerous the audience, the louder your voice and the bigger your gestures must be. Remember that screen actors can whisper and use subtle facial expressions, but stage actors need strong voices and broad movements to convey the same sorts of things. The more people in your audience, the louder you will have to speak because bodies and clothing absorb sound.

20. Move along quickly from one topic to the next. And when you have made your final point, *stop*. It is anticlimactic and boring for an audience to hear a well-made point watered down in subsequent repetition.

21. Well-executed visual aids can greatly enhance your audience's understanding of your message. Slides, overhead transparencies, white boards, a pad on which you can write with a felt marker, or even a chalkboard can each be used to your benefit.

22. When you use visual aids, be sure you have checked them out thoroughly *in advance*, not only at your office or at home, but *on-site, immediately before your presentation*. If you use PowerPoint, have transparencies and an overhead projector handy as back-up. Allow yourself the advantage of correcting or overcoming problems *before* you are up in front of your audience. A few minutes of preparation and thorough run-throughs can keep you from looking like a fool.

23. Be particularly conscious of how long you are expected to speak—or until what time. Use the minutes you have efficiently, and *do not exceed* your allotted time.

VISUAL AIDS

The adage runs, "One picture is worth a thousand words." And that is true with regard to speeches and presentations as well as printed materials. People find a speaker's message more interesting, grasp the meaning better, and remember it longer when visual aids are used. We live in a highly visual age. Motion pictures, television, and videos have trained us to expect visualization of material presented to us. The advantages of visual aids, then, are *interest, clarity*, and *retention*.

TYPES OF VISUAL AIDS

There are several types of visual aids from which you can choose in turning a simple speech into a dramatic *audiovisual* experience for your audience. The most effective are these:

- *Objects*—although many objects are too large to be taken along, others are too small to be seen clearly, and some (like a famous painting in an art museum) just might not be available to you. But you can use simple things like a tennis racquet, food, an article of clothing, and so on.
- *Models*—which can be both smaller than the original they represent, or larger. For example, a model sailing ship and a model of an oxygen molecule. Some models can be full-size, like medical models showing the internal organs.
- *Photographs*—good and credible visual support, but photographic prints must be enlarged sufficiently to be seen clearly by the entire audience. Naturally, there is a significant cost associated with photo prints, but their impact can often justify it—particularly since the room does not have to be darkened for them to be seen, unlike most projected images.
- *Drawings*—diagrams and sketches are sometimes good alternatives to photographs. And they can be as inexpensive as you wish. Useful ready-made drawings include posters and maps.
- *Slides*—35mm slides are an economical, versatile, and effective way to present visual information. Not only photographs from life, but mock-ups, charts, and key words can dramatically amplify the points of your presentation. You can advance (or reverse) them at any speed you want, unless you choose to have the sequence controlled by tape or a computer. Set-up of equipment can take time but is usually worth the effort.
- *Movies and videos*—very powerful additions to almost any presentation. Color, sound, and motion add an exciting and credible dimension. Time-lapse, stop-motion, high-speed, and other special effects are also possible. They tend to be expensive to produce, relative to some other types of visual aids, and equipment requires set-up time. But, overall, movies and videos can be an excellent addition to many presentations.
- *Graphs*—can be a great way to simplify and clarify, especially when a lot of numbers are involved. They can be on sheets or boards, or projected. The basic types are probably familiar to you:
  —Line graph—the most common and often used to illustrate trends.
  —Pie chart—good for things like distribution patterns, budgets, and the like.
  —Bar graph—an excellent way to illustrate comparisons.
- *Tables and lists*—useful for summarizing large blocks of information and for presenting steps in a process.

- *Physical demonstration*—where the speaker or an assistant can actually *use* something or physically show the audience how something is done. Not very effective for large groups unless supplemented by simultaneous video display.
- *Flipcharts*—long a popular form of visual aid, flipcharts formally prepared require advance preparation.
- *Newsprint pads*—large sheets of paper, quickly marked on, flipped, or torn off and taped to the wall can aid a lively presentation. No advance preparation is necessary as with flipcharts.
- *Overhead projectors*—transparencies (or cells) can be created from photographic materials, or line images transferred by office copiers. Inexpensive, fast, and easy to use.
- *White boards*—some find these easier to see, and more dramatic than chalkboards. *Photocopying* white boards permits the presenter to make a copy of what is written on the board at the touch of a button. The copy can then be duplicated and handed out to the audience while the white board is erased for the next series of points and copies.
- *Computer-assisted techniques*—more of this is coming! Currently, a wide range of special computer display equipment is available to project computer images. PowerPoint software has made slide-making relatively easy, but too many presentations of this type rely on lists of key words and cliché visuals from Microsoft.

TACTICS FOR USING VISUAL AIDS

Some of these points may duplicate a few points made in other contexts, but are included here for the sake of completeness.

- Your visual aids should be large enough to be seen easily from the farthest point in the room.
- Lines used in charts and diagrams should be dark and heavy to increase clarity. In other words, don't draw your pie chart with a #3 pencil!
- Do not include more details than are needed for your explanation. Keep your visual aids simple and uncluttered to avoid distraction and confusion.
- Put the visual aid in a place where everyone in the audience can see it, and be careful that no one's view is blocked.
- Talk to your *audience*—not to the visual aid.
- Be sure to explain everything on the visual aid, otherwise your audience will wonder about the unexplained details, and you will lose their attention.
- When you read from a visual aid, use exactly the words that appear. Paraphrasing the written word tends to reduce retention and even confuse the audience.
- Do not pass around a series of small objects like snapshots or coins. To avoid distraction, provide one for each person in the audience and place them at each person's seat *before* the presentation so you do not have to waste time passing them out.

- Generally try to avoid distributing printed materials before or during a presentation. It distracts the audience and draws them into searching for your conclusions before you are ready to deliver them.
- If you must hand something out, keep it simple, usually in list form, and with plenty of white space for note-taking.
- Keep visual aids out of sight except when they are being used.
- Do not play with the visual aid. Nervous toying with things is distracting, too.
- Rehearse your speech or presentation, *using the visual aid*, to foresee problems and to get comfortable with the extra activity.
- Remember that careful and deliberate control or your visual aids is as important as control of your spoken words, and control of your audience.

Chapter 35

Tradeshows, Seminars, and Open-House Events

Tradeshows, business shows, conventions, conferences, meetings, and seminars can all be extremely important parts of a strategic marketing program for several reasons:

- People go to such events because they are interested.
- They generally want to learn and make contacts.
- They are not distracted by day-to-day office matters while they are at such events.
- They are a captive audience to some extent.

CARDINAL RULES FOR SHOWS

The larger the show, the more complex the planning and implementation. But, whatever its size, four rules make things work efficiently:

1. Name one overall coordinator who has both *responsibility* and *authority*. The former without the latter can lead to disaster.
2. Write down specific responsibilities of every individual involved with the show, and see that they carry out their duties.
3. Encourage everyone to communicate clearly and regularly so every member of the team knows what everyone else is doing. Two marks of a bad manager are not wanting to be bothered with details, and changing plans every time he or she gets involved. Those are problems more commonly found with shows than with other forms of marketing communications.
4. Allow the people who are responsible to set time limits for alterations to plans, and employ "negative option approval," whereby if objection is not registered by a particular date, silence constitutes *agreement.*

STEPS TO SUCCESS

These are steps essential for successful planning. Take them in any order you want.

1. *Give yourself as much lead time as possible.* You often know a year or more in advance when a show is going to take place. Take advantage of advance knowledge, and use all the time available to do a first-class job. Rush jobs are seldom either excellent or satisfying.

2. *Set up a task force.* You can write your marketing plan by yourself; you can create ads and direct mail without any help at all; but you generally *do* need a team to develop and execute a successful show.

3. *Analyze your audience.* Start with a clear idea of exactly who your show audience will be. Don't be fooled by tradeshow promoters, many of whom make extravagant claims. Study certified show audits and reference guides available in most good business libraries for audience definition and information on who among show management is responsible for what. Use personal information, too, so you can direct the right message to the most receptive possible target segment(s). You should learn the size and composition of the prospective audience, as well as a realistic appraisal of *qualified attendees*. Not only the topic of the show and the industry which sponsors it, but also the part of the country where it is held may affect both audience size and composition.

4. *Move quickly to reserve space.* This is to obtain two important things: *good position* relative to the main entrance and major features or exhibits, and *good traffic flow*. Few things are more disappointing than to find yourself all alone in a back corner of a hall near the broom closet—with no visitors. With the exception of top powers in an industry who are regular participants, it's usually first come, first served. Try to lock up your space the same day that show management releases the floorplan.

5. *Check décor, design, and colors.* If possible, visit the place where the show will be held and take notes and pictures. Unless you are planning to drape a folding table and let it go at that, you'll also want to check lighting, ceiling height, columns, and access to the floor. I once did a business show in Ecuador where our local show coordinator didn't check access to the convention hotel first, and we had to haul our exhibit panels through second-floor windows since the hotel doors on the street level weren't large enough to accommodate them.

6. *Decide what you want to feature.* Again, the interests of the audience are prime. It's not as easy for service firms as for equipment manufacturers, but interesting exhibits *can* revolve around pure services. As in everything else, put your best foot forward. One of the reasons for having a task force is to get a range of ideas about vital subjects such as this. Brainstorming is a good technique in this activity.

7. *Keep your message simple.* As in other forms of marketing communications, it usually pays to boil your message down to the absolute essentials. Try to work in a clear audience *benefit* as well as product or service features. The message may be tailored to your theme, by the way—or vice versa.

8. *Establish a theme.* Themes are great for advertising, of course, and perhaps even *better* for shows and exhibits. An exhibit theme gives you a memorable point around which to build. It can be a copy line, a graphic, or both. It should be dramatic and appealing and should logically relate to your product(s) or service(s), and to the tastes and interests of the show audience. This is a tall order, to be sure. So development of a show theme is generally not a job for a committee but for someone who is creative and marketing oriented. Once you have a good, solid theme, use it on *everything* connected with your exhibit. And, if it is good enough, consider making it the theme for your *total* marketing communications program.

9. *Have separate sections of your exhibit for different customer or client needs.* A large exhibit can be segmented with partitions. But even a small exhibit will work better if different products or services are kept apart from one another.

10. *Consider building a scale model of your exhibit.* When you plan more than a basic 10-foot-by-10-foot space with a table and two chairs, making a scale model will help you determine placement of furniture and display materials, and calculate traffic flow to maximize the convenience of consultations with your sales people, and to minimize bottlenecks. A model will also help if you have to construct an exhibit.

11. *If you do build an exhibit, plan it for reuse.* Sometimes the same exhibit can serve you for many years. Just plan it so it can be disassembled and stored after each show. An economical alternative to a custom-built exhibit is one of the many portable stands available today. They can be just what you need and cost a fraction of one that you have built to your specifications. You can also consider using your exhibit at seminars and open-houses as well as shows.

12. *Schedule special events to conform to the show schedule.* You might want to have a hospitality suite in the show hotel or invite special customers and prospects to a dinner in connection with a particular exhibit or convention. Be sure that you do not schedule your event to conflict with parties, banquets, and other functions planned by show management. (Conflicting with your *competition*, on the other hand, is an altogether different matter.) Get a printed schedule of events from show management and ask to be kept up to date on changes.

13. *Promote your show participation.* Even a little slug at the bottom of your ads or at the end of your commercials that says, "Visit us at the [name] show," can help to build your attendance. And direct mail and e-mail are natural media for show promotion. Consider, too, the tactic of sending complimentary tickets (whether there's a charge for attendance or not) to prime customers and prospects with a courteous, businesslike covering letter inviting the recipient to stop by your exhibit.

14. *Get on the program if you can.* If the show is worthy of the investment of your marketing dollars, show management should realize that you probably have something important and interesting to tell attendees. Prepare a good speech along the lines suggested in Chapter 34 and send it or an outline to the program manager with a covering letter offering the services of one of your organization's top people as a speaker. It doesn't hurt to mention in the speech that

your firm is an exhibitor—but don't make the announcement sound like a commercial. If you can tie the theme of your exhibit to the theme of your speech, you will achieve that quality mentioned previously as "harmonics," the repetition of an idea in different contexts that can do so much for the memorability of your company or product name and marketing message.

15. *Obtain prospects' names for follow-up.* A show is a terrific place to build your marketing database. Be sure to get full information: name, title, organization, address, telephone number, and e-mail address. If you can also get an indication of their buying influence and the product or service in which they are most interested, so much the better. It will save your sales people time and help them to be better prepared when they make their personal calls. There are two ways to do this. Some people do not like raffles which require attendees to put their business cards in a bowl, but others use this to get raw lists. Frankly, if all you want is *names* instead of *qualified leads*, you can just get the registration list from show management and save time and trouble collecting business cards. It's more useful to have a formal register book at your exhibit with a full-time receptionist to give visitors a simple theme-related token of your esteem—something of modest value and noncommercial in appearance, like a lapel pin or appliqué—and ask them to sign the book and fill in the additional information, if they are willing—which they usually are. Alternatively, *literature request* cards can gather a lot of good information about interested visitors. If you decide to use literature request cards, you should not have racks of literature in your exhibit, of course. The advantages of this method are that (1) you get qualified names of interested prospects, (2) you cut down significantly on the amount of literature that is collected by visitors and later discarded, and (3) your literature is delivered to the prospect's office in an attractive package with a covering letter (see Chapter 26) and without competition. Your literature request cards can be collected at the show, but take the extra step of printing a business reply face on one side so people who take the cards away will be more inclined to mail them back to you. Some people have asked, "But what about the cost of *postage*?" That can be answered by another question: "What is a prospect *worth* to you?" If each prospect is worth at least a *dollar* they are well worth the cost of business reply mail. (See "Arithmetic Approach" in Chapter 37.)

16. *Of course, evaluate your results.* (See Chapter 38 for ways to do this.)

When you execute all these things well, you can be confident that your show activity will pay significant dividends.

SEMINARS AND OPEN-HOUSE EVENTS

Helpful, agreeable, inviting, hospitable, and genuinely friendly are words that have been used to describe the well-conducted business or professional seminar or open-house. This proven marketing communications tactic is effective because it can overpower the modern Praetorian Guards who seem to believe their mission is to prevent any useful information from reaching decision-makers within their organizations. Properly managed, a seminar or an open-house can reach those you might call the "unreachables," educate them, and persuade them in ways no other communications can.

Because such events are essentially *private business shows*, all attention is directed exclusively at the product or service message and the corporate image you wish to convey. In addition, because you are in complete control of all the marketing communications factors so essential to success, you can efficiently and effectively use every sense and every technique to please, amuse, delight, enlighten, impress, and persuade your target audience.

Properly executed, seminars and open-house events can be the most convenient, efficient, and effective methods yet devised to reach influential people, prime customers and prospects, and even your own managers and employees to do any or all of the following:

- expand present markets
- introduce new products and/or personalities
- show off new premises
- demonstrate product or service capabilities
- extend thanks for customer or client loyalty

Experience shows that well-run seminars or open-house presentations to a wide variety of audiences can produce results that are simply astonishing in terms of building a positive image and establishing or enhancing goodwill in a community or among a particular public.

An event will be productive when you can be sure of the following:

- the right audience is present
- the message is appropriate
- there are no major flaws in the performance
- careful attention is paid to every last detail

Consequently, the secret to success depends on two factors: *advance planning*, and *perfect execution*. To manage a successful seminar or open-house, you must pay close attention to *all* the details step by step. There can be no such thing for you as the old U.S. Army rule that "close enough is good enough."

By listing each step you must take in a *Ten-Week Countdown to Success*, found in Appendix 14, it becomes logical and easy for you to avoid common pitfalls and to complete your preparations successfully.

An executive summary of necessary steps follows, since (as for other tactics and techniques in this handbook) space limitations prevent an extensive treatment of the subject.

TACTICAL STEPS

You will see that this topic is sequenced a little differently than others, including shows and exhibits. You may take any of these tactical steps in any order you wish:

1. Start early.
2. Define your objectives and measurable goals.
3. Select products and/or services to be featured.
4. Identify your prime target audience.
5. Develop the message to be communicated.
6. Establish the tone of the event.
7. Create a theme.
8. Determine a reasonable budget.
9. Decide on materials.
10. Develop speeches and presentations.
11. Build your invitation list.
12. Plan decorations.
13. Arrange for refreshments and perhaps food.
14. Prepare and send invitations.
15. Train personnel.
16. Rehearse presentations.
17. Have everything ready early.
18. Use the telephone and e-mail to confirm attendance.
19. Hold subsequent sessions.
20. Thank attendees.
21. Follow up.
22. Evaluate results.

TYPE OF EVENT

The fundamental objective of most strategic marketing activities is, of course, to *increase business*—both short-term and, especially, long-term.

And *that* should be the primary objective of your seminar or open-house effort. But, as mentioned previously, these techniques offer you a rare opportunity to attain a number of important *secondary* marketing objectives as well.

You will probably want to meet with your senior salesperson(s) in a preliminary feasibility session before you call your planning meeting with full staff attendance. Among the options that you should consider at this point is the *type* of event that best fits your current marketing strategy. Your choices will generally fall within one of four main categories:

1. *Education or training on matters of interest to customers.* This is the most altruistic of reasons for gathering people together to hear what you have to say.

2. *Sales presentations* of specific products and/or services in specialized sessions to carefully selected audiences by special invitation. You may tend to favor this approach since it has the most immediate and measurable effect on revenues.

3. *General announcements* of major new products or services and/or public openings of new premises. Both of these types of events may be scheduled either as one-shots or as long-term (perhaps, one- or two-week) activities designed to host large numbers of walk-in or off-the-street visitors invited through media advertising and publicity notices.

4. *A combination approach* achieved by inviting selected customers and prospects to specialized private presentations held during a period of general activity. If you have major new products or services to offer, and/or new premises or new executive personnel, this combination approach might be the most productive of all.

Once you have selected the *type* of event you will host, you should consider how many of your secondary objectives can be accommodated without overtaxing your facilities or diluting your primary goal. It is important for you to decide just how much you should try to accomplish with your seminar or open-house before you call your first planning meeting.

When you consider that three days of presentations offering morning and afternoon sessions each day has the potential to reach six separate audiences, you might begin to wonder if you should present six separate product lines to six distinctly different prospect groups.

Very simply, the answer to that is NO, you should *not*. That would be overreaching, overtaxing resources, and expecting too much from both your personnel and your event. You will be far wiser to confine your efforts to six identical sessions aimed at similar types of customers and prospects, or perhaps three sessions (one each day) for two sets of prospects.

Secondary objectives such as the establishment of customer or client goodwill, the revival of present customer interest in your products or services, and the procurement of new prospects and customers are all obvious, so will not be treated here.

Equally obvious is a matter that heavily influences all your marketing efforts as well as day-to-day activities—*timing*. It is best to schedule your seminar or open-house sessions prior to crucial dates, allowing enough additional lead time for appropriate decisions to be made.

THE THEME

As mentioned elsewhere, a clear and meaningful theme is a vital factor in any comprehensive and effective marketing communications program, and it is especially important to successful and memorable seminar and open-house activities.

This does not necessarily mean either a slogan or a graphic symbol. But it should be simple, strong, and appropriate to the overall message you wish to convey. Like a solid foundation, an appropriate promotional theme—even if only in the form of a *title* for the event—supports all you wish to communicate and contributes positively to the persuasion process. Its productive lifespan extends from the very first invitation you send out through the presentations and the follow-up personal contacts. And if you have wisely integrated your theme into a useful, interesting, nondisposable gift item for attendees, it can continue to serve for years as your silent sales representative on your prospective customer's desk.

Here are the fundamental guidelines:

- A good theme should make a selling point or imply a clear and positive benefit.
- A good theme should lead to a catchy phrase or an easily remembered slogan.
- A good theme should provide continuity and generate enthusiasm among both audience *and* presenters.
- A good theme, above all, should maintain your prospect's and your salesperson's *focus* on your important marketing message.

See Appendix 13 for proven theme ideas.

WHERE TO START

Start with your treatment of those products and/or services that are going to be the *stars* of your presentations. Evaluate carefully what you intend to say about them. What message do you want most to get across to your customers and/or prospects? Does your message lie simply in the missing portion of the statement, "Come to us and get these things because . . ."?

There are other questions to answer:

- What role do you want your organization and/or your salespeople to play in the minds of your customers and prospects?
- Do you want to be known for your dependable goods and services, superior response, low prices, fast turn-around, or perhaps for your innovative and cost-conscious recommendations?
- Can you come up with a theme that will convincingly and entertainingly convey that message?

When you do, you will want to use that theme in *every one* of your seminar or open-house communication elements. Use your theme to inspire eye-catching invitations, provide continuity to your presentations, decorate your premises, enhance your handout materials, and spark a profitable follow-up effort.

This is not an easy task. But few worthwhile things are easy.

THE PLANNING MEETING

As early in the process as possible, you should call a planning meeting. In large organizations, it is wise to poll sales and customer service groups beforehand for their input on special prospect interest areas. To set the stage for your planning meeting, have the right people in attendance and allow sufficient time to define your specific goals clearly, to profile the target audience, to determine which products and/or services will star in your presentation, to consider a promotional theme, and to appoint a coordinator.

A typical agenda for a planning meeting should include discussion of the following: objectives, target audience, message, tone, theme, budget, planning calendar, materials, presentations and presenters, invitation list, invitation process, premises and personnel, showtime, follow-up—and appointment of the event coordinator, with authority from the very top. Your coordinator should be familiar with your products, your markets, and your organizational procedures. He or she should also know a bit about presentation techniques and printing production. All of the agenda items suggested are interrelated, of course, and occasionally the popularity (or lack thereof) of particular products or services will determine the objectives, the audience, and even the theme selected.

While it is apparent that the products and/or services you select for promotion will practically predetermine your invitation list, it is wise first to ask yourself several questions related to other important event opportunities before you make your final decision:

- Do you want to hold separate sessions for separate groups, or would it be more effective to mix your audiences?
- How about mixing new prospects with present customers? Should you invite a few satisfied users of products or services that you will be presenting to your new prospects? In-audience advocates can enhance a presentation; but if you use that approach, be sure you also provide enough *new* ideas to compensate the present customers for their endorsements. The introduction of new products that can be used by present customers offers a perfect opportunity for an audience of this type.
- Will you have new executive personnel to introduce or new premises to show? It is important that you distinguish such considerations clearly. Showing off new premises, for example, will require an entirely different type of event from one planned to present a new product to an exclusive audience of hot prospects.

Not everything can be decided at your first meeting but, at the very least, tentative dates can be set within the development time available. General objectives may be set, and the number and type of sessions per day may be agreed upon. Some method of consistent internal communication should be devised at that first meeting to keep everyone informed of intentions and progress. The coordinator should be made personally responsible for this.

Finally, at least the next formal meeting should be scheduled and assignments made as to who will be responsible for developing and presenting each of the agenda items.

PRINTING PRODUCTION SUGGESTIONS

A personal business letter may be the best form of invitation to a special seminar or open-house event. In some cases, though—particularly if you want to convey a very elegant image—an engraved, or formal printed invitation may produce the response you want. You are the best judge of invitation format. But certain information must *always* be conveyed: the *hours*, the *date*, the *purpose*, and the *place* where your seminar or open-house will be held.

Also, a cover envelope with a postage stamp many times suggests a more personal approach to an invitation than a self-mailer with indicia or metered postage. Often, too, a stamp on the reply card or reply envelope will pull better than a business reply face (the latter in the form of a card is called a *brc* and an envelope a *bre*).

Some people believe *handwritten* addressing of outer envelopes provides a personal touch. Others believe that, since most senior people don't open their own mail, an individually (even computer) typed address works very well. It is generally unwise, however, to label-address, as this method marks correspondence as "junk mail"—which is almost invariably discarded unopened by Praetorian Guards—as similar e-mail (except as a reminder) may be perceived as "spam."

Do not try to cut costs too much on this aspect of your event. A cheap fill-in facsimile letter or a cut-rate printing job—however good the envelope—will probably not get past the Guards either. Or, even if it does for some reason, it will still suggest a cheap, second-rate function which few prime prospects and respected customers will wish to attend.

Remember: Your business should have a reputation for *quality*, and all your event components from start to finish should reflect that fact. A major challenge for the event coordinator will be to obtain quality materials at fair and reasonable prices.

TIPS TO IMPROVE RESULTS

When your invitation, follow-up, and thank-yous are in *letter* form, they should be on your corporate letterhead. Except where a special impression dictates that formal engraved or printed invitations are appropriate, you should normally aim at a thoroughly personal, persuasive, business-letter approach to make your prospects feel both respected and wanted. (See Chapter 26 for more on this subject.)

If your standards of good taste permit, consider including with your invitation a postpaid reply card with a *door-prize stub*. Remind your printer to perforate the stub section of the reply card so your prospect can easily remove it. The door-prize device is recommended because it provides added motivation to attend—particularly if the prize is significant—and it adds an element of excitement to the event.

Be sure that members of the event committee have all known attendees' *name tags* printed and filled out in advance. Have blank name tags available for last-minute acceptances or unexpected arrivals.

Have all necessary signs and posters written, designed, and delivered to the silk-screener or printer as early as possible. Any special literature, seminar material, handouts, and folders or binders you may need for your event should be anticipated, prepared, and ordered well in advance of your show date.

If you are going to pass out a portfolio containing a company or product brochure, article reprints, and other literature, be sure that all the elements to be contained in the portfolio have been planned so that they fit, and that they are delivered at least a week ahead of showtime.

Be sure to include all information you need to know about your prospects' potential uses of your services.

Use your theme device tastefully on all portfolios and binders and (if possible) on other printed materials to provide continuity.

PRESENTATIONS AND PRESENTERS

Here you can be more important than a Hollywood director, because this part of the process can turn prospects into customers—small users into big users—doubters into believers—occasional customers in steady customers—lapsed business into renewed activity—and business acquaintances into business friends.

The key to success is *not* to think like a Hollywood director. For your seminar or open-house, remember that, as for other types of marketing communications, you are in the business of *persuasion*—not the business of entertainment. You will benefit by planning well-staged, in-depth sales presentations free of routine office interruptions, and with no business competitors in sight.

A marketing communicator can hardly ask for a better opportunity than a seminar or open-house to apply his or her craft, but there are still several vital preparation details to attend to before your show can go on. The coordinator should proceed as follows:

- Help contact personnel, customer service representatives, and general management organize their thoughts, prepare scripts, and perhaps visualize special presentations, remarks, and continuity bridges.
- Tailor and script each lecture and presentation so that it enhances and is enhanced by the event theme.
- Select the best available presenters and public speakers to deliver each product, service, or application presentation.
- Rehearse each packaged presentation and each individual presenter repeatedly. This includes even the President, Chairman, or CEO—however they may resist. Many top executives have made fools of themselves because they have tried to deliver an unrehearsed speech. *Nobody* is so good at public speaking that they do not have to prepare and rehearse.
- Draw from stock and/or print and package appropriate descriptive and application literature as handouts to support presentations.
- Decorate the event area in a style appropriate to the theme.
- Test all equipment before the event date and have service personnel on hand during the performance.
- Have all demonstration supplies on hand.
- Prepare appropriate prospect interest cards and/or survey materials and have them ready for use. They will, of course, be designed to capitalize on the event theme which will be established by the invitations, and reinforced throughout your presentations.
- Build reference to the cards or survey materials into the presentation scripts because it is much easier to get an interest card filled out or a survey appointment confirmed during and as an integral part of the presentation than it is later, amid the distraction of departure.

Historical footnote: Winston Churchill is said to have spent an average of *four hours* of preparation and rehearsal for every *minute* of time he spent addressing Parliament. As with athletics, and every other human activity, you don't get good at what you do unless you apply yourself, and practice conscientiously.

INVITATION LIST

If there is one key to a successful seminar or open-house, it is to have the right people in attendance. No matter how impressive your presentations, your sales results will depend entirely upon *whom* you are able to impress—so pay particular attention to your invitation list.

Your present customer and prospect database for regular promotional mailings may need updating and revision—probably right up to the day of the event—so be prepared. Your database is so important that it is a good idea to assign at least one person, exclusively, to the updating. Dust off and review your present and former customer files. By all means, exercise care in the spelling of prospect names and be watchful for position and title changes of individuals within your customer and prospect organizations. If you are going to make any errors in job titles, make them *upward*. When in doubt about either, your list person should telephone the organization involved for clarification.

The updating of your database provides you with two excellent opportunities to contribute to the success of your event and to smooth your salespersons' paths for follow-up activity: With the contact person's assistance, you can invite those decision-makers who seldom receive direct sales contact, but who are influential (behind the scenes) in contracting decisions. It has been estimated that these number roughly *70 percent* of executive ranks in the United States.

Prospects with special interests are particularly responsive to the seminar or open-house approach if the invitation and, of course, the presentations are directed toward their particular needs and application areas. Make a special effort to add all such prospects to your database.

Top executives of your prospect organizations are sometimes difficult to reach because, as noted, they are too well insulated by a Praetorian Guard of staff assistants or mail-screening clerks and call-screening secretaries. In such cases, a personal executive-to-executive invitation by telephone is often most productive. Special exclusively top-executive sessions, initiated by personal business letter and/or executive phone invitation, have proved effective to reach the thoroughly insulated prospect. But the gathering together of presidents and senior officers of prospect companies—or the top people of any type of organization—at a single session requires some very special handling. Success starts essentially with your executive personnel's ability and willingness to persuade top executives of prospect organizations to attend your event.

As suggested, you should be prepared to add names to your list up until the very eve of the presentation. These late invitees can be surprisingly responsive and productive, for among them you will find substitute attendees asked to attend by some of your best prospects who are unable to attend themselves.

Furthermore, and even more important, your contact people should ask original invitees to suggest other individuals from their organizations who should also be invited. You may be surprised at how many of these important contacts do not appear on your original mailing list. Invite them— even at the last minute—by phone call or personal contact, if necessary.

Occasionally you will find that some important prospects will commit themselves only via a *personal* invitation. Do not scratch them off your list just because you have not received a reply card. Ask your contact people to invite them personally because, once in a while, only a sense of personal obligation to a well-respected individual will motivate important (but busy or hesitant) prospects to leave their offices for a full- or a half-day of presentations.

Ex-customers can often be lured back via the allure of a *special* invitation to a seminar or open-house presentation, and that special invitation may require a personal visit to the offices of these former customers. But, if their past complaints were legitimate, be prepared to offer a solution to the previous problems during your presentation. Your promise of a solution to their problem with your organization is what makes it a special invitation, and each case must be handled on an individual basis. If your sales personnel have maintained solid, informal relationships with their former customers—even though their business has been lost—the special invitation could be as pleasant and casual, yet effective, as: "Hey, [name], come on out to our seminar so we can show you how our new [capability] will solve that [whatever] problem we used to have."

PREMISES AND PERSONNEL

Should you hold your event on-premises or in a hired hall? Much will depend, of course, on the type of show you want to put on, and your preferred method of presentation. Will it be audiovisual, stand-up, dramatization, or a combination of all three? Another factor in your decision will depend upon the results of your poll of your sales people regarding the areas of prospect interest. If you have adequate space on your own premises, by all means hold your sessions there, because—apart from the cost advantages—you will also be able to demonstrate your facilities and work environment first-hand. For walk-through demonstrations, arrange your equipment and personnel to provide a logical, progressive flow compatible with the application(s) being demonstrated.

Pay particular attention to these points:

- Your telephone operators should be well rehearsed in the use of scripts you provide for them because theirs is an extremely important function in the invitation process. A persuasive, quick-thinking operator with a well-modulated voice, working from a well-crafted script, can increase attendance by as much as 50 percent.
- Use well-made signs and flowcharts to reinforce your presentations and to lead your visitors along in an orderly fashion.
- All signage and decorations should reinforce your theme and graphic.
- Well-briefed personnel can often be used advantageously to succinctly explain points of interest at selected stops on a tour.
- Incoming guests should be greeted, registered, and escorted to the refreshment or presentation areas according to plan. Outside greeters assigned to or specially hired for the occasion should be well-briefed and rehearsed beforehand.

- Do not forget transportation and drivers. Having limousines or vans available, with drivers on duty, can turn a disappointing turnout into a full house.
- If necessary, arrange for free parking near your premises. If your own lot is not large enough to accommodate your crowd, contract with a commercial lot or arrange with local police for designated and marked curb space.

SHOWTIME

Here is where the *magic* happens. Now it all depends on you and how well you have planned and prepared.

You may have obtained help—or you and your staff may be the producers, directors, stars, stagehands, grips, prop people, sound engineers, greeters, caterers, projectionists, as well as the facilitators, demonstrators, teachers, consultants, and above all, *marketers.*

How does it all shape up? Are you ready? Let's start at the door:

- Have you anticipated your transportation needs? Are your drivers and limousines or vans ready?
- Are the hosts and/or hostesses on station?
- Is the guest register handy, with ample supplies?
- Do you have guests' name tags in place for pickup? Do you have someone assigned to prepare tags for unregistered and unexpected guests?
- Is there a deposit box for doorprize stubs (if that has been deemed appropriate)?
- The reception area and presentation rooms are already thematically decorated, of course, but has *all* demonstration, projection, and sound equipment been tested and found to be in perfect operating condition?
- Are extra supplies on hand?
- Are all demonstrators and presenters at their stations?
- Are the caterers (or your own responsible personnel) present and ready to serve good food and/or refreshments?
- Are gifts and/or mementos ready and literature packets on hand?
- Do you have someone assigned to the phones—ready to accept those reluctant, last-minute cancellations, *and* equally ready to reschedule the guests for subsequent performances?
- Are the telephones in the presentation areas cut off or shunted to the switchboard? Remember: There should be *no* unnecessary interruptions!
- Are prospect interest cards handy, and pens nearby?
- Is *everyone smiling*?

Then you're going to have a *smash hit* of a show!

Part VI

Quantitative Strategies
for Marketing

Chapter 36

Revenue Forecasting Strategies

TERMINOLOGY

Predicting how much of a product or service you can sell in the coming year begins with an understanding of several marketing terms, including the following:

- *Market potential*—the total amount of revenues in a particular industry or for a particular product line expected to be possible given maximum marketing activity.
- *Market demand*—the amount of revenues for a particular product or service in a defined geographic area by a particular target market segment within a certain time period, which is usually a calendar year.
- *Company potential*—the maximum amount of revenues that might be achieved by your organization given maximum marketing effort and minimal competitive pressures. The maximum company potential possible would be the same as market potential if yours was the only company in your industry (that is a pure monopoly) and you would have a market share of 100.
- *Company demand*—your organization's estimated portion of the market demand.
- *Market share* (or *share of market* or *brand share*)—your sales as a percent of total sales within your particular industry.
- *Company sales forecast*—your organization's future sales volume based on your anticipated marketing activity.
- *Area market potential*—sales within a particular geographic area for a given industry or type of product or service.
- *Market development index*—a number based on 100 that indicates the relationship between actual and potential customers for a particular product in a particular geographic area relative to the same relationship nationally.

- *Brand development index (BDI)*—a number based on 100 that indicates by geographics or demographics how a particular product is performing relative to average national sales for that product.

- *Brand potential index (BPI)*—reflects the relationship between a brand's *market development index* and *brand development index* in a particular geographic market area.

- *Category development index (CDI)*—a number based on 100 that indicates by geographics or demographics how a particular category of products is performing relative to average national sales in that industry. These several indexes are studied to indicate strengths, weaknesses, sales trends among competitive brands, to help predict sales, and to develop advertising and sales promotion budgets.

- *Sales quota*—the specific amount of sales required of each of your organization's sales territories, districts, and regions.

FORECASTING STRATEGIES

The following are the most commonly practiced strategies for predicting sales—sometimes called *"demand analysis."*

- *Chain ratio method*—about as simple as it gets, and used by many new businesses; estimate the number of customers you're likely to have the first year, and multiply by the amount of money you estimate each is likely to spend annually on your product(s) or service(s). The total represents your anticipated revenues.

- *Total market potential method*—a bit of a refinement of *chain ratio* whereby you multiply your estimate of the total number of likely customers in your draw area by the number of units they will buy per year by the average unit price you intend to charge.

- *Capacity method*—a new restaurant could look at its seating capacity, multiply by percent occupancy for various times of day and days of the week, multiply again by the number of settings (for a retail store, "turns") and then by the average meal tab to obtain approximate annual dollar revenues. Customers could also be segmented as to frequency of purchase and/or volume of each purchase for more accurate estimates.

- *Panel (syndicated) research*—buying behaviors for particular types of consumer products are available from syndicated-research sources such as *Simmons Selective and Mass Media Studies*, published by Simmons Marketing Research Bureau (called simply *"Simmons"*), *MRI Mediamark Research*, published by Mediamark Research, Inc. (called simply *"MRI"*), and trade associations. These are routinely used by national marketers to calculate future sales. Research studies based on panel information can also be tailored for additional fees. (See Appendix 3.)

- *Panel data applied locally*—to use national *panel research* figures for local operations, first calculate the population in your draw area. Then look at Simmons, MRI, or other published research to discover purchasing behavior for your type of product or service as a percent of the national population. Then multiply the percent by your draw area population (moving the decimal point two places to the left) to obtain approximate figures for purchasing of your type of product or service in your draw area. You might wish to factor in possible regional differences and, where units are reported rather than total dollars, multiply by average price to obtain estimated total market sales. Finally, multiply by your anticipated share of market to obtain your annual revenue.

- *Prior sales*—for existing businesses, this is the foundation for what is often called a *top-down* forecast, where you start with your records of past sales and divide them up by regions and territories and/or by product lines. This and the other forecasting strategies that rely on analyses of past trends to predict future revenues are collectively referred to as *barometric techniques*.

- *Trend extrapolation*—like "connecting the dots," where you extend points on your sales chart to extend the trend. Risky if information is too limited, especially for new businesses that may rely on *linear trend extrapolation* which, if early success has been achieved, may lead them to expect greater future revenues than will actually be achieved.

- *Prior sales plus a percentage*—where you add to your prior sales figures a reasonable amount (usually based on a percentage) to allow for inflation, market growth, and other factors you may identify.

- *Index analysis*—use BDI, CDI and other indexes just noted to compile a figure for total revenues, or apply an index to a national figure.

- *Direct forecast*—an estimate without any research generally made by a senior person who has experience in the industry. Also one of the *top-down* forecasting methods, it is sometimes remarkably accurate, but for new businesses often proves to be a *WAG*, or a "wild-ass guess."

- *Survey of expert* (or *executive*) *opinion* (or *consensus technique*)—upper-level people are asked what they believe sales will amount to, and averages are calculated. This is a relatively inexpensive forecasting method, with results called "*guesstimates*." When experts *outside* the company are polled and responses compiled and refined for reevaluation, the method is called the *Delphi technique*.

- *Survey of the sales organization*—the basic method of a *build-up* or *bottom-up* forecast where sales estimates by territory and region and/or by product line are summed to derive a total anticipated sales figure. A potential problem with this method is that sales reps and managers may realize that their quotas and their commission structures may be dependent on the figures they provide and therefore may tend to *low-ball* their estimates.

- *Channel* (or *distribution*) *forecast*—when you solicit the opinions of resellers in your channel(s) of distribution. Also a *build-up* or *bottom-up* method, and likely to be less biased (but perhaps no more reliable) than a survey of your sales organization.

- *Test market sales projection*—mentioned in connection with research, the test market approach can give you a factor which you can arithmetically translate to regional and/or national sales figures.

- *Survey of buyer intentions* (or *purchase-intent*)—where you ask how much prospective buyers think they will purchase in the coming year, and multiply the average by the anticipated number of buyers. This generally works better in business than in consumer market forecasting.

- *Lost horse forecast*—fun because of its name, this involves starting with the last known revenues, and considering how future buyers are likely to behave—as one would find a lost horse by starting where he was last seen and thinking through where he would go from there.

- *Simulations*—are of two types: *Computer* models simulate marketing performance based on hypothetical expectations about the marketplace and trend analysis research. *Physical* simulations involve consumers making buying decisions in as real a situation as can be devised, and projections being made from observations of buyer behavior.

- *Scenario analysis*—analysts develop subjective views of marketing results based on cause-and-effect relationships. This is commonly accomplished through computer models, which may not include all marketing considerations and market variables.

- *Regression analysis*—computerized models use advanced mathematics to assign causal values to various marketing elements that may affect revenues. This technique is complex, time-consuming, and of questionable accuracy, so it is rarely used outside of business schools.

Chapter 37

Budgeting Strategies

DIFFICULT TO TRACK SOME COSTS

Since much of marketing has to do with the quality of products, services, décor, attire and bearing of personnel, business courtesy toward customers and prospects, social contacts, entertainment, cultivation of referral sources, and so on, costs are likely to be ascribed to budgets *other* than the traditional marketing budget.

Expenditures that most practitioners think of as clearly marketing will normally fall within the area defined here as *marketing communications*— advertising, sales promotion, public relations, publicity, personal selling, and customer service or client relations.

We know investments in marketing communications, when executed properly, have positive effects, but it has proved impossible for most organizations to demonstrate an *exact* correlation between revenues and any marketing communications expenditures but those related to personal selling. This may be why *zero-based budgeting* is not popular in marketing.

The temptation in commerce and industry has traditionally been to spend *more* than necessary on marketing communications for fear of not spending *enough*.

But in these days of high costs and rapidly evolving communications methods, you will certainly want to keep close track of all your marketing investments and keep a particularly close eye on your advertising, sales promotion, public relations, and publicity budgets, lest you risk on the one hand spending more than you need to spend, but on the other hand failing to communicate effectively with your customers, clients, prospects, and other publics.

STANDARD STRATEGIES

Most marketing communications budgets are arrived at by one of the following eight standard strategies, methods, or techniques:

1. *Arbitrary method*—whereby a senior executive chooses a random number that seems reasonable. No kidding!
2. *Percentage of the previous year's revenues*—which a friend described as the equivalent of steering your automobile by looking in the rear-view mirror.
3. *Last year's budget, adjusted for inflation*—which isn't much better.
4. *Percentage of anticipated revenues*—which uses as a base one of the forecasting strategies suggested in the preceding chapter.
5. *"Unit technique"*—which means allocating a set dollar amount for each item expected to be sold in the coming year. This works rather well for goods like automobiles but is difficult for organizations whose product line is broad.
6. *Matching or exceeding competitors' spending*—which requires ethically researching competitive activity, which is sometimes very difficult to do.
7. *"All-you-can-afford" technique*—whereby all costs of running the organization are funded, and what is *left over* is used for marketing communications.
8. *Plow-back method*—often used for new product introductions, where net profits are reinvested in continued advertising and promotion.

A ninth method—the pure *objective and task method*—is highly recommended and covered in detail in the next section.

A LOGICAL PROCEDURE

The *objective and task method* of budgeting, or "task technique," as it is also known, seems to be the only intelligent approach to costing out a marketing communications program because it calculates a needed fixed amount and also guides the allocation of funds by category and medium.

Ideally, the size of your budget should be directly related to the scope of the job to be done. Thus, with a marketing communications budget tied to measurable advertising goals, as described in Chapters 5 and 6, the risks of both *over*spending and *under*spending can be minimized.

In actual practice, the process can take several *weeks* and may require computer assistance. Odds are it *cannot* be satisfactorily completed in a few hours of your spare time. But the results can be well worth all the effort, whether you do everything yourself or retain professional services to help you.

STEPS IN THE PROCESS

There are several steps for developing an accurate advertising or marketing communications budget:

1. Review all your objectives and goals that pertain to advertising or marketing communications to be absolutely certain of what you need to accomplish.

2. Define clearly in terms of geographics, demographics, and (if possible) psychographics and/or synchrographics exactly *whom* you wish to influence and the effect you wish your programs to have on them. (That is, identify specifically what you want them to *do*.)

3. List all media available to reach that target audience.

4. Collect all current rates and data on each appropriate media vehicle—all television and radio facilities, magazines, newspapers, Internet, and for other media average printing, mailing, and placement costs—plus the sizes of audiences for each media vehicle. (These data are as useful for publicity planning as for advertising and sales promotion, by the way.) With these figures you can calculate not only your costs but also your reach in terms of *gross impressions*. Use local reference sources such as Yellow Pages and advertising services directories, and/or *Standard Rate & Data Service* (SRDS), available in your public library's business section in separate volumes for each of the mass media. For the greatest accuracy and reliability of all, check directly and individually with the advertising sales department of *each* media vehicle on your preliminary schedule.

5. Estimate how many times participation in each medium will be required to attain the advertising goals specified, based on gross impression data. This sort of calculation was suggested in Chapter 5 as "Multiples of Ten" and will also suggest your *average frequency*. The fundamental *"three-hit"* theory of consumer advertising—that it takes a minimum of three ad exposures to achieve a significant level of awareness among consumers—should be considered here. And business marketers should keep in mind that the average business sale is not closed until the *fifth* personal call—so one should not expect a marketing communications message in any form to do better than a live person can do.

6. Alternatively, if you use broadcast media heavily, you can calculate *reach*, *frequency*, and *gross rating point* (GRP) figures and multiply out your budget estimate by working with *cost-per-rating* point (variously abbreviated CPP or CPR or CPGRP) averages. See Appendix 7 for useful media formulas for making these kinds of calculations.

7. On the basis of the preliminary gross impression (or reach, frequency, and gross rating point) numbers you have determined, total the corresponding time, space, and production costs required, applying all possible discounts.

8. If you wish to save the standard 15 percent ad agency commission by placing your advertising orders directly with the media, you must provide resources (either clerical or fiscal, or both) to cover the labor necessary to place and

formally confirm your media orders. You should also allow something to cover the source materials and time needed to monitor your schedule, to see that all your advertising actually appears as intended.

9. In addition, you must provide clerical and/or fiscal resources to cover what is called "traffic" in the advertising business: the production scheduling, supervising, and delivering of materials to the media by closing dates so that your ad schedule will run as planned.

10. And, again, if you are not going to use the services of a full-service advertising, promotion, or public relations agency, a capable marketing communications consultancy, or a media buying service you should provide funds for the time and expertise required to do your overall marketing communications planning, media planning, scheduling, and buying.

11. Whether you use a full-service agency, a "creative boutique," or freelance talent, you should allow 10 to 30 percent of your media budget (depending on its size) to cover the costs of creative development, copywriting, design, and also normal production costs for casting, photography and/or original art, recording, editing, typesetting, paste-up, printing production, delivery or dissemination, and the myriad of other details which are part of the implementation of your marketing plan.

12. Add 10 to 15 percent contingency.

13. The *total* is your budget, based on the *tasks* suggested by your communications objectives.

Use the same sort of discipline to calculate your sales promotion, public relations, and publicity budgets.

Your sales and customer service budgets will involve human resources considerations involving salaries, benefits, and travel and entertainment expenses of sales and customer service personnel, but a similar task approach is recommended.

ARITHMETIC APPROACH

It's often easier for professional practices and business marketers to calculate marketing communications costs than it is for consumer marketers because they can perhaps more easily estimate what a prospect is *worth* to them in terms of business to be derived.

If an accounting practice, for example, knows that a particular type of recurring annual service will average $5,000 in fees, and that they can close 1 in 20 respondents to a business letter direct mail solicitation, each respondent would be worth $250 to them.

Going one step further, if they expect a 4 percent return to their persuasive business letter mailing program (higher than should be expected for most consumer mailings), they would have 40 respondents to a mailing list of 1,000 names, 1 in 20 of which they could close, giving them 2 new customers at $5,000 each or $10,000 in first-year business. Each name on the original mailing list would be worth an average of $10 in initial (first-year) business to them.

That kind of arithmetic approach provides a point of reference for how much they might spend on direct mail and sales promotion. Certainly, a practice would not want to spend their *entire* anticipated revenues just generating one-shot contracts. But suppose they took 15 percent of the anticipated gross ($1,500) as a reasonable amount to invest in initial marketing communications, and another 15 percent ($1,500) to invest in cultivating their prospects, or actual respondents.

Then they could spend up to $1.50 on each of their *suspects* (or each of the names on their mailing list), and another $37.50 on each of their *prospects* (those 40 who actually *respond* to their solicitation). If they were to invest $0.80 each in contact letters, that would leave $0.70 per suspect to invest in some sort of lure, gimmick, or premium, commonly called an *action* (or *involvement*) *device*. That could be an attention-getter like an exotic postage stamp, a foreign coin, a tipped-on color photograph, a plastic novelty, or the like.

As to the *prospects*, if the firm invested $7.50 each in their fulfillment packages (an attractive folder containing literature, case histories, and a motivating covering letter) that would cost a total of $300, and they would still have $30 per person with which to incentivize their final offer through an executive gift, a book, or some such goodwill generator.

Thus, it would cost the practice $3,000 to obtain business worth $10,000 the first year. Although that might use up their first year's profit, they would have two new clients whom they could economically keep sold, and who would be continuing sources of future revenues and profits.

In addition to their use in generating response and new business, if those funds were wisely invested in premiums and gifts that could increase their *qualified response* by only 10 percent, and their conversion to clients by the same amount, it's easy to see how such an investment could be at least equally worthwhile.

BASIC PROBLEMS

In the case of an organization new to strategic marketing planning, advertising, and promotion, pure budgeting by the *objective and task* method probably cannot be done before the first year is over. After that they will be in a position to determine exactly what they need in order to accomplish their goals.

Several factors complicate the planning of marketing communications budgets. Each must be weighted and applied to the strategic planning process—although no purely scientific techniques for doing so have yet been discovered.

The primary considerations are these:

1. Marketing factors *other* than communications—such as quality of products and services, customer or client rapport, and price—affect customer and prospect decisions.
2. Competitors' activities—especially the levels of their spending on marketing communications—have a significant effect on customer and prospect perceptions.
3. Different marketing communications messages and strategies result in significantly different effects for similar dollar investments.
4. What is sometimes called the "impact" of a marketing communications program—including the strength of the offer, media effectiveness, timing, and creative execution—can vary enormously.
5. The unexplained psychic phenomenon called "zeitgeist" that makes masses of people receptive to certain products, services, and ideas only at certain times in history, and that accounts for fads and unexpected political upsets, also affects marketing communications efforts.

Because the relationship of expenditures to results is so difficult to control, track, and prove, allocation of dollars is often ill-conceived and even random. Many organizations still invest in advertising, sales promotion, public relations, publicity, and customer service simply because they *believe* that communicating with customers and prospects will help achieve marketing and sales objectives.

Thus *spending* sometimes becomes an end in itself without sufficient attention being paid to the total *strategic marketing planning* process.

Further complicating the matter, objectives *other than* marketing and marketing communications objectives—such as overall corporate objectives, and objectives related to manufacturing, human resources, and so on—are often the basis for planning.

SCOPE OF THE WORK

Obviously, if you have several different target markets or publics and/or several different messages in mind and expect to cover them individually during your marketing communications campaign, your planning, creative, and production will cost more and take more time than if you produce only one or two inclusive or general advertisements, pieces, or programs.

Although you wouldn't want to reduce the impact of your marketing communications by making them generic, you might realize economies by combining some activities. For example, advertisements run in business magazines could carry messages addressed to customers, prospects, dealers, distributors, suppliers, and perhaps referral sources, rather than just one or two of those targets.

If you have a modest budget, you may wish to use the staff production services offered by most newspapers, magazines, and television and radio stations. Often production is offered "free"—that is, the production cost is included in the rate you pay for your advertising space and time. However it is billed, the charge will usually be far less than that of an agency or art studio. The results will generally be quick and dirty, though—neither well thought out nor particularly well executed, as you would expect. But if you are on a tight budget, the media are resources you can consider— especially if you plan and write the ads yourself and require only mechanical production help.

Although you can get a lot of expert and valuable assistance from media and production sources such as radio and television stations, publications, and printers, experience proves that if you rely on them alone you can sometimes spend more than you should. You or the specialist who helps you should be cautious, disciplined, well organized, and businesslike in dealing with all suppliers of media and production services.

It's wise to get at least *three* competitive, firm, written quotes from qualified suppliers for printed materials so your budgeting in the planning stage is sufficient for execution. Be sure you give each vendor exactly the same specifications, including stock (type of paper), ink colors, scoring, folding, and any special instructions for handling, diecutting, and wrapping for shipment.

In the case of broadcast advertising production, even more detail is usually required, and the help of specialists such as an ad agency or production company for accurate estimating of costs is usually required.

In these ways you will be as well assured as you can be of comparable prices for the same quality of work, reasonable delivery, and no *unpleasant surprises* at the end of your jobs. Better to know your costs in the planning stage than to discover at the time of execution that you can't afford what you've decided you need.

Until you've had a few years experience with a full-fledged marketing program and can apply the objective and task technique of budgeting, you will probably want to use either an affordable budget figure of from 3 to 15 percent of your *anticipated revenues* (Standard Strategy 4), the *unit technique* based on the value of specific product sales or types of customers (Standard Strategy 5—and not recommended for most organizations), or the *all-you-can-afford technique* (Standard Strategy 7), and then divide the total dollars according to priorities of the marketing communications jobs to be done.

COMPARATIVE COSTS OF COMMUNICATIONS

The bigger your marketing communications effort, usually the lower your *unit* costs. For example, it might cost you several hundred dollars to hire someone to make one very important sales call on a prime prospect, but somewhat less per call if the same person were to visit several prospects at one address or call back on one customer several times.

It would certainly cost you less than either type of sales visit to write a personal letter to that prime prospect, a great deal less per contact to send a form letter to a hundred prospects at once, and less still per prospect to print your message on a postcard and send it bulk-rate to 10,000 addresses.

ACCOUNTANTS VERSUS MARKETERS

"All you marketing people want to do is *spend money*," the accountants complain. To which the marketer replies in the words of Oscar Wilde, "You know the *cost* of everything, and the *value* of nothing."

There may never be a resolution to the different perspectives of these budget adversaries.

Chapter 38

Evaluation and Testing Techniques

ACCOUNTABILITY

One of the major criticisms of marketing people—in addition to our liking to spend money—is that we are thought not to be sufficiently *accountable* for the results of our spending. The effectiveness, as well as the efficiency, of all elements of strategic marketing programs should be carefully and continuously evaluated. Are you producing the changes and the results you set out to produce? Where do you need to modify your strategic approach? Or must you scrap what you've been doing and develop something totally new?

Evaluation techniques should include the following, in order of importance:

1. Response of target market individuals in terms of new business, frequency of contact, sales volume, repeat business, and remarks or comments made is the most obvious method. Of particular value is relating *revenues* to marketing expenditures.

2. Direct marketing and sales promotion activities lend themselves naturally to *direct response* evaluation—that is, counting the returns.

3. Standard secondary research (primarily like Starch readership, Arbitron radio, and Nielsen television ratings) is useful in evaluating your advertising. These measure the effect upon the mass market, not necessarily your particular market segment(s), though, and such research is only available for mass-media advertising, not other types of marketing communications.

4. Results of primary research—especially if tracked over a period of time—among your customers, prospects, and other publics for *retention of infor-*

mation you wish to communicate, or *intention for action* you desire, is worthwhile. Your research should be constructed in such a way that information obtained relates directly to that specified in your objectives and goals.

5. Consider the opinions of your employees as to how resellers and customers are responding to your marketing efforts. Listening to and acting on feedback from your executives and staff is not only good marketing but also good management, the subject of Chapter 39.

6. The media vehicles in which you choose to advertise can also provide primary research, and even gather data for you, which is specially important for local advertisers.

7. Evaluation of your *creative strategy* should rely on pretesting as well as posttesting and will involve techniques described in Chapter 2.

8. *Public relations and publicity* are more difficult to evaluate objectively. Favorable appearance of articles in magazines and newspapers, minutes of air time, and inches of news or editorial space devoted to your organization, products, services, and activities (called "placement" by publicists) should be observed and recorded so that you have some sort of quantifiable measure of the results of your efforts. (I recommend hiring a *clipping service*, collecting your clips, and multiplying the column inches by the thousands of primary circulation, so that a mention in the *New York Times* gets more credit than one in the *Northport Journal*.) But you cannot get the secondary research information that is available for advertising for any of the other types of marketing communications.

9. No doubt some personal intuition will also enter into your evaluation and may help you in improving your total marketing program and your ads and publicity in particular, but more objective measures should be your primary guide.

10. The *least* reliable way to evaluate the success of your marketing communications is to do as Governor George Wallace suggested in his bid to be U.S. President and *ask any cabdriver*. Or ask your spouse.

As suggested in connection with *total quality marketing* in Chapter 4, plan on constant monitoring of all aspects of your marketing program and expect appropriate modification of strategies to be part of the execution of your plan.

You cannot improve on your work if you don't stop from time to time to see how well you've done. It may cost you time and even a little money, but that should be more than paid back in improved performance and the approval of senior management.

WAYS TO MEASURE DIRECT RESPONSE

Obtaining proof that your direct response program is working is more complex than simply counting returns. The full impact of direct response marketing communications (other than personal selling) in producing an order is directly traceable only in *direct* (or *mail order*) marketing. Otherwise, there are just too many other factors involved in a total marketing communications program to reliably ascribe causality.

Yet there are four accepted ways to measure the effectiveness of direct response marketing communications. Each depends largely on the objective(s) of the activity under consideration. If the objective is unclear, no amount of tabulating or survey activity will prove useful.

Measurement will be simplified greatly if instead of broad objectives you have set specific, measurable goals in numeric terms, as recommended in Chapter 6. For example, your marketing plan might include this goal: "Among CFOs in the 1,487 manufacturing firms in our region, to win acceptance of our computerized bookkeeping system by 20 percent (or 297) by the end of 20XX." Then, if your program produced only 149 clients, it would be considered to have been roughly 50 percent effective.

Applying this discipline is difficult, especially for those just beginning a strategic marketing program, and designating specific numbers in the form of measurable goals may at first be little more than an arbitrary choice. Also, in view of the overly optimistic goals some marketers set, the technique sometimes isn't practical. But you can still measure your success using one of four methods:

1. Evaluation of responses
2. Estimation of impact
3. Estimation of sales productivity
4. Surveying direct response (or mail) readership

EVALUATION OF RESPONSES

Simply counting replies is valid only when the primary objective of the program is to motivate some responsive action, such as sending in an inquiry, asking for a representative to call, or requesting that the recipient's name be retained in a database. Totaling responses is easy to do but seldom provides much really useful data. By itself it gives no indication of the *quality* of the responses. Thus, *evaluating* responses is a necessary second step.

To conserve personal contact time, some marketers send out one follow-up mailing to draw a *second* response before names are forwarded to field sales people. Other marketers maintain a check on response quality by recording the number of requests for a sales call and then comparing each rep's reports of such calls.

The most logical method for evaluating quality, is to use a *rating scale*. The factors to be graded and their weights should be based on the specific objectives and goals of each effort. They will differ from one industry to another—and even from one marketing communications effort to another by the same organization. Some factors, though, seem universally desirable. Here is an example of a rating scale, where five fundamental qualities of a prospective customer are weighted on the basis of 100 total maximum "points" of desirability. Such weights as these are normally determined by consensus among the marketer's senior people.

Factors to Be Graded	Maximum Points
Potential business in the responding company	25
Leadership of the responding company in its industry	10
Buying influence of the individual respondent	35
Door-opening effect (to new account or new person)	15
Degree of interest indicated by person responding	15
	100

Although determining desirable qualities and assigning points to develop ratings may be handled by a senior executive, it is preferable to seek the guidance of field sales personnel. After such a technique has been in use for a short time, standards of judgment develop and ratings tend to become generally consistent.

In the end, the average evaluation of all responses to a particular effort—plus the number of responses—provides a reasonably good measurement of the success of a marketing communications effort, and you might even develop such guidelines as, for example, that a program averaging less than a 60 score out of 100 should not be repeated in the future.

TECHNIQUES TO MEASURE IMPACT

What are often called *concept* communications are designed chiefly to influence recipients' views and attitudes—to stimulate acceptance of certain ideas or to change various perceptions of a company or its products and/ or services. In such cases, measuring results may seem impossible. And, in fact, measurement *is* difficult. But there are two techniques you can use to gain some idea of how effective your concept communications have been.

First, you can gather field sales or contact peoples' observations of recipients' reactions. The person in the field has a unique opportunity to assess the effects of marketing communications activities first-hand. If it can be arranged, tell your representatives in advance what information you want and provide a simple checklist for them to complete. To be fair, also ask their own personal opinions—but keep these separate from their more objective observations.

Second, you can conduct independent surveys of the opinions of and reactions to your communications. This process can be fairly expensive, but it is usually more objective than relying on your field personnel. Surveys may be conducted by personal interview, telephone, fax, the Internet, or mail. Questions should be simple and designed to draw out honest and uninhibited expressions of opinion. See Appendix 4 for suggestions on how to design a survey questionnaire.

Some specific suggestions for opinion surveys:

- Use a representative cross-section of your mailing list.
- Repeat the same survey at intervals. This (called "tracking research") shows the progress you have made in broadening or deepening a desired effect.
- Seek expert help for any survey project. If your organization has a good market research capability, by all means make use of it. Or use a qualified outside survey firm; a third party can help eliminate bias.

ESTIMATING PRODUCTIVITY

Sales productivity is, by far, the most difficult factor to relate to other types of marketing communications. But if you can demonstrate that your marketing communications have played a major role in the total selling process, you will have made an important contribution to the total strategic marketing effort.

Some marketers of modest means look at gross sales figures and are satisfied to look no further. More sophisticated organizations break sales activities down in a variety of ways to permit more careful strategic planning. A common method, mentioned elsewhere in this handbook, is to evaluate sales of four basic types:

- Old products or services to existing customers.
- New products or services to existing customers.
- Old products or services to new customers.
- New products or services to new customers.

New customers can be members of a previously served industry or a line of business the company has never served before. In addition to this categorization, it is often helpful to break the selling process into its component strategic steps, as suggested in Chapter 31:

1. Prospecting.
2. Completing the preapproach.
3. Making the approach.
4. Making the presentation.

5. Overcoming objections.

6. Closing the sale.

7. Collecting the money.

8. Following up.

9. Keeping the customer sold.

Marketing communications other than personal contact can play a significant part in Steps 1, 2, and 9, and they may help in 3, 7, and 8. It is necessary to determine the relative importance of each step in the sequence and perhaps even ascribe weights to each as suggested two sections ago. It then can become possible to make reasonable judgments about the amount of effort you should put into marketing communications efforts other than personal selling.

Two other methods for estimating a communication program's productivity should be mentioned. The first is to abstract information from sales representatives' *call reports* (or *conference reports* or *contact reports*), if you have established this discipline. From this you can learn what effects followed each effort. The second is to experiment. Use marketing communications to implement a sales drive in one or more territories and omit it in other well-matched territories. This is more of a test than a definite measuring device. But it can certainly provide useful information for larger organizations that have time and money to invest in such refinements.

MEASURING READERSHIP

A final measuring tool is the readership survey. When you conduct a readership study you are *not* trying to gather specific information about the recipients' knowledge, approval, goodwill, or receptiveness with respect to you or your company. Instead, such surveys measure how much pure *advertising* exposure you are getting as distinguished from direct response or sales.

Results of readership surveys can also help you make direct comparisons of cost efficiencies with other media and help you compare different mailings or other forms of direct distribution of your messages.

Surveys can be conducted by mail, telephone, fax, the Internet, or personal interviews. Preferably, they should be made within two to three weeks after a direct response effort is released. Like all other research, they should be conducted with a valid random sample of your audience or suspect list.

Personal interviews are normally too expensive to be practical. But they do let you aid recall, because you can display a sample of the marketing communication piece you're researching. Telephone interviews save money, but unless a mailing or piece is easily described, unaided recall is difficult. Mail surveys are least expensive although they generally produce the lowest total response. Recall can be aided by reproducing all or part of the mailing or piece.

If you do economize, for example, by reproducing only the cover of a printed piece, it should contain something distinctive to stimulate recall.

Typical questions you could ask by mail might be these:

The letter and folder shown here were recently mailed to a list on which your name appeared. To help us in a study we are making, would you please answer the following questions:

1. Do you remember receiving the mailing?

( ) Yes.   ( ) No.

2. If you received it, how much of it did you read?

( ) Read most of it. ( ) Read some of it. ( ) None.

3. If you received this mailing, did you take any of the following actions?

( ) Saved it or filed it.

( ) Routed or showed it to someone else.

( ) Requested literature.

( ) Requested a sales call.

Mailed surveys do have a major weakness: The group that replies to the survey may not contain the same proportion of readers of the mail as the group that *doesn't* reply. Perhaps some of the nonresponders did not see *either* the original mailing or the survey mailing. Thus, the telephone for surveys of business and professional people may produce more valid results.

As a rule, the higher your rate of response, the lower the probability of error.

WAYS QUANTITY OF RESPONSE MEANS SUCCESS

There are times when measuring simply the *number* of responses to a direct response effort is the best way to determine its effectiveness. Here are five specific instances:

- When the effort advertises a product or service low in cost and with a broad application, the more replies the better.
- When the effort is addressed to an audience so carefully defined and screened that a response from *anyone* in the audience is well worth a personal call, quantity counts.
- When the effort offers only a personal call for consultation, the number of replies from respondents with an active interest in your product or service is important.
- When the effort offers a brochure, manual, or other reference piece, the number of replies indicates the number of people interested in reading about the com-

pany and its products or services, and possibly becoming customers in the near future.

- When an exploratory research mailing asks for information, the number of replies indicates the interest generated in the project and its results.

TESTING YOUR MARKETING COMMUNICATIONS

Concentration so far in this chapter has been on measuring direct response marketing communications for evidence of accomplishment. But another goal of evaluation can be to *improve* future efforts.

You can gather data to help you achieve this aim using the techniques presented here. But often actual *testing* of various factors and devices is called for.

In no other area of marketing communications has testing become so important as in direct response. This is because the versatility and selectivity of such efforts make testing both possible and practical, and the ever-increasing costs of preparation, production, media, postage and the like make testing more desirable than ever before. Testing is like insurance. You should test those things you are not sure of—at low cost—and apply the results to your total effort. In this way you will get the best return on your marketing communications investment.

But remember that there are all kinds and degrees of testing. The tests you are likely to hear most about are done by very large-volume marketing communicators. For them, a small difference in a percentage of return may mean the difference between profit and loss, while for many others even a 10 percent difference in return might affect only a few ultimate sales.

So consider testing very carefully. While it can be vital to *direct marketing* (or mail order) advertisers, it may offer little or nothing to other marketers who simply wish to develop name recognition and/or build goodwill.

FACTORS TO TEST

Almost any aspect of your marketing message, your package, or your audience can be tested. You can even determine if the product or service you are promoting is suitable for the particular type of marketing activity you are considering.

When testing is indicated, most often you will want to check the following:

- Your target market.
- Your audience (such as your list for a mailing or the circulation of the magazine in which you advertise).
- Your basic message (including your offer).

- Your creative strategy.
- Your headline or lead.
- Your physical presentation (or your "package").
- The timing of your delivery.

TYPES OF TESTING

Without going into detail, suffice it to say that there are two basic types of testing for these types of evaluations. The first is *probability testing* which lets you check your basic approaches or the audience(s) you have chosen. You reach a small, representative segment of your target (the "sample") to determine whether appealing to the entire audience is likely to be productive. The second method, *comparison testing*, permits you to check one factor against an alternative. You test to determine, for example, whether one appeal is better than another or whether a predominantly blue background for your illustration is preferable to a predominantly red background.

Pretesting is where you show proposed marketing and creative ideas to sample audiences to try to predict response, and *posttesting* is where you research material *after* the sample audience has been exposed to try to judge effects. Types of *posttesting* are these:

- *Aided recall* (or *recognition-readership*)—where respondents are shown an ad and asked about effects. Daniel Starch and Associates Research (usually called simply "Starch") scores those who remember seeing the ad, called *ad-noters*, or those who *noted* (noticed) the ad, those who can identify the product or advertiser, called *seen-associated* or simply *associated* readers, and those who read at least half the copy, called *read most* readers.
- *Unaided recall*—respondents are asked to name ads they saw within the past 24 hours.
- *Attitude tests*—respondents are asked whether their attitude toward the product has changed as a result of the ad.
- *Inquiry tests*—offers of additional information, premiums, or product samples generate response, and higher levels assume greater ad effectiveness—even though it is fairly easy to "rig" this sort of research (that is, to affect the response rate by manipulating the incentive).
- *Sales tests*—relate advertising to sales. Cable systems and other media can be related to records of consumer purchases recorded by UPC scanners. Some fear "invasion of privacy" in this sort of research, but so far participation by consumers has been voluntary.

See Chapter 2 for more on primary research that you can apply to testing.

FUNDAMENTALS OF TESTING

Whatever you test and for whatever reason, you will be most successful if you follow these general principles:

1. *Test one thing at a time*—To obtain valid results, test only one thing at a time. Every factor must be identical except the one you are testing; otherwise you can't be sure what it was that was responsible for the different result. Even when testing one complete direct mail package against another, keep such things as the list, time of mailing, and class of postage used the same. To maintain consistency in your lists, by the way, just divide names from the same list alternately between the two test mailings (the *A/B method* defined in Chapter 2).

2. *Use a large enough sample to obtain reliable results*—Testing depends on mathematical laws of probability. A common rule for national marketers when testing similar samples is to use 2,000 names or 10 percent of a list, up to a maximum of 10,000. If a list has more than 100,000 names, the usual procedure is to conduct a series of tests in groups of 10,000 names each until a full 10 percent has been tested. In most cases if a list contains fewer than 1,000 names you should simply mail to the *entire* list and save the expense of a test.

3. *Mail all pieces at the same time, or try "two-flight" testing*—Mailing results can be affected by weather, current events, and other extraneous factors. So be sure to deliver all pieces in a test mailing to the post office at exactly the same *time*, and not just the same *day*. An alternative is to use the "two-flight" technique to ensure that some extraneous factor does not prejudice the test results. In this method, you mail duplicate sets of tests some time apart and compare results. Be sure, of course, that all sets are properly coded or "keyed," about which more in the next section.

4. *Make sure test lists are representative of the entire list*—To determine the value of a given list, make sure the portion chosen for your test is representative of the complete list. You can usually do this by selecting your sample on an "nth" name basis: Select every third, tenth, hundredth, or five-hundredth name. If you are testing a very large, geographically arranged list, the sample should include a proportionate number of names from each geographic area covered by the list. If this is impractical, select one major state, county, or ZIP Code area in each basic region included. Another rule is to keep track of the portions of every list used for testing. These names should be *eliminated* when you make any further tests and/or when you mail to the entire list. List suppliers are accustomed to doing this but are not likely to do so unless asked.

5. *When comparing lists, be sure they are equal in number*—If you use every tenth name from one list, use every tenth name from the second list. If you use the first 1,000 names from the first list, use the first 1,000 names from the second list. This assumes, of course, that each list has names arranged in exactly the same alphabetic, geographic, or other sequence. If they are not so arranged, try to have the two test lists formatted as nearly identically as possible. One unexpected benefit you can obtain from this procedure is to discover whether the two lists you are testing are actually the *same* list. Different list brokers may

describe the same list in different ways, which can cause costly and sometimes embarrassing duplication.

6. *Do not follow test results blindly, or make major decisions based on minor results*—You have made a test, and all the evidence seems to be in hand. But do not generalize too quickly. So many variables can affect direct response marketing communications that it is risky for you to accept the results of any single test as final. Remember, first, that the total quantity of returns may not constitute a large enough sample to be representative. And, second, that small differences in return are often caused by pure chance. Even more important, do not attempt to read nontested factors into the results. Whenever you are in doubt, *test again.*

7. *Keep good records over a long enough period of time*—This rule is especially important in list testing. Always suspect that test lists from rental sources may be slightly altered to provide a better-than-average response. And consider the *quality* of inquiries as well as the quantity when comparing one list to another.

8. *Follow up quickly*—When you have completed a test and believe you have the answers you need, follow up quickly with the total program you have planned. This is advisable because market factors can change rapidly, and future marketing efforts may face a whole new set of circumstances.

9. *Don't become "test happy"*—You probably should always keep testing. But it should always be a *secondary* activity. Do not let tests keep you from using direct response as an advertising and selling tool. Test only when the information you gain will be worth *more* than the time and expense required to get it.

TECHNIQUES TO "KEY" RESPONSES

To measure the results of a mailing—and for testing, in particular—some method for "keying" your responses is necessary. Keying is a way to identify each reply by its source. Here are six ways to do that:

1. *Change the key code*—The simplest—and most often used—technique to key is to print some code designation on the reply form. Usually it consists of a few letters and/or numbers printed in very small type in a lower corner of the reply card, form, or envelope.

2. *Alter the name of your organization*—It is easier than you might think to make minor changes in your firm name for keying purposes. For example: "Thomas, Perry & Associates, P.C." can be changed to "Thomas, Perry and Associates, P.C.," or "Thomas-Perry & Associates, P.C." The P.C. could be omitted or changed, Associates abbreviated in any of several ways, and so on.

3. *Change your address*—If mail is delivered to you through a post office box or simply by the name of your firm, it may be possible to add a fictitious street address. Or you might be able to change the designation "Street" to "Avenue" or "Lane" or "Road." Check with your local postal authorities for permissible modifications of address.

4. *Clip the corners of the reply form or card*—A printer's paper cutter—or even a pair of scissors—can help when you want to key a reply form. Cutting off one

corner, or a combination of corners, of reply cards can give you basic information about the source of the response. An alternative is to punch distinctive holes in them. Railroad conductor's punches are useful if you have small quantities of cards and lots of things to test. Large quantities of cards can be drilled or die-cut.

5. *Change department numbers*—On their reply forms, many marketers include a "department number," such as *Department B-23*, under the company name as a part of their address. When you key this way you can set up as many different departments as you have tests and even code by division, product, target audience, and so on.

6. *Print identification in invisible ink*—Ink that dries invisible and can be read under ultraviolet light or otherwise revealed has been used under some circumstances by direct response marketers who want to keep their keying a *secret*.

7. *Assign "finder numbers"*—A more sophisticated technique whereby you give each name on your list a sequential number, also called an *instant number*, and print that number on each reply form. This number (usually 15 digits or fewer) can be automatically scanned, and therefore greatly speeds electronic analysis of returns.

Note: A simple method for keying returns might seem to be the use of different colored papers or inks for the reply forms. *But avoid this*. It can invalidate your tests, because different colors can produce *different response rates*. In other words, the use of different colors introduces a *second variable* into a test, altering results in ways you might not be able to measure.

CONCLUSION

There is probably more in this chapter than you care to use at present, but please do keep this truism in mind: *Modern strategic marketing is impossible without measurement*. And that measurement should be an *ongoing* activity.

Part VII

Marketing Management Concerns

Chapter 39

Marketing Management Strategies

QUALITIES OF GOOD MANAGERS

Good management requires good leadership. A good leader is generally recognized as one with a genuine capacity for empathy, a clear mission or "vision," a consistently objective mood, and a sense of humor. Experts have suggested that to be a successful leader you should observe the following:

- Be true to yourself
- Have self-confidence
- Be willing to act intuitively
- Be honest with others
- Be open to the ideas of others
- Help others to succeed

RESPONSIBILITIES

The subject of management is probably as lengthy and complex as the subject of marketing, so this chapter touches only on highlights. The major responsibilities of a marketing manager, sales manager, advertising manager, and other marketing-related managers are these:

- *Recruiting*—considered by some to be the single most important responsibility. If a manager selects well-qualified people with a strong work ethic who are eager to take responsibility, the job of the manager is greatly facilitated. Human resources departments in larger companies try to help in this area, but many HR people don't fully understand what makes good marketing people, and the searching, screening, and inducting work should be handled by the manager personally for best results.

- *Training*—unless one hires previously qualified people, often major training efforts are necessary. Even when you hire experienced people, though, teaching them your corporate culture and style of doing business is vital, and ongoing training about products, applications, and skills—especially in the area of sales—is extremely important.

- *Supervising*—assigning people to areas or territories where they are likely to be most effective, seeing that they follow company procedures, and work to maximum productivity can take up a good deal of a manager's time.

- *Motivating*—as will be mentioned shortly, the principle of rewards versus punishments must be applied fairly, equitably, and consistently to keep people working at their best, for their own sakes as well as the sake of the company and its other stakeholders.

- *Compensating*—although sometimes not given enough attention by some managers, the matter of paying people for work performed is crucial. Related to motivation, but normally seen in the context of salaries, benefits, commissions, and bonuses, compensating your people fairly should be a major concern to managers.

- *Retaining*—since it's expensive to replace people managers neither want to fire them nor have them leave of their own accord. Handling all of the foregoing well should maximize employee retention.

It might be argued that there are as many management strategies as there are managers, but the basics can be categorized fairly simply. Of course, two or more strategies can be used simultaneously.

MINIMAL INVOLVEMENT STRATEGIES

Consider first strategies in which the manager does as little as possible.

- *Laissez-faire strategy*—as the French term translates, the manager "lets be" or just lays down basic rules and allows subordinates to manage themselves.
  - *Trust strategy*—a form of *laissez-faire* that works well with subordinates who have a strong work ethic and who are suitably motivated. The theory is that if you believe in them and support them, they will perform.
  - *Project team strategy*—another form of *laissez-faire* developed by the Japanese wherein employees ideally discover work that needs to be done, form responsible teams, and manage themselves.
  - *By-the-numbers strategy*—the manager lays down basic guidelines and then evaluates performance in an orderly and analytical fashion. Good for managers lacking interpersonal skills.

POSITIVE STRATEGIES

Strategies likely to have positive results for managers are these:

- *The carrot strategy*—based on the metaphor of the donkey moving ahead because its rider dangles a carrot in front of it. Although the term is not flattering to either manager or subordinate, the practice of providing rewards for good performance has proved effective.

  —*Buddy strategy*—the manager tries to be a pal to subordinates. The weakness of this strategy is that in time each assignment may become a matter of doing the manager a personal favor.

  —*Begging strategy*—goes beyond the *buddy* strategy with regard to manager humility. The manager pleads with subordinates to get the job done. Not good for either respect by employees or the manager's self-esteem.

  —*Management by walking around*—a good way to stay in touch with what's going on, to appear cordial and open, and to build camaraderie.

  —*Respect and recognition*—sometimes called "attaboys." Some managers believe compliments cause employees to slack off; others have found that *not* to be true, but rather that deserved praise is appreciated and encourages people to continue to do well, and even try to excel.

  —*Career development opportunities*—works well with ambitious subordinates.

  —*Participation in decision-making*—works well with self-confident subordinates.

  —*Pay for performance*—given lip service in many large organizations, and often a myth. If practiced conscientiously, this strategy is likely to be a good one— if it does not conflict with affirmative action programs.

  —*Piecework*—keeps employees on their toes, since they are retained and compensated only if they produce adequately.

  —*Commissions*—works best with sales people. It's hard to relate contributions to sales of other marketing personnel.

  —*Bonuses*—a particularly good executive management strategy.

  —*Stock options*—increasingly popular as a reward for good performance.

  —*Benefits*—taken for granted in some industries, but good to keep in mind in your planning if your organization does not offer such.

  —*Titles in lieu of salaries*—sometimes ridiculous, but favored in several industries, notably banking.

  —*Awards and lapel pins*—popular motivation device for sales representatives. Carried to an extreme in some industries where uniforms are worn, and sometimes decorated as in the military.

- *Management by objectives (MBO)*—popular subject on the business seminar circuit. Set mutually acceptable objectives (preferably in the form defined in this handbook as *goals*) and work jointly toward their achievement. Compensation, promotion, and other rewards are based on performance according to the MBO plan.

- *Critical path technique*—scheduling discipline used to manage complex work involving many steps; lists tasks, individuals or departments responsible, and assigns times for completion of each. May be diagrammed on a PERT chart (acronym for Program Evaluation and Review Technique) to graphically illustrate tasks, responsibilities, interrelationships, resources, and timing—optimistic and "drop dead" dates. PERT charts are particularly useful for new product introductions.

- *Quarterback approach*—where the manager calls the signals and relies on *teamwork* to move the ball.

NEGATIVE STRATEGIES

Management strategies less likely to succeed are these:

- *The stick strategy*—the philosophy contrary to *the carrot* strategy related to the donkey metaphor, holds that the manager must whip subordinates into doing required work. Normally the beating is verbal rather than physical, but can be damaging to the collective effort. Most managers who browbeat and threaten their employees appear to be flawed personalities who do so at least as much because they *enjoy* it as because it is an effective management strategy. The beaten employee will often find devious ways to get even, rather than putting full energies into the job.

  —*KITA strategy*—a form of the *stick* strategy and a common acronym for "kick in the ass." Popular in military basic training and probably rather effective there. A construction foreman once told me proudly, "I make my guys *mad* so they work harder." The drawback of *KITA* is that once you start kicking, you have to devote a great deal of your time to *continuing* to kick.

  —*What-have-you-done-for-me-lately strategy*—commonly practiced by clients to manage their advertising and public relations agencies, this is supposed to "keep their feet to the fire."

  —*Crisis strategy*—the manager runs around declaring "the sky is falling." Threats that the organization is in serious trouble and that employees are "lucky to have [their] jobs" are supposed to be motivators although, in fact, the contrary is often more likely.

  —*Authority strategy*—the manager is absolute dictator and all deference is due. A former federal government official had his desk raised on a dais so when employees entered his presence they had to look *up* at him, as if he were a king upon his throne. Like several of the strategies that follow, this is sometimes used, not maliciously, but simply for ego gratification and intended by the manager to "keep the peons in their place."

  —*"Just do it" strategy*—often linked with an *authority* strategy, the manager does not discuss any objections to orders. There's not enough money in your budget to buy the 30-second spot on the Super Bowl the boss wants? "Don't bother me with details; just *do* it!" Sometimes such orders are clarified with the capper,

"Or you're *fired!*" On the other hand, Winston Churchill reportedly used this strategy during the Second World War, and achieved historic success.

—*Yelling and slamming doors*—popular in several of our larger cities and probably limited to managers who were badly spoiled as children.

—*Derogation*—based on the assumption that a manager can insult subordinates into satisfactory performance. Another strategy practiced by managers with low self-esteem and/or a sadistic streak.

—*Terror and intimidation*—threats of demotion and firing of employees is presumed good motivation for those who survive. Morale may suffer and, as with the *KITA* strategy, possible retribution can result.

—*"A bitching ship is a healthy ship"*—an ex-Marine Corps officer I once worked with liked to use this metaphor to describe his management strategy, which seemed to be an outgrowth of *authority* strategy. In his view the more miserable his subordinates were the better he thought he was doing.

Obviously, if you believe in the power of positive reinforcement, you will favor many of the *carrot* strategies although sometimes, for some employees, the more heavy-handed strategies are called for.

Chapter 40

Information, Your Message, and Ethics

BASIC CONSIDERATIONS

Whether your marketing efforts are consumer, professional, commercial, industrial, reseller (or trade), institutional, or governmental, you are involved in the dissemination of useful and important information *in the public interest*. The fact that this might benefit you and your organization, is not in the least coincidental.

A vital part of marketing programs involves means by which you efficiently disseminate that useful information to select audiences and present your organization in *the most favorable light* that personal integrity and professional ethics permit.

Although few marketers will choose to answer all these questions in their communications, here are basic topics you should consider:

- *Who* are you, or what is your organization?
- *What* do you offer?
- *Where* are you located?
- *When* are you available?
- *Why* should prospects begin to deal with you?
- *Why* should customers continue to deal with you?
- *How* do you operate?
- *How much* do you charge?
- *What's in it for them?*

Remember, it's not what *you* are interested in that counts—it is what is in the interest of your customers and prospects.

THE ESSENTIAL FACTS

Some types of information—like product or service name and often organization name, location, telephone number, and Web site—are absolutely *essential*. Other items are less important and might well be omitted from your marketing communications.

What you must select is that information which is likely to be meaningful and significant to the particular target market segment you intend to address. Specifically, information should embody the following characteristics:

- *Important* to someone who buys your product or retains your services.
- *Interesting* to your target market—usually because it relates directly to their self-interest.
- *New* so it will be special to your prospects, and *newsworthy* so it will be significant to the media that might publicize it.

ADDITIONAL SUGGESTIONS

So much advertising, sales promotion, and publicity in the United States is tedious and boring because marketers fail to test their messages for the following common-sense suggestions:

- Do not bore your customers and prospects with *me-too* statements. Set yourself *apart* from your competition.
- Do not waste their time with comments on the obvious. Say something that is *worthy* of their attention.
- Keep all your marketing communications fresh and lively to maximize the probability of their prompting immediate *action*.

These basic elements are the blocks that should form the *foundation* of your marketing communications program. As such, it is likely that none will serve as the major attention-getter, nor what is sometimes called "the icing on the cake," which have been treated in preceding chapters.

SIMPLE IS BEST

The process of identifying your key information is somewhat like cleaning out your garage. You must strengthen your resolve and vow to *throw away* everything that is not *absolutely essential*.

According to *Business Week*, the average American is exposed to some 3,000 marketing messages every day. Because of what psychologists call *selective perception*, most of those messages are not noticed, understood, or remembered. First, people deliberately limit their exposure to marketing messages through what is called *selective exposure*; next, they adjust the content of messages in their minds to conform to their views of life in a process called *selective distortion*; and finally they remember only the messages they accept and to which they are frequently exposed through a third process called *selective retention*.

The information that registers, that is retained, that can be recalled, and that leads to action is information which has been reduced to its *simplest form*, and which is most closely related to the *needs and wants* of the audience.

Henry David Thoreau's advice on life itself is therefore appropriate here: *Simplify, simplify, simplify*.

For example, think of the retailer who does well by erecting a sign that reads simply "SALE," or think how effective are the signs along our interstate highways that say only "GAS" or "EAT." To the person who is low on fuel or hungry, such signs almost always do their job well by appealing directly and simply to immediate needs.

You know from your study of the fundamentals of marketing that there must be a *need*—be it for gasoline, a hot meal, or a new article of clothing. And although you should never overlook the importance of the need, you should also make all of your communication of information relating to its satisfaction no more complex than it has to be. A popular acronym you may recall is *KISS*, which stands simply, although rather rudely, for "Keep It Simple, Stupid."

YOUR MESSAGE

Your *message* is the meal. Your *information* is the potatoes and gravy, your *offer* is the meat, and your *appeal* is its aroma. Your "creative" is the dining atmosphere. Thus, your creative should attract attention, the aroma should create desire for your product or service, and your offer itself should lead to action by your customers and prospects. Of course, your supplementary basic information creates interest and makes an exchange or transaction possible.

Depending on how you structure your marketing communications, your message will often guide you to what is called your "grabber," your "hook," your "headline," or, in the case of publicity, your "lead," or your "news peg." The most powerful marketing messages go beyond being simply *interesting information*, and sometimes are perceived as being *exciting*.

Some messages are very simple and direct, such as "Drink Coca-Cola®." Some are terrifically complex—like those of firms seeking contracts to develop new aerospace programs or to install satellite-linked telecommunications systems.

There's a lot to remember in most marketing messages, and a proven way to keep track of it all is suggested in Appendix 7, "Your Marketing Communications Work Plan."

BEWARE OF HYPERBOLE

Try to keep a balanced perspective with regard to how you express your message. Many otherwise honest marketers seem to lapse into the philosophy that "the end justifies the means" when preparing statements of their message. That is to say, some people think that exaggeration and distortion are an essential part of the marketing communications process. This can lead to unwanted consequences.

So do not be seduced by the siren *Hyperbole*, whose song is sweet but whose kiss can be death.

Which relates to the subject of ethics. You are familiar with your code of ethics for your particular industry or profession, so consider here ethics as social and business philosophy, and as related specifically to *marketing*.

BASIC ETHICAL SYSTEMS

Most business and professional people can be expected to scrupulously uphold the *law*, but recent experience has shown that many are somewhat less conscientious when their behavior involves *ethics*. This is probably because the matter of ethics, and the related subject of *social responsibility*, are so poorly defined and open to such a wide range of individual interpretation.

Laws and government regulations are written, published, and enforceable in our courts of law. But ethics and social responsibility involve moral principles and values that are closer to folklore and that vary from one group of people to another—even within the same country.

Some people believe that the pressure on American businesspeople today to make a profit above all else, conform to the demands of diverse interest groups, and tolerate or at least rationalize asocial and even antisocial behavior have all contributed to an erosion of our traditional ethical and moral fiber. So the subject of ethics ranges from the classic "*caveat emptor*" (Latin for "let the buyer beware") to "*caveat venditor*" (Latin for "let the *seller* beware").

There are many complex systems for categorizing ethics, but the following is easy to use with regard to marketing activities:

• *Moral idealism*—many academic and clerical thinkers subscribe to the notion of *moral idealism* as a guide to ethical conduct. This means, in simplest terms, that there is only *one* system for guiding the rights and duties of individuals and organizations, and that system should be applied *universally*, regardless of the particular situation or the anticipated results. The Golden Rule of "do unto others as you would have them do unto you" is about as simple as can be. The Consumer Bill of Rights, formulated in 1962 under President Kennedy, codified the ethics of buying and selling in the absolutist fashion of *moral idealism.*

- *Utilitarianism*—the philosophy of *utilitarianism* is a more liberal approach that stresses "the greatest good for the greatest number of people." This reflects the *ideal* of our form of free-market capitalism, wherein the basic test of ethical behavior is whether the effects of a person's or organization's action(s) significantly benefit the majority, or at least a plurality, among their stakeholders, publics, or target markets.

- *Situational ethics*—people who do business internationally, or even among subcultures in our own country, tend to accept the idea of *situational ethics.* This has been summed up by the ancient phrase, "When in Rome, do as the Romans do." It recognizes different values and moral standards among people and does not seek to impose one system upon another. The only difficulty with this approach is that it may conflict with U.S. *law* as, for example, if one were to offer *"baksheesh"* to a Middle Eastern business contact. What is standard business practice there could be construed as a clearly illegal *bribe* by U.S. government authorities.

- *Optional ethics*—and, speaking of the Middle East, one of my acquaintances from Qatar introduced me to a fourth philosophy that he called "optional ethics." He explained that this is a common orientation of business and professional people in his culture. And it explains why our diplomats seem to have trouble negotiating with the Iraqis, for example, and why business executives are sometimes disappointed in their dealings in Arab countries. *Optional ethics* means, the fellow explained, that "you do or say whatever is necessary to get what you want." This standard is not recommended, of course, but is included here for the sake of completeness.

- *Consumer sovereignty*—in the book *Ethics in Marketing*, N. Craig Smith suggests that marketing managers will be best served by an ethical system which is founded on the marketing concept and which therefore requires that they weigh three factors:

  —*Capability* of the consumer, which involves vulnerability factors including age, education, and income.

  —*Information* availability and quantity sufficient to judge whether purchase expectations will be satisfied.

  —*Choice* involving the opportunity to switch, the level of competition, and the costs of switching.

If we balance Smith's idea with the first three rules suggested in connection with public relations in Chapter 29 (do no harm, tell the truth, and do nothing that would embarrass you if reported as news) we should be fairly safe.

Please see Appendix 15 for the code of ethics of the American Marketing Association, and Appendix 16 for the AMA code with regard to the Internet which treat this subject in greater detail.

Part VIII

Conclusion

Chapter 41

How to Write a Marketing Strategy Statement

Once you have decided what your strategy is to be—whether overall, for a specific section of a marketing plan, or for tactical execution—it is fairly simple to construct a succinct strategy statement.

State the marketing problem or opportunity, and then the marketing strategy to solve or take advantage of it. This can normally be done in one sentence. For example, a product-related overall strategy might read as follows:

> Because we have exclusive patents covering the technology of our antigravity device, we will launch a *pioneer market strategy* immediately to be the first company to offer antigravity products to the transportation industry.

Or, a specific strategy with regard to marketing communications might read like this:

> Our antigravity device will benefit from a *news story communications strategy* to convey the innovation and excitement of our revolutionary new products.

Alternatively, your strategy can evolve from your specific goal. Because measurable marketing and advertising goals have been defined as objectives that have been made specific in terms of (1) the job to be done (or the fundamental objective), (2) the target market or public to be affected, (3) the amount of change to occur, and (4) the time period for the activity, those elements should be included in your *goal* statement, and not necessarily in your *strategy* statement. If, however, you have not developed one or more measurable goals, you will find execution facilitated by including that pertinent information in your strategy statement.

This discipline is particularly important in written marketing plans. It is also advisable in formal plans to put your goal(s) in quantifiable terms, such as the number of prospects to be influenced or sales volume to be achieved, so you can measure your success. And, finally, the inclusion of a time-frame will help keep execution of your marketing program on schedule.

You might use this handbook to develop only a single strategy for one of the basic components of your marketing activities. Or you might want to develop strategies for an entire formal, written marketing plan. In that case, please see Appendix 2 for a basic framework for your plan and develop one or more strategies for each of the appropriate sections enumerated there.

Chapter 42

How to Evaluate Strategic Marketing Cases

GETTING STARTED

Whether you are working on a strategic marketing case as a corporate problem-solving assignment, a seminar exercise, or for a business or marketing course, you may wish to take the following steps:

1. Consider whether your case is business, marketing management, concentrated on pricing, dependant on advertising, or what have you.

2. Perhaps copy the case, especially if work is to be a team project.

3. Read the entire case first to see the *big picture*.

4. Be sure to clearly identify the central issue or issues; these should lend themselves to strategic marketing solutions. You should not simply reiterate the facts of the case but sort them out and develop your own interpretations of the facts.

5. Distinguish *relevant* facts and discard the others; be sure you are dealing with *root causes*, not the results or symptoms. For example, "declining sales" may not be the root problem, but the result of poor recruiting, hiring, and training of field sales personnel; or booming sales may not be the result of product quality, but of low price relative to perceived value.

6. Don't be concerned about lack of information; many marketing decisions have to be made with little or no substantive data or specific information. So you'll often have to trust your own assumptions.

7. Do a thorough *situation analysis*, along the lines indicated in Chapter 4, and include a SWOT analysis if that seems appropriate. If yours is a group project, this is an excellent opportunity to practice *brainstorming*.

8. Don't offer what are called in this handbook the *easy answers*. For example, if marketing communications seems to be a weakness in a case, don't just

suggest "hire an advertising agency," but devise a specific solution that relies on basic advertising media and creative *strategies*.

9. Make specific, confident recommendations; avoid vague and ambiguous statements.

10. Use proper marketing terminology and names for strategies for each marketing discipline which you can find in this handbook.

11. Double-check your conclusions to be sure they are *reasonable*; don't come up with pie-in-the-sky promises based on an unrealistic road to success. Can what you propose reasonably be done and result in what is necessary?

12. Keep in mind *when* the case occurred; don't assume twenty-first-century market situations for twentieth-century cases.

13. Allow yourself sufficient time to complete your work.

14. If yours is a course project, write carefully and cogently, and type double-spaced so there will be room for your instructor to comment where appropriate.

15. Students should normally attach one copy of the original case to their recommendations.

QUESTIONS TO ANSWER

Before you begin to write your recommendation, see that you can answer the following questions. Then concentrate on the answers you obtain to develop your marketing strategies.

1. What is the nature of the person(s) or organization represented in the case?

2. What is the product, service, or idea to be marketed?

3. What consumer or customer need(s) or want(s) can the product satisfy?

4. What specific type(s) of people potentially need or want the product? (Be sure to use standard target market segmentation variables to define them, as noted in Appendix 5.)

5. What market research has been done, or should be done?

6. What are the specific features of the product, and the corresponding benefit(s) to the target market?

7. Does the organization or product need a new name?

8. What are the product's packaging requirements?

9. What prices or fees should be charged, both to the ultimate buyer, and to intermediaries?

10. How will the product reach consumers or customers, or the service reach clients? (Define exactly the distribution channel(s), intermediaries, and logistics.)

11. What is the nature of the competition, both direct and indirect?

12. What is the company's or product's reputation and/or the brand image?

13. What is the product's positioning?

14. What is the nature of the product/business offer?

15. What is the primary problem or opportunity?

16. What is a reasonable marketing objective, and measurable marketing goal(s)? (The latter should include the target market, task to be accomplished, amount of change to occur, and the time period for completion.)

17. What should the message be, including the specific appeal and offer?

18. What should the marketing communications include? (Consider advertising, sales promotion, trade promotion, publicity, public relations, personal selling, sales management, and customer service.)

19. What should the marketing budget be? (Cover *SADA*: sales, advertising, distribution, and marketing administration expenses.)

20. What are the anticipated results of the proposed marketing program?

CHECKLIST FOR MAJOR CASE STUDY

If your project requires a full-fledged *marketing plan* based on a case study, consider the following checklist:

1. Identify the *organization's core competency* or the *product's major feature or benefit*.

2. Identify the *primary problem or opportunity* facing the business.

3. Develop an organizational *mission statement*.

4. Summarize the state of the industry.

5. Describe the product or service.

6. Explain pricing considerations.

7. Describe distribution and logistics.

8. Describe marketing communications to date.

9. Describe the organization's or product's *direct competition*, and comment on indirect competition.

10. Define specifically at least one *target market* to concentrate on for strategic planning.

11. Create a succinct *SWOT analysis* (strengths, weaknesses, opportunities, and threats). This can also precede #5.

12. Define key planning *assumptions and/or forecasts*.

13. Establish at least one essential *marketing objective*.

14. If feasible, convert each objective to at least one *measurable goal*.

15. Create a *core strategy* for the case product or organization.

16. Develop at least one *market strategy*.

17. Develop at least one *product* or *service strategy*.

18. Identify the *name* or *branding strategy*.

19. Specify the *packaging strategy*.

20. Develop at least one *pricing strategy*.

21. Develop at least one *distribution* or *logistics strategy*.

22. Develop at least one *competitive strategy*.

23. Develop at least one *positioning strategy*.

24. Develop at least one *offer strategy*.

25. Develop at least one *marketing communications strategy*.

26. Develop at least one *advertising media strategy*.

27. Develop at least one *advertising creative strategy*.

28. Supplement 27 with at least one *advertising design strategy*.

29. Develop at least one *sales promotion strategy*.

30. Develop at least one *public relations strategy*.

31. Specify at least one *publicity strategy*.

32. Specify one *personal selling strategy*.

33. Specify one *customer service strategy*.

34. Specify one *budgeting strategy*.

35. Specify how the program will be *evaluated*.

36. If appropriate, note recommended *marketing management strategy*.

37. Describe the kind(s) of *market research* that the organization should conduct to obtain information that would be useful in future marketing strategic planning.

38. Determine whether *tactical executions* based on your marketing strategies are reasonable.

CONCLUSION

The strategic case method provides an opportunity for the equivalent of on-the-job-training. It will not replace what can be learned from books and personal experience, but it will allow for the application of the kind of thinking necessary in real-life marketing situations.

As in the workaday world, there are seldom clearly right or absolutely wrong answers to questions of applied strategic marketing. What is important in the case study method is how each situation is analyzed, the imagination used in recommending strategies, how well decisions are justified, and how clearly strategic plans are communicated.

The objective here is to show how well one can reason and think innovatively. There should be no hesitation to suggest alternative strategies because there is not always "one best answer," as on multiple choice examinations.

As a supplement to strategies, those who prepare case studies should suggest marketing *action items*—that is, who is to do what, when, where, and why.

Here's to your great success in strategic marketing planning!

Appendixes

Appendix 1

The Fundamentals of Marketing

No marketing strategy can make a sustained success out of a product or a service for which there is no present or potential need or want, nor one that is unknown, of poor quality or value, difficult to obtain, or offered at the wrong time.

Academic discipline defines marketing in terms of the *4Ps*, which represent (1) product (or service, or idea), (2) price (or cost, or value), (3) place (or logistics, or distribution), and (4) promotion (or marketing communications). The 4Ps is a good mnemonic device, despite the need to explain what the words really mean, but there are several important aspects of marketing today that it does not cover. Here is a more complete enumeration of the fundamentals of modern marketing:

1. Discover a need and provide the means to satisfy it.

2. Identify the special group of people (usually a "target market" segment) who share the need and have the means and the authority to deal with you.

3. Let those particular people know what you have to offer.

4. Make your product appealing and desirable to them.

5. Make it easy for them to deal with you.

6. Distinguish yourself from your competition.

7. Keep your customers or clients sold, and your prospects interested.

8. Make an honest profit.

The best way to accomplish all these things is to develop a *written* strategic marketing plan.

There is no secret incantation, or magic formula, or easy answer that will guarantee the results you desire. The best path to success seems to involve serious reflective thinking, and dedication to your task.

Appendix 2

Topical Outline for a Marketing Plan

Cooking up a marketing program is similar in style to the method of a French chef making soup. You never completely empty the contents of your pot, but keep adding whatever good stuff is available to you, allowing it to simmer on the back of the stove, continuously stirring it, and serving up portions from time to time, as needed.

But that does not mean your planning should be random or haphazard. The discipline of marketing planning can be as regimented and formal as you choose, but it must involve a combination of observation, insight, logic, and creativity.

Strategic marketing planning tends to:

- clarify and organize your thoughts
- facilitate the setting of priorities
- help establish your objectives and goals (Chapters 5 and 6)
- lead logically to the means whereby you can accomplish your objectives and goals
- make more obvious the sharpening and specifying of each step in the marketing process
- establish performance standards for evaluation (Chapter 38)
- marshal the use of your resources (money, material, time, personnel, and so on)
- help you avoid doing those things that are nonproductive and hence wasteful of time, money, and other resources.

Although there are more detailed lists of components of a strategic marketing plan, you should be successful if you include the following elements:

1. Executive summary
2. Mission statement

3. Overview of the organization (including history and reputation)
4. Financial analysis of operations
5. Evaluation of the industry (including trends)
6. Description of the product, service, or idea
7. Pricing (may include discounting plans)
8. Logistics (including physical distribution)
9. Competition (both direct and indirect)
10. Target markets (details of segmentation)
11. Marketing communications activities to date
12. Other market influences
13. Strengths, weaknesses, opportunities, and threats (SWOT) analysis
14. Sales forecast (current and/or anticipated sales) or demand analysis
15. Distributors and dealers (if not marketing direct)
16. Market research (completed and proposed)
17. Assumptions (educated guesses)
18. Objectives and measurable goals
19. Customer and prospect needs, wants, and motives
20. Strategies (overall means to achieve objectives)
21. Image (name, trademark, logotype, trade dress, and so on)
22. Packaging (graphics, design, colors, and so on)
23. Positioning (concept, statement, or slogan)
24. Message (information, appeal, and offer)
25. Advertising (including the creative rationale)
26. Mass media (television, radio, magazines, and newspapers)
27. Alternative media (direct mail, point-of-purchase, tradeshows, and so on)
28. Media schedule (including gross impressions, reach, frequencies, CPMs)
29. Sales promotion (coupons, premiums, contests, and so on)
30. Trade promotion (terms, co-op, displays, and so on)
31. Public relations (making product or organization look good)
32. Publicity (including ongoing media relations plans)
33. Customer relations and customer services
34. Human resources (personnel and employee relations)
35. Investor relations
36. Industry relations
37. Government relations
38. Special interest groups
39. Sales management
40. Personal selling

41. Outside services (reps, consultants, agency, and so on)
42. Budget (detail of budgets for individual sections)
43. Program evaluation technique (how to measure success)
44. Conclusion (recapitulation in more detail than in the executive summary)

Note 1: This basic sequence may be changed in many ways to suit your particular needs. Delete whatever does not apply.

Note 2: If anticipated results can be specified and the timing of each element predicted and incorporated into your marketing plan, so much the better.

Note 3: There are four crucial qualities of well-crafted strategic marketing plans:

- Plans should be *flexible*—capable of being changed as new information or conditions require.
- Plans should be *realistic*—neither overly optimistic nor overly pessimistic.
- Plans should be *firmly committed*—subscribed to wholeheartedly by those responsible.
- Plans should be adequately *funded and staffed* for successful execution.

Appendix 3

Secondary Research Sources

If you want to save money by doing your marketing research yourself, you might wish to follow this procedure:

First, define *exactly what you need to know.*

Then search *your own records.* Always start searching there. Valuable insights can be gained by tabulating information on exactly who has been doing what type(s) of business with your organization in the past. It's also useful to get a picture of how your people have been approaching and serving customer needs.

Then seek out the *secondary data*—usually published materials and formal reference sources—that will provide the information required at little or no cost to you.

Some people feel they realize big savings by asking marketing professors at local colleges to have their students conduct studies at no direct charge. This is certainly good experience for the students, but the results are sometimes not of the quality you might wish to influence the success or failure of your organization. And, as for savings, the time you are likely to spend lining up and administering such an arrangement probably will be equivalent to just doing the job yourself.

The first place to look for basic secondary research information is your *public library.* In larger metropolitan areas this may be the only source required. In smaller communities you may have to search further.

The Internet can provide a wealth of information quickly and easily. However, *beware* of your sources, as there is a lot of misinformation, disinformation, and lies on the Web.

Chambers of commerce can often provide information about the business community, particular lines of business and industries, trends, and the like.

Local government agencies can sometimes do the same or even more, if you are able to discover a cooperative employee who knows what he or she is doing.

Business, trade, and professional organizations are good sources, particularly for information about professional, commercial, and industrial markets.

College and university libraries, business libraries, and *special libraries* may also be able to provide you with published data that you cannot find in more general archives.

Also, check *database retrieval services; tradeshow management; consulting firms; direct mail proprietors, compilers, and brokers;* and *Yellow Pages.*

Usually only as a last resort do you need to purchase syndicated research.

In the list that follows, only titles are provided, since that's all you need to find the sources in the business section of your library. Several sources (especially under "Media Sources") are useful for discovering information *other* than pure research.

INDUSTRY CLASSIFICATION SOURCES

- *North American Industry Classification System (NAICS)*—The new standard for classifying industries, products, and organizations. The old SIC manual has not yet been superseded, though. Also available on the Web at: http://www.census.gov/epcd/www/naics.html.

- *Standard Industrial Classification Manual 1987*—Defines and outlines the Standard Industrial Classification (SIC) used to classify industries, products, and organizations. Also on the Web at http://www.osha.gov/oshstats/sicser.html.

- *Standard and Poor's Industry Surveys*—Excellent source for major industries, and includes composite company information.

- *U.S. Industry & Trade Outlook*—U.S. Department of Commerce publication focusing on the outlook for more than 350 industries; includes narratives and statistical tables.

- *County and City Data Book*—From U.S. Bureau of the Census, provides population, personal income, education, and other demographic data useful in segmenting markets.

- *Survey of Buying Power*—Published by *Sales and Marketing Management.* Excellent indices by metro area.

- *Encyclopedia of Emerging Industries*—Focuses on some of the newer industries, such as cyber cafés, homeopathy, and virtual reality.

- *Services Industries U.S.A. Industry Analyses, Statistics, and Leading Organizations*—Comprehensive guide to economic activity in 150 service industries, both profit and nonprofit. Includes 4,000 leading organizations and local data for 620 major metropolitan areas.

- *Dun and Bradstreet's Industry Norms and Key Business Ratios*—Multiple volumes cover five major industry groupings and examine 800 industries. Provides typical balance sheet information for each industry based on median assets of that group. Information is consolidated by two- and four-digit SICs, by geographic area for the two-digit SICs and by three to five asset ranges for both two-digit and four-digit SIC numbers.

- *RMA Annual Statement Studies*—Provides common-size balance sheets and ratios for some 350 industries. Each table covers one SIC number, gives percentages of data derived from financial statements submitted to member banks for loans and calculations for 17 ratios. Comparative historical data, together with current data, can be used to analyze the financial situation of each industry over the past several years.
- *Survey of Current Business*—Published by the U.S. Department of Commerce.
- *Economic Indicators*—Published by the U.S. Council of Economic Advisors.
- *Consumer Price Index*—Published by the U.S. Government Printing Office.
- *American Statistics Index*—Published by the Congressional Information Service.
- *Statistical Reference Index (SRI)*—Published by the Congressional Information Service.
- *U.S. Industrial Outlook*—Published by the U.S. Government Printing Office.
- *County Business Patterns*—Published by the U.S. Government Printing Office.
- *Encyclopedia of Associations*—more than 16,000 national and regional associations compiled by Gale Research.
- *National Trade and Professional Associations of the U.S.*—some 4,500 listings.
- *National Trade Show Exhibitor's Association*—information on trade shows, conventions, and conferences nationwide.
- *Trade Directories of the World*—by Croner Publications.

RESOURCES FOR SMALL BUSINESSES

- *Telephone directories*—Many different phonebooks are now available.
- *Cole Directory*—This allows you to look up street addresses and find occupant names and telephone numbers. The directory is useful for drawing geographic samples and for a professional service or small business to discover prospective individual clients or customers convenient to their office. Local telephone companies now also offer this type of listing.
- *Contacts Influential*—Lists organizations, corporations, annual sales information, and individuals in buying positions by name.
- *Marquis Who's Who*—Several volumes, including special industry editions such as *Who's Who in Finance and Industry*, useful in prequalifying prospects for direct business-to-business sales.

DEMOGRAPHIC, ECONOMIC, AND STATISTICAL RESOURCES

- *Statistical Abstract of the United States*—Published by the U.S. Bureau of the Census, this answers many statistical questions about industrial, social, political, and economic topics. Gives an overview on each section, and sources for gathering further information.

- *American Generations*—Provides demographic information on five American generations: those born between 1977 and 1994, 1965 and 1976, 1946 and 1964, 1933 and 1945, and before 1933. Calculations presented in charts are based on data from Census, Bureau of Labor Statistics, the National Center for Education Statistics, and the National Center for Health Statistics.
- *Americans at Play*—Demographics on outdoor recreation and travel.
- *Census of Retail Trade*—Statistics for SICs from 52 to 5999. Data includes number of establishments, sales, payroll, and paid employees for a pay period.
- *Census of Service Industries*—Statistics for SICs ranging from 70 to 8999. Data includes number of establishments, sales, payroll, and paid employees for a pay period.
- *Demographics U.S.A. County Edition*—Consists of more than 1,500 pages of maps and demographic, economic, commercial, and industrial estimates.
- *Household Spending*—Guide to consumer spending, including apparel, entertainment, financial products and services, health care, gifts, housing, and transportation. Provides an overview of spending trends.
- *Lifestyle Market Analyst*—Provides demographics, market profiles, lifestyle profiles, and consumer segment lifestyles for 211 designated market areas (DMAs), as well as a list of consumer magazines and direct marketing lists targeting more than 70 lifestyle interests and activities.
- *Sourcebook of ZIP Code Demographics*—Population, demographics, household, and income data by ZIP Code.
- *Statistical Reference Index*—Indexes and abstracts state and local government materials and publications of nonprofit organizations, business associations, universities, and private publishers. Complete documents referred to are available on microfiche.
- *The Lifestyle Market Planner*—Compiled by Standard Rate & Data Service.

FINANCIAL RESOURCES

- *Moody's Manuals*—Company financial information compiled from 10-Ks and annual reports. Includes history, description, list of officers and basic financial data.
- *S&P Corporation Records*—Company information compiled from 10-Qs and other SEC filings. Includes most current information on financial data, management changes, and so forth. Updated semimonthly.
- *S&P Stock Reports*—Two-page overviews of financial information and outlook for companies traded on the NYSE, ASE, and NASDAQ exchanges. Includes company betas.
- *SEC-Filings*—10-Ks and annual reports on microfiche.
- *Value Line Investment Survey and Expanded Edition*—In-depth coverage of 1,700 stocks arranged within industry. Comparative historical data, together with

the current data, can be used to analyze the financial situation of the industry over the past few years. Also available on the Web at http://www.valueline.com for subscribers. There is also a CD-ROM version.

COMPANY RESOURCES

- *Directory of Corporate Affiliations*—Contains more than 120,000 public and private companies. Lists parent companies and U.S. and international subsidiaries. Indexes include company names, geographic location, SIC, and personnel. Has a separate international volume.
- *Dun's Directory of Service Companies*—Includes companies whose primary source of income is from a service, for example, lodging, business, recreation, health, legal, social, technical, and so forth. Companies are listed alphabetically, geographically, and by SIC.
- *Dun & Bradstreet Directories*—annual listings of U.S. firms, including *Middle Market Directory* and *Million Dollar Directory*.
- *Million Dollar Directory*—Includes 160,000 private and public companies, arranged alphabetically, geographically and by SIC code.
- *Standard & Poor's Register of Corporations, Directors and Executives*—Includes 55,000 private and public companies and 450,000 officers, directors, and other principals.
- *Macmillan Directory of Leading Private Companies*—list of more than 7,000 privately held companies.
- *Standard Directory of Advertisers*—"The Red Book" that lists national advertisers and indicates their management personnel and media activities.
- *Standard Directory of Advertising Agencies*—Indicates who is handling what accounts and media specialization.

MEDIA SOURCES

- *Editor and Publisher Market Guide*—Marketing information for every city or community where a daily newspaper is published. Describes population and commerce for each market.
- *Simmons Selective and Mass Media Studies*—Simmons Marketing Research Bureau information that relates product use to media consumption.
- *MRI Mediamark Research*—National consumer consumption patterns and related media exposure.
- *Standard Rate and Data Service (SRDS)*—A multivolume set that provides an alphabetical listing and classified subject listings for the identification and advertising rates of consumer magazines, business publications, agri-media, community periodicals, newspapers, spot radio, spot TV, and direct mail lists. SRDS also provides separate volumes for magazine editorial calendars for the coming 12 months with closing dates and detailed production specifications for magazines.

- *Ayer Directory of Publications*—newspapers and magazines listed by state and city.
- *Leo Burnett Worldwide Advertising and Media Fact Book*—basic media information country-by-country worldwide.
- *Bacon's*—Guides to where to send news releases and articles.
- *Gale Directory of Publications*—Newspapers and other periodicals.
- *Ulrich's International Periodical Directory*—A publicity and advertising information resource that includes international publications.
- *Nielsen Report on Syndicated Programs* and *Nielsen Station Index*—Television ratings, shares, and impressions.
- *Arbitron Reports*—for radio.

REGULATORY SOURCES

- *Code of Federal Regulations*—These are U.S. federal regulations. Also on the Web at http://www.access.gpo.gov/nara/cfr/cfr-table-search.html.
- *Regulations for states, counties, parishes, and municipalities*—Available locally.
- *Information U.S.A.*—extensive listing of U.S. government departments, bureaus, and agencies and their areas of responsibility.

GENERAL BUSINESS SOURCES

- *Encyclopedia of Business Information Sources*—Provides a directory of sources for numerous business, financial, or industrial subjects.
- *Small Business Sourcebook: The Entrepreneur's Resource*—Bills itself as "A guide to the information services and sources provided to 100 small businesses."
- *Standard and Poor's Industry Surveys*—Composite company information for major industries.
- *Market Share Reporter*—Annual compilation of market share data for companies, products, and services.
- *Handbook of Business Information*—Concise description of business sources, including on-line services.
- *Marketing Information: A Professional Reference Guide: Part I*—Guide to Associations and Organizations; *Part II*—Guide to Sources of Marketing Information.
- *Business Information: How to Find It, How to Use It*—sources and practical advice.
- *Using Government Information Sources: Print and Electronic*—Searching by subjects and agencies, special techniques.

ELECTRONIC INFORMATION SOURCES

The electronic resources that follow vary in how they are accessed. Check with your local librarian for guidance. If you use another ISP (such as

America Online), follow their instructions to set up your browser for remote access.

- *ABI/Inform*—Some full-text and full-content matter available online. Index and abstracts of business and management topics. Provides access to U.S. and international, scholarly, and trade publications. Contains selected full-text articles beginning in 1991.
- *Academic Universe*—A Web version of the popular service from Lexis-Nexis. Has full-text documents from newspapers, journals, trade publications, wire services, newsletters, case law, and law reviews.
- *Associations Unlimited*—This is a directory of numerous international, U.S., state, regional, and local nonprofit membership organizations. Includes mailing and Web addresses. This is a good source to use for identifying organizations in a particular industry.
- *CenSTATS*—This source provides statistics, including business ZIP Code patterns for 1994 and 1995, international trade data, occupation by race and sex, and the Annual Survey of Manufacturers.
- *DIALOG*—A broad-based database with access to numerous business and industry databases that provide full-text articles, SEC filings, corporate directories and profiles, and so forth. Includes international coverage.
- *Disclosure*—Selected financial information on publicly owned companies in the United States.
- *Findex*—A guide to published, commercially available market and business research. The reports are NOT available full-text online.
- *Gale Business Resources: Integrated*—Contains detailed information on 445,000 U.S. and international companies, thorough histories and chronologies of major companies, and in-depth coverage of more than 1,000 major U.S. and global industries including full-text essays, rankings, market shares, trade, and professional associations.
- *General Business File ASAP*—Business Periodical Article Index, Company Profiles, and Investext: Covers about 1,000 business publications, including the *Wall Street Journal* and the *New York Times*. Full text provided to more than 450 titles. Includes links to Company Profiles, and to about 40 percent of the Investext database which provides investment bankers reports for companies and various industries. Updated monthly.
- *Northern Light*—This search engine retrieves relevant Web sites related to a topic as well as articles from its Special Collection. Results are organized into custom folders for easier selection.
- *Predicasts PROMT*—Predicasts provides overviews of markets and technology. PROMT is useful for researching companies, the products and technologies they produce, and the markets in which they compete. Includes summaries and full text from nearly 1,000 business and trade journals, industry newsletters, newspapers, market research studies, news releases, and investment and brokerage firm reports.

- *ReferenceUSA*—Directory of more than 10 million U.S. private and public companies. Provides addresses, contact names, and estimated sales and employee figures for private companies. Ability to search by Yellow Pages heading, SIC code, geography, and size of business.
- *Statistical Universe*—A comprehensive index to statistical publications of the United States federal government. Links to many of the full-text documents published by U.S. government agencies. Includes access to Statistical Abstracts of the United States.
- *WorldScope*—Selected financial information on publicly owned companies worldwide.

WORLD WIDE WEB RESOURCES

- *Advertising Age*—http://www.adage.com: *Advertising Age* magazine's home page. Provides articles and data for advertising, marketing, and media. There is a fee for searching the backfiles.
- *American Demographics/Marketing Tools*—http//www.marketingtools.com: This page provides links to various marketing tools, including the magazine *American Demographics*. Fee required to access the full service.
- *BIZWEB*—http://www.bizweb.com: Links to company and product information.
- *Bureau of Labor Statistics*—http://www.bls.gov: Home page for the Department of Commerce's Bureau of Labor Statistics. Provides U.S. economic and labor statistics as well as data for ten U.S. regions.
- *Business Week*—http://www.businessweek.com: *Business Week*'s home page. Provides many of the articles in the current issue as well as links to past issues. Fee required to access the full site.
- *Census Home Page*—http://www.census.gov: U.S. Census Bureau home page. The official site for economic, demographic, and social statistics.
- *Census Lookup Server*—http://venus.census.gov/cdrom/lookup: From the U.S. Department of the Census, this site provides a simple-to-use tool for finding census information.
- *CEO Express*—http://www.ceoexpress.com: organizes links to a vast range of Internet information sources for business executives.
- *County and City Data Book*—http://fisher.lib.Virginia.edu/ccdb: World Wide Web access to 1988 and 1994 state, county, and city data.
- *Forbes*—http://www.forbes.com/: Home page for *Forbes* magazine. Provides links to the most recent issues and several past issues. Fee required to access the full service.
- *Fortune*—http://pathfinder.com/fortune/: Home page for *Fortune* magazine. Provides a link to articles from the most recent issue. Fee required to access the full service.
- *Hoovers Online*—http://www.hoovers.com: Links to more than 5,000 corporate Web sites and offers 2,700 private and public company profiles. Subscription required to obtain access to all the profiles.

- *The Industry Standard*—http://www.thestandard.com/: Publication dealing with the Internet economy. Subscription is required to access the entire contents.
- *IndustryLink*—http://www.industrylink.com: Links to companies in 20 industry categories.
- *PRARS Annual Reports*—http://www.prars.com/: Access to more than 3,600 public company annual reports. Provided by The Public Register's Annual Report Service.
- *SEC Edgar Database*—http://www.sec.gov/edaux/searches.htm: Access to corporate electronic filings submitted to the SEC directly from the SEC EDGAR database.
- *Small Business Administration Home Page*—http://www.sbaonline.sba.gov: A key site for small business entrepreneurs to identify available resources for starting and continuing their businesses.
- *Wall Street Journal Interactive*—http://www.wsj.com: Online version of the *Wall Street Journal*. Fee based but does provide access to quotes and articles from the recent issue.
- *Yahoo—Companies*—http://dir.yahoo.com/Business and Economy/Companies: From Yahoo, numerous company-related links.

OTHER ELECTRONIC SOURCES

- *ABI/inform*—via FirstSearch
- *Academic Universe*—from Lexis-Nexis
- *American Banker Financial Publications*
- *American Business Disc*
- *Asia & Pacific Business Journals*
- *Bond Buyer Full Text*
- *CenStats*
- *CIAO (Columbia International Affairs Online)*
- *Columbia International Affairs Online*
- *Commerce Business Daily*
- *Data Times*
- *DIALOG Finance and Banking Newsletter*
- *DIALOG Investment Research Index*
- *Ebsco Online*
- *Econbase*—Time series and forecasts
- *EconLit*
- *Eventline*
- *General Businessfile ASAP*
- *Globus & National Trade Data Bank (NTDB)*—via STAT-USA
- *Harvard Business Review*

- *International Hospitality and Tourism (1988–1996)*
- *JSTOR*
- *Knight-Ridder/Trib. Business News*
- *LegalTrac*—via INFOTRAC
- *Lexis-Nexis*—via Academic Universe
- *National Trade Data Bank (NTDB)*—via STAT-USA
- *New York Times Full Text* (most recent 90 days only)
- *Northern Light*
- *NTDB (National Trade Data Bank)*—via STAT-USA
- *NTDB*—Foreign Trader's Index
- *Political Risk Yearbook Online*
- *PR Newswire*
- *Predicasts PROMT*—via INFOTRAC
- *Predicasts US & Int'l.*
- *PROMT*—via INFOTRAC
- *ReferenceUSA*
- *SEC Online—10-K and 20-F Reports*
- *SEC Online—10-Q Reports*
- *SEC Online—Annual Reports*
- *SEC Online—Proxy Reports*
- *South American Business Information*
- *Standard & Poor's Daily News*
- *Standard & Poor's Register—Biographical*
- *Standard & Poor's Register—Corporate*
- *STAT-USA*
- *Statistical Universe*
- *Thomas Register Online*—directory of manufacturers and their products
- *Value Line*
- *Wall Street Journal Abstracts*
- *World Data (1994)*
- *WorldScope*
- *Zack's University Analyst Watch*

NOTE

Special thanks to Esther L. Gil, Assistant Professor/Business Reference Librarian, Penrose Library, University of Denver.

Appendix 4

How to Prepare a Survey Questionnaire

Key factors in developing a survey questionnaire are these:

- First, be sure the objective of your research project is clear in your mind.
- Decide exactly what you need to know and ask questions *only* about those things.
- Establish that your respondents are representative of your target market(s) by including questions pertaining to geographics, demographics, and perhaps psychographics (the latter primarily to aid in media selection).
- It is normally wise also to include questions about needs and/or wants and usage patterns.
- Don't ask the obvious, such as "Do you like fast delivery?"
- Define your terms. For example, in a question like "Do you want convenience?" what is meant by the word "convenience"?
- Ask only one question at a time. For example, "Do you seek high speed and economy?" should be two separate questions.
- Don't try to gather too much information all at once. Winnow your list of potential questions to the fewest you reasonably can since the amount of response will fall off as the length of your questionnaire increases. If possible, keep the number of questions fewer than 12.
- Ask general questions first, personal questions (such as age and income) last, and consider making them optional so you don't repel respondents at the beginning.
- Try to make your questions interesting and perhaps challenging to respondents so they are inclined to cooperate. To do this, consider a variety of questions: fill-in-the blank or "open-ended" questions; multiple-choice or "aided recall" questions; rating scales; and true/false, yes/no, or "dichotomous" questions.

- Consider using surveys that permit respondents to remain anonymous for especially confidential or personal information. Your results will be more honest and accurate in most cases.

- Phrase questions so that they will draw out free expressions of opinions. To this end, keep direct yes-or-no questions to a minimum. Instead, use multiple-choice questions and/or provide opportunities for respondents to indicate various degrees of approval or disapproval.

- Encourage volunteered remarks and suggestions by leaving spaces or by supplying the first few words of sentences and asking respondents to complete them in any way they wish.

- Phrase all questions as pleasantly, invitingly, and with as little implied judgment as possible. And don't inadvertently stack the deck by the way you phrase your questions. For example, answers to the following question would probably do you little good in your marketing planning: *Are you considering changing suppliers, or would you prefer to stay with our company, which provides the highest product quality, charges fair prices, and treats you as a friend?*

- Arrange your questions in a *logical* order, building from matters of lesser importance to those of greater importance.

- Regardless of how much thought you put into designing your survey questionnaire, it is wise to check it out by *pretesting*. Usually a pretest sample of as few as a dozen people is enough to reveal possible problems in design, interpretation, and content. You can evaluate your questions orally, but a good pretest should approximate the final test situation. Produce a small quantity of pretest survey questionnaires and administer them in the same way you intend for your formal research.

- If you mail your questionnaire rather than hand it out in a public place or on a visit, include a short covering letter that briefly explains your objective (if that will not bias results) and asks for a response as a favor. Experience has shown that this modest business courtesy will significantly improve your response.

- Inclusion of a self-addressed *postage-paid* reply envelope with a mailed questionnaire will also significantly increase the number of replies.

- It may be in bad taste to attach money to mailed questionnaires as an incentive. But some other token of your appreciation, if appropriate to the person addressed and the nature of the research, can boost response.

- Repeat the same survey at intervals. This so called "tracking research" shows the progress you have made in broadening or deepening a desired effect.

- Seek expert help for any survey project. If your organization has a good potential market research capability, by all means make use of it, or use a qualified outside research firm. Use of a third party can help eliminate bias.

Appendix 5

How to Define Your Target Markets and Publics

Here is a list of idea-starters for your definitions of *consumer* target market segments (for most marketing planning) or publics (for PR). You should continually refine all your profiles.

GEOGRAPHIC FACTORS

- Live locally
- Work locally
- Travel from afar
- ZIP Code area(s) and postal routes
- Region (large areas, such as Pacific, New England, South Central, and so on)
- County definition (by name)
- County size (A, B, C, D)
- City or metropolitan area definition (Standard Metropolitan Statistical Area [SMSA] or Consolidated Metropolitan Statistical Area [CMSA], both defined by U.S. Office of Management and Budget; Designated Market Area [DMA], TV market definition by A. C. Nielsen; Area of Dominant Influence [ADI], defined by Arbitron; Total Survey Area [TSA] for radio coverage; and so on, depending on the research organization. Be sure to compare *exactly the same* definitions.)
- Community population (under 5,000; 5,000–19,999; 20,000–49,999; 50,000–99,999; 100,000–249,999; 250,000–499,999; 500,000–999,999; 1,000,000–3,999,999; 4,000,000 and over)
- Population density (urban, suburban, exurban, rural)
- Climate (semitropical, Great Lakes, and so on)

- Census tract analysis
- Municipal boundary analysis
- Draw area pattern (or access) analysis
- Other descriptor(s)

DEMOGRAPHIC FACTORS

- Age range (various breaks—the most common being: children under 6, 6–11, teens 12–17, young adults 18–24, adults 25–34, 35–49, 50–64, and retired or seniors 65+)
- Gender (male, female, perhaps gay or lesbian, and Nielsen's *working women*)
- Income (individual employment income OR household income—various breaks— the most common being: under $5,000; $5,000–7,999; $8,000–9,999; $10,000– 14,999; 15,000–24,999; $25,000–49,999; over $50,000—more affluent targets require additional breaks)
- Education (grade school or less, some high school, graduated high school, some college, graduated college, postgraduate degree)
- Occupation (professional & technical; managers, officials & proprietors; clerical & sales; craftsmen & foremen; operatives; farmers; students; housewives; retired; unemployed)
- Type of residence (own or rent; apartment or condo, detached home; dollar value; and so on)
- Marital status (single, married, divorced, widowed)
- Number of children (1–2, 3–4, 5+)
- Family life cycle (*bachelor state*—young & single; *newly married*—young, married & no children; *full nest I*—young, married & youngest child under 6; *full nest II*—young, married & youngest child 6 or over; *full nest III*—older, married, with children; *empty nest I*—older, married, no children living at home and head of household still employed; *empty nest II*—older married couples with no children at home and head of household retired; *solitary survivors*—older and living alone, may or may not be retired. With roughly 50 percent of American marriages ending in divorce, and with only about a fourth of the U.S. population part of what is called a "traditional family," we probably need some new definitions in this category.)
- Religion (Roman Catholic, Protestant, Jewish, others—may be refined to specify exact denominations)
- Politics (Republican, Democrat, Socialist, independent, other)
- Race (Caucasian [white], African-American [black], Native American [Indian], Hispanic [Mexican, Cuban, etc.], Oriental [can specify], Aborigine, Oceanic, Eskimo [Aleut], and so on)
- Language or nationality (American, British, French, Scandinavian, Eastern European, Latin American, Middle Eastern, Japanese, Filipino, and so on)

- Social class (lower-lower, upper-lower, lower-middle, middle-middle, upper-middle, lower-upper, upper-upper; many other breaks also used in the United States and abroad; some cute names like "Pools & Patios" and "Shotguns & Pick-ups")
- Consumption patterns (such as alcohol, drugs, sweets)
- Other significant objectively measurable characteristics

PSYCHOGRAPHIC FACTORS

- Style of living (swinger, status seeker, social climber, plain Joe, and so on)
- Personality (compulsive, gregarious, conservative, ambitious, and so on)
- "Values & Lifestyles" (VALS 1 & 2 from SRI [Stanford Research International]—arrange everyone into one of several categories, including in VALS 1: Achievers, Societally Conscious, Belongers, Experiential, Emulators, I-Am-Me, Sustainers, Survivors, and Integrated; and in VALS 2: Actualizers, Fulfillers, Believers, Achievers, Strivers, Experiencers, Makers, and Strugglers)
- Attitudes (toward social issues, money matters, and so on)
- Interests (such as watching professional sports, fishing, gardening, and so on)
- Opinions (these last three are designated "AIO")
- Taste in décor, furniture, and so on
- Type of music preferred
- Favored entertainment
- Hobbies
- Club membership(s)
- Ambitions
- Fears
- Aspirations
- Other subjective factors, concerns, or involvements

SYNCHROGRAPHICS

This relates in some ways to consumer behavior models that include *reference groups* composed of: *membership group* (where they think they belong psychographically), *aspiration group* (where they would like to be), and *dissociative group* (whom they dislike or wish to avoid, which can be important in political and some nonprofit marketing). But more specifically *synchrographics* refers to major events, occasions, or significant "rites of passage" in people's lives that allow them to be segmented for marketing purposes.

- Entering school
- Graduating at various academic levels

- Obtaining a license of some sort
- Getting married
- Having children
- Buying a home
- Occasions of other major purchases
- Attending a significant event
- Changing career or lifestyle
- Suffering illness or injury
- Retiring
- Other major events in life

NEEDS

- What specific needs do you *think* they have?
- What do they *say* they need?
- What do they *really* need?
- Why do they *use* your product or service?
- How frequently? [*Note*: See also "Usage" that follows.]
- What is their perception of the quality of your product or service?
- Other perceived attributes of your product or service

ALSO CONSIDER CATEGORIZING SIMPLY, ACCORDING TO

- Benefits sought (economy, expertise, convenience, dependability, convenient hours, prestige, and so on)
- Purchase location (related to method of distribution)
- Season, day-of-the-week, or time of purchase
- Uniqueness of product, service, or organization
- Satisfaction of wants or needs other than the obvious
- Hidden qualities in your product, service, or organization
- Emotional qualities sought

USAGE

- Frequency of use of product or service
- Seasonality of use
- User status (nonuser, potential user, first-time user, regular user, ex-user [why?])
- Usage rate (light user, medium user, heavy user)
- Loyalty status (none, medium, strong, absolute)

- Readiness stage (unaware, aware but unconvinced, informed, interested, desirous, intending to take action, has taken action)

COMPANIES OR OTHER ORGANIZATIONS

Here are factors to consider when you segment *business marketing* targets:

- Geographic location
- Standard Industrial Classification (SIC) category or North American Industrial Classification (NAIC) which includes the United States, Canada, and Mexico
- Organizational revenues or company sales volume (annual dollars)
- Company production volume (units, tonnage, etc.)
- Number of employees
- Nature of customer or client requirement (need)
- Specific benefit(s) to customer or client
- Decision-maker title(s)
- Who makes recommendations versus final decisions
- Organization's purchasing policies
- Uniqueness of the product
- Nature of product use
- Frequency of product use
- Usage rate (light to heavy), or size of orders
- Where product is used
- Seasonality of product use
- User status (non-user, ex-user, and so on)
- Nature of business relationship and loyalty status
- Method of buying-decision-making and/or purchasing (for example, individual decision-making versus buying centers, and centralized versus decentralized purchasing departments)
- Buyer readiness stage within the business buying cycle
- Reliability (credit rating) and promptness of payment

FUNDAMENTAL SEGMENTATION STRATEGIES

- *Mass market*—target everyone
- *Basic segmentation*—three levels: high tier, middle tier, low tier
- *Subsegmentation technique*—five levels: high tier, middle tier, low tier, very low tier, ultra-low tier
- *Matrix* (or *niche*) segmentation—customer or client needs are assumed to be related to the three qualities of price, feature(s), and application(s). These are laid

out on a grid or matrix where patterns or "clusters" are plotted, akin to the perceptual mapping discipline but related to acceptance of price, desire for a feature, or need for an application. The densest clusters normally indicate prime target market segments. This is very useful in packaged-goods marketing but rather complex for marketing a professional organization.

Note: For purposes of implementation of your marketing plan, be sure that when you profile your target markets or publics you specify categories that are compatible with (and preferably identical to) categories used to profile the audiences of the marketing communications *media* you select. See Appendix 6 for media options.

Appendix 6

Types of Marketing
Communications Media

Here are categories for the various ways marketers can communicate with their target markets:

MASS (MEASURED) MEDIA

1. Television (market-by-market [or local or "spot"], network, cable, satellite, and entertainment videos)
2. Radio (AM, FM, student, community stations, and "storecasts")
3. Magazines (consumer, broad reach [mass] or special interest [class]; specialized business publications [trade or professional]; national, regional, and local)
4. Newspapers (broadsheet or tabloid; daily, weekly, Sunday, monthly; local, national, and special interest; ads in the form of display, classified, and free-standing inserts [FSIs])
5. Outdoor (billboards, painted buildings, and other structures that carry advertising messages)
6. Transit ("car cards" inside buses and subway trains, "dash cards" on exteriors, posters in and on buses and trains, fully illustrated buses, station platform posters, and kiosks; also panels on *trucks* and *taxicabs* carrying commercial messages other than identification of owners)

ALTERNATIVE ADVERTISING MEDIA

7. Display (posters around sports stadiums, racetracks, rinks, and public buildings)
8. Other visual outdoor (sandwich boards, skywriting, blimps, images projected on floors in airports, or pressed in sand on beaches, etc.)

9. Visual indoor, or in-home (ad imprints on metered postage, calendars, blotters, thermometers, and the like that carry advertising messages)

10. Direct mail (first class for business and personalized letters; pre-sorted first class for lower postal rate; second class for educational materials and mailings by nonprofit organizations; third class or bulk-rate which may smack of "junk mail"; either priority or parcel post for "dimensionals" and executive gifts; and for greatest economy card packs, or "marriage mail," and co-ops); courier services for high impact

11. Handbills or "throwaways" (doorknob hangers, broadsides, flyers under automobile windshield wipers, and so on)

12. Point-of-purchase (signage, banners, tags, flipcharts, video, handouts, and projected images in stores and other commercial outlets)

DIMENSIONAL MEDIA

13. Advertising specialties (premiums and gifts such as imprinted ballpoint pens, paperweights, caps, and so on)

14. Awards (trophies, plaques, and so on)

15. Tradeshows and exhibits

ENTERTAINMENT MEDIA

16. Audiovisuals (slides, movies, videos, and disks) for presentation

17. Audiocassettes and audio disks for distribution

18. Videocassettes and video disks for distribution

19. Cinema (slides or motion picture footage shown in movie theaters)

20. Product placement (a brand-name product appears in a movie or TV program)

PRINTED MEDIA

21. House organs (internal and external newsletters, and periodicals for customers, prospects, and/or employees)

22. Literature (product and applications flyers, folders, and brochures; article reprints; "educational" booklets)

23. Annual reports

24. Directories and annuals—where advertising space is sold (Yellow Pages, association member lists, yearbooks, and the like)

25. Book bind-ins

ELECTRONIC MEDIA

26. Telemarketing (incoming or inbound and outgoing or outbound telephone, voice mail systems that include commercial messages, cellular networks, and fax transmission)

27. Computer-based systems (computer bulletin boards, commercial online services, Web sites, and the Internet)

PERSON-TO-PERSON MEDIA

28. Seminars, training programs, meetings, and open-house events
29. Live speakers ("the platform medium" from pitches to executive speeches)
30. Personnel trained to transmit specific marketing messages person-to-person, other than through personal selling (customer service specialists, client relations staff, detail reps, and so on)
31. Personal selling representatives (counter clerks, rack jobbers, manufacturer's reps, sales engineers, field sales representatives, and so on)

Note 1: These are *media* or the types of vehicles that can carry marketing messages; the *means* to carry messages—such as commercials, advertisements, slogans, jingles, news releases, feature articles, and so on—are communications considerations that involve *content* and are covered in Parts III and IV of this handbook.

Note 2: Some of these media have been defined as sales promotion or public relations, but they may also be thought of as advertising, since there is a cost attached to each, and a marketing effect unique to each from which advertisers can benefit.

Appendix 7

Advertising Media Formulas

All of the following are translatable to any media target and, except as noted, to any media vehicle, type, or schedule.

AUDIENCE

1. Print only: Audience = Circulation × RPC (Readers per Copy).
2. TV only: Audience = TV Homes Audience × Target VPVH (Viewers per Viewing Household).
3. Composition: Audience of Demographic Group ÷ Total Audience = Composition (as a percent).

ADVERTISING WEIGHT

1. Gross Impressions = Sum of Impressions (Messages) in the Media Schedule.
2. Gross Impressions = Average Audience × Number of Advertisements (or Occasions, or Insertions, or Spots).
3. Gross Impressions = Gross Rating Points ÷ 100 × Population Base.
4. TV only: Commercial Minutes = Average Minute Audience × Length of Commercial, summed over all commercials in a schedule. (By convention 60" = 1.0, 30" = 0.5).
5. Gross Rating Points (GRPs) = Sum of Individual Ratings in a Media Schedule.
6. GRPs = Reach (as a percent) × Average Frequency.

RATINGS

1. Rating = Vehicle's Audience ÷ Population in Area.
2. TV Homes Rating = Percent Homes Using TV × Vehicle's Share of TV Audience.
3. TV Target Rating = TV Homes Rating × Target VPVH ÷ Target Population per TV Household in Area.
4. TV Target Rating = TV Homes Rating × % of Target Using TV ÷ % of TV Homes Using TV. (More general than method number 3.)

RATING/HOMES USING TELEVISION (HUT)/SHARE

Solve for Rating: HUT × Share = Rating.
Solve for Share: Rating ÷ HUT = Share.
Solve for HUT: Rating ÷ Share = HUT.

Formulas work the same when Sets in Use (SIU)—an antiquated term—Persons Using Television (PUT), Persons Viewing Television (PVT), and Persons Using Radio (PUR) are substituted for HUT and/or HUR.

REACH AND FREQUENCY

1. Reach (as a percent) × Frequency = Gross Rating Points.
2. Or: Reach (in thousands) = Gross Impressions ÷ Average Frequency.
3. Reach (as a percent) = GRPs ÷ Average Frequency.
4. Average Frequency = Gross Impressions ÷ Reach (in thousands).
5. Average Frequency = GRPs ÷ Reach (as a percent).

COVERAGE/RATING

Audience of Demographic Group (e.g. 18–49) ÷ Population Universe of Same Demographic Group = Coverage.

READERS-PER-COPY (RPC) OR PASSALONG

Total Audience ÷ Circulation = Readers per Copy (RPC).
Circulation × RPC = Total Audience.

COST EFFICIENCY (COST PER THOUSAND)

1. Cost per Thousand (CPM) = Cost ÷ (Audience ÷ 1000).
   Or: CPM = Cost ÷ Audience × 1000.

2. Cost per Minute = Cost ÷ Commercial Minutes.
3. Cost per Rating Point = Cost ÷ GRPs.
4. Cost per TV Target Rating Point = Cost per TV Home Rating Point × Target Population per TV Home in Area ÷ Target Viewers per Viewing Household.
5. CPM × Audience (in thousands) = Cost.
6. Cost ÷ CPM = Audience (in thousands).
7. GRPs × Cost per Rating Point = Cost.
8. Budget ÷ CPM = Gross Impressions.
9. Budget ÷ Cost per Rating Point = GRPs.
10. Cost per Unit = Rating × Cost per Rating Point for the Unit.

COST-PER-RATING-POINT (CPP) [or CPR or CPRP]

Cost per Unit (e.g. :30) ÷ Rating per Unit = CPP.

CONVERTING CPP TO CPM

CPP × 100 ÷ Market Population (in thousands) = CPM.

CONVERTING CPM TO CPP

Market Population (in thousands) × CPM ÷ 100 = CPP.

BRAND DEVELOPMENT INDEX (BDI)

Market × Percent Brand Sales ÷ Market × Percent Population = BDI.
Market × Share of Market ÷ U.S. Average Share of Market = BDI.

CATEGORY DEVELOPMENT INDEX

Market × % Category Sales ÷ Market × % Population = CDI.

COST-PER-INQUIRY (CPI) OR COST-PER-ORDER (CPO)

(List Rental + Creative Cost + Package Production + Postage + Fulfillment − Bad Debt − Returns) ÷ Number of Inquiries or Orders = CPI or CPO.

Appendix 8

Items for a Creative Work Plan

Here are things you should *get down on paper* and check before, during, and after you create an advertisement or other type of marketing communication:

1. *Exact name of what you intend to advertise.* This can be a product, a service, an organization, a location, an individual, or an idea. Use this name *often* in your copy, and *exactly the same way* every time. Frequency of exposure and consistency of appearance will significantly enhance recognition and recall of the name you wish to have remembered by individuals in your target audience.

2. *Exact definition of the target audience for this advertising effort.* Clear definition of your audience is essential to effective advertising. You need to remind yourself as you work on your creative products of *exactly whom* you are communicating with. Develop a mental image of *one person* who best represents your target audience and write directly to that person alone. No one else should matter to you at this time.

3. *What you want the target to do or think; your objective.* Creative planning for most advertising falls marvelously into place when you know *whom* you are addressing and *what you want them to do or think.* Keep your objective clearly in mind as you ponder and write.

4. *The needs, wants, and motives of the target.* Needs, wants, and motives should be clearly specified in the marketing plan upon which your advertising efforts are based. Even if they're not, get down on paper a succinct statement of what your product will satisfy among your particular target, and what other factors are likely to motivate them.

This guidance first appeared in *Journal of Business & Industrial Marketing*, Volume 10, Number 2 (1995), as "How to Create Advertising that Works," by Stuart C. Rogers.

5. *Why the target should do what you want them to do: your appeal and your offer.* You've identified basic needs or wants, and you know about the motives of your target related to your product. Remember that many purchases are made for purely *emotional* reasons, and that customers look for rational reasons for their actions often *after* the sale. Give them both emotional and rational reasons, if possible. Think how you can express what is called your *appeal,* or *what's in it for them* if they do what you want them to do. What makes the thing you're advertising *special*—and (especially) special *to them*? Think about converting your product's best features into *benefits*. And make a clear, reasonable, and appealing *offer*. That's what will persuade your target logically and ethically. No tricks, no smoke and mirrors. Just explain what your offer can do for that one person you're addressing in your particular target audience. You must look at your product honestly and objectively from the perspective of your target, and, when you do that, you'll have a good chance of winning both heart and mind!

6. *Your organization's and product's history.* Describe in the fewest, simplest, and most vivid words you can find what is significant about your company's experience, expertise, customers, personnel, and so on. Be completely honest, but *put your best foot forward.*

7. *Your method of doing business.* Whether you expect to use it or not, make a simple statement of your organization's business philosophy here. Often you'll find that in the *mission statement* toward the beginning of the marketing plan. It should include a clear definition of the organization's values and special concerns for customers. Especially if this is business advertising, you should also mention special price considerations or payment terms that you might offer.

8. *Why and how you are better than your competitors.* Of course, you do not want to "brag and boast," as the Madison Avenue types say, and you do not want to directly derogate others in your industry. But your customers and prospects want to receive superior products and services and deal with the most reputable organization they can afford. So help them out by explaining that for them.

9. *Information.* No matter how sure you are of your facts, you need a *checklist* to be absolutely certain you include all essential information about your product and your offer. Don't be too sure of yourself. Even the most seasoned of marketing pros can make significant mistakes. For example, a major publishing firm made a large mailing to solicit mail order sales for one of my books—and *forgot to mention the price.* Needless to say, few people placed orders without that vital piece of information and the publisher was terribly disappointed with direct mail as a medium to generate direct sales. Basic information should be in an agency's job-jacket, but often is incomplete, and among in-house operations advertising creative people normally have to dig up all information themselves. Summarize vital points in this section of your Creative Work Plan.

10. *Your measurable goal(s).* In addition to what you want your target to do or think, you should have a clear definition in *exact* numeric terms of what you expect your advertising effort to accomplish. That is to say, the *objective* is the

broad aim, the goal specifies (1) target audience, (2) task, or what you must do to accomplish the objective, (3) quantity or amount of change (such as "20 percent awareness" or "15,000 direct orders"), and (4) timeframe. As an old saying goes, "if you don't know where you are going, any road will take you there." An example of a goal to keep a business advertiser on track might be, "Among the 1,257 retail establishments in our draw area, persuade managers and owners of 10 percent (126) to make an appointment this year to discuss our computer bookkeeping system." A corresponding consumer goal might be, "In our test market of Rochester, N.Y., to stimulate 50,000 trial retail purchases of our new brand of toothpaste by December 31." This sort of thing helps enormously in focusing your strategic planning as well as your advertising and sales promotion execution.

11. *Your positioning.* The positioning concept, statement, or slogan for your product or organization should appear here as a reminder—for the sake of consistency at the very least. Recall that basic positioning reflects the *unique niche* in the mind of *your target* that *only your product* can occupy, unless you choose the *preemptive positioning* strategy. (See Chapter 14.) Don't confuse this with blather—which will be meaningless to your target—about how proud the company is of the product you are advertising.

12. *Your graphic identity.* The reason for including a concise but complete definition of your graphic identity in your Creative Work Plan is so that you will offer a *consistent image* of the visual aspects of your product. This consistency in all of your marketing communications will help to create the whole that is greater than the sum of the parts of your marketing program. Include specifics of logotype, symbol, trademark treatment, typography, corporate colors, trade dress, and any special design and format considerations, such as preference for two-page spreads, half-page-verticals, or 60-second spots.

13. *Your message.* Boil down information from sections 1, 5, 6, 7, 8, 9, and 11, which is the basic information your target *needs to know*. Be absolutely certain you include the product name, your offer, and why the target should do what you wish. Explain to your *friend* to whom you wish to advertise just why this is the best deal he or she can make to satisfy important needs or wants.

14. *Mandatories.* Every company and client has certain things that *must* be included in their advertisements, such as a copyright notice, phrases like "We are an equal opportunity employer," or "If symptoms persist, consult your physician." In some industries they are required by law, such as the familiar "Warning: The Surgeon General has determined that cigarette smoking is dangerous to your health." Normally legal counsel will provide these *mandatories*, but sometimes they are simply part of the corporate culture of the advertiser company.

15. *The medium in which you will be working.* A television commercial will take a different form than a radio spot, and a direct mail piece will be different from either. A billboard needs no more than six words, while a trade magazine ad may need a thousand or more. The message and the medium will be the primary considerations in developing the last item you must select and add to your Creative Work Plan: your *creative strategy*.

16. *Your creative strategy.* How you can *package* all of this material in one attention-getting, interest-arousing, desire-provoking, and action-getting piece of advertising is a mystery to most businesspeople. And how you *make it appropriate* for the particular medium through which you wish to communicate is almost as bewildering. Part III of this handbook provides a variety of advertising creative strategies that you can use individually or in combination with one another. The key factor is to use *your own good judgment* in selecting the appropriate strategy or strategies for your particular message and medium.

What you have in the first 15 items here is vitally important (1) as guidance while you are preparing your creative product, (2) as a *checklist* for review after you've finished copy and layout to assure that you've included everything, (3) in preproduction, and (4) in final production (when you do ads for release) to be sure you have not omitted anything.

HOW TO PACKAGE YOUR MESSAGE

Depending on the advertising medium or media you select you can package your marketing message an infinite number of ways. Just how you do that is an important consideration in your planning of advertising that does what you have every right to expect it to do.

Of course, the medium both defines and limits your choices. The illustration in print ads and visualization for several other media normally serve as attention-getters and/or as proofs of claims. But many good ads rely only on a strong headline to draw readers in. However you supplement the words of your advertising, don't let the medium dictate your creative treatment. For example, it's easy to get lured into using music or a jingle in a television or radio commercial. But jingles are generally not appropriate for business advertising. On the other hand, appeals to senses other than sight and hearing can be very effective. The tactile sensation of a new type of floor tile, for example, a distinctive scratch-and-sniff aroma, or the memorable taste of a small enclosure can help distinguish you from your competitors. So don't limit your thinking to conventional advertising approaches.

This is an area where the nature of your message, your choice of copy approach, the medium or media you have chosen, and your budget will all have to be weighed carefully as you decide how to communicate most persuasively.

BASIC RULES

When you observe the basic rules that follow, you will not fall into the trap that has caused so much American advertising to fail. Note that like any good rules these can sometimes be broken safely—but only when there is sound reason to do so. Most of the advertising that doesn't work suffers from careless or ignorant violation of one or more of the following:

- *You should concentrate on persuasion rather than on entertainment*—Remember you are in business when you create advertising. You should not be involved simultaneously in higher education, comedy, erotica, or dramatic entertainment. People will not avail themselves of your products or services today merely because you have enlightened, amused, titillated, or otherwise entertained them—particularly if your product or service is higher-priced or related to a serious business decision.

- *You should make your message easy to receive*—Your guide to media selection and advertising production should be what the people you wish to affect are used to, hence what they find most familiar and with which they are most comfortable. You do not have the time or resources to change people to new patterns of reading, listening, and viewing. So save yourself waste and disappointment by using established marketing communication methods instead of trying to discover new media and different ways to use existing media. For example, although printing your magazine advertisement upside down might get some attention, it will generally decrease readership and recall among most audiences. And ads printed on toilet paper placed in public restrooms (a medium once actually offered) could seem innovative, but might convey negative implications about your product or service.

- *You should assume relative ignorance on the part of your audience*—Your audience is not as familiar with your products and services as you are. So part of the job of your advertising is to inform adequately—ethically of course, yet persuasively. Many packaged goods advertisers aim at a 7- to 9-year mental age in their ads. Some even test broadcast copy on preschool children to assure broad comprehension. Business and industrial audiences can be effectively approached at roughly the same level, unless the product or service is particularly sophisticated.

- *You should assume lack of interest on the part of your audience*—Bombarded as they are with so many marketing messages, your audience is not as interested in your message as you might think they should be. So at least as big a part of your job as informing them is to interest and involve them in your message. It's all too easy for your prospective customers to turn a page, switch a channel, toss away a letter, or click to another home page. A fundamental part of your task as a marketing communicator—after you have fairly gained the audience's attention—is to hold them so persuasion can take place.

- *You should provide significant information*—You must give people reasons to make intelligent choices. Despite the assumption of limited intellectual level and the effects of commercial clutter, the old sales adage still holds true: "The more you tell, the more you sell." And be sure to repeat important points through your ads, in your printed materials, and in every other medium you employ. The body of advertising is information, its heart is imagination, and its soul is repetition.

- *You should be assertive*—Media for which you have to pay is no place to demonstrate your modesty. People who criticize what they call "self-serving" advertisements clearly are not paying the media bills. To be self-serving is the very reason for most advertising. You should serve yourself, your fellow employees, your company, your investors, your suppliers, your dealers and distributors, and your customers and prospects as well as you can, using every ethical device available to you. In advertising, as in athletics, politics, and war, you should play to win.

COMMON SENSE

At the risk of appearing to comment on the obvious, here are three supplementary rules worthy of note in this context:

- *Generally speaking the larger the print ad and the longer the broadcast spot, the greater the attention and recall it will receive*—As to what size ad to run, ideally your impact should be proportional to cost, but it's not. Experience shows you can expect roughly one-third the attention for single pages that you get with multi-page inserts, and only about 10 percent of that for small display ads. Budget is often your key to deciding how much space or time to buy for each advertisement. Although size (or length) of your ad is important, you do not always get awareness in proportion to what you pay. For example, if a half-page ad in a magazine costs 60 percent of what a full-page ad costs, but you discover through readership research that it gets 75 percent as much attention as a full page, the half page is a more efficient investment than the full page—all other factors being equal.

- *All elements in your ad should work together, complement one another, and contribute to delivery of the persuasive message*—The visual aspect of your print advertisement should clearly relate to the headline and the body copy. Similarly the copy should "pay off" the headline and/or visual—something many ads fail to do. This again is just common sense. In a world overloaded with advertising and other types of messages, you should stick to the essence of your subject and try very hard not to confuse your audience with anything else.

- *Don't model your business advertising on consumer packaged goods advertisements, which probably have different target markets and very different objectives than you have*—Your ads should probably be more like those for other business and industrial marketing efforts—but, best of all, they will be uniquely crafted on the basis of your clearly defined audience and your particular objectives.

NO GENIUS NEEDED

Some of the greatest advertising ideas of all time have been produced by people who had little or no apparent talent or experience in creative planning or copywriting.

For example, President Theodore Roosevelt is credited with having coined the still-famous line for Maxwell House coffee, "good to the last drop," when he observed no grounds at the bottom of his cup.

And George Eastman, a banker by training and a manufacturer by experience, created all of Kodak's early advertising personally, including their then-famous line, "You push the button and we do the rest."

So have faith in yourself: You, too, can produce top-quality creative work. But don't wait for a muse to whisper in your ear. Do what you no doubt do in other aspects of your business: Follow a careful plan.

Before you begin the creative process, be sure you have a positive attitude toward marketing communications and advertising. Remember that you will be providing useful information in the public interest. You are not a flack, a fake, or a phony when you try to persuade people to let you help them with their business or personal needs. You are delivering the first part of a very important service of significant value.

Appendix 9

A Test for Honest Advertising

Common sense should demand that companies not deceive their customers with their advertising, lest they lose the loyalty and goodwill that mean the repeat purchases essential to marketing success.

But many advertisers seem to think, somewhat contrary to Abraham Lincoln, that they *can* in small ways fool most of the people much of the time. Today truth is often treated as a relative value rather than an absolute, *situational ethics* prevail, and personal integrity in some business quarters is at risk of becoming an anachronism.

HYPERBOLE OR DECEPTION?

We may forgive simple enthusiasm or "puffery" in advertisements, as when a business claims its products are "absolutely the best." That might be their honest belief and is justified under the First Amendment to the U.S. Constitution, whether it is true or not. But we should not permit such grandiose claims as a garment being "made of 100 percent virgin nylon," or a piece of Queen Anne style furniture being a "genuine guaranteed authentic facsimile." These are not simply hyperbole, but inflations, obviously intended to mislead, if not deceive.

Perhaps codes of ethics for advertising are so often ignored because they are too complex. A simple and ancient test, on the other hand, proven over many centuries in British and American courts of law, could help keep our advertising honest, if intelligently and conscientiously applied.

The test envisioned would be based on the oath sworn prior to witnesses testifying in our courts of law. Every witness is required to tell *the truth, the whole truth, and nothing but the truth*. Although this might sound like pompous legal redundancy, there are good reasons for each of the three qualities of truth specified.

QUALITY #1: THE TRUTH

The truth means, in simple terms, that which is not false. What is right and honest. Real things, events, and facts.

The Federal Trade Commission (FTC) has neatly defined truth as that which can be *documented* and *substantiated* by factual and statistical data—a good test, no doubt. Exceptions involve humor, irony, or obvious fantasy, as when we're told that Keebler cookies are "baked by elves in a hollow tree." As long as no *reasonable* person would believe such a claim, it is not judged to be deceptive. But it appears that today we need something *better* than the FTC's rules of documentation and substantiation.

Despite a few landmark FTC actions, many retailers still advertise "sales" or merchandise discounts that are clearly fraudulent. Often, the "original" price is an inflated fiction—a price never charged. This far too common advertising and promotion tactic would certainly fail both the documentation and *the truth* tests.

A classic television commercial for Rapid Shave® shaving cream attempted to demonstrate dramatically the product's efficacy by supposedly shaving *sandpaper*. It was a ridiculous test, to be sure, and difficult to execute. So to get the effect of shaving real sandpaper, the producers reportedly sprinkled sand on an acetate sheet, then ran the camera, applied Rapid Shave, scraped the mess away with a safety razor, and later applied a grating noise to the film's soundtrack. This production technique was rightly deemed by the FTC to be deceptive.

The Rapid Shave people could have saved a lot of money, trouble, time, and bad publicity by asking themselves if their commercial simply presented *the truth*—which, of course, it clearly did not. Instead of the faked test, they could have shaved a bearskin rug or a hairbrush to show the extra softening power of their product. Or, if those materials wouldn't work satisfactorily, they should have concentrated on a creative approach that did not require a demonstration, or another feature of the product, such as its pleasant fragrance.

QUALITY #2: THE WHOLE TRUTH

The whole truth means that nothing is *left out* of the pitch. Now, obviously it is impossible to tell a prospective buyer literally *everything* about a product. Bombarded by an estimated 3,000 commercial messages a day, the average American does not even *want* exhaustively complete information, any more than judges and juries want every detail related to a case presented in court. But the prospective customer *should* be provided with enough of the truth to make a rational buying decision. The key to passing *the whole truth* test is for marketers, like litigants, not to deceive through the deliberate *omission* of anything important.

For example, Profile® bread once claimed that it contained "fewer calories." Actually, the bread by weight reportedly contained at least as many calories as other breads, but Profile slices were cut *thinner*, so each slice did indeed have fewer calories than a traditional thicker slice of competitive bread. Thus, although the advertising was literally true, it did not cover all the pertinent facts, so it would have failed *the whole truth* test.

One of the best-kept secrets in over-the-counter pain-reliever advertising is that acetaminophen, the active ingredient in Tylenol® and several other headache remedies, can ease headache pain, but may result in an equal or greater headache later. Although marketers of acetaminophen products suggest consumers take no more than 6 or 8 doses a day for no more than 10 days, they deliberately omit the fact that their medications can actually *cause* the very problem they are advertised to correct. If their advertising ever begins to include the important point that persistent "rebound" headache pain is a common result of consuming their products, those companies will finally pass *the whole truth* test.

QUALITY #3: NOTHING BUT THE TRUTH

Nothing but the truth means that unrelated or extraneous elements that can cloud or conceal the essential truth should not be communicated.

A common advertising approach that some may find innocent enough and that is called in this handbook *related factor* creative strategy is exemplified by the classic exhortation, "Enjoy ice cold Coca-Cola®." This would fail the *nothing but the truth* test because, although Coca-Cola is sweet, carbonated, flavorful, dark brown, and even good for the stomach in some cases, it is not inherently *ice cold*.

Similarly, the phrase "Eat Wheaties® with plenty of *strawberries and dairy cream*" does not reflect simple truth in advertising because, while the suggested combination might be delicious, plain old Wheaties and milk are not nearly as tasty.

Applying the *nothing but the truth* test would mean that the popular creative advertising strategy called "borrowed interest"—where consumers are lured into an advertising pitch by something appealing, such as sex or sports, that is in no significant way related to the product—would have to be discarded. And, although persuasive messages might not be as entrancing or exciting after passing this test, advertisers who stuck to *nothing but the truth* would be dealing with their customers accurately, fairly, and honestly.

Campbell's® soup got blasted by the FTC in a famous case where the quantity and variety of the inclusions in their vegetable soup was illustrated by *marbles* placed in the bowl to hold the vegetables on the surface of the soup.

Many marketers found that to be an innocent act necessitated by the circumstances of studio photography, and akin to the trick of using mashed potatoes in place of ice cream, which would melt under studio lighting. But the FTC ruled that Campbell's was wrong and had deceived the public.

Intelligent application of the *nothing but the truth* test might well have saved the company the strife it suffered.

THE THREE QUALITIES TOGETHER

The truth, the whole truth, and nothing but the truth as a test for honesty in advertising might kill a few creative concepts, to be sure. But American consumers could benefit from advertising that is more simple and precise than much of what they are now exposed to. And *marketers* would benefit as well, in the long term, because their claims would become more reasonable and accurate and, hence, more *credible.*

Consistent application of this easy little test surely would prevent recurrence of such advertising travesties as Volvo® automobiles' visualization of competitive makes of cars collapsing under the weight of a monster truck, while a Volvo remained intact. This dramatic demonstration was reportedly accomplished by technicians cutting the roof supports of the competitive cars, and reinforcing the Volvo roof to withstand the weight of the truck. That was by no means innocent, and certainly violated *all three* aspects of the proposed test.

Perhaps judicious application of the ancient and familiar oath of English Law would also free us of the newer style of advertising (called in this handbook *non-ingredient* creative strategy) that tells us what products *do not* contain, such as the Kellogg's® corn flakes television commercials in which we have been told in hushed tones of amazement that the product *doesn't contain fat* because it *isn't fried*—thereby implying that competitive brands *are* fried.

Is it true that *any* breakfast cereal is fried—or even "shot from guns"? Wouldn't you like to know the truth, the whole truth, and nothing but the truth?

Appendix 10

Techniques for Writing a News Release

The *news release* is the workhorse of the publicity program for a product, service, or organization.

What follows is an idealized form, where the numbers at the right refer to notes that follow. They are included only for your guidance and *should not be included in your releases*. If you use the general form presented here, editors and news directors should assume you know what you are doing and pay more attention to what you have to offer.

Of course, your topic must not only be well presented, but also *newsworthy* and potentially *interesting* to their readers, listeners, or viewers.

SAMPLE NEWS RELEASE

Thomas-Perry & Associates, P.C.   (1)
2700 East Salem Drive
Mallow, Idaho 90011

CONTACT: Bradstone Perry, CPA   (2)
    Telephone: (239) 555–4343

FOR IMMEDIATE RELEASE   (3)

FIRM APPOINTS SENIOR ASSOCIATE   (4)

6/26/XX, MALLOW, ID—Crockett E. Sherman, CPA has been   (5)
appointed Vice President of Marketing and a senior associate of
Thomas-Perry & Associates, P.C., one of the Rocky Mountain's

more prestigious accounting firms, according to Bradstone Perry, President.

"The appointment of Crockett Sherman is another example of (6)
Thomas-Perry's policy of hiring from within," Mr. Perry said. "And
we are sure that Mr. Sherman will continue to make the kinds of
innovative contributions he has made during his eleven years with
the firm."

Mr. Sherman, who serves on the Executive Committee in his new (7)
capacity, was previously Assistant to Mr. Perry, and responsible for
new business development.

A graduate of the University of Idaho, with a major in Accounting, (8)
Mr. Sherman received his MBA degree from the University of
Denver. He is a native of Cheyenne, Wyoming, and currently lives
with his wife, Marguerite, and their two daughters in the Golden
Valley subdivision in Mallow.

(MORE) (9)

THOMAS-PERRY—PAGE 2 (10)

Thomas-Perry & Associates specializes in auditing and accounting; (11)
individual income tax returns; tax planning, advice, and return
preparation; small business interim compilation and review; and
corporate and partnership income tax preparation.

Mr. Sherman replaces Dudley Blanchard, who resigned last month to (12)
pursue other business interests.

(13)

KEY TO INFORMATION ON RELEASE

News releases in hard-copy form should be typed *double-space*, with
margins of no less than *one inch* to permit editor's notations and changes.

Allow some "air" or extra line spacing at the top so that the source,
contact information, and headline are not crowded together.

Text should be *printed on only one side* of each sheet to permit "cut-
and-paste" editing.

Keep paragraphs together—also to help with cut-and-paste editing—and
never split a paragraph between pages of a release.

Preferred paper is 8–1/2 × 11, 20-pound white bond in the United States.
No odd sizes or unusual paper stock colors should be used.

(1) You must identify the *source* of the release. If you use your organization letterhead, use it only for the *first* sheet. Some firms that do a lot of publicity print special release stationery that identifies the source with a phrase like "NEWS from Thomas-Perry & Associates."

(2) Whether you use letterhead or not, the name and telephone number of a person *who will be accessible* during normal business hours should be included. The person responsible for the publicity item should have all information on the subject and be the official spokesperson for the organization on this particular subject. It's best if *one person* can handle all media inquiries, but dividing responsibilities is sometimes necessary. The vital thing is to have the person identified standing by to answer questions during normal business hours when the media are most likely to call.

(3) Publicity pieces are generally marked as this one FOR IMMEDIATE RELEASE, which means they can be used at any time. If you must for some reason hold an item, provide what is called an "embargo date" and mark the piece, for example, "FOR RELEASE ON OR AFTER JULY 1, 20XX."

(4) Editors seldom use the headline you provide. But you want something to attract *their* attention. This is a bland headline at best and could be more interesting if it used a rhetorical device like alliteration as in, "Mallow Man Made Marketing Manager," or if it revealed something more about the story, like, "Tax Firm Promotes from Within."

(5) What is called the "dateline" should appear at the beginning of the text. The date of release and the city and state where the story originated should appear first in solid capital letters, followed by a dash (or two hyphens). Then the first paragraph should continue on the same line and summarize the key news point of the story. This paragraph often will be used alone and the rest of the release ignored, so make that first paragraph good, and tightly written. Keep paragraphs to no more than six lines. Try to get news to newspapers at least a week in advance. Magazines need even *more* lead time. Remember the old observation in the newspaper business that "yesterday's news wraps the garbage."

(6) Quotes are important in releases not only to carry supplementary information, but also to lend credibility, and to give credit to important people. This spotlights the President, although the release is not about him, and also helps to enhance the image of the firm as practicing a philosophy of concern for and loyalty to its employees.

(7) More information should be provided to build the story, but each succeeding paragraph should be *less important* than what appeared before it. This is called "the inverted pyramid" form.

(8) The kind of information you see in this paragraph makes this release appropriate to the newspapers of the colleges mentioned, and also to local newspapers such as the one serving the community in which the Mr. Sherman lives. The firm would not expect the big Boise paper to publish all this information.

(9) Be sure the word MORE appears at the bottom of each page of the release except the last. It may be centered, or flush right as it appears here. It may be

in parentheses, or preceded by three dots. As noted, do not split paragraphs between pages.

(10) Identify the source of the release once again at the top of each new page, and indicate page number, in case pages get separated. Join pages only with a paperclip; *do not staple.*

(11) This is the so-called "boilerplate" that should appear at or near the end of each release. It is a succinct statement of what the firm is, does, or believes in. It's sort of a boiled-down mission statement or informational commercial that *may* be included in the published version if the editor needs to fill space.

(12) Blanchard has become a commercial real estate agent. They feel they should acknowledge him but don't want to help his cause. Frankly, they put this in to give editors something to *delete*—and hope they all *do.*

(13) The symbol # # # indicates the end of the release. Some journalists still use -30- but today this might appear somewhat affected and even presumptuous for someone who is not an old-time professional journalist. By the way, the general rule is that normally a release should be *no more than two pages.* So write tight!

Appendix 11

A Checklist of Idea-Starters for Publicity

You may need to get out a *newsworthy* release every couple of weeks to keep your name before the public. Your releases also have to have a strong *lead, hook, grabber*, or *news peg*. But often you may think you have nothing interesting or important to write about.

Curiously, like writing personal letters to someone once a day versus once a year, the *more often* you write, the more you discover about which you *can* write. So don't despair—there are lots of good stories around your organization if you just start keeping your eyes open.

To help you get started, here are possible subject areas among which you should find timely topics for news releases or feature articles. In fact, some might also work rather well for advertisements and public relations activities or events, too.

Check back over this list when you get stuck for a good approach.

HISTORICAL

[ ] Anniversaries or milestones in the organization.

[ ] Length of service of partners, officers, or staff.

[ ] Special contributions of employees.

[ ] History of office building or office.

[ ] Corporate parties or festivities regularly held.

[ ] State or national holidays that relate to the organization.

[ ] Past awards or honors received.

[ ] Long-time satisfied customers, suppliers, or representatives of other publics.

ORGANIZATIONAL

[　] Forecasts.

[　] Events and activities.

[　] Reorganization.

[　] Your organization's studies or research.

[　] Project or contract announcements.

[　] Status reports.

ACTIVITIES

[　] Current achievements or milestones.

[　] New facilities.

[　] New personnel.

[　] Response to industry news.

[　] Presentation of papers or speeches.

[　] Publication of books or articles.

[　] Future plans.

[　] Improvements in efficiency or productivity.

[　] New procedures developed or being used.

[　] New applications of existing products or services.

[　] Statistics that indicate trends.

PRODUCTS AND SERVICES

[　] New products or services.

[　] Improvements in products or services.

[　] Unusual product or service applications.

[　] New customers or clients (especially corporate or organizational).

[　] Successful bids or awards of contracts.

[　] Efficiency records with customers or clients.

[　] Comparative evaluations of products or services.

[　] Quality controls.

[　] Cost containment programs.

[　] Price increases or decreases.

TECHNICAL

[　] Effects of new laws on operations.

[　] New business regulations by governments.

[   ] Industry rule changes.

[   ] Corporate policy and procedures changes.

PROMOTION

[   ] Participation in tradeshows, fairs, and the like.

[   ] Presentations and speeches.

[   ] Training programs or seminars.

[   ] Open-house activities.

[   ] New media uses (for example, publication of a newsletter).

[   ] Contests, games, and sweepstakes.

[   ] Cooperative programs with other organizations.

[   ] Awards to customers, suppliers, and so on.

[   ] Modification of corporate symbol.

[   ] New symbol.

[   ] Creation of a slogan.

[   ] Tie-in with a nonprofit organization.

[   ] Endorsements by prominent individuals or groups.

[   ] New advertising campaign.

POLICIES

[   ] Change in policies.

[   ] Change in contract terms.

[   ] Response to government policies.

[   ] Response to community problems.

[   ] Employee training or policies.

PERSONALITIES

[   ] Interviews with senior personnel (include photographs).

[   ] Executive speeches.

[   ] Visits to facilities or offices by famous or prominent persons.

[   ] Visits by groups (e.g. students, politicians, foreign visitors).

[   ] Elections of officers and board members.

[   ] Personnel with interesting backgrounds.

[   ] Personnel accomplishments.

[   ] Personnel hobbies and sports activities.

[   ] Honors and awards.

[ ] Training and education completed.

[ ] Scholarships to employees and their families.

[ ] Donations made by employees as a group.

[ ] Community service work performed by employees.

[ ] Retirements, resignations, births, deaths and so on.

COMMUNITY

[ ] Involvement in community programs (clean-up, public health, and so on).

[ ] Leadership by senior people and/or employees in community activities.

[ ] Election or appointment to public office.

[ ] Community open-house.

[ ] Offers of facilities, goods, or services to the community.

[ ] Corporate donations to local organizations.

[ ] Involvement in community groups as advisors.

[ ] Awards to community individuals or groups.

[ ] Awards received from community organizations.

MEDIA SELECTION

While you're thinking of subjects for publicity, it's often a good idea to note at the same time the *media vehicles* you think would most likely carry your news. Or sometimes it works the *other* way and you decide first what *vehicle* you need to be in and then develop a story of special interest to *them.*

Either way, you can double-check your media choices against the vehicles you selected for advertising to see where tie-ins might help—or where tie-ins might best be *avoided.*

MAKING YOUR OWN NEWS

If you can't think of anything that has happened recently that relates to one of the topics listed, then you might want to *create* a good news item.

For example, if you ran an advertising agency, on a slow week you might telephone the Chair of the Marketing Department of your local college or university and invite a group of advertising students to your office for a tour. Treat them well, give them a brief overview of what you do and why your agency is special, and serve refreshments. Hire a local photographer to stop in for a few minutes and take pictures of the occasion, if you don't have someone on staff to do that.

The best of the photos, in the form of black-and-white glossy prints

(8 × 10 inches for a group photo) sent to local papers, business magazines, and the college newspaper can have a lot of appeal.

Or invite the town mayor, the lieutenant governor, or some such personage over to discuss some matter of importance, such as the possibility of applying sales tax to advertising services. Depending on how prominent your visitor is, you might even notify the local radio and television stations and they just might send a sound or film crew to record some pithy comments by you and/or the dignitary. When you aim for this sort of publicity prepare your remarks *well in advance*, and rehearse your delivery. You should be especially alert and organized for such possible "spontaneous" exposure.

The more you use your imagination in this game, the more fun you are likely to have—and the more *productive* your publicity program will prove.

As for writing publicity yourself, in addition to the form illustrated in Appendix 10, the suggestions that appear in Chapter 23, "Copywriting Techniques," should serve you well.

Appendix 12

Crisis Management

Public relations differs from other types of marketing communications, among other ways, with respect to its unpredictability. Creative litigation, arbitrary attacks by special interest groups, and even government action can take one by surprise and even destroy successful operations.

Therefore, many organizations have found it strategically helpful to develop and keep close at hand a *crisis management plan* that they can rely on if the going gets rough.

To begin, play a game like our military experts at the Pentagon do: develop a *worst-case scenario*—the most terrible thing you can imagine happening to your business and use that as a basis for constructive planning. For example, suppose that you are accused of laundering money for an illicit drug operation, that you are sued for racial discrimination by an unsuccessful job applicant, or that one of your senior people appears to have been misappropriating funds and commits suicide by jumping out his office window. What would you *do*?

Here is one way to approach such unpleasant but important possibilities—in advance:

- *Establish channels of communication.* There are two basic types of communication channels: *internal* and *external*. You must keep your employees informed, and you must be honest, open, and cooperative with the media. The media need to meet deadlines. But employees should learn what's happening directly from the company *before* they see or hear it in the media—and, if possible, before they get it through the rumor mill.
- *Establish a* single *point of contact.* Allow only *one* person in your organization to be spokesperson, for both internal and external communication. Things can

get terribly confusing for everyone when more than one person speaks for the organization. This person should have at least one prepared "understudy" in case the primary contact person is unavailable at the time of a crisis. You may also want to establish one or more *hotlines*—telephone numbers devoted to crisis management where either recorded messages are played or the spokesperson is on duty.

- *Establish a communication hierarchy.* Develop a list of people with *need to know* what is going on. Start with the top person in your organization, and then arrange the others in order of precedence or priority. This way, the persons most concerned in a crisis should be notified *first*.

- *Appoint callers.* Perhaps you want to hire this function out to a *reliable* 24-hour telephone service. There also are automatic systems available that connect numbers of key personnel and deliver a prerecorded crisis message. Or there may be dependable people in your organization you wish to appoint as dispatchers. Be sure you have at least one back-up for each person appointed.

- *Specify actions to be taken.* You should agree upon hard and fast rules about who goes where, and who initiates what action when. Think through what is likely to serve your interests best. For example, does the boss go to the office if alerted in the middle of the night—or to your attorney's office—or to a control center suite in a midtown hotel? Does someone notify the media—or do you wait for them to contact you? How should your single point of contact behave during a crisis? And so on.

- *Appoint an action team.* Specify, in addition to the primary contact person and understudy, exactly who will be on deck in case of a crisis to plan the right things to do. Also allow for substitutes in case of illness or absence. You cannot foresee everything, and you need quick thinkers to be on hand to guide the organization through the rapids.

- *Compile a media list.* Be sure to include all media people (reporters, editors, news directors, columnists, and so forth) who are acquainted with your organization and friendly, or at least positively disposed, toward your organization. Media on your advertising schedule are good ones to start with, but get the names of the *news* people, not the sales reps. National marketers should use *Bacon's* and *Gale Directory of Publications*, and international marketers should use *Ulrich's* to compile a list of media contacts. Prepare everyone on your list in advance by sending them a *media kit*, as described in Chapter 30. You may wish to *code* your list according to special interest or function; for example, matters related to technical information would go to science editors, whereas matters involving personnel would better be sent to business or social pages editors, depending on the slant of the release. Be sure to keep your list updated through periodic telephone or e-mail contact since people in the communications business tend to change jobs often.

- *Materials to be dispatched.* Review your publicity materials to see that you have things that could help your position should something horrible happen. Things like history of the organization, biographical sketches of your top people, community service activities, types of products and services offered, awards, complimentary articles, and so on. Someone should be appointed to sort these materials and send out the appropriate ones to the appropriate media in the event of a crisis.

- *Public statements.* Prepare a variety of statements from which the best can be chosen for various types of crises. You might wish to check them with your legal counsel, so you and counsel both are satisfied that they seem not to contain anything that might hurt you or your organization.

- *Likely questions.* Brainstorm a list of questions likely to be asked by the media in the event of a crisis, and work with top management and your legal counsel on how best to answer them. Questions and answers should be organized by category or type of crisis and kept in a *briefing book*, normally a tabbed binder, for the contact person to use when responding to media people and issuing announcements. Briefing books are also useful at annual meetings of shareholders and other occasions when executives must answer questions.

- *Rehearse responses.* Your key contact person and also the understudy should regularly be engaged in role-playing exercises where questions are fed to them at random, and they rehearse answering as succinctly, cogently, and confidently as possible. Like the effective delivery of executive speeches, media relations require practice.

- *Emergency releases.* As you ride out a crisis, you should issue *news releases* or *alerts* or *bulletins* to the media. Someone must write these, have them approved by management and perhaps legal counsel, neatly type them, proof carefully, print or duplicate, and distribute them either in hard-copy form or electronically promptly to the right media vehicles. This may involve a lot of work, so be sure the function is adequately staffed.

- *Logistics for a news conference.* Do *not* call a news conference unless what you have to say is *enormously* important to the media and their audiences. But know in advance where you will hold it, how you will invite media representatives, who will present information, and how the information should be presented. Like everything else, successful news conferences are thoroughly *planned* in advance.

- *Advertising.* If the media won't cooperate in presenting your situation fairly, be prepared to plan, produce, and place *advertising* to reach your important publics. There's an old saying in the PR business that "Good publicity is what you *pray* for, while advertising is what you *pay* for." And that's why it's nice to have a "slush fund," or contingency, built into your advertising budget in the event of a crisis.

Additional guidance appropriate to this topic appears in Chapters 29 and 30.

Appendix 13

Special Event List for Retailers and Proven Themes for Sales Managers

Here is a list of proven themes for sales incentive contests, tradeshows, retail sales, and other promotional activities.

In addition, consider themes that involve local and national holidays, special festivities, historical events, and points of interest in your marketing area.

The themes are arranged in straight alphabetical order, and also by topic: Sports, Sales, Travel, Animals, Historical, and Store Events.

ALPHABETICAL LIST

All Aboard
All for One and One for All
Anniversary Sale
Are You a Pro?
Around the World
Bandwagon
Bargains (some retailers spell this backwards: "Sniagrab") Sale
Be a Buccaneer
Be a High Flyer
Be a Touchdown Hero
Beat the Bushes
Beauty Contest
Big Bad Wolf

Big Bear Hunt
Big Birthday Party
Big Bonus
Big Build-up
Big Business
The Big Game
Big Game Hunt
The Big Pay-Off
Big Reward
Blast-Off
Bonanza
Boom Time
Break Par
Bring 'Em Back Alive
Bring in a Gusher
Build Your Security
Business Builders
Buyer's Day Sale

Canadian Caper
Championship
Chart a New Course
Chase for Sales
Christmas Shoppers
Climb to the Top
Cook Up a Sale
Corner the Market
Crusaders
Dealer's Choice
Dividend Days
Do-It-Yourself
Early Bird
Everybody Loves a Winner
Expansion Sale
Farming for Futures
Fire Sale

Five-Alarm Fire
Flood Sale
Follow the Train
Football Game
Founder's Day Sale
Get in the Swim
Get on the Bandwagon
Get the Big Ones
Get the Extra Point
Get the Vote
Go-Getters
Going Out of Business
  Sale
Going Places
Gold Rush
Gopher Gold
Grand Opening Sale
Great Performers
Happy Holiday
Harvest Contest
Heads Up
Heavyweight Champions
Hit a Homer
Hit the Bull's Eye
Hit the Line
Hit the Prize Route
Jamboree
Join the Winners
Kentucky Derby
Key Person
Kick-Off
Knights of the Round
  Table
Let Yourself Go
Line Drive
Live It Up!
Lord of the Manor
Lucky Money
Make a Record
Man Hunt
Man in Motion
Manager's Sale
Marathon
Master Builders
Mexican Fiesta
Millionaire's Contest
Millionaire's Holiday
Minute Man

Mountain Climber
Mountain Men
Mystery Weekend
Open Season on Sales
Out of This World
Over the Top
Par Stars
Partners in Performance
Partners in Progress
The People's Choice
Perk Up Sales
Pick a Trip
Play Ball for Prizes
Post-inventory Sale
Pre-inventory Sale
President's Month
Prize Jubilee
Prize Magic
Prize Partners
Profit Prophet
Prosperity Drive
Quota Busters
Quota Makers
Reaching the Moon
Remodeling Sale
Ring the Bell
Road to Success
Roman Holiday
Roundup Time
Sale Away
Salemaker the Magician
Sales Aces
Sales Agent 007
Sales Carnival
Sales Circus
Sales Derby
Sales Magic
Sales Open
Sales Power
Sales Races
Sales Round-Up
Sales Safari
Sales Showdown
Sales Sleuths
Sales Track-down
Sell in Style
Sellalot
Sellathon

Sellebration
Selling Bee
Selling Jamboree
Selling Spree
Sell-O-Drama
Sellstakes
Shoot for the Moon
Shoot the Goal
Shoot to Kill
Sky Raiders
Spotlight on Sports
Spring Training
Springtime in Paris
Strike While the Iron's
  Hot
Swing Away
Take Off
Tee Off
Thar She Blows
Top Dog
Top Gun
Touchdown
Treasure Island
Treasure Trove
Turkey Contest
Turkey Shoot
Turn on the Heat
Two on the Isle
Up and At 'Em!
Up the Ladder
War!
Westward Ho
Wild Game Hunt
Win Your Wings
Winner Take All
Winner Wonderland
Winnerama
Winning Ticket
World Series
Write Your Own Ticket
Your Shining Hour
You're the Top

SPORTS THEMES

Are You a Pro?
Be a Touchdown Hero
Big Bear Hunt

The Big Game
Big Game Hunt
Break Par
Championship
Climb to the Top
Everybody Loves a
    Winner
Football Game
Get in the Swim
Get the Extra Point
Heavyweight Champions
Hit a Homer
Hit the Bull's Eye
Hit the Line
Join the Winners
Kentucky Derby
Kick-Off
Line Drive
Marathon
Mountain Climber
Open Season on Sales
Par Stars
Play Ball for Prizes
Shoot the Goal
Spotlight on Sports
Spring Training
Swing Away
Tee Off
Touchdown
Winning Ticket
World Series

SALES THEMES

Anniversary Sales
Chase for Sales
Cook Up a Sale
Open Season on Sales
Perk Up Sales
Quota Busters
Sale Away
Salemaker the Magician
Sales Aces
Sales Agent 007
Sales Carnival
Sales Circus
Sales Derby

Sales Magic
Sales Open
Sales Power
Sales Races
Sales Round-Up
Sales Safari
Sales Showdown
Sales Sleuths
Sales Track-down
Sell in Style
Sell-O-Drama
Sellalot
Sellathon
Sellebration
Selling Bee
Selling Jamboree
Selling Spree
Sellstakes

TRAVEL THEMES

All Aboard
Around the World
Blast-Off
Canadian Caper
Chart a New Course
Follow the Train
Going Places
Happy Holiday
Hit the Prize Route
Let Yourself Go
Mexican Fiesta
Millionaire's Holiday
Mountain Men
Mystery Weekend
Out of This World
Pick a Trip
Reaching the Moon
Road to Success
Roman Holiday
Roundup Time
Sale Away
Sales Carnival
Sales Safari
Springtime in Paris
Take Off!
Treasure Island

Two on the Isle
Westward Ho
Win Your Wings
Winner Wonderland
Write Your Own Ticket

ANIMAL THEMES

Beat the Bushes
Big Bad Wolf
Big Bear Hunt
Big Game Hunt
Early Bird
Gopher Gold
Open Season on Sales
Roundup Time
Sales Circus
Sales Round-Up
Sales Safari
Shoot to Kill
Thar She Blows
Top Dog
Turkey Contest
Turkey Shoot
Wild Game Hunt

HISTORICAL THEMES

All for One and One for
    All
Be a Buccaneer
Crusaders
Gold Rush
Knights of the Round
    Table
Lord of the Manor
Minute Man

STORE EVENTS

Anniversary Sale
Bargains (some retailers
    spell this backwards:
    "Sniagrab") Sale

Buyer's Day Sale
Expansion Sale
Fire Sale
Flood Sale

Founder's Day Sale
Going Out of Business
    Sale
Grand Opening Sale

Manager's Sale
Post-inventory Sale
Pre-inventory Sale
Remodeling Sale

Appendix 14

Ten-Week Open-House Countdown
to Success Planning Checklist

This appendix is a supplement to Chapter 35, "Tradeshows, Seminars, and Open-House Events."

WEEK ONE

[ ] Start to use planning checklist.
[ ] Appoint coordinator.
[ ] Define marketing and communications objectives.
[ ] Poll contact people about prospective attendees and service interests.
[ ] Make initial selection of topics, products, and/or services to be presented.
[ ] Investigate potential themes.
[ ] Hold planning meeting.
[ ] Set approximate budget.
[ ] Establish theme.
[ ] Assign responsibility for updating present mailing list.
[ ] Set dates for event.
[ ] Discuss types of presentations.
[ ] Inspect own premises for suitability, capacity, and traffic flow.

WEEK TWO

[ ] Inform employees of intentions.
[ ] Cull customer and prospect database or mailing list to provide initial invitation list.

[ ] Continue update of invitation list as information comes in from sales people.

[ ] Revise selection of promotable products and/or services if new information requires.

[ ] Make final decision on topics, products, and services to be presented.

[ ] Make final decision on number and types of presentations (or mix) to use.

[ ] Make final decision on suitability of own premises; if inadequate, look into rented facilities.

[ ] Check present inventory of appropriate equipment, supplies, audiovisuals, presentation materials, flip-charts, literature, and so on.

[ ] Polish theme and begin work on final copy and graphics.

[ ] Lay out all printed materials (invitations, name tags, and so on).

[ ] Consider advertising specialties (premiums or gifts).

WEEK THREE

[ ] Make first estimate of potential number of attendees per session.

[ ] If your own premises are inadequate, reserve rental facilities immediately.

[ ] Continue update of invitation list.

[ ] Inspect premises and determine requirements for signage, flow-charts, and so forth.

[ ] Begin process of personnel selection for seminar leaders and presenters. If any sales or other contact personnel are to be used, advise them.

[ ] Complete finished art for graphics and signage, and have all text typeset.

[ ] Contact printers for competitive bids.

[ ] Select telephone operators and receptionists.

[ ] If required, contract for actors, models, entertainers, musicians, and the like.

WEEK FOUR

[ ] Update invitation list.

[ ] Hold progress meeting.

[ ] Finalize presentation mix.

[ ] Begin thematic customization of presentations and telephone scripts.

[ ] Begin arrangements for extra parking and/or limousine or other transportation.

[ ] Contact caterers for competitive bids.

[ ] Finalize printing order and delivery schedule.

[ ] Check your premiums and gifts inventory, and/or investigate local sources for appropriate specialty items, portfolios, binders, and mementos.

[ ] Order signs and charts.

[   ] Finalize presentations and sequence of sessions. If you are holding alternate sessions on different topics or services, do not forget to segment your invitation list.

[   ] If required, order decorative materials.

WEEK FIVE

[   ] Update invitation list.

[   ] Practice presentations and demonstrations.

[   ] Instruct telephone operators on procedures.

[   ] Make final revisions and adjustments to presentations.

[   ] Compile list for miscellaneous materials needed: pads, pens, and so on.

[   ] Select printer and confirm delivery.

[   ] Order local specialty items if required.

[   ] Finalize premises decoration plans.

[   ] Rehearse telephone operators.

[   ] Confirm contracts of extra personnel (receptionists, actors, models, entertainers, musicians, and so on).

WEEK SIX

[   ] Make final update of initial invitation list.

[   ] Expedite deliveries of all materials.

[   ] Begin equipment installation and decoration of premises.

[   ] Arrange service checks of all equipment.

[   ] Assign support personnel for event duties.

[   ] Separate prime prospects; make list for personal contact invitations.

[   ] Contact local newspapers, magazines, radio and TV stations, and associations for publicity.

[   ] Check items delivered.

WEEK SEVEN

[   ] Address and mail invitations and reply cards for sessions; if planning separate sessions on different days, mail daily in order.

[   ] Invite prime prospects by telephone or personal call.

[   ] Ask sales and other contact people to extend personal invitations on calls.

[   ] Add prospect-recommended guests to invitation list.

[   ] Begin your acceptance list with first returns from personal invitations.

WEEK EIGHT

[   ] Check returns from mailings and reinvite nonrespondents.

[   ] Encourage sales and contact people to continue to extend personal invitations on calls.

[   ] Add to acceptance list.

[   ] Rehearse all personnel.

[   ] Make final checks on all supplies, AV material, projectors, screens, tape units, computers, and the like.

[   ] Finalize parking and/or limousine or other transportation arrangements.

WEEK NINE

[   ] Update acceptance list.

[   ] Complete installations and decorations.

[   ] Assemble and package literature and visitor mementos.

[   ] Rehearse, rehearse, rehearse.

[   ] Compare all acceptances with mailing list.

[   ] Telephone and/or e-mail all prospects still not heard from.

[   ] Mail reminder cards to all expected guests.

[   ] Telephone all prospects who said "NO" on reply card.

WEEK TEN

[   ] Make final count of acceptances.

[   ] See that food/beverage, literature, and memento quantities are sufficient.

[   ] Make final checks on all equipment, supplies, decorations, and so on.

[   ] Hold final rehearsals.

[   ] Telephone all prospects expected Day 1 and confirm; arrange transportation, if required.

[   ] Assign transportation duties for first day.

[   ] Register all attendees and hold #1 event.

[   ] Phone prospects expected Day 2 and confirm.

[   ] Phone all Day 1 no-shows and reinvite for Days 2 or 3 (offering transportation).

[   ] Register all attendees and hold #2 event.

[   ] Phone prospects expected Day 3 and confirm.

[   ] Phone all Day 2 no-shows and reinvite for Day 3 (offering transportation).

[   ] Register all attendees and hold #3 event.

[   ] Use guest register to compile mailing list for thank-you letters.

[   ] Record all hot prospects, interest areas, appointments, and the like.

[   ] Collapse; then get ready for Monday.

Appendix 15

American Marketing Association Code of Ethics

The American Marketing Association has codified the subject of ethics as it pertains specifically to marketing, and recommends a comprehensive system, appropriate portions of which are quoted here with their permission:

RESPONSIBILITIES OF THE MARKETER

Marketers must accept responsibility for the consequences of their activities and make every effort to ensure that their decisions, recommendations and actions function to identify, serve and satisfy all relevant publics: customers, organizations and society.

Marketers' Professional Conduct must be guided by:

1. The basic rule of professional ethics: not knowingly to do harm;
2. The adherence to all applicable laws and regulations;
3. The accurate representation of their education, training and experience; and
4. The active support, practice and promotion of this Code of Ethics.

HONESTY AND FAIRNESS

Marketers shall uphold and advance the integrity, honor and dignity of the marketing profession by:

Reprinted with permission from www.ama.org/about/ama/fulleth.asp, published by the American Marketing Association.

1. Being honest in serving customers, clients, employees, suppliers, distributors, and the public;
2. Not knowingly participating in conflict of interest without prior notice to all parties involved; and
3. Establishing equitable fee schedules including the payment or receipt of usual, ocustomary and/or legal compensation for marketing exchanges.

RIGHTS AND DUTIES OF PARTIES IN THE MARKETING EXCHANGE PROCESS

Participants in the marketing exchange process should be able to expect that:

1. Products and services offered are safe and fit for their intended uses;
2. Communications about offered products and services are not deceptive;
3. All parties intend to discharge their obligations, financial and otherwise, in good faith; and
4. Appropriate internal techniques exist for equitable adjustment and/or redress of grievances concerning purchases.

It is understood that the above would include, but is not limited to, the following responsibilities of the marketer:

In the area of product development and management:
- disclosure of all substantial risks associated with product or service usage;
- identification of any product component substitution that might materially change the product or impact on the buyer's purchase decision;
- identification of extra-cost added features.

In the area of promotions:
- avoidance of false and misleading advertising;
- rejection of high-pressure manipulation, or misleading sales tactics;
- avoidance of sales promotions that use deception or manipulation.

In the area of distribution:
- not manipulating the availability of a product for the purpose of exploitation.
- not using coercion in the marketing channel;
- not exerting undue influence over the reseller's choice to handle a product.

In the area of pricing:
- not engaging in price fixing;
- not practicing predatory pricing;
- disclosing the full price associated with any purchase.

In the area of marketing research:

- prohibiting selling or fundraising under the guise of conducting research;
- maintaining research integrity by avoiding misrepresentation and omission of pertinent research data;
- treating outside clients and suppliers fairly.

Organizational relationships:

Marketers should be aware of how their behavior may influence or impact the behavior of others in organizational relationships. They should not demand, encourage or apply coercion to obtain unethical behavior in their relationships with others, such as employees, suppliers, or customers.

1 Apply confidentiality and anonymity in professional relationships with regard to privileged information;

2 Meet their obligations and responsibilities in contracts and mutual agreements in a timely manner.

3 Avoid taking the work of others, in whole, or in part, and representing this work as their own or directly benefiting from it without compensation or consent of the originator or owner; and

4 Avoid manipulation to take advantage of situations to maximize personal welfare in a way that unfairly deprives or damages the organization or others.

This is a good checklist for every marketer to review from time to time. It seems to cover the major areas *in marketing* where one is most likely to go astray or even get into trouble. The next appendix relates to ethics and the Internet.

American Marketing Association Code of Ethics for Marketing on the Internet

PREAMBLE

The Internet, including online computer communications, has become increasingly important to marketers' activities, as they provide exchanges and access to markets worldwide. The ability to interact with stakeholders has created new marketing opportunities and risks that are not currently specifically addressed in the American Marketing Association Code of Ethics. The American Marketing Association Code of Ethics for Internet marketing provides additional guidance and direction for ethical responsibility in this dynamic area of marketing. The American Marketing Association is committed to ethical professional conduct and has adopted these principles for using the Internet, including online marketing activities utilizing network computers.

GENERAL RESPONSIBILITIES

Internet marketers must assess the risks and take responsibility for the consequences of their activities. Internet marketers' professional conduct must be guided by:

1. Support of professional ethics to avoid harm by protecting the rights of privacy, ownership and access.
2. Adherence to all applicable laws and regulations with no use of Internet marketing that would be illegal, if conducted by mail, telephone, fax or other media.

3. Awareness of changes in regulations related to Internet marketing.

4. Effective communication to organizational members on risks and policies related to Internet marketing, when appropriate.

5. Organizational commitment to ethical Internet practices communicated to employees, customers and relevant stakeholders.

PRIVACY

Information collected from customers should be confidential and used only for expressed purposes. All data, especially confidential customer data, should be safeguarded against unauthorized access. The expressed wishes of others should be respected with regard to the receipt of unsolicited e-mail messages.

OWNERSHIP

Information obtained from the Internet sources should be properly authorized and documented. Information ownership should be safeguarded and respected. Marketers should respect the integrity and ownership of computer and network systems.

ACCESS

Marketers should treat access to accounts, passwords, and other information as confidential, and only examine or disclose content when authorized by a responsible party. The integrity of others' information systems should be respected with regard to placement of information, advertising, or messages.

Appendix 17

Marketing, Advertising, and Management Professional Associations

---

Academy of Management, Box 3020, Briarcliff Manor, NY 10510-8020

American Advertising Federation, 1101 Vermont Avenue NW, Suite 500, Washington, DC 20005

American Management Association, 1601 Broadway, New York, NY 10019

Association of National Advertisers, 708 Third Avenue, New York, NY 10017

Business Marketing Association, 400 North Michigan Avenue, 15th Floor, Chicago, IL 60611

Council of Better Business Bureaus, 4200 Wilson Boulevard, Suite 800, Arlington, VA 22203-1804

International Association of Business Communicators, One Halidie Plaza, 6th Floor, San Francisco, CA 94102

National Management Association, 2201 Arbor Boulevard, Dayton, OH 45439

Public Relations Society of America, 33 Irving Place, New York, NY 10003-2376

Appendix 18

Marketing, Management, and General Business Magazines

AAF Communicator, American Advertising Federation, 1101 Vermont Avenue NW, Suite 500, Washington, DC 20005

Across the Board, Conference Board, Inc., 845 Third Avenue, New York, NY 10022

Ad Business Report, Executive Communications, Inc., 185 East 85th Street, 11th Floor, New York, NY 10028

Administrative Assistant Adviser, 370 Technology Drive, Malvern, PA 19355-1315

Advances in Applied Business Strategy, 100 Prospect Street, Box 811, Stamford, CT 06904-0811

The Advertiser, Association of National Advertisers, 708 Third Avenue, New York, NY 10017

Advertising Age, Crain Communications, Inc., 740 North Rush Street, Chicago, IL 60611

Advertising & Marketing Review, 622 Gardenia Court, Golden, CO 80401

Advertising-Communications Times, 121 Chestnut Street, Philadelphia, PA 19106

ADWEEK [multiple editions],1515 Broadway, New York, NY 10036

Agency, Custom Communications Partners, Inc., 38 Newbury Street, 5th Floor, Boston, MA 02116

American Advertising, American Advertising Federation, 1101 Vermont Avenue NW, Suite 500, Washington, DC 20005

American Demographics, P.O. Box 4949, 11 River Bend Drive South, Stamford, CT 06907

ASK!, 9711 MacArthur Boulevard, Bethesda, MD 20817

AWNY Matters, Advertising Women of New York, 153 East 57th Street, New York, NY 10022

Better Business, Council of Better Business Bureaus, 4200 Wilson Boulevard, Suite 800, Arlington, VA 22203-1804

Brand Marketing, 7 West 34th Street, New York, NY 10001

BRANDWEEK, 1515 Broadway, New York, NY 10036

Business Marketing, Crain Communications, Inc., 740 North Rush Street, Chicago, IL 60611-2590

The Business Owner, 16 Fox Lane, Locust Valley, NY 11560-1119

The Business-to-Business Marketer, Business Marketing Association, 150 North Wacker Drive, Suite 1760, Chicago, IL 60606

Business Week, 1221 Avenue of the Americas, 39th Floor, New York, NY 10020

Buzz, 500 Helendale Road, Rochester, NY 14609

Cheap Relief, 734 West El Alba Way, Chandler, AZ 85224-2408

Chicago Advertising & Media, K B Communications, Box 5353, Chicago, IL 60680-5353

Chief Executive Magazine, 733 Third Avenue, 24th Floor, New York, NY 10017

Communication World, International Association of Business Communicators, One Halidie Plaza, 6th Floor, San Francisco, CA 94102

Consulting Success, 3924 South Troost, Tulsa, OK 74105

Counsel, National Council for Marketing & PR, 4602 West 21st Street, Greeley, CO 80634-3277

The Counselor, Advertising Specialty Institute, 1120 Wheeler Way, Langhorn, PA 19047

Creative, Magazines/Creative, Inc., 42 West 38th Street, New York, NY 10018

Creative New Jersey, Box 327, Ramsay, NJ 07446

D&B Reports, 299 Park Avenue, New York, NY 10171

Direct, INTERTEC Publishing, Box 4949, 11 Riverbend Center Drive South, Stamford, CT 06907-0949

Direct Marketing, Hoke Communications, Inc., 224 Seventh Street, Garden City, NY 11530

Direction, Direct Marketing Consultants, Inc., 705 Franklin Turnpike, Allendale, NJ 07401-1637

DM News, Mill Hollow Corp., 100 Avenue of the Americas, New York, NY 10013

Downtown Promotion Reporter, Alexander Communications Group, Inc., 215 Park Avenue South, New York, NY 10003

Entrepreneur, 2445 McCabe Way, Irvine, CA 92614

Fast Company, 450 West 33rd Street, 11th Floor, New York, NY 10001

Forbes, 60 Fifth Avenue, New York, NY 10011

Fortune Magazine, 1271 Avenue of the Americas, New York, NY 10020

IAA World News, International Advertising Association, 521 Fifth Avenue, Room 1807, New York, NY 10175-0003

IDEAS, International Newspaper Marketing Association, 12770 Merit Drive, Suite 330, Dallas, TX 75251

Inc., G&J USA Publishing, 38 Commercial Wharf, Boston, MA 02110

Incentive, Bill Communications, Inc., 355 Park Avenue South, New York, NY 10010-1789

Industrial Marketing Management, Box 945, New York, NY 10159-0945

The Industrial Marketing Practitioner, 1551 South Valley Forge Road, Suite 246, Lansdale, PA 19446

Industry Week, 1100 Superior Avenue, Cleveland, OH 44114-2543

Inside Impact, 1546 Main Street, Dunedin, FL 34698

Inside P.R., 708 Third Avenue, 2nd Floor, New York, NY 10017-4201

Journal of Advertising, American Academy of Advertising, c/o School of Journalism & Mass Communications, University of Minnesota, 11 Murphy Hall, Minneapolis, MN 55455

Journal of Advertising Research, Advertising Research Foundation, 641 Lexington Avenue, New York, NY 10022

Journal of Business Strategies, Gibson D. Lewis Center for Business & Econ. Development, Sam Houston State University, Huntsville, TX 77341-2056

Journal of Business Strategy, EC Media Group, 11 Penn Plaza, New York, NY 10001

Journal of Management Consulting, 858 Longview Road, Burlingame, CA 94010-6974

Journal of Marketing, American Marketing Association, 311 South Wacker Drive, Suite 5800, Chicago, IL 60606

Journal of Marketing Research, American Marketing Association, 311 South Wacker Drive, Suite 5800, Chicago, IL 60606

Journal of Promotion Management, Haworth Press, Inc., 10 Alice Street, Binghamton, NY 13904

Magnet Marketing, 40 Oval Road, Quincy, MA 02170

Mainly Marketing, Drawer 973, Coram, NY 11727

Manage, National Management Association, 2201 Arbor Boulevard, Dayton, OH 45439

Management Review, American Management Association, 1601 Broadway, New York, NY 10019

Marketing Health Services, American Marketing Association, 311 South Wacker Drive, Suite 5800, Chicago, IL 60606

Marketing Management, American Marketing Association, 311 South Wacker Drive, Suite 5800, Chicago, IL 60606

Marketing News, American Marketing Association, 311 South Wacker Drive, Suite 5800, Chicago, IL 60606

The Marketing Report, 370 Technology Drive, Malvern, PA 19355-1315

Marketing Research, American Marketing Association, 311 South Wacker Drive, Suite 5800, Chicago, IL 60606

MC, 1515 Broadway, New York, NY 10036

Media Matters, 18 East 41st Street, Suite 1806, New York, NY 10017

MEDIAWEEK, 1515 Broadway, New York, NY 10036

Potentials, Lakewood Publications, Inc., 50 South Ninth Street, Minneapolis, MN 55402

PR Strategist, Public Relations Society of America, 33 Irving Place, New York, NY 10003-2376

PR Week, 220 Fifth Avenue, 14th Floor, New York, NY 10001

PROMO, Primedia Intertek Publishing, 11 River Bend Drive South, Stamford, CT 06907

Public Relations Quarterly, 44 West Market Street, Box 311, Rhinebeck, NY 12572

Public Relations Tactics, Public Relations Society of America, 33 Irving Place, New York, NY 10003-2376

RESPONSE, Advanstar Communications, Inc., 201 Sandpointe Avenue, Suite 600, Santa Ana, CA 92707

Sales & Marketing Management, 770 Broadway, New York, NY 10003-9595

Sales & Marketing Strategies & News, P.O. Box 197, 211 West State Street, Rockford, IL 61101

Selling Power, Box 5467, Fredericksburg, VA 22403-0467

Signs of the Times, 407 Gilbert Avenue, Cincinnati, OH 45202

Sloan Management Review, Massachusetts Institute of Technology, Sloan School of Management, 77 Massachusetts Avenue, E2, Cambridge, MA 02139

Strategic Sales Management, 24 Rope Ferry Road, Waterford, CT 06386

strategy & business, Booz Allen & Hamilton, 101 Park Avenue, New York, NY 10178

Strategy & Leadership, 435 North Michigan Avenue, Suite 1717, Chicago, IL 60611-4008

Target Marketing, North American Publishing Company, 401 North Broad Street, Philadelphia, PA 19108

Appendix 19

Marketing, Management, and General Business Newsletters

Advertising Club of New York Newsletter, 35 Park Avenue South, New York, NY 10003-1405

Agency Expertise & ICOM Newsletter, International Communications Agency Network, Inc., P.O. Box 490, 1649 County Road 12, Rollinsville, CO 80474-0490

Business Breakthroughs, 7811 Montrose Road, Potomac, MD 20854

Business Ethic Resource, Business Ethics Foundation, 150 Buckminster Road, Brookline, MA 02445-5806

Business Ethics Newsline, Institute for Global Ethics, Box 563, Camden, ME 04843

Certified Letter, Institute of Certified Professional Managers, James Madison University, Harrisonburg, VA 27807

Chief Executive Officers Newsletter, Center for Entrepreneurial Management, Inc., 180 Varik Street, Penthouse, New York, NY 10014

Communication Briefings, 1101 King Street, Suite 110, Alexandria, VA 22314

The Competitive Advantage, 1101 King Street, Suite 110, Alexandria, VA 22314

Consultants News, One Kennedy Place, Route 12 South, Fitzwilliam, NH 03447

Delaney Report, 149 Fifth Avenue, New York, NY 10010

Executive Newsletter, Academy of Management, Box 3020, Briarcliff Manor, NY 10510-8020

Executive Strategies, National Institute of Business Management, Box 9266, McLean, VA 22102-0266

Frohlinger's Marketing Report, 7 Coppel Drive, Tenefly, NJ 07670-2903

Geiger Report, Box 24248, Edina, MN 55424-0248

I'm Too Busy to Read Marketing Report Service, 16501 Franklin Road, Fort Bragg, CA 95437-8714

Jack O'Dwyer's Newsletter and *PR Services Report*, 271 Madison Avenue, New York, NY 10016

Management Matters, Box 15640, Plantation, FL 33318-5640

Management Strategy, 804 North Neil Street, Suite 100, Champaign, IL 61820

The Manager's Intelligence Report, PR Intelligence Report, and *Ragan's PR Review*, Lawrence Ragan Communications, 316 North Michigan Avenue, Suite 300, Chicago, IL 60601

Non-store Marketing Report, 522 Forest Avenue, Evanston, IL 60202-3005

PR News, 1201 Seven Locks Road, Potomac, MD 20854

PR Reporter, Box 600, Exeter, NH 03833

PR Watch, Center for Media & Democracy, Inc., 3318 Gregory Street, Madison, WI 53711

Practice Builders, 18351 Jamboree Road, Irvine, CA 92715-1011

Professional Advisor, Box 6432, Kingwood, TX 77325-6399

Sales & Marketing Executive Report, 4660 North Ravenswood Avenue, Chicago, IL 60640

Success Orientation, Box 487, Roswell, GA 30077

Recommended Related Reading

These books should provide additional insight into strategic marketing planning. There are hundreds of excellent business and marketing books available that can be found by browsing in local libraries and bookstores. I have listed here books of three types: textbooks I have used in my courses, practitioner books I have used for planning, and books on subjects related to this handbook that I believe may be interesting and helpful to readers. I have eliminated some classic out-of-print books that were on my original list because they are likely to be too hard to find; I have tried to include here the most recent editions as of this writing. Since many of these books (particularly the textbooks) are updated every few years you may find editions even more recent than those I have noted. Previous editions can also serve very well and, of course, are substantially less expensive. This list is not intended to be exhaustive, and I regret that many excellent books—particularly those with highly specialized focus—have not been included.

ADVERTISING CREATIVE STRATEGY

Jewler, A. Jerome, and Bonnie L. Drewniany. *Creative Strategy in Advertising*. 7th ed. Belmont, CA: Wadsworth Publishing Company, 2000.
Patti, Charles H., and Sandra E. Moriarity. *The Making of Effective Advertising*. Englewood Cliffs, NJ: Prentice Hall, 1990.

ADVERTISING DESIGN, ART, AND TYPOGRAPHY

Anonymous. *Pocket Pal*. 15th ed. Memphis: International Paper Company, 1992. (Free to marketing practitioners who write to the company at 6400 Poplar Avenue, Memphis, TN 38197, or through large paper distributors.)

Lem, Dean Phillip. *Graphics Master 6: A Workbook of Planning Aids, Reference Guides, and Graphic Tools.* 6th ed. Kihel, HI: D. Lem Associates, 1996.
Schlemmer, Richard M. *Handbook of Advertising Art Production.* Upper Saddle River, NJ: Prentice Hall, 1990.

ADVERTISING PRINCIPLES

Patti, Charles H., and Charles F. Frazer. *Advertising: A Decision-Making Approach.* Chicago: Dryden Press, 1988.
Wells, William D., John Burnett, and Sandra Moriarity. *Advertising Principles and Practice.* 5th ed. Upper Saddle River, NJ: Prentice Hall, 2000.

BUSINESS MARKETING

Bingham, Frank G., and Barney T. Raffield III. *Business to Business Marketing Management.* Chicago: Irwin/McGraw-Hill, 1990.
Rangan, V. Kasturi, Benson P. Shapiro, and Rowland T. Moriarity, Jr. *Business Marketing Strategy: Cases, Concepts, and Applications.* Chicago: Irwin/McGraw-Hill, 1995.

BUSINESS STRATEGY

Fahey, Liam, and Robert M. Randall. *The Portable MBA in Strategy.* New York: John Wiley and Sons, 1994.
Patti, Charles H., Susan Kennedy, with Steven Hartley. *Business-to-Business Advertising: A Marketing Management Approach.* Lincolnwood, IL: NTC Publishing Group, 1991.
Ulwick, Anthony. W. *Business Strategy Formulation: Theory, Process, and the Intellectual Revolution.* Westport, CT: Quorum Books, 1999.

COMPETITION

McGonagle, John J., and Carolyn M. Vella. *The Internet Age of Competitive Intelligence.* Westport, CT: Quorum Books, 1999.
Tylzak, Lynn. *Get Competitive! Cut Costs and Improve Quality.* New York: McGraw-Hill Professional Publishing, 1990.

CONSUMER BEHAVIOR

Hawkins, Delbert I., Roger J. Best, and Kenneth A. Coney (deceased). *Consumer Behavior: Building Marketing Strategy.* 8th ed. Chicago: Irwin/McGraw-Hill, 2001.
Peter, J. Paul, and Jerry C. Olson. *Consumer Behavior and Marketing Strategy.* 5th ed. Chicago: Irwin/McGraw-Hill, 1999.
Underhill, Paco. *Why We Buy: The Science of Shopping.* New York: Simon & Schuster, 2000.

COPYWRITING

Bendinger, Bruce H. *The Copy Workshop Workbook*. Chicago: Copy Workshop, 1993.

Caples, John, and revised by Fred E. Hahn. *Tested Advertising Methods*. Upper Saddle River, NJ: Prentice Hall, 1998.

Ogilvy, David. *Ogilvy on Advertising*. New York: Random House, 1985.

DIRECT MARKETING

Nash, Edward L. *Direct Marketing: Strategy, Planning, Execution*. 4th ed. New York: McGraw-Hill, 1999.

Stone, Bob (née Robert B.). *Successful Direct Marketing Methods*. 6th ed. New York: NTC Publishing Group, 1997.

DISTRIBUTION, LOGISTICS, AND CHANNELS

Lambert, Douglas, Lisa M. Ellram, and James R. Stock. *Fundamentals of Logistics Management*. Chicago: Irwin/McGraw-Hill, 1998.

Rolnicki, Kenneth. *Managing Channels of Distribution: The Marketing Executive's Complete Guide*. New York: AMACOM, 1996.

Rosenbloom, Bert, and G. Behrens Ulrich. *Marketing Channels: A Management View*. 6th ed. Fort Worth: Harcourt Brace College Publishers, 1998.

ELECTRONIC COMMERCE AND THE INTERNET

Emerick, Donald, and Kim Round. *Exploring Web Marketing and Project Management Interactive Workbook*. Upper Saddle River, NJ: Prentice Hall, 2000.

Seybold, Patricia B., with Ronni T. Marshak. *Customers.com: How to Create a Profitable Business Strategy for the Internet and Beyond*. New York: Times Business, Random House, 1998.

Silverstein, Barry. *Business-to-Business Internet Marketing: Seven Proven Strategies for Increased Profits Through Internet Direct Marketing*. Gulf Breeze, FL: Maximum Press, 1999.

Steinbock, Dan. *The Birth of Internet Marketing Communications*. Westport, CT: Quorum Books, 2000.

ETHICS

Chonko, Lawrence B. *Ethical Decision Making in Marketing*. Thousand Oaks, CA: Sage Publications, 1995.

Ciulla, Joanne B., ed. *Ethics, the Heart of Leadership*. Westport, CT: Quorum Books, 1998.

Smith, N. Craig, and John A. Quelch. *Ethics in Marketing*. Homewood, IL: Irwin/McGraw-Hill, 1993.

EVALUATION AND TESTING

Alreck, Pamela L., and Robert B. Settle. *The Survey Research Handbook*. 2nd ed. Chicago: Irwin/McGraw-Hill, 1994.

Breen, George Edward, and Albert B. Blankenship. *Do-It-Yourself Marketing Research*. 3rd ed. New York: McGraw-Hill, 1989.

FORECASTING

Kress, George J., and John Snyder. *Forecasting and Market Analysis Techniques: A Practical Approach*. Westport, CT: Quorum Books, 1994.

Mentzer, John T., and Carol C. Bienstock. *Sales Forecasting Management: Understanding the Techniques, Systems, and Management of the Sales Forecasting Process*. Thousand Oaks, CA: Sage Publications, 1998.

INTEGRATED MARKETING COMMUNICATIONS

Schultz, Don E., Stanley Tannenbaum, and Robert F. Lauterborn. *The New Marketing Paradigm: Integrated Marketing Communications*. Lincolnwood, IL: NTC Publishing Group, 1994.

Sirgy, M. Joseph. *Integrated Marketing Communications: A Systems Approach*. Upper Saddle River, NJ: Prentice Hall, 1998.

INTERNATIONAL MARKETING

Bradley, Frank. *International Marketing Strategy*. 2nd ed. Englewood Cliffs, NJ: Prentice Hall, 1995.

Jean-Perry, Jeannet H., and David Hennessey. *Global Marketing Strategies*. 4th ed. Boston: Houghton Mifflin, 1998.

MANAGEMENT STRATEGY

Dew, John Robert. *Managing in a Team Environment*. Westport, CT: Quorum Books, 1998.

Dolan, Robert J. *Strategic Marketing Management*. Boston: Harvard Business School Publications, 1991.

London, Manuel. *Principled Leadership and Business Diplomacy: Values-Based Strategies for Management Development*. Westport, CT: Quorum Books, 1999.

Pearce, John A. II, and Richard B. Robinson, Jr. *Strategic Management*. Chicago: Irwin/McGraw-Hill, 2000.

MARKETING COMMUNICATIONS AND MEDIA

Sissors, Jack, and Lincoln Bumba. *Advertising Media Planning*. 5th ed. Lincolnwood, IL: NTC Business Books, 1997.

Surmanek, Jim. *Media Planning: A Practical Guide*. Lincolnwood, IL: NTC Business Books, 1993.

Turk, Peter B., Donald W. Jugenheimer, and Arnold M. Barban. *Advertising Media Sourcebook*. 4th ed. Lincolnwood, IL: NTC Business Books, 1997.

MARKETING PLANNING

Hiebing, Roman G., and Scott W. Cooper. *The Successful Marketing Plan*. 2nd ed. Lincolnwood, IL: NTC Business Books, 1997.

Makens, James C. *The Marketing Plan Workbook*. Englewood Cliffs, NJ: Prentice Hall, 1985.

MARKETING STRATEGY

Cook, Kenneth. *AMA Complete Guide to Strategic Planning for Small Business*. Lincolnwood, IL: NTC Business Books, 1994.

Cook, William J., Jr. *Strategics: The Art and Science of Holistic Strategy*. Westport, CT: Quorum Books, 2000.

Cravens, David W. *Strategic Marketing*. 6th ed. Chicago: Irwin/McGraw-Hill, 2000.

Fantus, James E. *Encyclopedia of Marketing Strategies*. Brookfield, WI: Concept Management, 1994.

Hiam, Alexander, and Charles D. Schewe. *The Portable MBA in Marketing*. New York: John Wiley and Sons, 1992.

Walker, Orville C., Harper W. Boyd, and Jean-Claud Larreche. *Marketing Strategy: Planning and Implementation*. 3rd ed. Chicago: Irwin/McGraw-Hill, 1999.

MARKETING THEORY AND PRACTICE

Berkowitz, Eric N., Roger A. Kerin, Steven W. Hartley, and William Rudelius. *Marketing*. 6th ed. Boston: Irwin/McGraw-Hill, 2000.

Kotler, Philip. *Marketing Management: Millennium Edition*. 10th ed. Upper Saddle River, NJ: Prentice Hall, 2000.

NAMES, BRANDS, AND TRADEMARKS

Carter, David E. *Designing Corporate Identity Programs*. New York: Art Direction Book Company, 1982.

Carter, David E. *Designing Corporate Symbols*. New York: Art Direction Book Company, 1982.

LePla, F. Joseph, and Lynn M. Parker. *Integrated Branding: Becoming Brand-Driven Through Companywide Action*. Westport, CT: Quorum Books, 2000.

OBJECTIVES AND GOALS

Dutka, Solomon, and Russell H. Colley. *DAGMAR: Defining Advertising Goals for Measured Advertising Results*. Lincolnwood, IL: NTC Publishing Group, 1995.

PERSONAL SELLING

Bauer, Gerald J., Mark S. Baunchalk, Thomas N. Ingram, and Raymond W. La-Forge. *Emerging Trends in Sales Thought and Practice*. Westport, CT: Quorum Books, 1998.

Futrell, Charles M. *Fundamentals of Selling: Customers for Life*. 5th ed. Chicago: Irwin/McGraw-Hill Higher Education, 1996.

Hopkins, Tom. *How to Master the Art of Selling*. 2nd ed. New York: Warner Books, 1982.

Kimball, Bob. *AMA Handbook for Successful Selling*. Lincolnwood, IL: NTC Business Books, 1994.

POSITIONING

Ries, Al, and Jack Trout. *Positioning: The Battle for Your Mind*. 2nd ed. New York: Warner Books, 1986.

PRESENTATIONS AND PUBLIC SPEAKING

Brooks, William T. *High Impact Public Speaking*. Englewood Cliffs, NJ: Prentice Hall, 1988.

Osborn, Michael, and Suzanne Osborn. *Public Speaking*. 5th ed. Boston: Houghton Mifflin, 2000.

Worth, Richard. *Creating Corporate Audio-Visual Presentations: How to Commission and Manage Successful Projects*. New York: Quorum Books, 1991.

PRICING

Engelson, Morris. *Pricing Strategy: An Interdisciplinary Approach*. Portland, OR: Joint Management Strategy, 1995.

Nagle, Thomas T., and Reed K. Holden. *The Strategy and Tactics of Pricing*. New York: Simon & Schuster, 1994.

PRODUCT PLANNING

Ulrich, Karl, and Steven Eppinger. *Product Design and Development*. 2nd ed. Chicago: Irwin/McGraw-Hill, 2000.

PUBLIC RELATIONS

Marconi, Joe. *Image Marketing: Using Public Perceptions to Attain Business Objectives.* Lincolnwood, IL: NTC Publishing Group, 1996.

Seitel, Fraser P. *The Practice of Public Relations.* 8th ed. Upper Saddle River, NJ: Prentice Hall, 2001.

PUBLICITY

Goldstein, Norm, ed. *The Associated Press Stylebook and Briefing on Media Law.* Revised ed. Reading, MA: Addison-Wesley, 2000.

Various authors. *The Chicago Manual of Style.* 14th ed. Chicago: University of Chicago Press, 1993.

QUALITY

Dobyns, Lloyd, with Clare Crawford-Mason. *Quality or Else: The Revolution in World Business.* Boston: Houghton Mifflin, 1991.

Gryna, Frank M., Jr. *Quality Planning and Analysis.* 4th ed. Chicago: Irwin/McGraw-Hill, 2001.

RESEARCH

Churchill, Gilbert A., Jr. *Basic Marketing Research.* 4th ed. Fort Worth: Harcourt College Publishers, 2000.

Kinnear, Thomas C., and James R. Taylor. *Marketing Research: An Applied Approach.* 5th ed. Chicago: Irwin/McGraw-Hill, 1996.

Walle, Alf H. III. *Qualitative Research in Intelligence and Marketing: The New Strategic Convergence.* Westport, CT: Quorum Books, 2000.

RETAILING

Levy, Michael, and Barton A. Weitz. *Retailing Management.* 3rd ed. Chicago: Irwin/McGraw-Hill, 1998.

Samli, A. Coskun. *Strategic Marketing for Success in Retailing.* Westport, CT: Quorum Books, 1998.

SALES MANAGEMENT

Green, Thad P. *Developing and Leading the Sales Organization.* Westport, CT: Quorum Books, 1998.

Stanton, William J., and Rosann L. Spiro. *Management of a Sales Force.* 10th ed. Chicago: Irwin/McGraw-Hill, 1999.

SALES PROMOTION

Burnett, John J. *Promotion Management: A Strategic Approach*. Boston: Houghton Mifflin, 1993.

David, Bruce E. *Mercenary Marketing: How to Promote Your Business for Less than $1000*. Willoughby, OH: WorthPromoting, 1989.

SELLING-LETTERS

Flesch, Rudolf, and A. H. Lass. *The Classic Guide to Better Writing: Step-by-Step Techniques and Exercises to Write Simply*. New York: HarperCollins, 1996.

Strunk, William, Jr., and E. B. White. *The Elements of Style*. 4th ed. New York: Macmillan, 1999.

SERVICES MARKETING

Zeithaml, Valerie and Mary J. Bitner. *Services Marketing*. Revised ed. Chicago: Irwin/McGraw-Hill, 2000.

SITUATION ANALYSIS AND SWOT

Lehman, Donald R. *Analysis for Marketing Planning*. 4th ed. Chicago: Irwin/McGraw-Hill, 1997.

Peter, J. Paul, and James H. Donnelly. *Preface to Marketing Management*. 8th ed. Chicago: Irwin/McGraw-Hill, 2000.

Roney, C. W. *Assessing Business Environment: Guidelines for Strategists*. Westport, CT: Quorum Books, 1999.

STRATEGIC MARKETING CASES

Bernhardt, Kenneth L., and Thomas C. Kinnear. *Cases in Marketing Management*. 7th ed. Chicago: Irwin/McGraw-Hill, 1997.

Cravens, David W., Charles W. Lamb, and Victoria L. Crittenden. *Strategic Marketing Management Cases*. 6th ed. Chicago: Irwin/McGraw-Hill, 1999.

Index

About the Author

STUART C. ROGERS, for 10 years a professor of marketing at the Daniels College of Business, University of Denver, has taught a variety of courses and seminars in marketing and strategic planning. Before teaching, Professor Rogers' 40-year marketing career included executive positions with Eastman Kodak Company, Benton & Bowles advertising agency, the U.S. Information Agency, and his own marketing consultancy. He is the author of numerous articles, white papers, and six previous books on marketing.